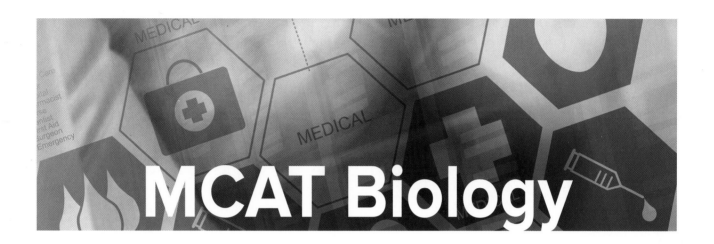

MCAT Biology

CONTENT REVIEW AND PRACTICE PASSAGES

NextStep
TEST PREP nextsteptestprep.com

Printed in the United States of America

Second Printing, 2017

ISBN 978-1-944-935-17-7

Next Step Test Prep, LLC
4256 N Ravenswood Ave
Suite 207
Chicago IL 60613

www.nextsteptestprep.com

Revision Number: 1.02 (2017-12-01)

FREE ONLINE FULL LENGTH MCAT

Want to see how you would do on the MCAT
and understand where you need to focus your prep?

TAKE OUR FREE MCAT DIAGNOSTIC EXAM
and **FREE FULL LENGTH**
Timed practice that simulates Test Day and provides
comprehensive analysis, reporting, and in-depth explanations.

Included with this free account is the first lesson
in Next Step's online course, a free sample
from our science QBank, and more!

All of these resources are provided free to students who have
purchased a Next Step book. Register for your free account at:

http://nextsteptestprep.com/mcat-diagnostic

iii

This page left intentionally blank.

STOP! READ ME FIRST!

The book you're holding is one of Next Step's six MCAT review books and contains both concise content review and questions to practice applying your content knowledge. In order to get the most out of this book, we strongly recommend that you follow a few simple steps:

1. Register for a free MCAT bundle at http://nextsteptestprep.com/mcat-diagnostic and begin your prep by taking the MCAT Diagnostic and Science Content Diagnostic to assess your strengths and weaknesses.

2. Begin working through the Next Step Review set starting with the Verbal, Quantitative, and Research Methods book. Complete this entire book at the start of your prep.

3. Use the Study Plan generator in your free account at nextstepmcat.com to generate a day-by-day study plan to take you through the rest of the Next Step Books.

4. Begin working through the rest of the Next Step MCAT review books, including this one. To get the most value out of these books, use spaced repetition to ensure complete mastery of the material. A spaced repetition approach would look something like this:

> I. Begin by skimming through the chapter to familiarize yourself with the key terms and content in the book. Then go back and read the chapter carefully.

> II. Sleep on it! Solidifying those long term memories requires sleep.

> III. Come back to the chapter **the next day**, re-skim it and then **complete the questions at the end of the chapter**. Carefully read all of the explanations, even for the questions you got right.

> IV. Take notes in your Lessons Learned Journal from the chapter. For a full explanation on what a Lessons Learned Journal is, watch Lesson 1 included in the free online bundle at nextstepmcat.com.

> IV. Sleep on it!

> V. Two days later, come back, briefly re-skim the chapter, re-do the questions at the end of the chapter, and review your Lessons Learned Journal.

Mastering the MCAT requires more than just a good set of books. You'll want to continue your prep with the most representative practice tests available. Your free bundle includes Next Step Full Length #1. After you've completed that, you can upgrade your account to include additional practice exams.

Finally, if you would like more extensive help, including daily live office hours with Next Step's senior faculty, contact us for more information about our online course. You can reach us at 888-530-NEXT or mcat@nextsteptestprep.com.

Group → Period ↓	1	2	3	4	5	6	7	8	9	10	11	12	13	14	15	16	17	18
1	1 H																	2 He
2	3 Li	4 Be											5 B	6 C	7 N	8 O	9 F	10 Ne
3	11 Na	12 Mg											13 Al	14 Si	15 P	16 S	17 Cl	18 Ar
4	19 K	20 Ca	21 Sc	22 Ti	23 V	24 Cr	25 Mn	26 Fe	27 Co	28 Ni	29 Cu	30 Zn	31 Ga	32 Ge	33 As	34 Se	35 Br	36 Kr
5	37 Rb	38 Sr	39 Y	40 Zr	41 Nb	42 Mo	43 Tc	44 Ru	45 Rh	46 Pd	47 Ag	48 Cd	49 In	50 Sn	51 Sb	52 Te	53 I	54 Xe
6	55 Cs	56 Ba	57 La	72 Hf	73 Ta	74 W	75 Re	76 Os	77 Ir	78 Pt	79 Au	80 Hg	81 Tl	82 Pb	83 Bi	84 Po	85 At	86 Rn
7	87 Fr	88 Ra	89 Ac	104 Rf	105 Db	106 Sg	107 Bh	108 Hs	109 Mt	110 Ds	111 Rg	112 Cn	113 Nh	114 Fl	115 Mc	116 Lv	117 Ts	118 Og

* 58 Ce | 59 Pr | 60 Nd | 61 Pm | 62 Sm | 63 Eu | 64 Gd | 65 Tb | 66 Dy | 67 Ho | 68 Er | 69 Tm | 70 Yb | 71 Lu

** 90 Th | 91 Pa | 92 U | 93 Np | 94 Pu | 95 Am | 96 Cm | 97 Bk | 98 Cf | 99 Es | 100 Fm | 101 Md | 102 No | 103 Lr

TABLE OF CONTENTS

This page left intentionally blank.

0. Introduction

Molecules are the building block of all life, and in order to understand the function of biological systems it is crucial to have a high-level understanding of the major types of biomolecules. The goal of this chapter is to focus on how major biomolecules contribute to biological processes and to provide the background information necessary for understanding the topics covered in the rest of this volume; more comprehensive information, with a focus on the underlying chemistry, is provided in the Biochemistry textbook.

1. Polarity and Functional Groups

Polarity is probably the single most important chemical concept for the MCAT, because it reappears at conceptual levels ranging from the very small-scale (atomic structure) to the very large-scale (physiology). The MCAT loves to test you on small-scale ways of understanding large-scale systems and on the large-scale implications of small-scale changes, so this is a very important topic.

Polarity describes the distribution of charge within a molecule as mediated by electrons. In nonpolar molecules, electrons are distributed fairly evenly, although transient and induced dipoles may be present. In polar molecules, however, one or more electronegative atoms attract electrons, creating areas of higher electron density (with a partial negative charge, indicated using the symbol δ-) or lower electron density (with a partial positive charge, indicated as δ+). Taking polarity to the next level, charged molecules have one or more full positive or negative charges. Recall that like charges repel each other and opposite charges attract; this means that molecules with partial or full charges will interact with each other more intensely. As we will see, this simple principle has tremendous ramifications, and can be used as a lens through which to analyze many physiological processes.

The concept of a functional group is a useful way to explain the reactivity and chemical/physical properties of classes of molecules. A functional group is a specific group of atoms that contribute in a predictable way to the behavior of a molecule. As shown in Figure 1, you can arrange functional groups on a spectrum of polarity. Here, "polarity" is used

> > **CONNECTIONS** < <

Chapter 2 of Chemistry

very broadly, encompassing the presence of permanent dipoles, the ability to engage in hydrogen bonding, and the presence of charges.

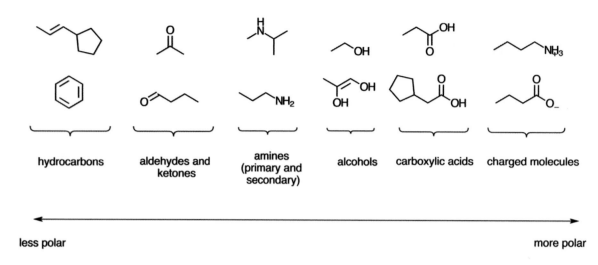

Figure 1. Functional groups and polarity (including charged groups).

MCAT STRATEGY > > >

On Test Day, if you encounter a puzzling question dealing with chemical structures, it's always a good idea to first think about whether polarity can provide any insight. Since polarity has so many effects throughout various biochemical systems, it's entirely possible for an intimidatingly worded question to boil down to "which of these molecules is most/least polar?"

What happens if a molecule has more than one functional group? Essentially, you have to make a qualitative assessment of the molecule as a whole. On the MCAT, you will often need to make a snap judgment about whether a molecule is polar or nonpolar, even though polarity is more properly thought of as a spectrum. Essentially, you have to use your judgment. Many "nonpolar" biological molecules do have some degree of polarity, but the polar functional groups are outweighed by much larger nonpolar structures. This is shown below in Figure 2, which illustrates some steroids, a large class of nonpolar hormones derived from cholesterol.

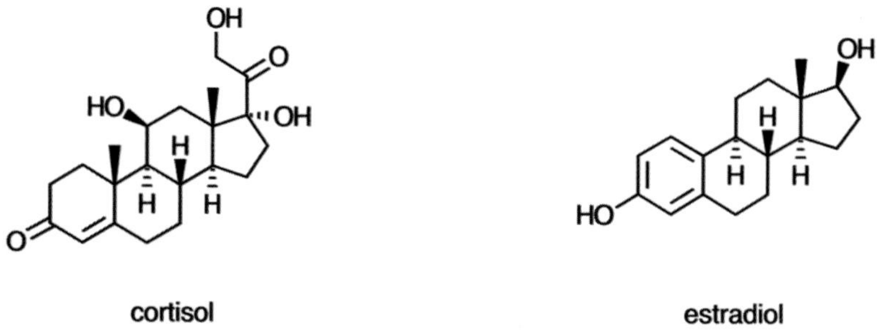

cortisol

estradiol

Figure 2. Nonpolar steroids.

Additionally, amphipathic molecules exhibit significant polar and nonpolar properties localized to different parts of the molecules. A common example of amphipathic molecules are fatty acids, which have a polar head and a nonpolar tail.

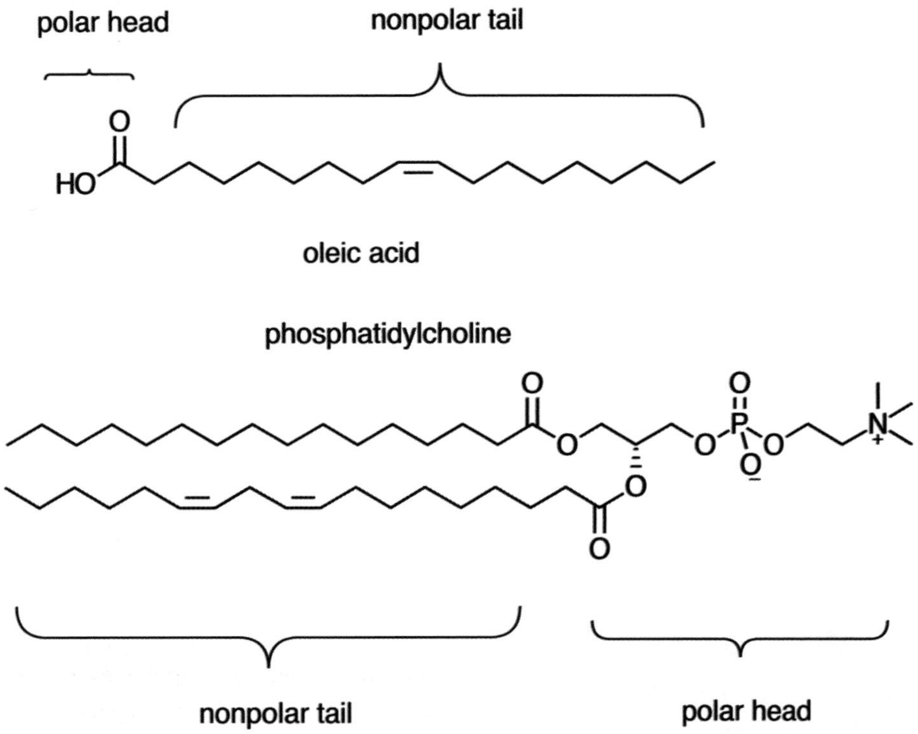

Figure 3. Amphipathic molecules.

When determining whether a molecule is polar or nonpolar, be sure to take its molecular geometry into account. A molecule can have polar bonds but be nonpolar if those polar bonds are arranged such that the dipoles cancel each other out. Two famous examples of this are carbon tetrachloride (CCl_4) and carbon dioxide (CO_2). Such molecules may occur as trap answers to questions about polarity, so be on the lookout!

Figure 4. Nonpolar molecules with polar bonds.

Polarity is also often discussed in terms of solubility. Based on the principle that like dissolves like, polar molecules are typically soluble in polar solvents (the most well-known of which is water), while nonpolar molecules are soluble in nonpolar solvents. In an organic chemistry lab, nonpolar solvents include compounds like hexane that are toxic physiologically, so in a biological context it often makes more sense to think of polar molecules as "liking" aqueous solutions and of nonpolar molecules as "liking" lipid-rich environments, since lipids are one of the most common

> > CONNECTIONS < <

Chapter 5 of Chemistry

nonpolar environments that can be found in the body. Thus, polar molecules can be described as water-soluble, hydrophilic, or lipophobic (although "lipophobic" is not commonly encountered). Nonpolar molecules can be described as non-water-soluble, hydrophobic, or lipophilic. For the purposes of the MCAT, these terms are essentially synonyms.

MCAT STRATEGY > > >

Recall that solubility is just a special case of intermolecular interactions. The MCAT could also ask you about which structures are likely to interact with each other in a more specialized environment, such as membrane receptors. The same basic principle applies: like interacts with like, and positive charges interact with negative charges.

Table 1 summarizes the key properties of polar/nonpolar compounds.

Nonpolar ↑ ↓ Polar	Examples	Major intermolecular forces	Soluble in water?	Lipophilic?
	Hydrocarbons (alkanes, alkenes, alkynes)	London dispersion forces	N	Y
	Aldehydes and ketones	Dipole-dipole forces	Y	N
	Amines	Dipole-dipole forces, hydrogen bonding (not tertiary amines)	Y	N
	Alcohols	Dipole-dipole forces, hydrogen bonding	Y	N
	Carboxylic acids	Dipole-dipole forces, hydrogen bonding	Y	N
	Charged compounds	Ionic and ion-dipole interactions	Y	N

Table 1. Key properties of polar and non-polar compounds.

2. Amino Acids and Proteins

Proteins are the building blocks of life, and amino acids are the building blocks of proteins. Amino acids are called amino acids because they have an amine ($-NH_2$) functional group and a carboxylic acid ($-COOH$) functional group. Although "amino acid" is a general chemical term that applies to many structures, in the context of the MCAT it refers to the 20 amino acids that are coded for by specific codons and are used in the body to build proteins. Amino acids have a structure characterized by a central carbon to which the following substituents are attached: $-NH_2$, $-COOH$, $-H$, and $-R$. The $-R$ group is termed the side chain of the amino acid, and it's where all the action is; that is, the properties of the side chain are what contributes to the function of the protein or peptide sequence that the amino acid is incorporated into.

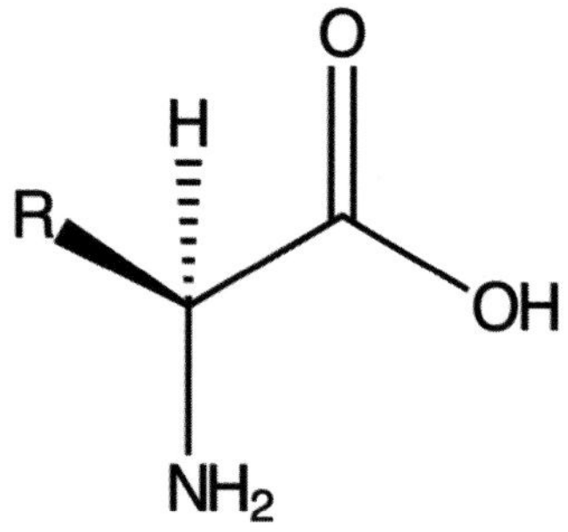

Figure 5. Generic amino acid structure.

There are multiple ways that side chains can be classified, and some of them intersect with each other. Probably the simplest classification is into nonpolar, polar uncharged, negatively charged (at physiological pH), and positively charged (at physiological pH). This classification is illustrated in Table 2, along with the three-letter and one-letter abbreviations for each amino acid, which are essential to memorize for the MCAT. Table 2 also presents subcategories of amino acids, such as aromatic amino acids, sulfur-containing amino acids, and special cases, and contains information about the pK_a values and pI values of the amino acids, which are discussed more in chapter 2 of the Biochemistry volume.

	Name	Side chain	pK_a values $pK_{a1} = COOH$ $pK_{a2} = NH_2$ $pK_{aR} = R$	pI
Nonpolar	Glycine (Gly, G)		$pK_{a1} = 2.34$ $pK_{a2} = 9.58$	5.97
	Alanine (Ala, A)		$pK_{a1} = 2.33$ $pK_{a2} = 9.71$	6.00
	Valine (Val, V)		$pK_{a1} = 2.27$ $pK_{a2} = 9.52$	5.96
	Isoleucine (Ile, I)		$pK_{a1} = 2.26$ $pK_{a2} = 9.60$	6.02
	Leucine (Leu, L)		$pK_{a1} = 2.32$ $pK_{a2} = 9.58$	5.98
	Methionine (Met, M)		$pK_{a1} = 2.16$ $pK_{a2} = 9.08$	5.74
	Proline (Pro, P)		$pK_{a1} = 1.95$ $pK_{a2} = 10.47$	6.30
	Phenylalanine (Phe, F)		$pK_{a1} = 2.18$ $pK_{a2} = 9.09$	5.48
	Tyrosine (Tyr, Y)		$pK_{a1} = 2.24$ $pK_{a2} = 9.04$ $pK_{aR} = 10.10$	5.66
	Tryptophan (Trp, W)		$pK_{a1} = 2.38$ $pK_{a2} = 9.34$	5.89

Polar uncharged	Serine (Ser, S)		$pK_{a1} = 2.13$ $pK_{a2} = 9.05$	5.68
	Threonine (Thr, T)		$pK_{a1} = 2.20$ $pK_{a2} = 8.96$	5.60
	Asparagine (Asn, N)		$pK_{a1} = 2.16$ $pK_{a2} = 8.76$	5.41
	Glutamine (Gln, Q)		$pK_{a1} = 2.18$ $pK_{a2} = 9.00$	5.65
	Cysteine (Cys, C)		$pK_{a1} = 1.91$ $pK_{a2} = 10.28$ $pK_{aR} = 8.14$	5.07
Positively charged (basic)	Arginine (Arg, R)		$pK_{a1} = 2.03$ $pK_{a2} = 9.00$ $pK_{aR} = 12.10$	10.76
	Histidine (His, H)		$pK_{a1} = 1.70$ $pK_{a2} = 9.09$ $pK_{aR} = 6.04$	7.59
	Lysine (Lys, K)		$pK_{a1} = 2.15$ $pK_{a2} = 9.16$ $pK_{aR} = 10.67$	9.74
Negatively charged (acidic)	Aspartic acid (aspartate) (Asp, D)		$pK_{a1} = 1.95$ $pK_{a2} = 9.66$ $pK_{aR} = 3.71$	2.77
	Glutamic acid (glutamate) (Glu, E)		$pK_{a1} = 2.16$ $pK_{a2} = 9.58$ $pK_{aR} = 4.15$	3.22
Special cases				
Achiral: Gly		Sulfur-containing: Cys, Met		
Aromatic: Phe, Try, Trp		Breaks up secondary structure: Pro		

Table 2. Amino acid structures and properties.

One complication to be aware of is that amino acids with polar side chains can show hydrophobic behavior. This may seem paradoxical, but recall from Section 1 that hydrophobicity/hydrophilicity is determined on the level of the molecule as a whole, and a molecule that is predominantly nonpolar can still behave in a hydrophobic manner even if it has one or more polar functional groups (see, for example, the steroid molecules in Figure 2). This is the case for cysteine because the C–S bond is actually nonpolar (with an electronegativity difference of only 0.03), as is the S–H bond (electronegativity difference of 0.38, less than the cutoff of 0.5 usually used to determine whether a covalent bond is polar), *but* the –SH group can participate in hydrogen bonding, meaning that the side group is usually classified as polar. However, its polarity is so weak that cysteine generally displays nonpolar behavior. The side chain of tyrosine has a polar –OH group, but the polar –OH group is attached to a bulky aromatic nonpolar benzyl group, which largely dictates the behavior of tyrosine overall.

In addition to this high-level classification, there are some special cases you should be aware of:

> Glycine is the only achiral amino acid because its central carbon is bonded to two hydrogens (one corresponding to the R group of glycine and one that is part of the general structure of amino acids).
> Cysteine and methionine contain sulfur.
> Cysteine residues form disulfide bridges (2 RS–H → RS–SR), resulting in cystine. Disulfide bridges form a crucial part of tertiary structure.
> Tyrosine, phenylalanine, and tryptophan are the aromatic amino acids.
> Proline is unique because its side chain binds to the nitrogen of its own amine. This locks it in place, and so-called proline kinks often disrupt the alpha-helices and beta-sheets that form the secondary structures of a protein.

> Arginine, lysine, and histidine are basic amino acids, while aspartic acid and glutamic acid are acidic amino acids. The conjugate bases of aspartic acid and glutamic acid, which predominate at physiological pH, are known as aspartate and glutamate.
> Histidine is often classified as a positively-charged amino acid, although it is not generally positively charged at physiological pH (the pK_a of the side chain NH is 6.04, which means that it *can* serve as a buffer at pH levels slightly more acidic than physiological pH, but the deprotonated, non-charged form is prevalent at physiological pH).

Amino acids are joined together through peptide bonds, in which the –COOH group of one amino acid binds with the $-NH_2$ group of another, releasing water. Peptide bonds have important biochemical properties that are discussed in Chapter 2 of the Biochemistry volume. Sequences of two amino acids are called dipeptides, and sequences of three amino acids are called tripeptides. The term "oligopeptide" is used to as a catch-all term to refer to sequences of relatively few amino acid residues (generally 2-20), while polypeptides have more. Peptide chains have an N-terminus (the terminal $-NH_2$ group) and a C-terminus (the terminal $-COOH$ group), and are conventionally written from the N-terminus to the C-terminus, which also corresponds to the order that they are synthesized in.

> > **CONNECTIONS** < <

Chapter 2 of Biochemistry

Proteins are biologically relevant molecules that are made up of one or more long amino acid chain. They have up to four levels of structure, which are essential to know for the MCAT:

> Primary structure is defined as the sequence of amino acids itself.
> Secondary structure is formed by hydrogen-bonding interactions between the carboxyl and amine components of the amino acid backbone—that is, *not* the side chains. Two common types of secondary structure are alpha-helices and beta-sheets.
> Tertiary structure is defined by side-chain interactions, including:
  − Hydrophobic interactions between side chains
  − Hydrogen bonding between side chains
  − Salt bridges formed by interactions between charged side chains
  − Disulfide bonding between cysteine residues
> Quaternary structure is formed by interactions between polypeptide chains.

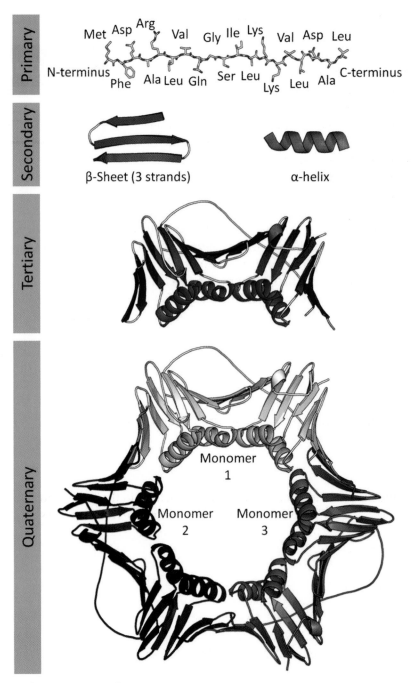

Figure 6. Primary, secondary, tertiary, and quaternary structure.

All proteins have primary, secondary, and tertiary structure, but not all proteins have quaternary structure. In general, predicting the secondary and especially the tertiary structures of proteins is computationally challenging: these levels of structure reflect protein folding that maximizes entropy, but it is very difficult to predict exactly what the optimal outcome can be. A tremendous amount of computational resources has been dedicated to protein folding simulations because it is a fundamentally important question for drug design and many other aspects of medical research, and it is an area of ongoing research.

Polarity is the driving force that determines how proteins interact with their surroundings. Nonpolar amino acid residues "like" to interact with other nonpolar substances, while polar and charged amino acid residues "like" to interact with other polar substances. The MCAT can test this principle in many ways, with some common contexts provided below:

> In aqueous solution (which corresponds to the majority of the human body), nonpolar amino acids tend to be part of the internal core of a protein's three-dimensional structure, while polar and charged amino acid residues tend to be on the outside.

> Transmembrane proteins cross through the lipid bilayer plasma membrane of cells and have three domains: an extracellular domain (facing the outside of the cell), an intracellular domain (facing the cytosol), and a transmembrane domain that spans the plasma membrane. The extracellular and intracellular domains interact with aqueous solution and are therefore largely composed of hydrophilic amino acid residues, while the transmembrane domain is dominated by hydrophobic residues because it crosses through the nonpolar layer of the lipid membrane.

> Proteins interact with other molecules at specialized areas known as binding sites. Altering the binding site by replacing one amino acid with another that has similar characteristics in polarity and charge is unlikely to significantly affect the behavior of the protein, whereas replacing one amino acid residue with another one that has different polarity/charge properties is likely to significantly disrupt the behavior.

> > CONNECTIONS < <

Chapter 3 of Biochemistry

Although proteins are also thought of primarily in terms of structure, they also play a major role in signaling, most notably in peptide hormones and in intracellular signaling pathways. Another crucial role of proteins is that they serve as enzymes, or biological catalysts. The enzymatic function of proteins is essential in regulating the reactions necessary for life.

3. Lipids

Lipids are hydrophobic, and have a diverse range of structural functions in the body, contributing to energy storage, structure, and signaling. For the MCAT, you should be aware of four main classes of lipids: (1) fatty acids and derivatives thereof; (2) cholesterol and its derivatives, such as steroid hormones; (3) eicosanoids, including prostaglandins; and (4) terpenes and terpenoids.

Fatty acids are relatively long-chain carboxylic acids. Short-chain fatty acids are defined as those with five or fewer carbons on the chain, medium-chain fatty acids have six to 12 carbons, long-chain fatty acids have 13 to 21 carbons in their tail, and very long chain fatty acids have even more. Most of the fatty acids you will see for the MCAT are long-chain fatty acids, although it is occasionally useful to note the presence of medium-chain fatty acids as well.

> > CONNECTIONS < <

Chapter 9 of Biochemistry

Triacylglycerols have three fatty acid chains (R–COOH) attached to a glycerol backbone. The esters formed between the –COOH groups of the fatty acids and the –OH groups of the glycerol can be broken down under basic conditions in a process known as saponification.

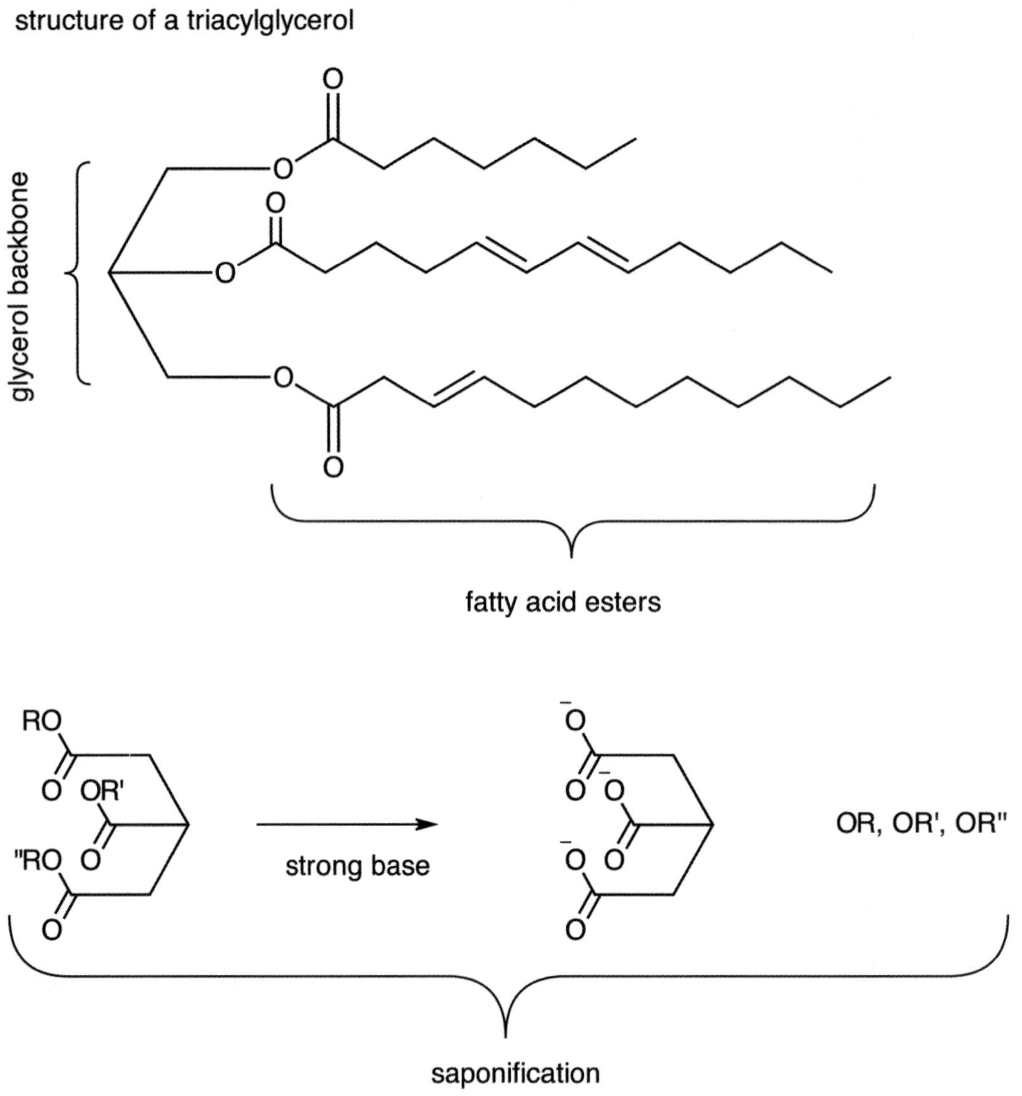

structure of a triacylglycerol

Figure 7. Triacylglycerols and saponification.

MCAT STRATEGY > > >

Recall from our discussion above that fatty acids, one of the components of triacylglycerols, are amphipathic molecules with a polar head and nonpolar tail. How would we expect triacylglycerols to differ from fatty acids? Unlike carboxylic acids or alcohols, the ester functional groups in triacylglycerols cannot participate in hydrogen bonding, so we would expect markedly less polar behavior. To succeed on the MCAT, it is essential to make a habit of engaging in this sort of reasoning that connects structure to function.

A diverse range of lipids can be generated by replacing one of the fatty acid chains with something else. In phospholipids, this "something else" is a polar phosphate group, which itself can be modified by the addition of other organic substituents. Phospholipids are most well-known for being the major components of the lipid bilayer of the plasma membrane in eukaryotic cells.

Sphingolipids are based on a molecule known as sphingosine, and all have a fatty acid residue bonded to the amine group of sphingosine. The simplest sphingolipids are known as ceramides. However, the terminal –OH group of sphingosine can be additionally modified, resulting in derivatives including glycosphingolipids and sphingomyelins. These molecules are generally found on the outer side of the plasma membrane and play a crucial role in signaling systems.

Additionally, for the MCAT you should be aware of waxes, which are complicated, naturally-occurring mixtures of lipids that include fatty acid, long-chain alcohols, aromatic compounds, and other functional groups. They are secreted by plants and animals, are solid at room temperature, and have a range of applications.

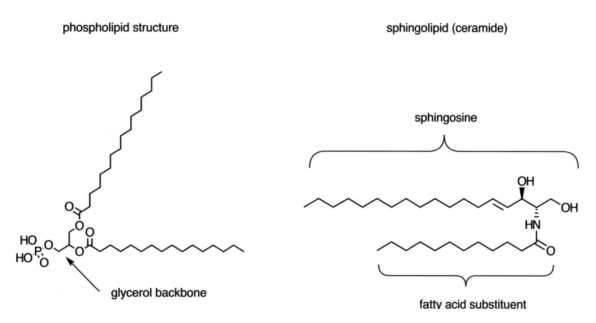

Figure 8. Phospholipids and sphingolipids.

The next major class of lipids includes cholesterol and its derivatives, including steroid hormones and vitamin D. Cholesterol has a characteristic four-ring structure, as do its derivatives. While people often associate cholesterol with heart disease risk, the real story is more complicated. Although cholesterol does play a role in the formation of atherosclerotic plaques, it is also an essential component of life, as it contributes to the fluidity of the plasma membrane and serves as the precursor for steroid hormones and other biologically essential molecules, such as vitamin D.

> > **CONNECTIONS** < <

Chapter 11 of Biochemistry

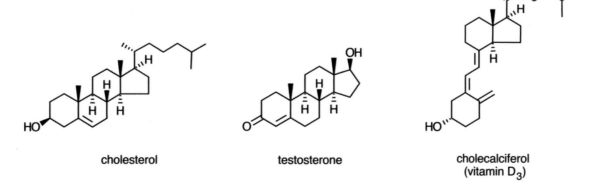

Figure 9. Cholesterol and its derivatives.

Eicosanoids form a very broad family of signaling molecules, the most important subclass of which is prostaglandins. Prostaglandins are synthesized from arachidonic acid, and have 20 carbons and a 5-carbon ring, although the other aspects of the structure of prostaglandins may vary widely. Prostaglandins have a wide range of effects. You will have ample opportunity to explore the details in medical school, but one of the most well-known effects of prostaglandins is the regulation of inflammation. Certain prostaglandins contribute to pro-inflammatory environments, while other prostaglandins have anti-inflammatory effects. This is noteworthy because emerging research indicates that inflammation may play a role in the pathophysiology of a surprising amount of diseases.

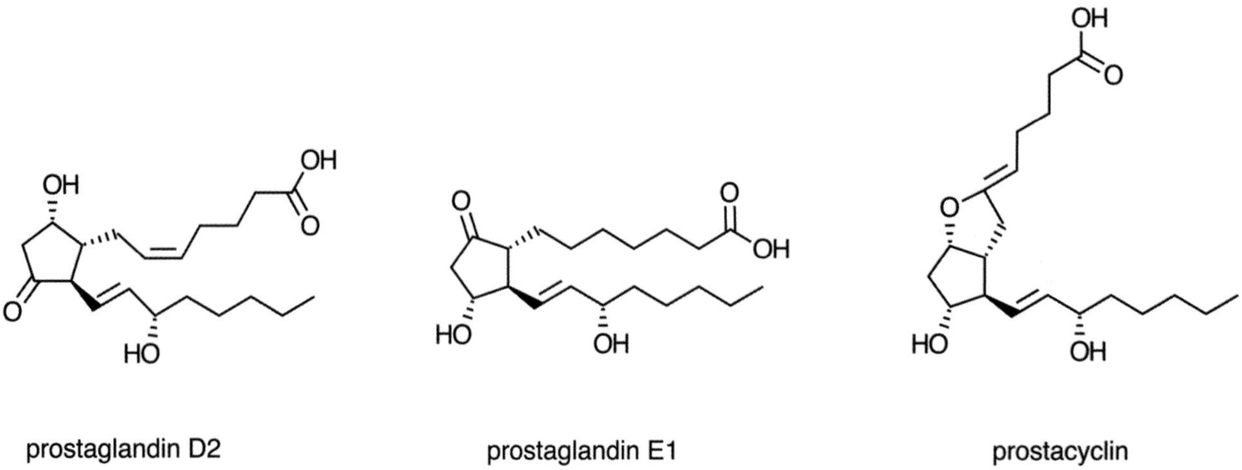

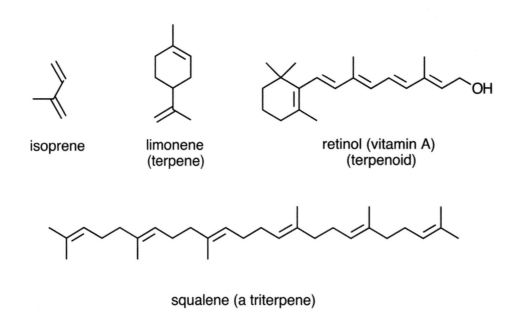

prostaglandin D2   prostaglandin E1   prostacyclin

Figure 10. Prostaglandins.

Finally, the MCAT expects you to be aware of terpenes and terpenoids. Terpenes are hydrocarbons composed of repeating isoprene units (C_5H_8), and terpenoids are terpenes that are modified with other organic substituents. Terpenes are produced by many plants and have a variety of applications; in fact, terpenoids and terpenes make up the majority of all naturally produced compounds. However, they are relevant for the MCAT for two major reasons. First, vitamin A is a terpene derivative. Second, squalene, which is a 30-carbon terpene, is a precursor for the synthesis of cholesterol, steroid hormones, and vitamin D.

isoprene   limonene   retinol (vitamin A)
                  (terpene)   (terpenoid)

squalene (a triterpene)

Figure 11. Terpenes, terpenoids, squalene, and vitamin A.

We've covered two lipid-soluble vitamins, vitamin A (a terpene derivative) and vitamin D (a cholesterol derivative), but vitamins E and K are lipids as well. Their structures are shown in Figure 12, but they do not belong to any larger classes of lipids that are tested on the MCAT. For more details about the function of vitamins, see Chapter 10 on the digestive system and Chapter 3 of the Biochemistry volume, which deals with enzymes.

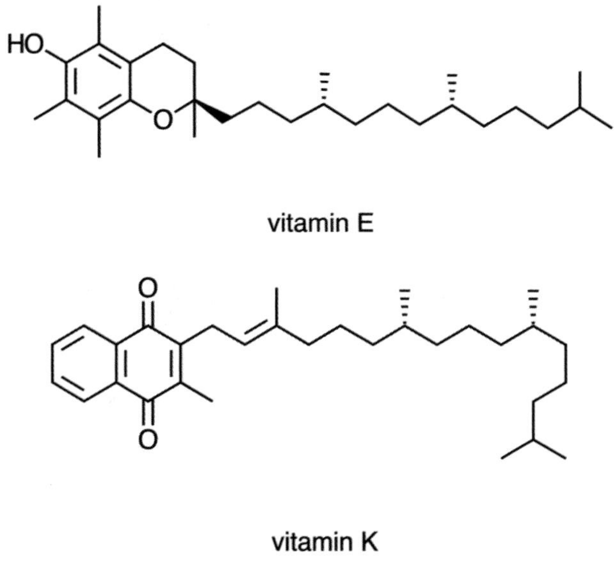

vitamin E

vitamin K

Figure 12. Vitamins E and K.

> > **CONNECTIONS** < <

Chapter 10 of Biology

> > **CONNECTIONS** < <

Chapters 6, 7, and 8 of Biochemistry volume

4. Carbohydrates

Carbohydrates are a major source of energy. Their metabolic and biochemical properties are very important topics for the MCAT, and are discussed at length in Chapters 6 through 8 of the Biochemistry volume. In this section, we will briefly review the classification, structure, and terminology associated with carbohydrates in order to provide a scaffold for understanding how they fit into the cellular and physiological systems explored in other chapters of the present volume.

Carbohydrates get their name because they fit the formula $C_x(H_2O)_y$— that is, they are composed of carbon and water. They contain a carbon backbone, a carbonyl group (C=O), and at least one hydroxyl group (–OH). If the molecule contains a terminal carbonyl group, it is known as an aldose (because it is an aldehyde), while if the carbonyl group is non-terminal, it is known as a ketose (because it is a ketone). Depending on the number of carbons, carbohydrates can be referred to as trioses (3 carbons), tetroses (4 carbons), pentoses (5 carbons), or hexoses (6 carbons).

Carbohydrate chemistry can be challenging in the context of the MCAT for several reasons, the most important of which are outlined below.

> Carbohydrates generally have multiple stereocenters, meaning that their stereochemistry is complex, to the point that a separate nomenclature system has been developed for it. For the purposes of this chapter, it suffices to know that in eukaryotes, carbohydrates occur in their D-isomers. This system of nomenclature

(D/L) is based on the orientation of glyceraldehyde and is not equivalent to *either* R/S or dextrorotatory/levorotatory.

> Carbohydrates exist in linear forms and ring forms, and it is important to be familiar with both.
> Carbohydrates bond with each other to form chains. Isolated carbohydrates are known as monosaccharides, groups of two are known as disaccharides, and long carbohydrate chains are known as polysaccharides. For the MCAT, you must be familiar with biologically relevant monosaccharides and disaccharides, as well as some important polysaccharides.

The stereochemistry of carbohydrates and the interconversion between linear and ring forms is beyond the scope of this chapter, but a familiarity with the nomenclature and structure of the essential carbohydrates will prove helpful in understanding much of the biology content of the MCAT.

MONOSACCHARIDES				
Name	**Type**	**Linear structure**	**Ring form**	**Notes**
Glucose	Aldohexose			Main source of fuel for the organism
Fructose	Ketohexose			Produced by many plants/fruits, commonly used as a sweetener
Galactose	Aldohexose			Found in dairy products and sugar beets; can be rapidly converted to glucose

DISACCHARIDES			
Name	**Composition**	**Ring form**	**Notes**
Sucrose	Glucose + fructose		Table sugar

| Lactose | Glucose + galactose | | Lactose tolerance depends on continued expression of lactase |
| Maltose | Glucose + glucose | | Found in beer, cereal, pasta, and potatoes; produced by breakdown of starch |

POLYSACCHARIDES		
Name	**Composition**	**Notes**
Amylose	Linear chains of glucose linked by α(1→4) glycosidic bonds	A major component of starch (20%-30%); less easily digested than amylopectin
Amylopectin	Linear chains of glucose linked by α(1→4) glycosidic bonds + branching due to α(1→6) glycosidic bonds every 24-30 units	Comprises approximately 70%-80% of starch; broken down more easily than amylose
Starch	~20%-30% amylose, ~70%-80% amylopectin	Major energy store produced by most green plants; most common form of carbohydrate in most diets
Glycogen	Linear chains of glucose linked by α(1→4) glycosidic bonds + branching due to α(1→6) glycosidic bonds every 8-12 units	Similar to amylopectin, but more branched; synthesized in liver and stored primarily in liver cells and muscle cells; how the body stores glucose to be used
Cellulose	Linear chain of glucose units linked by β(1→4) bonds	Produced by many plants; not digestible by humans; often referred to as dietary fiber

Table 3. Structure and properties of important carbohydrates.

5. Nucleic Acids

Nucleic acids are involved in the storage and transmission of biological information. The discovery that nucleic acids are the mechanism through which genetic information is stored and transmitted is one of the most important and fascinating scientific stories of the 20th century, and you should be aware of some of the important experiments and discoveries along that path (see Chapter 3 on molecular genetics). They are made up of nucleotides, which have three components: a nitrogenous base, a five-carbon sugar, and a phosphate group. You may sometimes encounter the term nucleoside, which refers to a nitrogenous base and a five-carbon sugar.

> > CONNECTIONS < <

Chapter 10 of Biochemistry

The nitrogenous bases include adenine (A), cytosine (C), guanine (G), thymine (T), and uracil (U). Deoxyribonucleic acid (DNA) uses A, C, G, and T, while ribonucleic acid (RNA) uses A, C, G, and U (that is, T is replaced by U in RNA). A and G have two-ring structures and are classified as purines, while C, T, and U have one-ring structures and are classified as pyrimidines. Strict rules govern which nitrogenous bases pair with each other across strands: C and G pair with each other and A and T pair with each other in DNA, while in RNA, U pairs with A. A consequence of this is known as the Chargaff rule, which states that in a double-stranded DNA molecule, the percentage of A equals the percentage of T and the percentage of C equals the percentage of G.

The structures of the nitrogenous bases are presented below in Figure 13. They are less high-yield than amino acid structures but are still worth being familiar with at least on the level of recognition. In particular, note that U is a demethylated version of T.

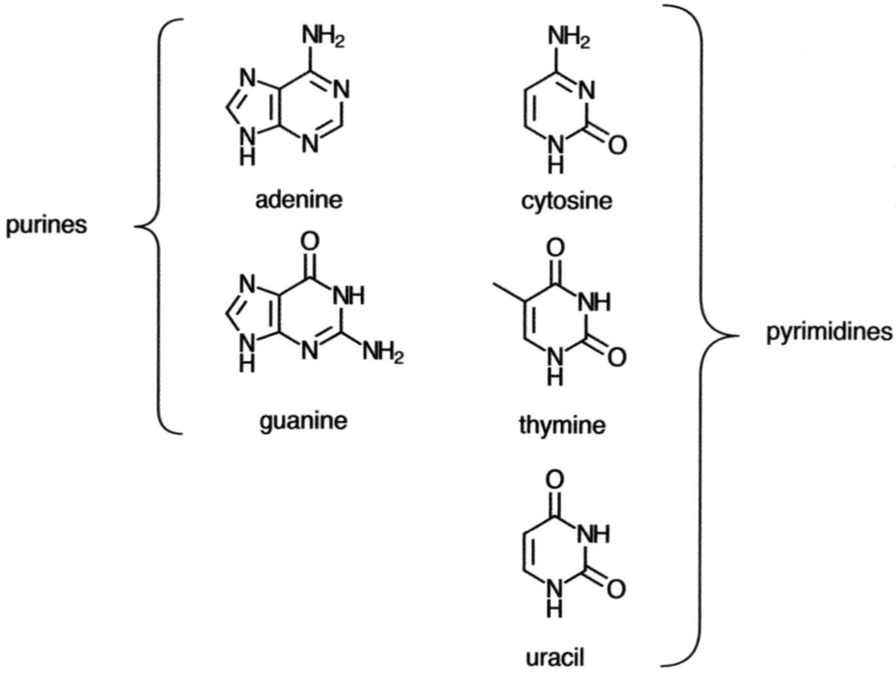

Figure 13. Nitrogenous bases.

MCAT STRATEGY > > >

To remember which nucleobases are purines and which are pyrimidines, you can use the following mnemonics. For purines, think *pure as gold*—i.e., that the *pur*ines are *A* and *G*. For pyrimidines, think *cut the pie*—*cut* is for C, U, and T, and *pie* sounds like pyrimidine.

There are two possibilities for which five-carbon sugar is present in a nucleic acid: ribose or deoxyribose, in which the 2' hydroxyl group is missing. Ribose is used in RNA (*ribo*nucleic acid) and deoxyribose is present in DNA (*deoxyribo*nucleic acid).

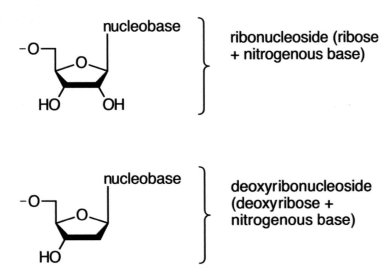

Figure 14. Ribonucleoside vs. deoxyribonucleoside.

Nucleic acids are chained together in what is termed a sugar-phosphate backbone, connected by phosphodiester linkages. In these bonds, a phosphate group forms an ester bond to the 3' carbon of one sugar molecule and the 5' carbon of another. Using this, we can talk about sequences running in the 3' → 5' direction or in the 5' → 3' direction. As we will see, most processes operate in the 5' → 3' direction.

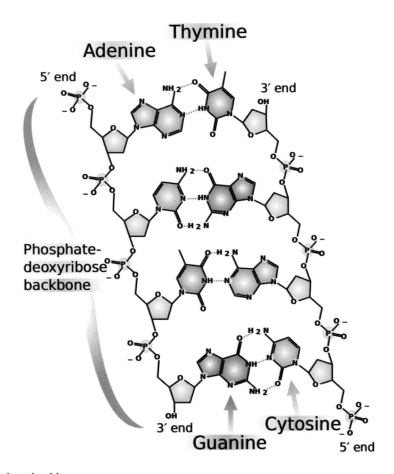

Figure 15. Sugar-phosphate backbone.

Nucleic acids can be either single-stranded or double-stranded. DNA is generally double-stranded, unless the strands are temporarily separated as part of some biological or laboratory process (a process known as denaturing), and RNA is generally single-stranded, although double-stranded RNA does occur as part of some viral genomes and as part of RNA interference in eukaryotes. Additionally, DNA-RNA hybrids can occur, most notably as a temporary step in the transcription of eukaryotic genes. The formation of double-stranded DNA relies on hydrogen-bonding interactions between complementary bases. Two hydrogen bonds are formed between A and T, and three are present between C and G. A result of this is that sequences in which C and G bases predominate require higher temperatures for the strands to denature (or separate).

Double-stranded DNA has an antiparallel orientation: that is, if the 5' → 3' direction of one strand runs "up" the page, the 5' → 3' of the other strand runs "down" the page. Double-stranded DNA is also characterized by a helical shape known as a double helix. The double helix can occur in three different major geometrical forms. In B-DNA, the most common form, the double-helix is right-handed, has approximately 10.5 base pairs per turn, and extends approximately 34 Å per 10 base pairs. A-DNA can be thought of as "tighter," with 11 base pairs per turn and 23 Å per 10 base pairs. Z-DNA, on the other hand, is "looser," with 12 base pairs per turn but 38 Å per 10 base pairs.

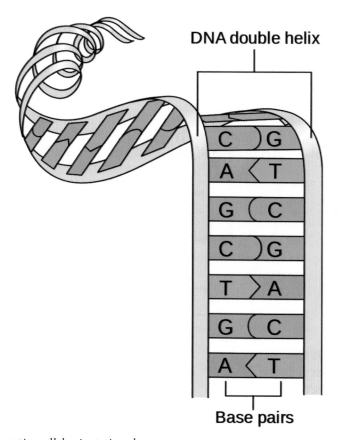

Figure 16. Double helix with antiparallel orientation shown.

DNA and RNA play fundamentally different roles in the cell. DNA is used for the long-term storage of genetic information, either in the nucleus (which contains the 23 chromosomes of the human genome) or the mitochondria (which contain mitochondrial DNA, or mtDNA, which is inherited maternally). In contrast, RNA is involved in gene expression. The most familiar example of RNA is messenger RNA (mRNA), which is transcribed from DNA and passed to the ribosomes for translation, but you should be aware of some other types of RNA with more diverse functionality as well. Heterogeneous nuclear RNA (hnRNA) is the precursor of mRNA, which is generated by several post-transcriptional modifications. Transfer RNA (tRNA) serves as the physical link between mRNA sequences and the amino acids that they code for during the translation process in the ribosomes. Ribosomal RNA (rRNA) makes up more than 50% of the ribosome by weight and plays an essential role in ensuring that translation successfully happens. Small interfering RNA (siRNA) and micro-RNA (miRNA) are RNA sequences that inhibit the expression of specific genes by interfering with the corresponding mRNA. Although these functions of RNA are diverse, a common thread is that they reflect various steps in gene expression-that is, actually *building* the products that genetic sequences code for-instead of long-term storage.

> > CONNECTIONS < <

Chapter 3 and 5 of Biology

Table 4 summarizes the major structural and functional differences between DNA and RNA.

PARAMETER	DNA	RNA
Five-carbon sugar	Deoxyribose (no 2' -OH)	Ribose (+2' -OH)
Nucleobases	A, C, G, T	A, C, G, U
Single- or double-stranded?	Double-stranded	Single-stranded
Basic role	Long-term storage of genetic information	Gene expression
Location in cell	Nucleus, mitochondria	Nucleus, cytoplasm, mitochondria
Subtypes	mtDNA	mRNA, tRNA, rRNA, hnRNA, siRNA, miRNA

Table 4. Major structural and functional differences between DNA and RNA.

6. Must-Knows

> Polarity:
  - Polar covalent bonds create permanent dipoles in molecules.
  - Polarity is driving force behind intermolecular forces and physical/chemical compounds of various functional groups.
  - Alkanes = nonpolar, alcohols = polar, carboxylic acids = very polar, charged molecules = extremely polar.
  - Symmetrical polar bonds → nonpolar molecule (CCl_4, CO_2).
> Amino acids:
  - Central carbon with –NH$_2$, –COOH, –H, and –R groups.
  - Nonpolar: glycine (Gly, G), alanine (Ala, A), valine (Val, V), isoleucine (Ile, I), leucine (Leu, L), methionine (Met, M), proline (Pro, P), phenylalanine (Phe, F), tyrosine (Tyr, Y), tryptophan (Trp, W)
  - Polar uncharged: serine (Ser, S), threonine (Thr, T), asparagine (Asn, N), glutamine (Gln, Q), cysteine (Cys, C)
  - Positively charged/basic: arginine (Arg, R), histidine (His, H), lysine (Lys, K)
  - Negatively charged/acidic: aspartic acid (Asp, D), glutamic acid (Glu, E)
  - *Know the structures!*
> Proteins
  - Building blocks of body, structure and signaling

- Primary structure = amino acid sequence, secondary structure = H-bonding between amino acid backbone components, tertiary structure = side-chain interactions, quaternary structure = interactions between polypeptides.
> Lipids: know the structure and functions of the following classes:
  - Signaling, structure, energy storage
  - Fatty acids and derivatives (triacylglycerols, phospholipids, sphingolipids)
  - Cholesterol and derivatives (steroid hormones and vitamin D)
  - Prostaglandins
  - Terpenes and terpenoids
> Carbohydrates
  - Energy storage; used in metabolism
  - Important monosaccharides: glucose, fructose, galactose
  - Sucrose = glucose + fructose, lactose = glucose + galactose, maltose = glucose + glucose
  - Polysaccharides (starch and glycogen): polymers of glucose used for energy storage in plants and animals, respectively.
> Nucleic acids: differences between RNA and DNA
  - DNA: deoxyribose base, RNA: ribose base
  - DNA: A ~ T, C ~ G; RNA: A ~ U, C ~ G
  - DNA: long-term storage of genetic information, RNA: gene expression
  - DNA: double-stranded, RNA: single-stranded

This page left intentionally blank.

Practice Passage

Research investigating the diet of medical students has highlighted problems associated with consumption of ethanol mixed with energy drinks. These problems include reduced perception of alcohol intoxication and greater alcohol consumption, resulting in more negative consequences.

Most energy drinks contain high amounts of carbohydrates and taurine, an amino sulfonic acid (Figure 1). Taurine is a conditional amino acid and in proper doses it can be used as medicine to treat congestive heart failure, high blood pressure, hepatitis, high cholesterol, and cystic fibrosis. The ethanol component of the combined drink contributes 6.9 kcal/g to the energy needs of the body.

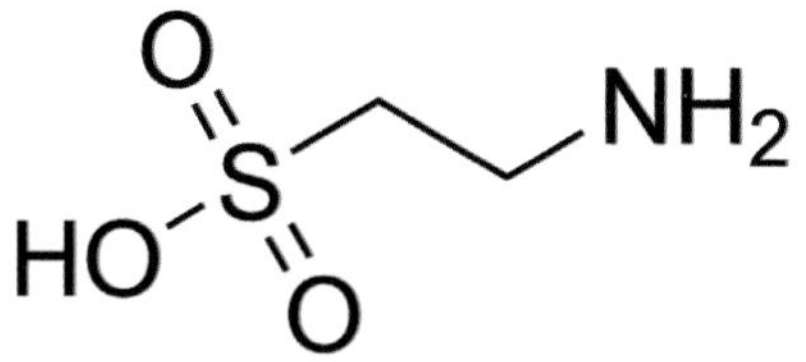

Figure 1. Taurine

Naturally occurring amino acids, monosaccharides, and disaccharides were among the most common compounds in the commercial drinks analyzed. Select identified compounds in the drinks analyzed are included in Figure 2.

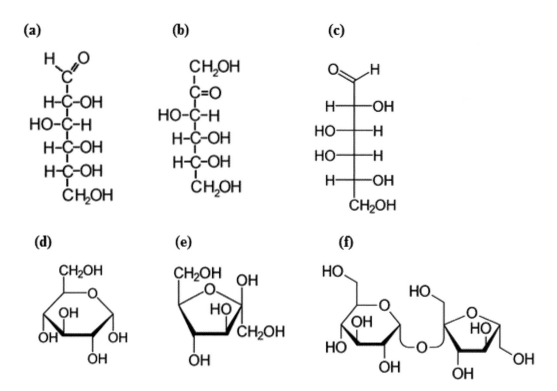

Figure 2. Linear forms of (a) glucose, (b) fructose, and (c) galactose; ring forms of (d) glucose (e) fructose, and (f) sucrose

The effect of these drinks on students' kidney function and carbohydrate metabolism was assessed via urinalysis. Subjects provided 300 ml urine samples and Benedict's test for non-reducing sugars was performed.

Adapted from Alford, C., Scholey, A., & Verster, J. C. (2015). Energy drinks mixed with alcohol: are there any risks? Nutrition Reviews, 73(11), 796–798. under CCBY 4.0

1. Glucose and galactose are which of the following types of stereoisomers?
   A. Enantiomers
   B. Rotomers
   C. Epimers
   D. Constitutional isomers

2. Which of the following types of reactions are involved in the formation of sucrose from glucose and fructose?
   A. Hydrolysis
   B. Dehydration
   C. Esterification
   D. Addition

3. A student in an organic chemistry class was given a sample of an unknown monosaccharide and was asked to identify the compound. The student performed an elemental analysis and found that the sample was 40.0% carbon, 6.7% hydrogen, and 53.3% oxygen. Which of the following monosaccharides could be the unknown based on this experiment?
   I. Glucose
   II. Galactose
   III. Fructose
   A. I only
   B. II only
   C. I and II only
   D. I, II, and III

4. What best explains the difference between the three-dimensional arrangement of phospholipids and that of fatty acids inside the human body?
   A. Hydrophilic interactions
   B. Hydrophobic interactions
   C. Steric hindrance
   D. Non-covalent assemblies

5. The disaccharide maltose, shown below, is composed of which of the following monosaccharides?

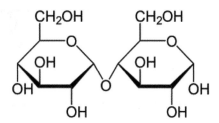

   I. Glucose
   II. Galactose
   III. Fructose
   A. I only
   B. II only
   C. I and II only
   D. I and III only

6. What is the proper order of nutritional energy density from smallest to largest?
   A. Carbohydrates < lipids < proteins
   B. Lipids < proteins < carbohydrates
   C. Ethanol < carbohydrates < lipids
   D. Carbohydrates < ethanol < lipids

7. Which of the following molecules is in the same macronutrient category as taurine?
   A. Serine
   B. Linoleic acid
   C. Lactose
   D. Galactose

Practice Passage Explanations

Research investigating the diet of medical students has highlighted problems associated with consumption of ethanol mixed with energy drinks. These problems include reduced perception of alcohol intoxication and greater alcohol consumption, resulting in more negative consequences.

Key terms: ethanol, energy drinks

Cause and effect: combination of energy drinks + EtOH reduces perception of EtOH consumption

Most energy drinks contain high amounts of carbohydrates and taurine, an amino sulfonic acid (Figure 1). Taurine is a conditional amino acid and in proper doses it can be used as medicine to treat congestive heart failure, high blood pressure, hepatitis, high cholesterol, and cystic fibrosis. The ethanol component of the combined drink contributes 6.9 kcal/g to the energy needs of the body.

Key terms: taurine, conditional amino acid

Cause and effect: taurine can be used as a medicine; ethanol contributes to dietary energy

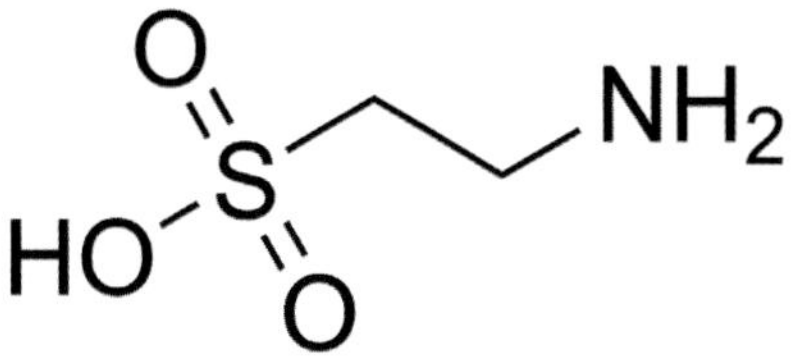

Figure 1. Taurine

Naturally occurring amino acids, monosaccharides, and disaccharides were among the most common compounds in the commercial drinks analyzed. Select identified compounds in the drinks analyzed are included in Figure 2.

Key terms: naturally occurring, saccharides, amino acids

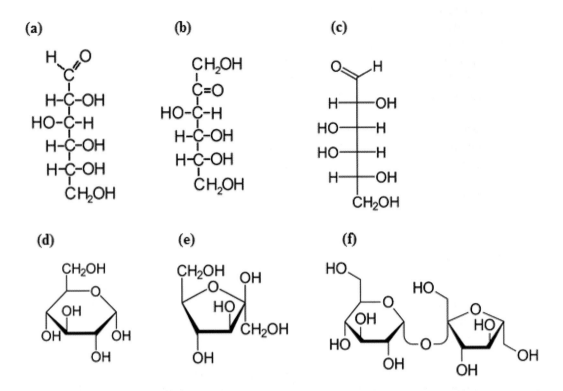

Figure 2. Linear forms of (a) glucose, (b) fructose, and (c) galactose; ring forms of (d) glucose (e) fructose, and (f) sucrose

Figure 2 contrasts the linear/ring forms of common sugars; linear forms have carbonyl groups, making it possible to classify them as either aldehydes or ketones, both of which are capable of undergoing tautomerization and rearrangement

The effect of these drinks on students' kidney function and carbohydrate metabolism was assessed via urinalysis. Subjects provided 300 ml urine samples and Benedict's test for non-reducing sugars was performed.

Cause and effect: aldoses can be oxidized to carboxylate groups, which forms the basis for Benedict's test, in which basic aqueous solutions of Cu^{2+} get reduced to insoluble Cu^{+}

Adapted from Alford, C., Scholey, A., & Verster, J. C. (2015). Energy drinks mixed with alcohol: are there any risks? Nutrition Reviews, 73(11), 796–798. under CCBY 4.0

1. C is correct. Looking closely at Figure 1 (a and c) shows that the only difference between glucose and galactose is the stereochemical arrangement of groups on C(4). Note that the aldehyde carbon establishes the order of numbering. Epimers are stereoisomers that differ in the stereochemistry of a single chiral center. Choice C is the correct answer.
   A. Enantiomers are stereoisomers that are mirror image structures. For compounds with multiple chiral centers, each chiral atom would have opposite configurations to be enantiomers. Choice A can be eliminated.
   B. Rotamers result from different rotational conformations that can exist. Glucose and galactose are not rotomers.
   C. Constitutional isomers, also known as structural isomers, occur when two compounds have the same formula but different connectivity. Stereoisomers are not constitutional isomers.

2. B is correct. When sucrose (a disaccharide) is formed from glucose and fructose (monosaccharides), an ether group is formed from two alcohols by loss of a water molecule.
A, C, D: Hydrolysis is when water is added to a compound, therefore choice A can be eliminated. Esterification is when an organic acid and an alcohol are combined by way of dehydration to form an ester. Choice C can be eliminated. As stated in the passage, addition typically occurs when an unsaturated molecule such as an aldehyde, ketone, or alkene becomes saturated. Choice D can be eliminated.

3. D is correct. There are three basic ways to answer this question. The longest method would be to assume that you have 100 g of the unknown and then determine the mole ratio by dividing the resulting mass of carbon, hydrogen, and oxygen by the corresponding atomic masses. A shorter method would be to first determine the empirical weight:

$$C_6H_{12}O_6 \rightarrow C_1H_2O_1 \rightarrow 1(12) + 2(1) + 1(16) = 30 \text{ g/mole}$$

Next determine the percentage of carbon, hydrogen, and oxygen.
$(12/30) \times 100 = 40\%$
$(2/30) \times 100 = 7\%$
$(16/30) \times 100 = 53\%$
A, B, C: These answers are a result of miscalculation. The most efficient method to the answer the question would be to notice that glucose, fructose, and galactose all have the same molecular formula ($C_6H_{12}O_6$) and therefore the same empirical formula ($C_1H_2O_1$). Thus, all the sugars given must be correct.

4. C is correct. In aqueous environments, phospholipids and glycolipids do not form spherical micelles like fatty acids do. This is because phospholipids and glycolipids have two hydrocarbon chain tails while fatty acids only have one. As a result, phospholipids and glycolipids are too bulky to orient themselves into a micelle.
   A. Lipids and fatty acids do not experience significant hydrophilic interactions in aqueous environments.
   B. Both phospholipids and fatty acids will experience hydrophobic interactions in the aqueous environment of the human body.
   D. Cell membranes are non-covalent assemblies. In an actual cell membrane, the constituent protein and lipid molecules are held together by many non-covalent interactions, which act cooperatively.

5. A is correct. If we look closely at the orientation of the hydroxyl groups in the maltose, we see that the orientations are the same, eliminating choice C. We now can compare the orientations of the hydroxyl groups in the maltose to the sucrose, which is composed of glucose and fructose.

Glucose   **Galactose**   **Fructose**

Notice that the six-membered ring structure in sucrose is identical to the six-membered ring on the left in the structure of maltose. Therefore maltose is composed of two glucose molecules, connected by an ether link at the 1,4 positions of the rings.
II: The rings shown in the question are not galactose.
III: Looking closely at the ring structure of the maltose, you can see that there are six atoms in the rings, eliminating fructose as one of the component monosaccharides.

6. D is correct. While fats (lipids), carbohydrates (sugars), and proteins are the three primary macronutrients, other molecules humans consume have an energy density. The passage tells us that alcohols have an energy density of approximately 6.9 kcal/g. Do not worry when you encounter unknown or unfamiliar information in the passage. We can combine it with our required knowledge about macronutrients. Fats have the greatest amount of food energy per gram (8.8 kcal/g) while proteins and most carbohydrates have about 4 kcal/g.

    A. Proteins have a lower energy density (~ 4 kcal/g) than lipids (~ 9 kcal/g).
    B. Both proteins and carbohydrates have a lower energy density (~ 4 kcal/g) than lipids (~ 9 kcal/g).
    C. According to the passage, ethanol (~ 7 kcal/g) has a higher energy density than carbohydrates (4 kcal/g).

7. A is correct. The passage describes taurine as an amino acid. The only amino acid listed among the answer choices is serine.

    B. Linoleic acid is a fatty acid.
    C. Lactose is a carbohydrate.
    D. Galactose is a carbohydrate.

Independent Questions

1. Which of the following lists the monomers that make up carbohydrates, nucleic acids, and proteins, respectively?
   A. Monosaccharides, amino acids, nucleotides
   B. Triacylglycerols, nucleotides, amino acids
   C. Monosaccharides, nucleosides, amino acids
   D. Monosaccharides, nucleotides, amino acids

2. The alpha-helical structure of a protein is held together by which of the following?
   A. Hydrogen bonding between carbonyl oxygen and amino hydrogen atoms
   B. Hydrogen bonding between amino nitrogen atoms and hydrogen atoms attached to the alpha carbon
   C. Disulfide bridges between side chain sulfur atoms
   D. Hydrogen bonding between side chain hydrogen and oxygen atoms

3. In a transmembrane protein, an isoleucine residue is replaced by an arginine residue. This mutation will most likely:
   A. allow the protein to form more disulfide bridges.
   B. render the protein more hydrophilic than before.
   C. render the protein uncharged at physiological pH at the position of the mutation.
   D. disrupt the protein's alpha-helical structure through the formation of a kink.

4. Consider the triacylglycerol shown below.

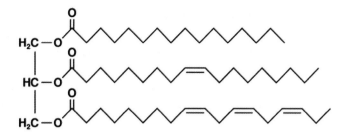

   This molecule:
   A. consists of three short-chain fatty acids connected to a backbone via ether linkages.
   B. consists of three medium-chain fatty acids connected to a backbone via ester linkages.
   C. consists of three long-chain fatty acids connected to a backbone via ester linkages.
   D. consists of three short-chain fatty acids connected to a backbone via ester linkages.

5. Which of the following is NOT true of squalene?
   A. It is classified as a carbohydrate.
   B. It is classified as a terpene.
   C. It is a precursor of testosterone.
   D. It is involved in cholesterol synthesis.

6. The structure of D-galactose is depicted below.

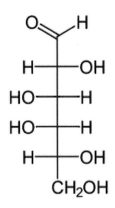

Galactose can be accurately described as:

I. a hexose.

II. an aldose.

III. a ketose.

IV. an isomer of glucose.

A. III only

B. I and II only

C. I, II, and IV only

D. I, III, and IV only

7. A researcher is using a biochemical technique to learn the exact sequence of a nucleic acid. He discovers that the 100th unit in the sequence is the molecule shown below.

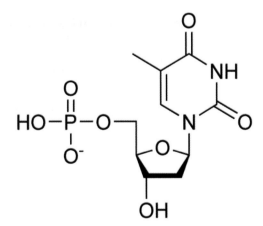

Which of the following choices accurately describes this structure?

A. It is a ribonucleotide.

B. It is a ribonucleoside.

C. It is a deoxyribonucleotide.

D. It is a deoxyribonucleoside.

8. One end of a segment of double-stranded DNA reads 5'-CATTG-3'. How many hydrogen bonds are contained between complementary nucleotides in this five-base-pair segment?

A. 4

B. 10

C. 12

D. 13

Independent Question Explanations

1. D is correct. Carbohydrates, nucleic acids, and proteins are polymers, which means that they are composed of smaller repeating subunits known as monomers. Carbohydrate monomers are called monosaccharides, nucleic acid monomers are nucleotides, and protein monomers are amino acids. Triacylglycerols are lipids, while nucleosides lack the phosphate groups that nucleotides contain.

2. A is correct. Alpha helices are a form of secondary structure, which does not directly involve side chains. Instead, secondary structure is held together by hydrogen bonding between the carbonyl and amine regions of protein residues. Specifically, amino hydrogen atoms form H-bonds with carbonyl oxygen atoms. (The hydrogen atoms attached to the alpha carbon cannot be involved, since they are not bound to O, F, or N.)

3. B is correct. Arginine is a basic amino acid, meaning that it can become protonated, causing it to carry a positive charge. As such, arginine is more polar than isoleucine, a nonpolar amino acid. The mutation described in the question would thus render the protein more hydrophilic ("water-loving") than before. Disulfide bridges are associated with cysteine, while kinks in the secondary structure are caused by proline.

4. C is correct. Triacylglycerols consist of three fatty acid subunits connected to a three-carbon glycerol backbone. These connections are ester linkages (note the presence of three ester functional groups in the molecule above). Long-chain fatty acids are those with between 13 and 21 carbons in their tails, which is true of all three fatty acid components of this molecule.

5. A is correct. Squalene is a terpene, or a compound composed of isoprene (C_5H_8) units. Terpenes are hydrocarbons, but they do not contain oxygen, which means they cannot possibly be classified as carbohydrates. Squalene is a precursor to cholesterol, which in turn is the major precursor to the formation of steroid hormones (of which testosterone is one).

6. C is correct. From the given diagram, we can easily tell that galactose contains six carbons, making it a hexose (I is correct). Sugars that contain or are derived from aldehydes are also called aldoses; the molecule shown clearly contains an aldehyde functional group, making II correct as well. (Ketoses are sugars that contain ketones, which galactose does not.) Finally, galactose is shown as having a molecular formula of $C_6H_{12}O_6$. This is identical to the formula of glucose, making the two molecules isomers (IV is correct).

7. C is correct. The structure shown contains deoxyribose as its five-carbon sugar, which is evidenced by the lack of a 2' hydroxyl group. This molecule is also a nucleotide, as it includes phosphate. (Nucleosides contain only a nitrogenous base and a five-carbon sugar.)

8. C is correct. Complementary C and G nucleotides are held together by three hydrogen bonds, while A and T nucleotides are connected by two H-bonds. When in the form of double-stranded DNA, the segment above contains two C-G pairings and three A-T pairings. This yields a total of 2 (3) + 3 (2) = 12 hydrogen bonds.

This page left intentionally blank.

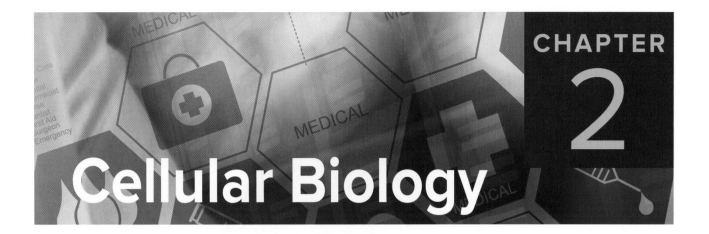

CHAPTER 2

Cellular Biology

0. Introduction

Cellular biology forms much of the basic groundwork for MCAT biology. This subject is important not just because it can be directly tested—although it is very likely that you will encounter at least a few questions on this material—but because it is often a prerequisite for understanding the information presented in passages, especially experimental passages. When studying cellular biology for the MCAT, be sure not to limit yourself to memorizing isolated details. While you do certainly have to know the basic factual material thoroughly, it is also important for you to be able to integrate the material and understand how cells function in response to various stimuli, how that functionality can be disrupted, and how cells contribute to the larger-scale functionality of the organism.

1. Cell Theory

From 1650 until the mid-19th century, the basic composition of life was a major subject of research, and this process led to the formulation of the following basic tenets of cell theory (the first two were proposed in 1839 and the third was proposed in 1855):

1. All living organisms are composed of one or more cells.

2. The cell is the most basic unit of life.

3. All cells arise only from pre-existing cells.

More modern versions of cell theory also incorporate the idea that genetic information encoded by DNA is transmitted from cell to cell. While the statements in cell theory may be easy to take for granted, each of them reflects a remarkable intellectual journey. The MCAT expects you to be familiar with the basics of cell theory and its historical impact on the field of biology, so it is worth reviewing some of the key experimental findings that provided the foundation of cell theory.

The first experiment that identified evidence of cells was conducted by Robert Hooke in 1665, who constructed a simple compound microscope and used it to examine cork, which is composed of dead tissue from the bark of trees. He observed what seemed to be a honeycomb-shaped lattice, and he dubbed the components of that structure "cells" because they reminded him of cells (or rooms) within monasteries. In 1674, the self-taught scientist and lensmaker Anton van Leeuwenhoek observed so-called "animalcules" ("little animals") under his microscopes; his observations included bacteria and spermatozoa.

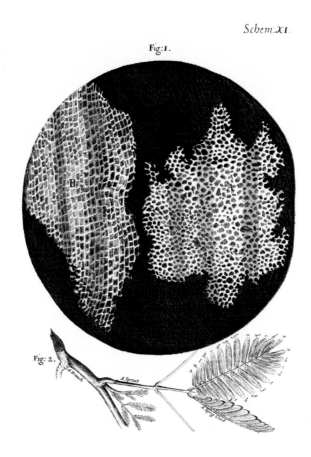

Figure 1. Hooke's observations of the microscopic structure of cork.

2. Eukaryotic Cell Structure

Eukaryotes are defined by three major structural/functional features: the presence of a membrane-bound nucleus, the presence of organelles, and mitotic division. In this section, we will discuss the structure of eukaryotic cells.

As mentioned above, eukaryotes are defined by the presence of a membrane-bound nucleus, although there are some exceptions to this rule (as is almost always the case in biology). Red blood cells, or erythrocytes, are the most notable exception that you should know for the MCAT: these cells do not contain nuclei. It is also possible for cells to have more than one nucleus. The MCAT does not expect you to be aware of any specific instances of this, but it could potentially be presented to you in a passage, so don't let it surprise you.

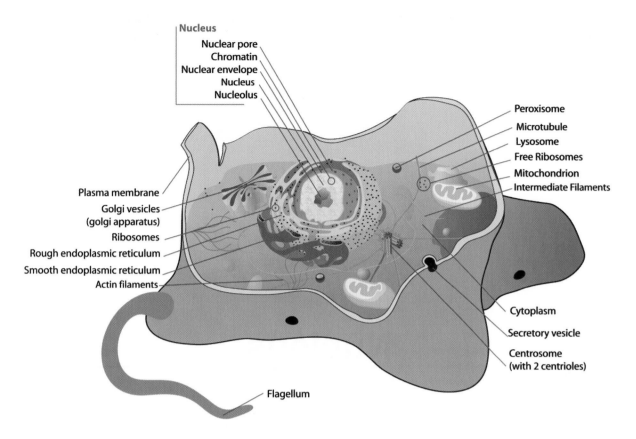

Figure 2. Diagram of a eukaryotic cell.

The basic function of the nucleus is to compartmentalize and store genetic information, which is encoded in DNA in the form of linear chromosomes. The structures that allow the nucleus to carry out this function are the nuclear membrane and the nuclear pores. The nuclear membrane, also known as the nuclear envelope, is a bilayer membrane composed of two phospholipid layers. Nuclear pores are protein complexes that cross the nuclear membrane and allow the selective transport of larger molecules (>40 kDa, most importantly RNA and protein molecules) into and out of the nucleus, while smaller molecules such as ions and fluids can simply diffuse through the membrane. Additionally, the nucleus contains a sub-organelle known as the nucleolus ("little nucleus"), which is responsible for ribosome assembly.

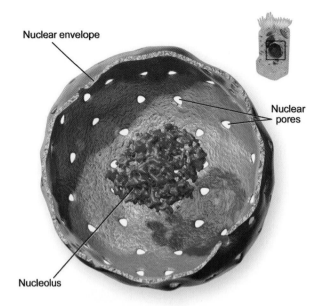

Nucleus

Figure 3. Nucleus.

The cytoplasm is defined as everything else within a living cell (i.e., everything besides the nucleus and the external membrane). It includes all the other organelles and the cytosol, which is the dense, gel-like, aqueous solution that comprises the liquid found inside cells. The terms "cytoplasm" and "cytosol" are often used almost interchangeably, but you should be careful to be able to differentiate them if necessary, because terminological precision is an essential component of MCAT success.

The next most basic function of the cell is energy production or metabolism. Metabolism is a huge topic, and is covered at length in the Biochemistry volume. However, when thinking about metabolism from a high-level point of view, you can keep the following points in mind. Adenosine triphosphate (ATP) can be thought of as synonymous to energy in the cell, so generating energy essentially means generating ATP. ATP is produced by ATP synthase, which is powered by the proton gradient generated by the electron transport chain, which is in turn fed by electron carriers such as NADH and $FADH_2$—meaning that when you see NADH and $FADH_2$, you can essentially think of them as energy precursors. A chain of metabolic processes generate energy. First, glycolysis takes place in the cytoplasm and generates a net payoff of two NADH molecules and two ATP molecules per glucose, as well as two molecules of pyruvate. Glycolysis is common in both prokaryotes and eukaryotes, but eukaryotes (and aerobic prokaryotes) take metabolism to the next level by deploying the citric acid cycle (also known as the Krebs cycle, tricarboxylic acid cycle, or the TCA cycle) and oxidative phosphorylation to squeeze every last bit of energy out of the pyruvate generated by glycolysis. In addition, energy can be generated from fatty acids via beta-oxidation, and even from amino acids when necessary.

The citric acid cycle, beta-oxidation of fatty acids, and oxidative phosphorylation take place in organelles known as the mitochondria (singular = mitochondrion), which are the energy powerhouses of the cell. In combination with the products of glycolysis, the citric acid cycle and oxidative phosphorylation allow 30+ molecules of ATP to be obtained from a single molecule of glucose, which is at least a 15-fold increase from what is possible using glycolysis alone. As you can imagine, this was a transformative evolutionary leap in the history of life, and the mitochondria are therefore essential to the functioning of all eukaryotic organisms.

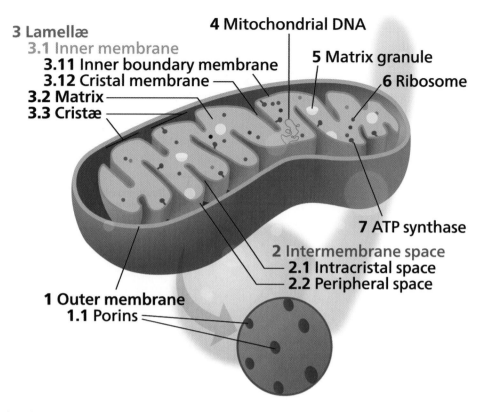

3 Lamellæ
3.1 Inner membrane
3.11 Inner boundary membrane
3.12 Cristal membrane
3.2 Matrix
3.3 Cristæ

4 Mitochondrial DNA

5 Matrix granule

6 Ribosome

7 ATP synthase

2 Intermembrane space
2.1 Intracristal space
2.2 Peripheral space

1 Outer membrane
1.1 Porins

Figure 4. Mitochondrion.

The mitochondria are separated from the rest of the cytoplasm by two membranes (an outer membrane and an inner membrane), both of which are composed of a phospholipid bilayer. The structure of mitochondria can therefore be subdivided into the outer membrane, the intermembrane space, the inner membrane, and the mitochondrial matrix, which is the innermost part of each mitochondrion. The mitochondrial matrix is the site of the citric acid cycle, and oxidative phosphorylation takes place via the action of protein complexes embedded in the inner membrane of the mitochondrion. As part of oxidative phosphorylation, the electron transport chain causes a buildup of protons in the intermembrane space, and the resulting proton gradient is used to power the activity of ATP synthase.

Mitochondria are also unique in that they are self-replicating organelles. They contain their own DNA (mitochondrial DNA, or mtDNA), which is circular in structure and inherited maternally, and undergo binary fission. This remarkable fact has been explained through the endosymbiontic origin hypothesis, popularized by the pioneering 20th-century biologist Lynn Margulis. According to this proposal, mitochondria derive from an original prokaryotic cell capable of aerobic metabolism that became engulfed in another cell, resulting in an endosymbiotic lineage. Deleterious mutations in mtDNA can cause mitochondrial disorders, which can vary dramatically in severity, cause wide-ranging symptoms dealing with malfunctioning oxidative metabolism, and are inherited maternally. These disorders are an area of intense ongoing research, and are worth being aware of because they could conceivably be discussed in a passage on the MCAT. Additionally, mtDNA has proven quite useful in research into the genetic history and dispersion of humans, as a result of its maternal inheritance pattern.

Lysosomes can be thought of as the garbage disposal system of the cell; material from outside the cell enters the lysosomes through endocytosis, while material from inside the cells enters through autophagy. They are membrane-bound vesicles that contain a diverse range of enzymes that hydrolyze various polymers. These enzymes operate best at acidic pH levels, and the lysosomes are therefore kept at a pH of 4.5-5.0.

The endoplasmic reticulum (ER) is a net-like organelle that extends out from the nuclear membrane. It is composed of cisternae, which are flat, round or tube-like structures that are enclosed by double membranes. It is divided into the rough ER and the smooth ER. The rough ER is rough because it is covered with ribosomes, which are the site of protein synthesis. In contrast, the smooth ER does not have ribosomes, and is involved in lipid metabolism (both synthesis and breakdown), the production of steroid hormones, and detoxification. Of note, the fact that the smooth ER is involved in lipid production means that it produces the phospholipid components of membranes throughout the cell.

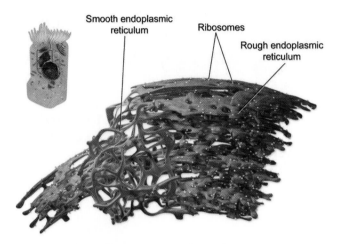

Endoplasmic Reticulum

Figure 5. Endoplasmic reticulum.

Once proteins are synthesized, the Golgi apparatus modifies them and packages them into membrane-bound vesicles that are then sent to the ultimate destination of the proteins. It is composed of stacks of pancake-like chambers known as cisternae (similar to those in the ER), and plays a major role in preparing proteins for secretion.

MCAT STRATEGY > > >

The Golgi apparatus is often analogized to a post office. Comparisons like this are sort of silly, but can be helpful to remember the basic functionality of various organelles. As part of your own study process, get creative in thinking about ways to conceptualize how organelles function and what would happen if their function was negatively impacted by some external factor.

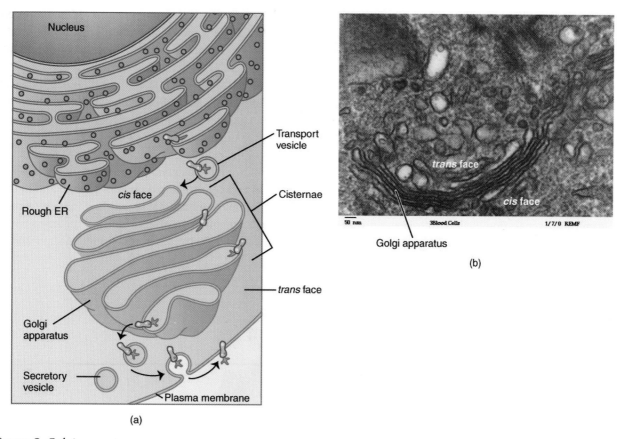

Figure 6. Golgi apparatus.

Peroxisomes are the final membrane-bound organelle that you should be aware of for the MCAT. As the name implies, peroxides (such as hydrogen peroxide or H_2O_2) accumulate in the peroxisomes. Functionally, peroxisomes play a major role in the metabolism of very-long-chain lipids by breaking them down to medium-chain lipids that are transported to the mitochondria for further processing. Peroxisomes also play a role in detoxification of substances such as ethanol.

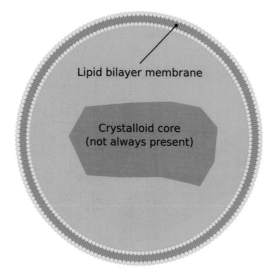

Figure 7. Peroxisomes.

The cytoskeleton is also a crucial component of the structure of eukaryotic cells. It is sometimes considered an afterthought, but the MCAT considers it to be of comparable importance to the membrane-bound organelles discussed above, so be sure not to skim over it in your study process! Essentially, the cytoskeleton is what provides structural support to a cell and helps it move.

The major components of the cytoskeleton are microfilaments, microtubules, and intermediate filaments. Microfilaments are composed of two strands of actin polymers, and play a role in cell motility (or movement), as well as endocytosis and exocytosis. Additionally, microfilaments contribute to the process of cell cleavage during division and to the ability of cells to contract. The actin components of microfilaments also interact with myosin as part of muscle contraction. Microtubules are slightly wider than microfilaments and are composed of polymeric dimers of proteins known as alpha-tubulin and beta-tubulin. They help maintain the structure of the cell and make up cilia and flagella. They also help facilitate intracellular transport and make up mitotic spindles, which play a role in chromosome separation during mitosis and meiosis. Intermediate filaments are a diverse family of proteins that provide structural support and are involved in cell-cell adhesion processes. Keratin, which makes up our hair and nails, is a well-known example of an intermediate filament.

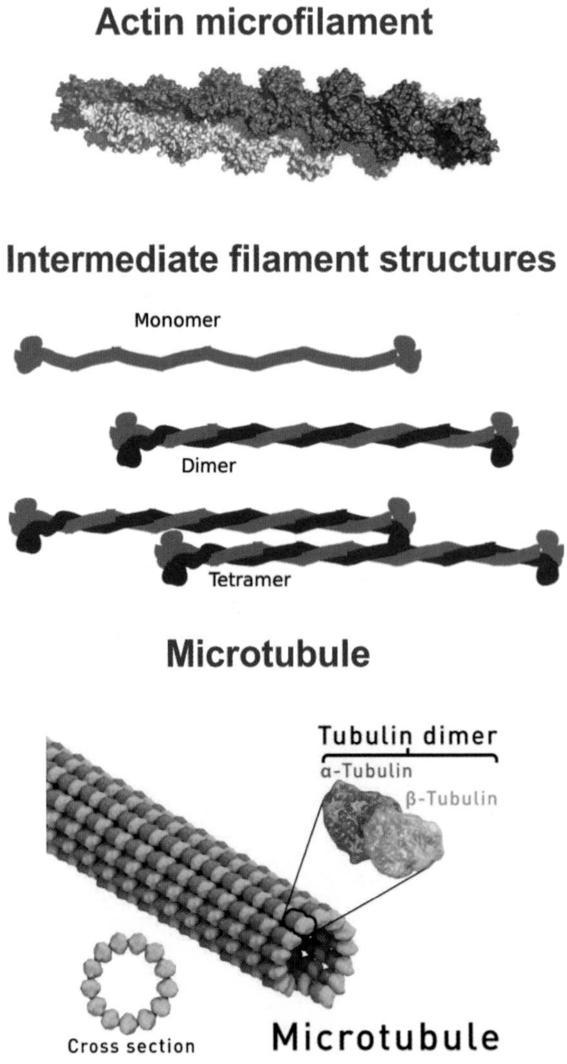

Figure 8. Microfilaments, microtubules, and intermediate filaments.

Centrioles are cylindrical structures made up primarily of tubulin that help organize the mitotic spindle and are an important constituent of the centrosome, which is the major microtubule organizing center within the cell.

Flagella and cilia are two structures involved in cell motility that are formed from microtubules. Flagella (singular = flagellum) are tail-like appendages that protrude from a cell and allow it to move, although they also can serve as sensory appendages. Flagella are found in both prokaryotes and eukaryotes, but they are structurally distinct. Cilia are relatively small projections that help move substances along the cell surface. A well-known example in the human body is the presence of cilia in the respiratory tract to help move mucus out of the lungs. In eukaryotes, both cilia and flagella are characterized by what is known as a 9+2 structure, in which an outer ring of nine pairs of microtubules surrounds an inner ring of two microtubules. Eukaryotic flagella flap back and forth and their movement is powered by ATP. In contrast, prokaryotic flagella use a rotary motion, are powered by a proton gradient, and are composed of a protein known as flagellin.

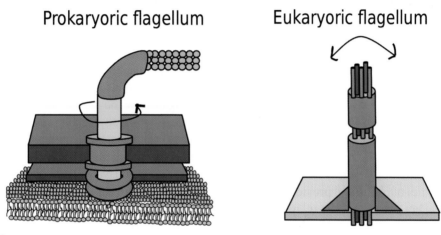

Figure 9A. Flagella.

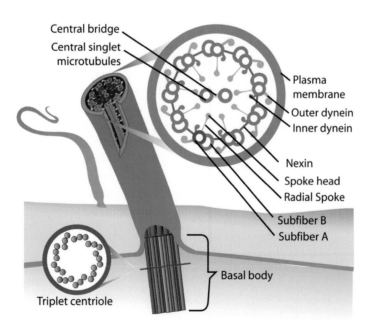

Figure 9B. Cilia.

MCAT STRATEGY > > >

A danger when reviewing eukaryotic cell structure for the MCAT is that this material may be quite familiar—perhaps even deceptively familiar, since it is all too easy to allow your eyes to skim over familiar-sounding content without really double-checking it. To combat this tendency, consider making it a point to learn something new about all of the organelles, either from this textbook or from external sources. Even if the new content you learn isn't technically speaking MCAT content, just the act of learning something new (even if you forget it before Test Day) will force you to consolidate your knowledge and identify potential gaps.

3. Transmembrane Transport and Signaling

The plasma membrane of a cell separates the cell from the extracellular environment surrounding it, and therefore is critical for maintaining cellular integrity and for mediating the communication of a cell with its surroundings. Biological membranes are discussed in more detail in Chapter 11 of the Biochemistry volume, but it is worth reviewing some high-level points in the context of eukaryotic cell structure.

The plasma membrane is primarily composed of lipids and proteins. It is defined by the presence of a lipid bilayer, created by two layers of phospholipids with hydrophilic heads and hydrophobic tails. The hydrophilic heads face towards the aqueous solutions present in the cytoplasm and the extracellular space, while the hydrophobic tails face inward. Phospholipids are a relatively diverse class of molecules that can also be involved in signaling cascades, depending on how the phosphate group is modified (with an example being phosphatidylinositol, a major secondary messenger). Sphingolipids are present in the membrane as well, with roles in signaling. Cholesterol is another major component of the cell membrane and promotes fluidity at low temperatures by preventing crystal structures from being formed among phospholipid tails and stability at high temperatures by inhibiting the movement of phospholipids in the lipid bilayer. Waxes are present in the cell membrane of some types of plants and provide structural support and waterproofing. Carbohydrates are also present in the cell membrane, but only on the outer layer (due to their hydrophilicity), where they modify proteins and lipids in a variety of ways, usually with implications for signaling and/or recognition pathways.

MCAT STRATEGY > > >

Let's integrate this information about the plasma membrane with what we learned about amino acids and proteins in Chapter 1. Recall that some amino acids are nonpolar and others are polar. We'd expect nonpolar amino acids to predominate on the inside of the cell membrane and polar amino acids to predominate on the outsides. Always be on the lookout for ways to integrate pieces of biological knowledge!

The structure of the plasma membrane is commonly described in terms of the fluid mosaic model. The fluid mosaic model states that the plasma membrane can be thought of as a two-dimensional liquid in which the lipid and protein components can shift relatively freely. It is possible for phospholipids to shift from one side of the membrane to another (i.e., from facing the cytoplasm to facing the extracellular space), but this is energetically costly and is catalyzed by enzymes known as flippases. As a result of these structural aspects of membrane dynamics, very small and nonpolar molecules can diffuse easily through the cell membrane, whereas large and polar molecules must be transported.

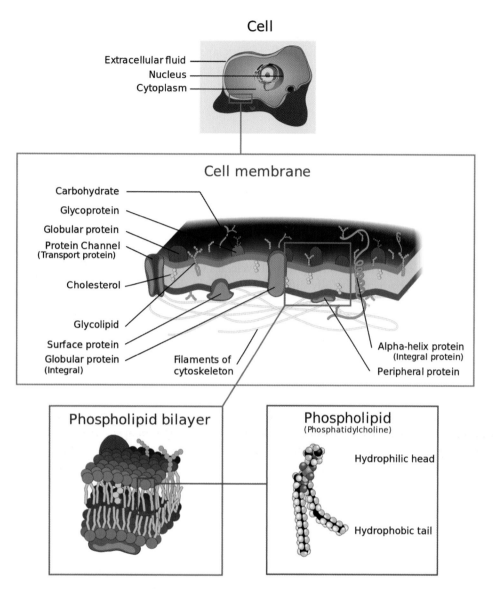

Figure 10. Plasma membrane structure.

The fluid mosaic of the plasma membrane contains some structures of note in addition to the phospholipid bilayer. Lipid rafts are held together by large amounts of cholesterol and contain relatively high concentrations of sphingomyelins. They can diffuse within the lipid bilayer, and their main functions include contributing to the fluidity of the membrane and helping to regulate signaling processes. The interior and exterior surfaces of the plasma membrane contain embedded proteins, which are closely rooted in the interior of the membrane but do not span it, and membrane-associated proteins, which are held in place by non-covalent interactions with other structures present on the surface of the plasma membrane. The plasma membrane is also traversed by many different types of proteins, including membrane receptors and transport proteins (channels and pores).

> > CONNECTIONS < <

Chapter 11 of Biochemistry

> > CONNECTIONS < <

Chapter 7 of Biology

The details of transmembrane transport and signaling are discussed in Chapter 11 of the Biochemistry textbook, but you should be aware that transmembrane transport is tightly regulated and that the chemical properties of signaling molecules shape how they interact with the cell. Smaller nonpolar molecules, such as steroid hormones, can diffuse directly into the cell, while polar signaling molecules generally exert their effects on cells by interacting with membrane-bound receptors.

4. Cell Cycle and Mitosis

The cell cycle describes the rhythm of a cell's life as it goes through phases of division. In this section we will cover the cell cycle and mitosis, or asexual reproduction. The cell cycle can be divided into a resting phase, interphase, and cell division.

Resting phase is also known as Gap 0 (G_0). As the name implies, during resting phase nothing in particular happens from the point of view of cell division: essentially, during this period, the cell just goes about its business. However, although we tend to skip over G_0 when covering the cell cycle, it's worth remembering that G_0 is an extremely common state for cells in the body: many fully-differentiated cells in the body remain in G_0 for long periods of time. Because it can last for an essentially indefinite period of time, resting phase is often considered not to be a proper part of the cell cycle itself.

Interphase is when a cell prepares for division, and it can take up approximately 90% of the time of the cell cycle. Two major things happen during interphase: growth and DNA replication. However, interphase is broken into three stages: Gap 1 (G_1), synthesis (S), and Gap 2 (G_2). During G_1 and G_2, the cell grows, and during S, DNA is replicated.

Why, then, does S happen in between, meaning that this phase has three stages for two functions? This may seem inefficient, but it has the crucial advantage of allowing checkpoints. The G_1 checkpoint, also known as the restriction point, is when a cell commits to division. The presence of DNA damage or other external factors can cause a cell to fail this checkpoint and not divide. The G_2 checkpoint that takes place before cell division similarly checks for DNA damage after DNA replication, and if damage is detected, serves to "pause" cell division until the damage is repaired. Throughout interphase, chromatin is loosely packaged (euchromatin) to allow transcription and replication.

MCAT STRATEGY > > >

Don't neglect interphase! Many MCAT students remember focusing more intensely on mitosis in introductory biology coursework and carry over that tendency into MCAT prep. However, when studying for the MCAT, you should always keep an eye out for areas of content that have potential implications for disease processes. The fact that two major checkpoints happen in interphase tells you that interphase plays a major role in regulating cell division, with potential implications for cancer.

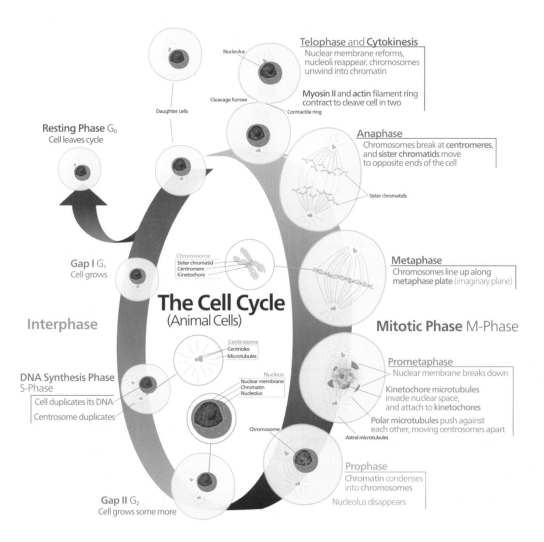

Figure 11. The cell cycle.

Cell division, or mitosis, takes place in four phases: prophase, metaphase, anaphase, and telophase. For the MCAT, you must be very familiar with these stages, because it is likely that you will have to apply your knowledge of mitosis rapidly in a potentially unfamiliar context. Mitosis (and meiosis, described in the next section) is a subject that virtually every pre-med student has studied at least twice in various classes, if not more—yet it has a way of remaining a source of confusion.

Essentially, the point of prophase is to prepare the cell to go through mitosis. This preparation involves condensing the DNA such that distinct chromosomes become visible, as sister chromatids (or copies of a given chromosome) joined at a region known as the centromere. The kinetochore assembles on the centromere, and is the site where microtubule fibers that extend from the centrosome and form the mitotic spindle attach to pull the sister chromatids apart in later stages of mitosis. In addition to microtubules that attach to the kinetochore, other microtubules known as asters extend from the

MCAT STRATEGY > > >

If you find yourself coming back to study mitosis/meiosis again and again, the best way to solidify your knowledge for the long term is to actively rehearse it. Obtain some pipe cleaner or any other bendy colored structure that you can use to simulate chromosomes and walk through it. Doing so may seem silly, but all measures are on the table for transforming passive knowledge into active knowledge!

centrosome to anchor it to the cell membrane (from the Latin word for "stars"—asters are known for forming star-like patterns around the centrosome) The other major aspect of prophase is preparation of the rest of the structures involved in mitosis. The nuclear envelope and the nucleolus disappear, and the mitotic spindle forms.

In metaphase, the chromosomes line up at the middle of the cell along an imaginary line that is known as the metaphase plate. This alignment takes place in the center of the cell because the microtubules attached to the kinetochores generally exert the same force. Metaphase is especially important because a final cell checkpoint occurs, during which the cell checks to make sure that the kinetochores are attached properly to the microtubules of the mitotic spindle. This serves as a way to prevent improper separation (leading to potential nondisjunction and aneuploidy) in the next phase.

In anaphase, the sister chromatids are separated and pulled to opposite sides of the cell by shortening of the microtubules attached to the kinetochores. At this point, each side of the cell should have a complete set of chromosomes.

Telophase can be thought of as the opposite of prophase. A new nuclear envelope appears around each set of chromosomes and a nucleolus reappears within each of those nuclei. The process of mitosis is completed by cytokinesis, which is sometimes considered to be part of telophase and is sometimes presented as an independent process.

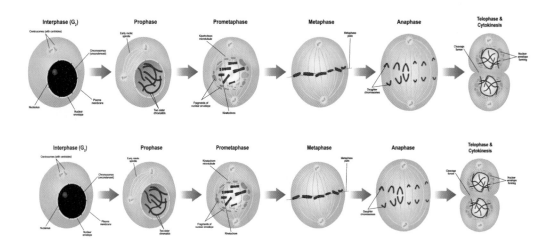

Figure 12. Mitosis.

5. Meiosis

Meiosis is a form of cell division that is essential for sexual reproduction. It takes place in germ cells (also known as sex cells). In humans, meiosis can be subdivided into spermatogenesis (how sperm cells are formed) and oogenesis (how eggs are formed). For more detail, see Chapter 8, which discusses the human reproductive system.

> > CONNECTIONS < <

Chapter 8 of Biology

Meiosis differs from mitosis in that it results in the formation of four daughter cells, each of which has only one copy of each chromosome (haploid, n), in contrast to mitosis, which generates cells with two copies of each chromosome (diploid, 2n) that are essentially identical to their parent cell (with the exception of any newly occurring mutations). These daughter cells are known as gametes. In sexual reproduction, two haploid cells fuse to create a new diploid daughter cell, known as a zygote, which is different from its parents. The variability allowed by sexual reproduction was a tremendously important development in the history of life.

Meiosis and mitosis include the same basic sequence of prophase, metaphase, anaphase, and telophase, but meiosis involves two rounds of cell division and some of the stages are crucially different from their counterparts in mitosis. In the following discussion, we'll focus on the ways in which meiosis and mitosis differ; if not otherwise specified, you can assume that the mechanics involved in the various stages of mitosis transfer over.

Meiosis I is the first round of division, and results in the formation of two haploid daughter cells that contain duplicate sister chromatids. In prophase I, homologous chromosomes (i.e., the maternal and paternal copies of a given chromosome) pair up with each other in a process known as synapsis, forming tetrads. While paired up, homologous chromosomes may exchange genetic information in a process known as crossing over. The crossing-over points are known as chiasmata. This process results in recombinant DNA that is another source of variation in sexual reproduction, in addition to the variability inherent to the process.

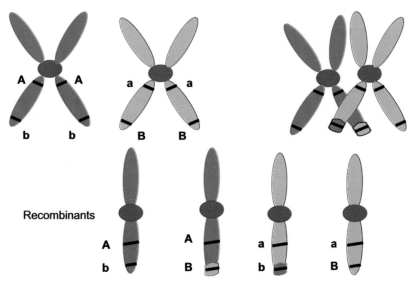

Figure 13. Crossing over.

> > CONNECTIONS < <

Chapter 4 of Biology

In metaphase I, homologous pairs, which take the form of tetrads, line up at the metaphase plate. The orientation of the homologous pairs is random in terms of which side of the metaphase plate the maternal or paternal copy of a given chromosome in a homologous pair winds up. This is an important point to recognize because it is the mechanical reason for the principle of independent assortment in genetics.

In anaphase I, the homologous pairs are separated, and one member of each pair is pulled to each side of the cell. This is when the cell is converted from a diploid cell (maternal and paternal copies of each chromosome) to a haploid cell (only the maternal or paternal copy of each chromosome). Note, however, that each individual member of the homologous pair still has two chromatids.

Meiosis II operates essentially the same way as mitosis. In meiosis II, the sister chromatids are split up into two haploid daughter cells.

Table 1 below summarizes the essential differences between mitosis and meiosis.

MITOSIS	MEIOSIS
Single-stage process	Two-stage process
No pairing of homologous chromosomes	Pairing of homologous chromosomes in synapsis, resulting in tetrads
Results in two diploid cells	Results in four haploid cells
Daughter cells are genetically identical to parent cell, except for incidental mutations or malfunctions	Crossing over in prophase I leads to genetic recombination
	Random orientation of homologous pairs in metaphase I leads to principle of independent assortment
Takes place in somatic cells	Only takes place in germ (sex) cells

Table 1. Mitosis versus meiosis.

6. Prokaryotic Cells

Prokaryotes are the simplest and oldest form of cellular life, and have tremendous effects, both positive and negative, on human health, so a basic knowledge of their structure is fundamental for all physicians.

Prokaryotes are defined by the absence of a nucleus and membrane-bound organelles, and are classified into two domains of life: Bacteria and Archaea. Archaea are single-celled organisms that are traditionally known as extremophiles, capable of inhabiting environments with high salinity or extreme temperatures. Archaea can be thought of as being somewhere between prokaryotic and eukaryotic life; structurally, they resemble bacteria in that they do not have nuclei or membrane-bound organelles, but they resemble eukaryotes in terms of certain genes and enzymes used in metabolic pathways. A notable fact about Archaea is that they use a broad range of energy sources, including organic compounds, ammonia, metal ions, and even hydrogen. Additionally, some Archaea are photosynthetic. The MCAT places a much heavier emphasis on bacteria than on Archaea, so the rest of this section will deal with bacteria and viruses.

Bacteria are ubiquitous: at any given time, it has been estimated that approximately 10^{30} bacteria exist on Earth, with a biomass comparable to that of plants. It is often stated that there are 10 times more bacterial cells than human cells in the body; this has been argued to be an overestimate, but it is still absolutely certain that bacteria, especially in the gastrointestinal tract, are present in huge numbers and play a crucial role in the maintenance of human health. Many bacteria are commensal, meaning that the body provides them with nutrients but they have no particular positive or negative effects on the body, except for the marginal effect provided by helping to prevent the overgrowth of harmful bacteria. Some bacteria have a symbiotic relationship with the body, which means that they have positive effects on the body. A classic example of this is the fact that vitamins K and B_7 are produced in the gut by bacteria.

Other bacteria, however, are pathogens, and can cause infections that negatively impact the organism. The pathogenicity of a bacterium may vary depending on context. For example, methicillin-resistant *Staphylococcus aureus* (MRSA), which is a major problem in hospitals, can asymptomatically colonize the skin of healthy individuals for extended periods of time, but can also cause life-threatening infections, especially in individuals with a weakened immune system. Pathogenic bacteria can damage their human hosts in a variety of mechanisms; while we often think of an infection as simple out-of-control reproduction, there are some bacteria that must reproduce intracellularly (like *Chlamydia*) and others that can reproduce either within host cells or outside of host cells (such as *Yersinia pestis*, the causative agent of plague). Moreover, some bacteria exert a negative effect by producing specific toxins; this is the case for *Clostridium tetani*, which causes tetanus. Treating infections of such pathogens can be tricky, because immediately killing off all of the bacteria could cause a massive release of toxins, which would harm the patient.

Although bacteria do have specific genus and species names, they are commonly described in terms of their shape and their ability to engage in certain types of metabolism. The reason for this is that it can be quite time-consuming and challenging to specifically characterize the type of bacteria observed in a patient or in a culture; although the cost of genomics-based identification techniques has dropped tremendously over the last 20 years, it is still often more feasible to discuss bacteria in terms of macro-level properties such as morphology and metabolism.

Spherical bacteria are known as cocci, rod-shaped bacteria are called bacilli, and spiral-shaped bacteria are known as spirilli. The shape of a bacterium may be reflected in its name, so you should be able to guess that *Staphylococcus aureus* is spherical and *Lactobacillus acidophilus* is rod-shaped (moreover, the *acidophilus* part of that name is a clue that this bacterium likes low-pH environments—and in fact, *Lactobacillus acidophilus* is a major component of the gut and vaginal microbiota, as well as a common ingredient in yogurt).

MCAT STRATEGY >>>

Of course, there is no rule saying that the genus and species name of bacteria have to provide any useful information, but you should cultivate the habit of absorbing all the relevant clues you can.

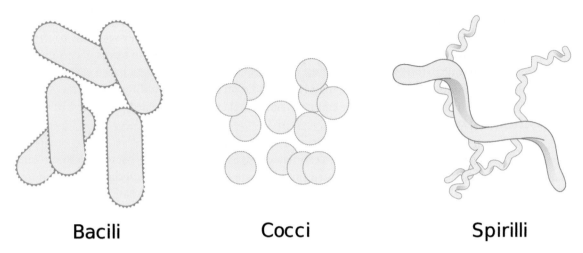

Bacili   **Cocci**   **Spirilli**

Figure 14. Shapes of bacteria.

Bacteria are also classified in terms of how they use oxygen in metabolism. Bacteria that do not require oxygen for metabolism are known as anaerobes, and there are several types of anaerobes depending on the details of their relationship with oxygen. For obligate anaerobes, oxygen is toxic. (As a historical aside, developing the ability to handle the presence of oxygen in the atmosphere was a major step in the evolution of life. Oxygen is, in many ways, a toxin, because it generates reactive oxygen species that induce major cellular damage. While the MCAT does not expect much familiarity with evolutionary history, you are expected to know about antioxidants, the importance of which derives from this fact.) Aerotolerant anaerobes are similar to obligate anaerobes in that they cannot engage in aerobic metabolism, but as their name implies, oxygen is not toxic for them. Other bacteria, known as facultative anaerobes, can engage in either aerobic or anaerobic metabolism, depending on the circumstances. Bacteria that require oxygen for metabolism are known as obligate aerobes.

Figure 15 shows where you would find different types of bacteria in a culture medium contained in a test tube with a loosely fitting cap. Oxygen would be expected to be present at the top of the tube and absent at the bottom. Therefore, obligate aerobes (#1 in Figure 15) would only be found at the top, and obligate anaerobes (#2) only at the bottom. Facultative aerobes (#3) would be found throughout the tube, but with a greater distribution at the top due to the increased efficiency of aerobic metabolism. So-called microaerophiles (#4) are a group of microorganisms that require oxygen for metabolism but are poisoned by high concentrations. Aerotolerant anaerobes (#5) would be spread evenly throughout the tube.

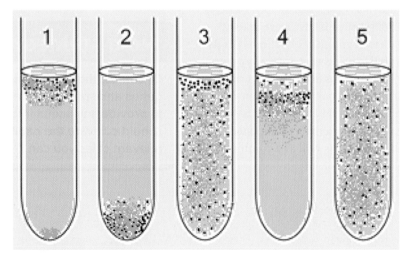

Figure 15. Aerobes and anaerobes in a test tube.

Since bacteria by definition do not have membrane-bound organelles, their structure is simpler than that of eukaryotes. Nonetheless, there are some key aspects of the structure of bacteria that help differentiate them from eukaryotes and have clinical implications. In fact, these points are intimately related on a conceptual level. The goal of antibiotics is to kill prokaryotes without negatively affecting eukaryotic (host) cells, so any major structural difference between prokaryotes and eukaryotes can potentially be exploited for that goal.

Unlike eukaryotes, bacteria have a cell wall that encloses a cell membrane. The cell membrane is similar to that of eukaryotes, but the cell wall is a major structural difference. The basic point of the cell wall is to provide structural support for bacteria in a range of environments. Bacterial cell walls are characterized by the presence of a polysaccharide known as peptidoglycan, which gives the cell wall its rigidity.

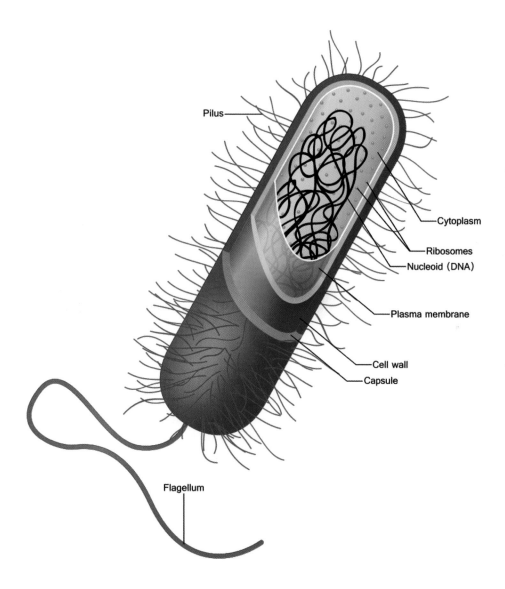

Figure 16. Bacterial cell.

There are two main types of bacterial cell walls, containing different quantities of peptidoglycan. They are differentiated in a process known as Gram staining (named after the Danish scientist Hans Christian Gram, not after the metric unit of weight). Gram-positive bacteria have cell walls with extensive cross-linked peptidoglycan structures, whereas Gram-negative bacteria have a thin peptidoglycan layer surrounded by a lipopolysaccharide outer membrane. Gram staining depends on a dye that remains trapped within the cross-linked peptidoglycan layers of Gram-positive, while being washed away from the Gram-negative cells. The steps of Gram staining are as follows:

1. Crystal violet is applied as a primary stain to heat-fixed bacteria.

2. Iodide is added. Iodide binds to the crystal violet stain and traps it within the peptidoglycan layer.

3. An ethanol or acetone wash is applied. This washes away the lipopolysaccharide membrane of Gram-negative bacteria and allows the crystal violet-iodide complexes to be washed away as well.

4. Safranin is applied as a counterstain to visualize Gram-negative cells as pink (otherwise they would just be unstained).

After Gram staining, Gram-positive cells are a deep purple, while Gram-negative cells are pink. Gram staining is a common first step in the identification of bacteria in clinical settings because, although it has some limitations (not all bacteria yield consistent results), it does correlate to meaningful differences in clinical behavior. Gram-negative bacteria are generally not susceptible to antibiotics such as penicillin that target peptidoglycan cross-linking; however, specific antibiotics exist that target Gram-negative bacteria. The lipopolysaccharide membrane of Gram-negative bacteria also has clinical implications because it can induce an innate immune response in humans, causing inflammation and complicating the clinical course of treatment.

Prokaryotes lack mitochondria, but aerobic bacteria carry out aerobic respiration, which we usually associate with mitochondria in humans. How can this be? The electron transport chain, which generates a proton pump that powers ATP synthase, requires a membrane. In eukaryotes, the inner membrane of the mitochondria is used for this purpose, but prokaryotes use the cell membrane for this purpose.

Prokaryotes do have ribosomes (note that these are not *membrane-bound* organelles), but they structurally differ from those of eukaryotes. Prokaryotic ribosomes are made of 30S and 50S subunits, which add up to a 70S ribosome, while eukaryotes have an 80S ribosome composed of a 60S and a 40S component. The unit "S" is a non-metric unit, known as Svedberg units, that describes sedimentation rate. It is defined as 10^{-13} seconds, and it refers to how long it takes a particle to sink to the bottom of a test tube under high-intensity centrifugation. The key point here is that Svedberg units are proportional to mass, because larger particles take longer to sediment, but it is not a linear relationship, meaning that Svedberg units are not directly additive. This is why we observe that the 30S and 50S components of the bacterial ribosome add up to 70S. From a clinical point of view this fact about bacteria is important because the structural differences between the subunits of bacterial and eukaryotic ribosomes mean that ribosomes can be a target of antibiotics.

Bacteria also have flagella that are used for movement. Unlike in eukaryotes, where the flagellum works by whipping, bacterial flagella act as a motor that rotates. They have three components: the basal body, which is the motor of the flagellum and also anchors it to the membrane; the filament, which is a hollow helical structure made up of flagellin; and the hook, which connects the basal body and the filament. Movement in response to chemical signals is known as chemotaxis.

As already mentioned, bacteria lack a nucleus. Their genetic material is contained in a single circular chromosome that tends to congregate in a region of the cell known as the nucleoid region. Interestingly, prokaryotes can carry out transcription and translation simultaneously. In

MCAT STRATEGY > > >

Throughout this chapter, we've explored several differences between prokaryotes and eukaryotes. As always, remember that your goal for success on Test Day is to learn this material actively, not just passively. It may be useful here to draw a Venn diagram exploring the similarities and differences between eukaryotes and prokaryotes.

addition to the main chromosome, prokaryotes often contain small circular pieces of DNA known as plasmids. Plasmids generally code for advantageous but non-essential abilities, and play a major role in antibiotic resistance. Plasmids also often code for virulence factors, which refers to anything that allows a bacterial infection to be more virulent, or harmful to the host. For instance, *Vibrio cholerae*, the causative agent of cholera (a disease responsible for millions of deaths in the last two centuries), has virulence factors including motility, adhesion to the intestinal wall, and a toxin. Without these virulence factors, *V. cholerae* would be much less harmful.

Bacteria reproduce through a process known as binary fission. Remember that although binary fission may be *similar* to mitosis in that it results in two daughter cells that are identical to the parent cell with the exception of any incidental mutations that may take place, it is a *different* process. Mitosis occurs in eukaryotes and binary fission occurs in prokaryotes: do not let any question trick you into answering otherwise! Mitosis crucially involves linear chromosomes lining up on the metaphase plate and being pulled to opposite sides of the cell by elements of the cytoskeleton, while bacteria have neither linear chromosomes nor a proper cytoskeleton. Binary fission involves the following steps: replication, in which the chromosome is duplicated while the cell grows; segregation and growth of a new cell wall, in which the chromosomes are pulled towards different sides of the cell and the cell envelope begins to grow towards the middle of the cell; and then the separation of two daughter cells.

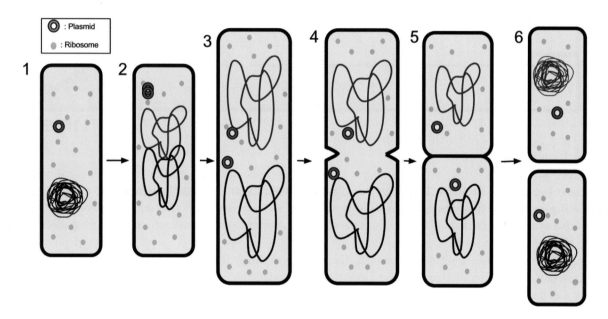

Figure 17. Binary fission.

Binary fission can take place very quickly, and it is easy for bacteria to exhaust the resources available to them in a given setting. The bacterial growth curve describes this process. First, when bacteria are introduced to a new environment, they adapt to it during the lag phase, which takes place before appreciable growth. After adapting to the environment, they embark on an exponential growth process, known as the exponential or log phase. Eventually, the environment stops being able to sustain exponential growth, and growth ceases in the stationary phase. Finally, the resources in the environment are exhausted completely and the bacteria die in the death phase. This is illustrated in Figure 18. Note that the y-axis of this graph is logarithmic, so the linear increase observed in the log phase actually reflects exponential growth.

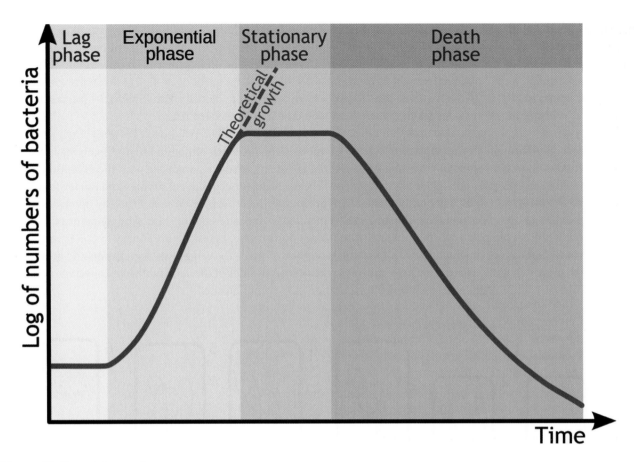

Figure 18. Bacterial growth curve.

Bacteria have the remarkable ability to engage in horizontal gene transfer. You can think of this as a way of compensating for the fact that binary fission excludes any genetic variability except for what is introduced by chance. There are three mechanisms through which this takes place: transformation, transduction, and conjugation.

Transformation is the simplest of these mechanisms, and refers to the ability of some bacteria to absorb genetic material directly from the environment. Transformation was actually identified before it was securely established that DNA was the material containing genetic information. The first experiment involving transformation was conducted in 1928 by Frederick Griffith, and it was found that harmless strains of *Streptococcus pneumoniae* could be made virulent by exposing it to virulent bacteria that had been lysed with heat. In 1944, the Avery-MacLeod-McCarty experiment did something similar but showed that it was specifically an extract of DNA that led to the transformation of *S. pneumoniae* into a virulent form. This experiment was one of the pieces of evidence suggesting that DNA contains genetic information.

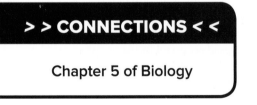

> > **CONNECTIONS** < <

Chapter 5 of Biology

Transduction is virus-mediated gene transfer. The lack of nuclei in bacteria makes it relatively easy for viruses that infect bacteria (bacteriophages) to incorporate part of the bacterial genome during their assembly. Bacteriophages can then infect another bacterial cell, taking the genetic material from a previous cell along for the ride, because it can become integrated into the genome of the new cell after infection. As discussed further in Chapter 5, transduction has been widely applied in biotechnology.

Conjugation can be thought of as the bacterial equivalent of sexual reproduction, and involves the transfer of a plasmid through a bridge that is created when a sex pilus on one bacterium (often known as F⁺, which refers to the presence of the fertility factor, or as male) attaches to another bacterium (generally known as F⁻). During this process, the fertility factor itself is duplicated and transferred, creating a new F⁺ cell. This is a major mechanism contributing to the spread of antibiotic resistance.

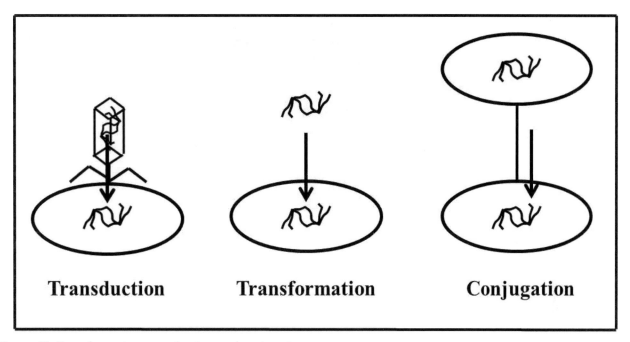

Figure 19. Transformation, transduction, and conjugation.

7. Viruses

Viruses are obligate intracellular parasites, which means that they must hijack host cells to replicate. Many do not consider them to be forms of life based on the postulates of cell theory, but they have interacted with prokaryotic and eukaryotic life for billions of years and are a routine part of the clinical practice of medicine.

Viruses exhibit tremendous structural variation, but they all have at least genetic material and a protein coat known as a capsid. Some viruses also have an envelope made up of phospholipids and proteins. Somewhat counterintuitively, lipid envelopes are quite sensitive to the environment; viruses with envelopes can easily be destroyed through light, heat, or desiccation, whereas viruses without envelopes are more resilient. For instance, human immunodeficiency virus (HIV) has an envelope, and cannot survive for long at all in the environment, which explains why it must be transmitted through specific bodily fluids. In contrast, rotavirus, which causes diarrhea in virtually every child worldwide before the age of 5, is a non-enveloped virus that is quite persistent in the environment. The term virion is used specifically to refer to the fully-assembled, infectious virus; although "virus" and "virion" may often be used interchangeably, you should be aware of the difference. Figure 20 presents the structure of the tobacco mosaic virus, a common RNA virus.

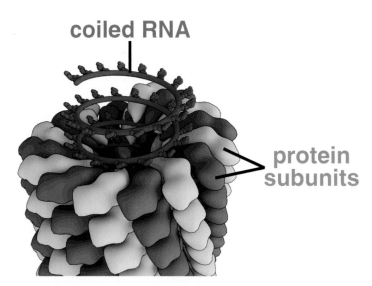

coiled RNA

protein subunits

Figure 20. Tobacco mosaic virus structure.

Viruses are very small, generally ranging from 20 nm to 250-400 nm, although some rare exceptionally large viruses have been discovered. Their genomes also vary tremendously in size; for example, the hepatitis B virus encodes only four genes, while a virus known as megavirus encodes approximately 1,100 protein-encoding genes. Viruses can come in a variety of shapes, with some common examples including helical and icosahedral forms.

The genetic material of viruses can be in the form of either single-stranded or double-stranded DNA or RNA. Single-stranded RNA viruses are further subdivided into positive-sense and negative-sense viruses. Positive-sense RNA viruses can be thought of as simply containing mRNA that can immediately be translated by the cell. In contrast, negative-sense RNA viruses contain RNA that is complementary to mRNA, meaning that mRNA must be synthesized by an enzyme known as RNA replicase that is carried in the virion.

Bacteriophages are viruses whose host cells are bacteria. A distinctive fact about them is that instead of entering the cell completely, they inject their genetic material into their host through a syringe-like structure known as a tail sheath. They also contain tail fibers, which are used to attach to the host cell.

MCAT STRATEGY > > >

On one hand, you're not expected to have any specific knowledge about antiviral medications for the MCAT (plenty of time for that in medical school!), but on the other hand, thinking about some of the potential targets for antiviral medications may help you understand the viral life cycle better. Some major approaches include interfering with binding/cell entry, interfering with the process of synthesizing new genetic material, blocking translation, and interfering with the assembly of viral proteins.

Retroviruses are a distinct class of single-stranded RNA viruses with special clinical, evolutionary, and laboratory-related importance. Retroviruses use an enzyme known as reverse transcriptase to synthesize DNA from their RNA genome. This DNA is then incorporated into the genome of the host cell, where it replicates along with the host. This makes pathogenic retroviruses very difficult to treat, because they cannot be killed without killing their host cells. Human immunodeficiency virus (HIV), the cause of AIDS, is a retrovirus that is responsible for the deaths of approximately 35 million people worldwide since the HIV pandemic emerged in the late 1970s and early 1980s. The retroviral nature of HIV is one of the reasons why it has been so challenging to develop effective treatments, although combination therapies of antiretroviral drugs now allow persons with HIV to live essentially normal lives. Moreover, it has been proposed that retrotransposons, which account for approximately 40% of the human genome, are fossilized remnants of retroviral infections. On a very practical level, reverse transcriptase is used in the lab to generate complementary DNA (cDNA) sequences from RNA; such applications are discussed more in Chapter 5.

The life cycle of a virus within an infected cell depends largely on its genetic material. The basic "goal" of a virus is to reproduce by ensuring that its protein-coding genes are expressed. RNA viruses can accomplish this goal in the cytoplasm directly, while DNA viruses are transported to the nucleus for mRNA to be synthesized. The viral genome must also be replicated. Using the machinery of the host cell, new virions are packaged. Virions can be released from a host cell through a process known as extrusion, which is similar to exocytosis and does not damage the host cell, or virions can be produced in such quantities that they cause the host cell to lyse and spill out into the environment.

> > CONNECTIONS < <

Chapter 5 of Biology

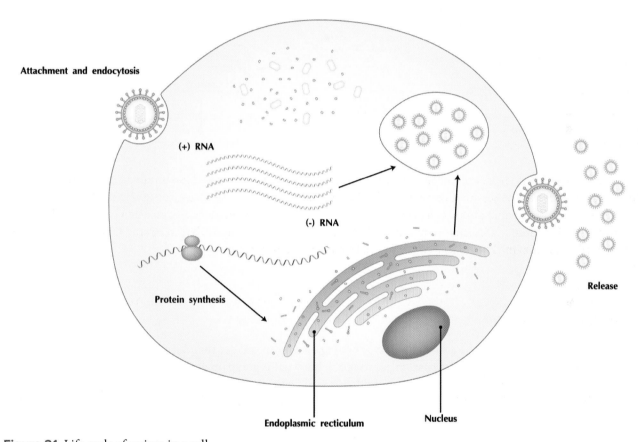

Figure 21. Life cycle of a virus in a cell.

Bacteriophages have two distinct life cycles: lytic and lysogenic. During the lytic cycle, the bacteriophage essentially works to replicate at full speed, making full use of the host cell's machinery. Eventually, the host cell is filled with virions to the point that it bursts or lyses, and a tremendous number of new virions spill out into the environment. Alternately, in the lysogenic cycle, bacteriophages can integrate themselves into the host genome, at which point they are referred to as a prophage or a provirus. In response to environmental signals, the prophage can re-emerge from the host genome and resume a lytic cycle.

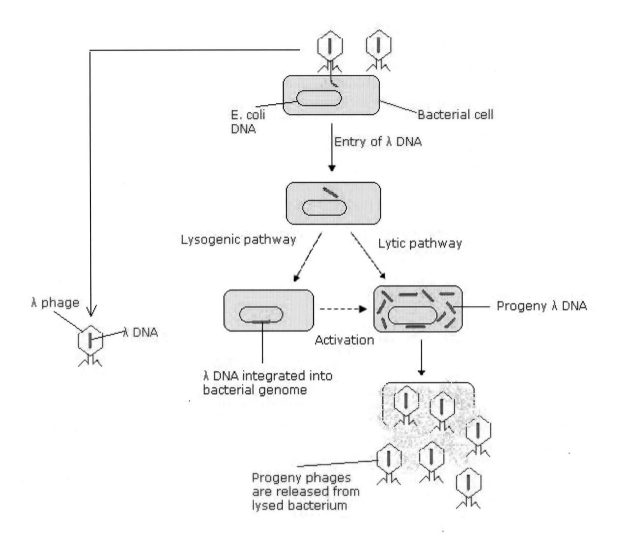

Figure 22. Lytic and lysogenic cycles.

The MCAT also expects you to be aware of two types of particles even smaller than viruses: prions and virioids. Prions are infectious proteins. This may seem paradoxical, but what is going on with prions is that they are misfolded proteins that cause other proteins to become misfolded as well, with implications for cellular function. In humans, prions cause Creutzfeldt-Jakob disease (essentially the human form of "mad cow disease"), fatal familial insomnia, as well as a disease known as kuru that was transmitted by cannibalism. Virioids are small infectious particles found in plants that can silence gene expression by binding to specific RNA sequences. In humans, it has been argued that hepatitis D virus, which is dependent on co-infection with hepatitis B virus, evolved from a viroid.

8. Must-Knows

> Eukaryotic cell structure:
  – Nucleus: contains DNA and nucleolus; site of DNA replication and transcription.
  – Mitochondria: site of aerobic metabolism; "powerhouses" of the cell; self-replicating and contain mtDNA
  – Cytoskeleton: made up of microfilaments, microtubules, and intermediate filaments; helps maintain structure of cell and carry out basic functions
  – Plasma membrane: composed of phospholipid bilayer with lipid rafts and transmembrane proteins; regulates signaling and transport

> Cell cycle:
  − Resting phase: cell carries out normal activities
  − Interphase: preparation for division, DNA synthesized and G_1/S and G_2 checkpoints make sure that cell is ready for division
  − Mitosis: cell division
> Mitosis:
  − Prophase: nuclear membrane disappears, chromosomes condense, mitotic spindle forms
  − Metaphase: chromosomes line up along metaphase plate
  − Anaphase: chromosomes pulled apart
  − Telophase/cytokinesis: nuclear envelope and nucleolus reappear, cells divide
> Meiosis:
  − Takes place in sex/germ cells, turns diploid (2n) parent cell into 4 haploid (n) daughter cells; has two stages
  − Meiosis I → two haploid daughter cells with duplicate sister chromatids
  − Prophase I: homologous chromosomes pair up in synapsis, exchange genetic information in crossing over
  − Meiosis itself + homologous chromosomes → major source of genetic variability in sexual reproduction
> Prokaryotes and viruses:
  − Bacteria: no membrane-bound organelles, no nucleus, circular genome
  − Bacteria shapes: cocci = spheres, bacilli = rods, spirilli = spirals
  − Metabolism: obligate aerobes require oxygen, obligate anaerobes require oxygen-free environments, facultative anaerobes can do both
  − Bacterial cell walls contain peptidoglycan
  − Gram-positive: turn purple in Gram staining, have thick peptidoglycan cell walls
  − Gram-negative: turn pink in Gram staining, have thin wall with outer lipopolysaccharide layer
  − Ribosomes (70S) are structurally different than in eukaryotes (80S)
  − Transformation: DNA from environment, transduction: virus-mediated gene transfer; conjugation: like sexual reproduction for bacteria
  − Viruses: obligate intracellular parasites, protein capsid coat around genetic material
  − Lytic cycle: machinery hijacked, host cell killed; lysogenic: virus incorporates itself into host genome and waits. Only in bacteriophages.

Practice Passage

The universally conserved signal recognition particle (SRP) mediates co-translational targeting of proteins to membranes. In eukaryotes, SRP—ribosome nascent chain complexes (RNCs) are targeted to the endoplasmic reticulum by guanosine-5'-triphosphate- (GTP-) dependent interaction with the membrane-bound SRP receptor.

The two largest proteins, SRP68 and SRP72, form a heterodimer and bind to a regulatory site of the SRP RNA. The tight interaction was confirmed by isothermal titration calorimetry (ITC; K_D of 33 nM). Next, the crystal structures of the SRP68 protein-binding domain (PBD) in complex with SRP72-PBD and of the SRP72-ribosome binding domain (RBD) bound to the SRP S domain were determined (Figure 1).

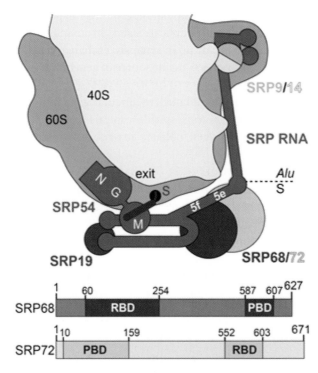

Figure 1. Upper panel: Scheme of human SRP bound to a ribosome—nascent chain complex. Exit: polypeptide tunnel exit; S: signal sequence; NGM: domains of SRP54; 5e/5f: loops of SRP RNA. Lower panel: Domain architecture of human SRP68/72

The subunits of the SRP68/72 heterodimer (Figure 1) bind individually to SRP RNA. The N-terminal SRP68 RNA-binding domain (RBD) locates to a central RNA three-way junction between RNA helices. SRP68 binding to the RNA kinks the S domain RNA and remodels the nearby 5f-loop. Kinking is important for ribosome interaction.

While the majority of DNA in a eukaryotic cell is nuclear, it has been discovered that a small amount of non-nuclear DNA resides within the mitochondria. Mitochondrial DNA (mtDNA) contains 37 genes, all of which are essential for normal mitochondrial function. Thirteen of these genes produce the enzymes involved in oxidative phosphorylation.

Mitochondria that function improperly due to problems with mtDNA can be devastating to cellular viability. Retinitis pigmentosa (NARP) syndrome is an example of this. Upon entering early adulthood, most people with NARP syndrome begin to experience tingling and/or pain in their extremities and problems with balance. As the disease progresses, the patient may experience light sensitivity and vision loss.

Adapted from Becker, M. & Sinning, I. (2017). Structures of human SRP72 complexes provide insights into SRP RNA remodeling and ribosome interaction. Nucleic Acids Research, 45(1), 470–481. under CCBY 4.0

1. A mother with NARP syndrome has two children, a son and a daughter. Which child is more likely to inherit the disease?
   A. The son
   B. The daughter
   C. Son and daughter have equal likelihood of inheriting the disease
   D. The mtDNA composition of the father is needed to determine the answer

2. The endosymbiotic theory states that the mitochondrion developed when a prokaryote entered a eukaryotic cell through endocytosis and led to a symbiotic relationship where both organisms were able to thrive. If true, what is the most plausible size of the ribosomes coded for by mtDNA?
   A. 40S
   B. 50S
   C. 70S
   D. 80S

3. According to the researcher's findings, what is the minimum number of nucleotides that are found in between the RBD and PBD in human SRP68?
   A. 331
   B. 333
   C. 992
   D. 999

4. In an individual free of mitochondrial disease, which of the following cell types would still lack functioning mitochondria?
   A. Red blood cells
   B. Muscle cells
   C. Neurons
   D. White blood cells

5. Which of the following does NOT contribute to genetic diversity in spermatogenesis?
   A. Centriole activity near the poles during metaphase I
   B. Chromosomal fragment separation and reattachment to the centromere during prophase I
   C. Random chromosomes are replicated prior to the onset of meiosis I
   D. Crossing over during prophase I.

6. The structural interactions shown in Figure 1 are most likely to occur at which cellular structure?
   A. Nucleus
   B. Mitoribosomes
   C. Rough endoplasmic reticulum
   D. Lysosome

7. All of the following have a double membrane structure EXCEPT:
   A. mitochondria.
   B. Golgi body.
   C. endoplasmic reticulum.
   D. peroxisomes.

Practice Passage Explanations

The universally conserved signal recognition particle (SRP) mediates co-translational targeting of proteins to membranes. In eukaryotes, SRP—ribosome nascent chain complexes (RNCs) are targeted to the endoplasmic reticulum by guanosine-5'-triphosphate- (GTP-) dependent interaction with the membrane-bound SRP receptor.

Key terms: SRP, RNCs, GTP- dependent interaction

Cause and effect: GTP-dependent interactions allow SRP-RNCs to move to endoplasmic reticulum

The two largest proteins, SRP68 and SRP72, form a heterodimer and bind to a regulatory site of the SRP RNA. The tight interaction was confirmed by isothermal titration calorimetry (ITC; K_D of 33 nM). Next, the crystal structures of the SRP68 protein-binding domain (PBD) in complex with SRP72-PBD and of the SRP72-ribosome binding domain (RBD) bound to the SRP S domain were determined (Figure 1).

Key terms: SRP68/72, heterodimer, ITC, PBD, RBD, crystal structure

Cause and effect: SRPS form heterodimer with strong interactions between subunits

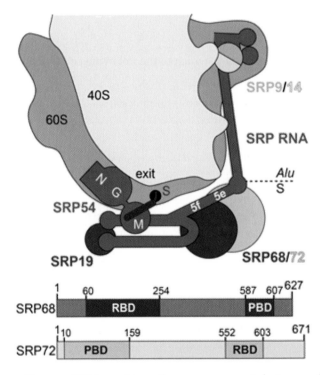

Figure 1. Upper panel: Scheme of human SRP bound to a ribosome—nascent chain complex. Exit: polypeptide tunnel exit; S: signal sequence; NGM: domains of SRP54; 5e/5f: loops of SRP RNA. Lower panel: Domain architecture of human SRP68/72

Figure 1 is very detailed, so avoid getting bogged down unless the questions demand more analysis; the ribosome is a eukaryotic cytosolic ribosome (60S/40S); the bottom figures show the AA lengths for the SRPs

The subunits of the SRP68/72 heterodimer (Figure 1) bind individually to SRP RNA. The N-terminal SRP68 RNA-binding domain (RBD) locates to a central RNA three-way junction between RNA helices. SRP68 binding to the RNA kinks the S domain RNA and remodels the nearby 5f-loop. Kinking is important for ribosome interaction.

Key terms: RNA kinks, 5f-loop

Cause and effect: helical junctions (kinks) in the secondary structure of RNA are crucial for SRP-RNA interactions

While the majority of DNA in a eukaryotic cell is nuclear, it has been discovered that a small amount of non-nuclear DNA resides within the mitochondria. Mitochondrial DNA (mtDNA) contains 37 genes, all of which are essential for normal mitochondrial function. Thirteen of these genes produce the enzymes involved in oxidative phosphorylation.

Key terms: non-nuclear DNA, mtDNA

Cause and effect: mitochondria have unique DNA to carry out their specialized function

Mitochondria that function improperly can be devastating to cellular viability. Retinitis pigmentosa (NARP) syndrome is an example of this. Upon entering early adulthood, most people with NARP syndrome begin to experience tingling and/or pain in their extremities and problems with balance. As the disease progresses, the patient may experience light sensitivity and vision loss.

Key terms: NARP syndrome

Cause and Effect: malfunctioning mitochondria → neuropathies, coordination issues, possible loss of vision

Adapted from Becker, M. & Sinning, I. (2017). Structures of human SRP72 complexes provide insights into SRP RNA remodeling and ribosome interaction. Nucleic Acids Research, 45(1), 470–481. under CCBY 4.0

1. C is correct. The final paragraph discusses mtDNA but does not mention inheritance. We should know for test day that the mtDNA in the zygote is exclusively inherited from the ovum. If the mother has NARP syndrome, then she has an equal likelihood of passing it on to her children via her mtDNA.
   A, B, D: There is no gender difference in mtDNA inheritance. Since mtDNA is exclusively inherited from the mother, the father's disease status is irrelevant.

2. C is correct. The question suggests that the mitochondria evolved evolutionarily from a prokaryote entering a eukaryote. The passage also provides evidence for this by suggesting that the mitochondria have their own set of DNA that is separate from nuclear DNA. Prokaryotic ribosomes are 70S, comprised of a small (30S) subunit and a large (50S) subunit.
   A. This is the size of the small subunit in a eukaryotic ribosome.
   B. This is the size of the large subunit in a prokaryotic ribosome.
   D. This is the size of the eukaryotic ribosome.

3. D is correct. In Figure 1, the lower panel shows the protein domain architecture. How do we know this? In general, symbols for genes are italicized (e.g., IGFα), whereas symbols for proteins are not italicized (e.g., IGFα). This means we go from residue 255 to 586, inclusive, in SRP68 (586 – 255 = 331 + 2 = 333). Each amino acid residue is coded for by 3 nucleotides so 333(3) = 999. Note this is the minimum possible since there may be introns.

4. A is correct. In order to provide maximum space for hemoglobin, red blood cells lack a nucleus and most organelles, including mitochondria.
   B. Muscle cells require a high amount of energy, and thus definitely must undergo aerobic respiration and have mitochondria.
   C. Neurons require a high amount of energy, and thus definitely must undergo aerobic respiration and have mitochondria.
   D. White blood cells are unlike red blood cells in that they have organelles and a nucleus (since they do not need to accommodate high amounts of hemoglobin).

5. C is correct. Prior to meiosis I, germ cells replicate all of their nuclear genetic information. Afterwards, the homologous chromosomes always pair up. There is nothing random about this process.
   A. During metaphase I, the centrioles control the spindle apparatus, which allows for the division of homologous chromosomes. This division is random. Each daughter cell has a 50% chance of getting the father's chromosome and 50% chance of getting the mother's.
   B, D: Read carefully, as these are, in effect, the same answer. The detachment, rearrangement, and reattachment of chromosomal fragments to the centromere is known as crossing over. Sister chromatids will not be exactly identical due to this crossing over. Each daughter cell has a 50% chance of getting one chromatid over the other.

6. C is correct. Figure 1 shows interactions between RNA and the ribosome. Ribosomes in the eukaryotic cell can be found on the rough endoplasmic reticulum.
   A. The nucleus is the site of DNA and DNA→RNA transcription, but not ribosomes.
   B. Figure 1 shows a 60S and 40S subunit on the ribosome. Mammalian mitochondrial ribosomes (55S) differ from bacterial (70S) and cytoplasmic ribosomes (80S).
   D. Lysosomes are membrane bound organelles that contain enzymes capable of breaking down all types of biological polymers (e.g. proteins, nucleic acids, carbohydrates, and lipids).

7. D is correct. In eukaryotic cells, the double membrane-bound organelles are the mitochondria, endoplasmic reticulum, Golgi body, and nucleus. Peroxisomes are small, single membrane-enclosed organelles which contain enzymes involved in a variety of metabolic reactions (e.g. fatty acid oxidation).

Independent Questions

1. Cytochalasin B (CB) is a small, hydrophilic molecule that interferes with microfilament polymerization without measurably affecting microtubule function. Eukaryotic cells treated with CB *in vitro* are most likely to display abnormal:
   A. chromosomal alignment during prophase.
   B. chromosomal separation during anaphase.
   C. cytokinesis.
   D. mitochondrial replication during early prophase.

2. Anterograde vesicles leaving the ER will most immediately dock with:
   A. the Golgi apparatus.
   B. the nuclear membrane.
   C. larger, endocytic vesicles.
   D. lysosomes.

3. Which of the following would most significantly increase the fluidity of the plasma membrane in an experimental model?
   A. Increasing the percent composition of phospholipids containing saturated fatty acids
   B. Reducing the temperature
   C. Decreasing the percent composition of cholesterol at high temperature
   D. Increasing the percent composition of cholesterol at high temperature

4. Acid proteases would most likely be found within:
   A. lysosomes.
   B. peroxisomes.
   C. the mitochondrial matrix.
   D. chloroplasts.

5. Which of the following is not a principal component of the extracellular matrix in any animal tissues?
   A. Collagen
   B. Elastin
   C. Glycosaminoglycans
   D. Triglycerides

6. The lumen of the rough endoplasmic reticulum most resembles which of the following?
   A. The mitochondrial intermembrane space
   B. The lumen of a lysosome
   C. The extracellular space
   D. The cytoplasm

7. In the context of cell biology, the 'bystander effect' refers to the death of healthy cells adjacent to a cell undergoing apoptosis. This effect is thought to involve the transfer of proapoptotic factors via gap junctions. Such factors could include:
   A. cytochrome c, a soluble protein normally associated with mitochondria.
   B. lamin B, a nuclear membrane structural protein known to break down during apoptosis.
   C. caspases, enzymes that cleave cellular proteins.
   D. calcium ions, which are normally present in low concentrations in the cytoplasm.

8. Gram-positive bacteria:
   A. stain pink due to the adhesion of crystal violet to their thick peptidoglycan layer.
   B. stain purple due to the adhesion of crystal violet to their thick peptidoglycan layer.
   C. stain pink due to the adhesion of crystal violet to their outer membrane.
   D. stain purple due to the adhesion of crystal violet to their outer membrane.

Independent Question Explanations

1. C is correct. Cytokinesis involves a contractile ring complex, consisting of actin filaments (microfilaments) and myosin motor proteins. Interference with microfilament polymerization is likely to compromise contractile ring function and disrupt cytokinesis. Chromosomal alignment occurs during metaphase (making Choice A incorrect), and mitochondrial replication occurs during interphase (Choice D is wrong). Chromosomal separation involves the spindle apparatus, which is composed of microtubules, not microfilaments.

2. A is correct. Anterograde traffic refers to vesicles leaving the ER with newly synthesized protein cargo, bound for the Golgi apparatus for further modification. Once modified, proteins are packaged into vesicles, sent away from the Golgi, and either secreted or kept within the cell.

3. C is correct. Reducing temperature and adding more saturated phospholipids will always reduce membrane fluidity, eliminating choices A and B. At high temperatures, cholesterol stabilizes phospholipid bilayers and reduces fluidity. Therefore, an increase in temperature coupled with a decrease in cholesterol would most likely result in a greater increase in fluidity than a temperature increase with a concomitant increase in cholesterol.

4. A is correct. Lysosomes are involved in the catabolism of proteins. They feature an acidic lumen that facilitates peptide bond hydrolysis by acid proteases. Peroxisomes perform functions related to the pentose phosphate pathway and the neutralization of reactive oxygen species.

5. D is correct. Collagen and elastin are fibrous proteins found in many connective tissues. Glycosaminoglycans (GAGs) are polysaccharides that are often bound to extracellular matrix proteins to form proteoglycans. Triglycerides are not extracellular matrix components. They are synthesized in the cytoplasm or absorbed from dietary sources, but they do not generally reside in the extracellular environment.

6. C is correct. Secreted proteins and transmembrane proteins are synthesized and modified in the rough ER lumen. For such proteins to properly function, they must fold under conditions similar to those of the extracellular environment. Unlike the cytoplasm, which is a reducing environment, the rough ER lumen facilitates the oxidation of cysteine residues to form disulfide bridges.

7. D is correct. Gap junctions are large relative to a typical ion channel, but they do not allow passage of macromolecules such as nucleic acids and proteins. Although all four choices describe molecules involved in the apoptotic pathway, only calcium ions could feasibly be transferred via gap junctions.

8. B is correct. A Gram-positive bacterium contains a thick peptidoglycan cell wall outside its cell membrane. Crystal violet stain adheres to the cross-links within the peptidoglycan structure, causing the bacterium to appear purple when visualized at the end of the procedure. Gram-negative bacteria, not Gram-positive bacteria, contain both an outer and an inner cell membrane.

Molecular Genetics

0. Introduction

It is common to distinguish between molecular genetics and genetic inheritance, at least partially for historical reasons: the principles of genetic inheritance were largely worked out in the late 19th to early 20th centuries, before scientists elucidated the actual mechanisms of how genetic information is transmitted. However, we're going to reverse the historical path of research into genetics and cover the mechanisms first, because having a solid understanding of how inheritance works on the molecular level can help you make sense of inheritance patterns and evolution, which are discussed in Chapter 4.

> > **CONNECTIONS** < <

Chapter 4 of Biology

1. Central Dogma and the Genetic Code

The central dogma of molecular genetics, also sometimes known as the fundamental dogma, states that information flows from DNA to RNA to protein. The term "dogma" may seem somewhat strange in this context because it is frequently encountered when discussing religion or philosophy, but this is a historical relic from a period when scientists were still debating where genetic information was contained. It was only in the 1950s that a series of experiments conclusively showed that nucleic acids-specifically DNA-were the medium in which genetic information was stored.

One of the most decisive experiments that showed that DNA contains genetic information was the Hershey-Chase experiment, which was conducted in 1952 and led to Hershey being awarded the 1969 Nobel Prize in Physiology or Medicine. The researchers used radiolabeled sulfur and phosphorus as a way of distinguishing between proteins (which contain sulfur atoms present in cysteine and methionine residues, but not phosphate groups) and nucleic acids (which contain phosphate groups but no sulfur). It was known at this point that bacteriophages inject genetic material into bacterial cells. Radiolabeled bacteriophages were added to cell cultures of bacteria, and it was determined that the bacterial cells post-transduction contained radiolabeled phosphate, not sulfur, which therefore indicated that the genetic material in question is DNA.

The idea that information flows from DNA to RNA to protein is familiar to anyone who has taken a college-level biology course, but it's still important not to skip over it too quickly, because it is a good problem-solving tool to apply to difficult passages and because some noteworthy exceptions/complications have been discovered. The simplest version of this framework states that genetic information is stored over the long term in DNA, and is then transcribed into messenger RNA (mRNA), which are then translated into proteins. This does correctly describe the basic chain of events in most cells, but it is not the whole story. Most remarkably, reverse transcriptase (present in retroviruses; see Chapter 2) allows DNA to be transcribed from RNA, reversing the normal flow of information. Additionally, several forms of non-coding RNA exist, including transfer RNA (tRNA), which assists in translation, and forms of RNA that affect gene expression (discussed in more depth in Chapter 5). Figure 1 presents the central dogma; the basic logic of the principle is shown on the left side of the image, while the right side of the image contains details that we will discuss in this chapter. It may be worth revisiting Figure 1 after studying this chapter to see how the details align with the big-picture principles.

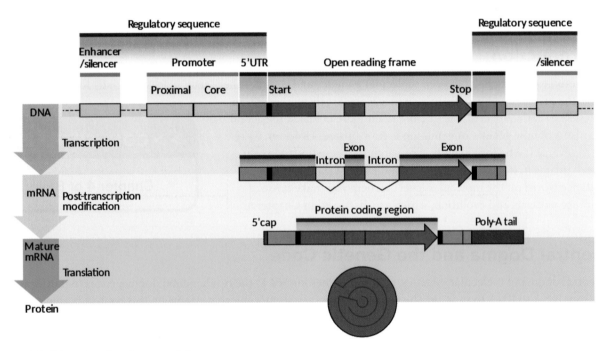

Figure 1. Information flow in central dogma.

The central dogma is also limited in that it deals with the flow of *genetic* information. Signaling pathways also transfer information throughout the organism using a wide range of mechanisms: proteins can influence other proteins in secondary messenger systems, steroid hormones can upregulate gene expression, and so on. However, in the context of an MCAT passage, you can apply the central dogma to predict some of the ways a cell might react to a stimulus. For instance, a steroid hormone can bind to a nuclear receptor, increasing the rate at which a specific gene (DNA) is transcribed into RNA, which then is translated into the protein of interest.

> > CONNECTIONS < <

Chapter 2 and Chapter 5 of Biology

In order to understand how information contained in the form of nucleic acids can be translated into proteins, it is useful to think of DNA/RNA as containing a genetic code. DNA and RNA each contain four bases (A, C, G, and T for DNA and A, C, G, and U for RNA), and these must be combined to code for 20 amino acids. A system in which each base corresponds to an amino acid would clearly be too simple, as would a system in which combinations of two nucleobases coded for amino acids (in such a system there would be $4^2=16$ combinations, which falls short of what we need). Instead, we have a system in which combinations of three nucleobases, known as codons, code for amino acids. There are 64 (4^3) combinations of bases, which is much more than the 20 amino acids that need to be coded for, but this is actually advantageous in that it provides a certain degree of resilience and tolerance for error. This property of the genetic code is known as degeneracy. The genetic code also contains three stop codons that cause the translation process to be halted, and a start codon (coding for methionine) that indicates where translation begins.

The genetic code is presented below in Table 1. However, you do not have to, and should not, memorize it. You should know the stop and start codons. Also, note that nearly half (eight of the 20) amino acids are completely specified by the first two base pairs in the codons, and that almost all of the amino acids have are definitively specified by the first two base pairs and have some room for error in the third. As discussed below in the section on mutations, this room for error, which leads to the third base of the codon sometimes being referred to as the "wobble" position, provides some degree of protection against mutations. It is a piece of evidence that suggests that the three-base-pair codon system emerged evolutionarily from an early system with two base pairs.

> **MCAT STRATEGY >>>**
>
> A mnemonic for the stop codons is: U Are Annoying (UAA), U Are Gross (UAG), and U Go Away (UGA).

		Second nucleotide			
		U	C	A	G
First nucleotide	U	UUU, UUC Phenylalanine	UCU, UCC, UCC, UCA Serine	UAU, UAC Tyrosine	UGU, UGC Cysteine
		UUA, UUG Leucine		UAA, UAG (STOP)	UGA (STOP)
					UGG Tryptophan
	C	CUU, CUC, CUA, CUG Leucine	CCU, CCC, CCA, CCG Proline	CAU, CAC Histidine	CGU, CGC, CGA, CGG Arginine
				CAA, CAG Glutamine	
	A	AUU, AUC, AUA Isoleucine	ACU, ACC, ACA, ACG Threonine	AAU, AAC Asparagine	AGU, AGC Serine
		AUG Methionine (START)		AAA, AAG Lysine	AGA, AGG Arginine
	G	GUU, GUC, GUA, GUG Valine	GCU, GCC, GCA, GCG Alanine	GAU, GAC Aspartic acid	GGU, GGC, GGA, GGG Glycine
				GAA, GAG Glutamic acid	

Table 1. Genetic code.

2. DNA Structure and Chromosomes

The structure of nucleic acids (DNA and RNA) was presented in Chapter 1 on biomolecules, but the basic points of the Watson-Crick model of DNA structure are presented below for review:

> DNA is organized in a double helix of antiparallel strands, with a sugar-phosphate backbone connected by phosphodiester bonds on the outside and nitrogenous bases on the inside.
> Complementary base-pairing dictates that adenine (A) pairs with thymine (T) and cytosine (C) pairs with guanine (G).
> The interior of the structure is stabilized by hydrogen bonds between base pairs (two hydrogen bonds for AT pairs and three for CG pairs), as well as hydrophobic interactions between stacked nitrogenous bases.

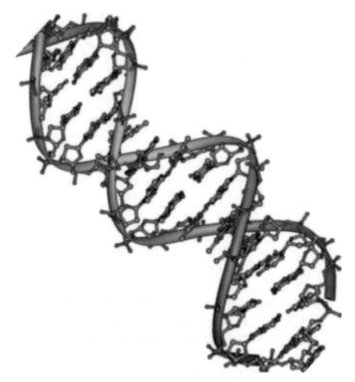

Figure 2. Double helix structure.

The MCAT may ask you to identify the complementary DNA/RNA sequence for a given strand of DNA, either directly or as a step in a more complicated problem. Be very careful about directionality when answering such problems! This is a common source of avoidable missed points on the exam. Standard practice is to list DNA sequences in the 5'-3' order, but remember that the actual complementary sequence must both be complementary *and* antiparallel. Let's work through a sample problem illustrating the correct process and some possible pitfalls.

Example problem: What is the complementary strand for the DNA sequence AACC?

Solution:

> Step 1: Recognize that the implied directionality in this sequence is 5'-AACC-3'.
> Step 2: Generate a complementary sequence through base pairing: TTGG.
> Step 3: Recognize that this complement must have the directionality of 3'-TTGG-5'.
> Step 4: Be alert to the directionality of the answer choices: the correct answer could *either* be 3'-TTGG-5' (although it is standard to give DNA sequences in 5'-3' order, it is not actually mandatory) or 5'-GGTT-3'.

Let's consider some potential trap answer choices here. One set of incorrect answer choices might rely on confusion about base pairing. Those are pretty simple to handle, though: knowing the base pairs is an absolute must, and on the MCAT, it will be assumed that most test-takers will have that knowledge. Therefore, we need to look for some more subtle possible missteps. If the answer choices do not specify directionality, then you need to understand that the implied directionality is 5'-3'. A potential trap answer along these lines would be TTGG, because in the absence of explicit marking of directionality, that answer choice would be understood to be 5'-TTGG-3', which would be incorrect. Another possibility would be to include *both* 5'-TTGG-3' (the incorrect answer) and *either* of the two ways of presenting the correct answer (3'-TTGG-5' or 5'-GGTT-3').

In eukaryotes, DNA is organized into linear chromosomes, which each contain part of the genome. Human cells normally have 22 distinct chromosomes known as autosomes; somatic cells (i.e., non-germline cells) contain two copies of each of these chromosomes, one inherited maternally and the other inherited paternally. Additionally, humans generally have two sex chromosomes, with females having two X chromosomes (one inherited maternally and one inherited paternally) and males having an X chromosome and Y chromosome, with the Y chromosome inherited paternally. Therefore, in the standard human cell, there are 46 chromosomes, with two copies of each of 22 autosomes and either two X chromosomes or one X chromosome and a Y chromosome.

> ## MCAT STRATEGY > > >
>
> A good way of studying this would be for you to attempt to write an MCAT-style question and generate incorrect but tempting answer choices. Regardless of how you do this, work through this carefully and slowly until it becomes reflexive, because this is an instance where investing a relatively small amount of time into really *getting* it is very likely to pay off on Test Day. On Test Day, use your whiteboard to write out your work so that you can clearly visualize what's going on.

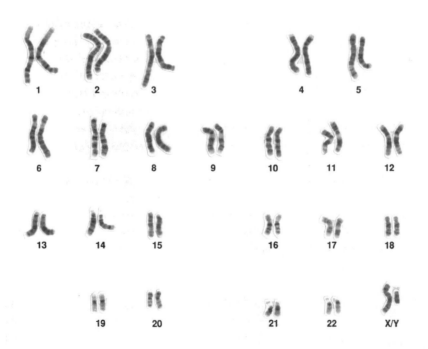

Figure 3. Human chromosomes.

The human genome contains approximately 3 billion base pairs, meaning that in diploid somatic cells that contain two copies of each chromosome, there are approximately 6 billion base pairs. One base pair corresponds to approximately 3.4 Å (340 pm or 3.4×10^{-10} m). This means that if stretched out linearly, every body cell would contain approximately 2 meters of DNA. This is obviously incompatible with the size of human nuclei, which are generally about 6 μm (6×10^{-6} m) in size. How do we squeeze so much DNA into the nuclei of our cells? One way is by subdividing the genome into linear chromosomes, but that only accomplishes a relatively small part of the task. The rest of the job is done by histones and chromatin.

Histones are proteins that act as spools for DNA to wind around. They are composed of various subproteins known as H1, H2A, H2B, H3, and H4. The core of a histone contains two dimers of H2A and H2B and a tetramer of H3 and H4, while H1 serves as a linking unit. Approximately 200 base pairs of DNA can be wound around a histone, and the complex formed by DNA and a histone is known as a nucleosome. The phrase "beads on a string" is often associated with the appearance of nucleosomes under electron microscopy, and chromatin refers to the structure formed by many nucleosomes. Two distinct forms of chromatin exist: euchromatin and heterochromatin. Euchromatin is a loose configuration that is difficult to see under light microscopy and allows DNA to be readily transcribed. Throughout interphase (i.e., most of the cell cycle), DNA generally exists as euchromatin, which makes sense because this is the form that allows transcription to happen and for cellular activities to be carried out. Heterochromatin is the tightly coiled, dense form of chromatin that is visible during cell division and is present to a lesser extent even during interphase.

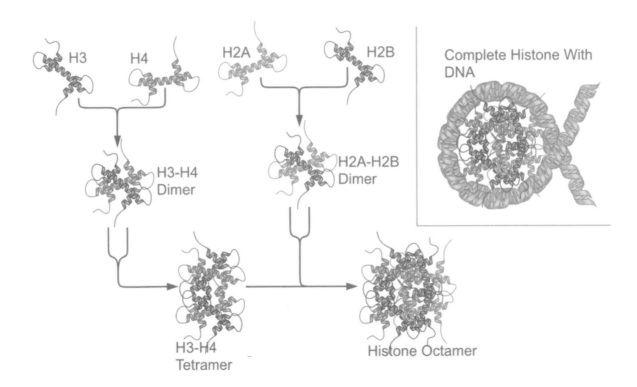

Figure 4. Histones.

On a biochemical level, charge plays a major role in the interactions between histones and DNA. Histones are highly alkaline and are positively charged at physiological pH, which facilitates their interaction with the highly negatively charged phosphate groups on the backbone of DNA. Modifications like acetylation of histones reduce that positive charge, making histones interact with DNA less closely, which in turn facilitates transcriptional activity.

> > CONNECTIONS < <

Chapter 5 of Biology

3. DNA Replication

DNA replication is the basis for genetic inheritance, because it is the process that allows DNA to be passed on to a daughter cell. In replication, a DNA helix unwinds and a new complementary sequence is synthesized from each strand. This process is known as semiconservative replication, because each new DNA sequence contains one strand from the original DNA molecule and one newly synthesized complement.

The fact that DNA replication is semiconservative was discovered in 1958 in the Meselson-Stahl experiment, which is worth familiarizing yourself with because it provides an elegant example of experimental design related to a specific point of testable content (the semiconservative nature of replication). Given the basic structure of DNA, there are three possibilities for how replication works: (1) the entire DNA molecule could serve as a template for the synthesis of a new DNA molecule, in a process in which the original DNA molecule would denature, replication would take place, the new DNA molecule would be separated, and the original DNA molecule would re-anneal (the conservative hypothesis); (2) each strand of the original DNA molecule could serve as the template for a complementary strand, with the new molecule composed of an old strand and a new strand (the semiconservative hypothesis); and (3) each of the two resulting DNA molecules could contain equally mixed segments of entirely old strands or entirely new strands (the dispersive hypothesis).

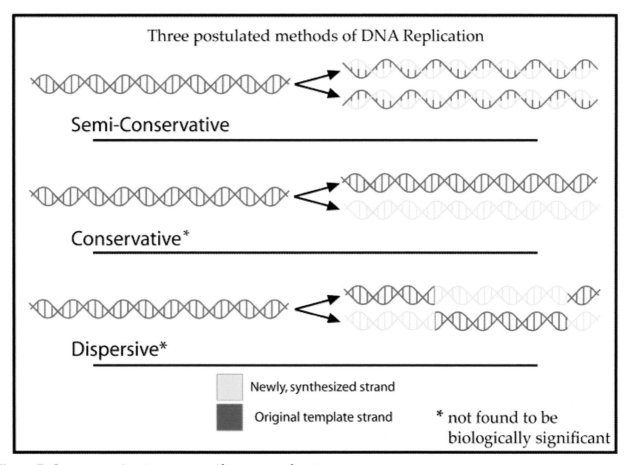

Figure 5. Conservative/semiconservative/dispersive replication.

The insight of the Meselson-Stahl experiment was that the researchers found a way to distinguish between "old" and "new" DNA. They grew *E. coli* in a medium enriched with ^{15}N (heavier than the normal isotope ^{14}N) until all of the nitrogen atoms in the bacterial DNA were ^{15}N. They then transferred the bacteria to a medium containing ^{14}N. At this point, the "old" DNA would contain ^{15}N and therefore be heavier than the newly-synthesized DNA containing ^{14}N. The researchers carefully used centrifugation to assess the density of DNA samples as a proxy for identifying the mass of the various strands. The three different theories about replication made different predictions for what would happen in these experimental conditions:

> Conservative replication: No DNA molecules would have intermediate density. Over progressive rounds of replication, the amount of ^{15}N-containing molecules would remain constant but be drowned out by exponentially-growing quantities of ^{14}N-containing molecules.
> Semiconservative replication: After one round of replication, the DNA molecules would have an intermediate weight (something like $^{14.5}$N, although you should note that there is no such isotope in reality). The second round of replication would lead to one set of DNA molecules with only ^{14}N, and one set of molecules with an intermediate weight because the original ^{15}N strands were used as templates.
> Dispersive replication: After one round of replication, the DNA molecules would have an intermediate weight (something like $^{14.5}$N). Remember that the fundamental idea behind dispersive replication is that the original DNA would be evenly distributed over new rounds of replication, so with successive rounds of replication, you would expect to observe uniform intermediate weights converging towards ^{14}N (e.g., first $^{14.5}$N, then $^{14.25}$N, then $^{14.125}$N, etc.), as more and more ^{14}N is incorporated into the molecules.

The results of this experiment clearly confirmed that DNA replication is semiconservative.

Next, let's turn to the actual mechanics of DNA replication. Replication must start somewhere, and that somewhere is known as the origin of replication; this is not just a random place, but specific sequences that bind with a protein complex known as the pre-replication complex and tend to have high AT content. Bacterial genomes have one origin of replication, from which replication proceeds bidirectionally. Eukaryotic chromosomes have multiple origins of replication, and the centromere (which was discussed in Chapter 2 in mitosis) connects the sister chromatids that are created during this process.

DNA replication involves several important enzymes:

> Helicase unwinds the DNA helix and separates the two strands of DNA.
> Single-stranded DNA-binding proteins keep the separated strands from immediately re-annealing.
> Primase synthesizes a short RNA primer with a free 3' OH group that is used as the starting point for the synthesis of a new strand. (Evolutionary history generally goes beyond the scope of the MCAT, but the curious fact that RNA is needed for DNA replication is one piece of evidence that scientists have pointed to as evidence that RNA was the original form of genetic material.)
> DNA polymerase reads the DNA template in a 3' to 5' direction and synthesizes the complementary strand in the 5' to 3' direction. This may seem counterintuitive at first, but draw it out: imagine DNA polymerase reading a template from left to right and generating complementary base pairs as it goes, and remember that the new strand is antiparallel to the original strand. This means that the synthesis must proceed from 5' to 3'.
> DNA gyrase, also known as DNA topoisomerase II, alleviates the supercoiling that would otherwise be created as helicase works its way down the DNA molecule.
> Ligase links together Okazaki fragments, which are created from the lagging strand of DNA replication.

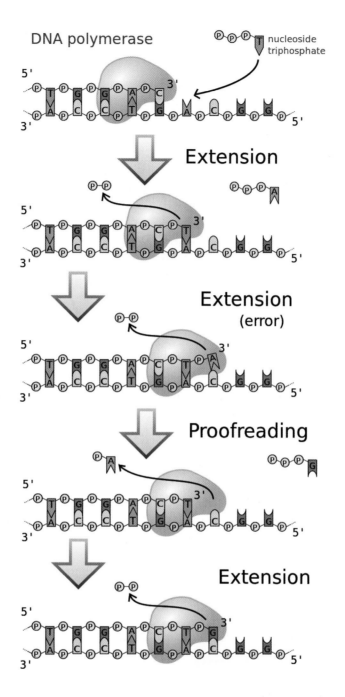

Figure 6. DNA replication.

While most of these enzymes have relatively straightforward functions, DNA polymerase is associated with some complications that you have to be aware of for the MCAT. First, its directionality has important implications. Recall that DNA polymerase only works in one direction (reading in the 3'-5' direction and synthesizing in the 5'-3' direction). This means that, as helicase works its way in one direction, DNA polymerase can operate straightforwardly on one strand (known as the leading strand) but not on the other strand (the lagging strand). This problem is solved by having DNA

MCAT STRATEGY > > >

Draw out the function of DNA polymerase as many times as it takes to convince yourself that reading in the 3'-5' direction means synthesizing in the 5'-3' direction. In general, genetics is a subject best approached through understanding rather than just superficial memorization, but this is especially the case for the directionality of DNA.

polymerase work piece by piece as the lagging strand is unraveled. The resulting small pieces of DNA are known as Okazaki fragments, and are eventually joined back together by ligase.

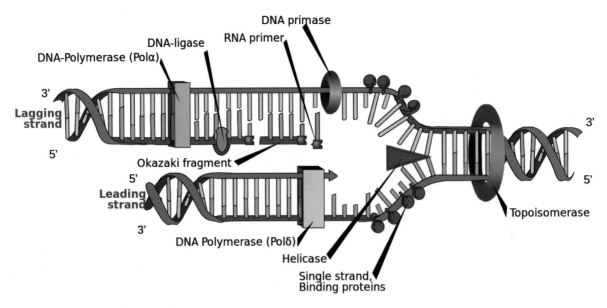

Figure 7. Leading and lagging strands.

Additionally, DNA polymerase is more accurately thought of as a family of enzymes, rather than a single enzyme. Roman numerals are used to refer to the different types of DNA polymerases in prokaryotes, and Greek letters are used for the same purpose in eukaryotes. The MCAT does not expect you to be aware of all of the many types of polymerases that exist, but you should be familiar with some especially important examples, listed below.

In prokaryotes, DNA polymerase I (Pol I) assists with Okazaki fragments and removing the RNA primer through excision repair. DNA polymerase II (Pol II) is primarily involved with repair, and DNA polymerase III (Pol III) is involved in the main process of DNA synthesis.

In eukaryotes, DNA polymerase α initiates synthesis in replication in both the leading and lagging strands, and then DNA polymerase δ takes over because it operates more efficiently. Additionally, DNA polymerase δ adds DNA nucleotides when the RNA primer is removed. DNA polymerase ε specifically assists in extension of the leading strand, and also assists in DNA repair, as does DNA polymerase β. DNA polymerase γ replicates mitochondrial DNA.

MCAT STRATEGY > > >

The different types of DNA polymerase are relatively low-yield but potentially fair game. They're worth investing a little bit of time into understanding, but don't stay up all night worrying about them at the expense of biochemistry fundamentals (for instance).

Some special types of DNA polymerase have their own names. Reverse transcriptase, which is discussed in greater depth in Chapter 2 in the context of retroviruses, is a special kind of DNA polymerase that operates with an RNA template. Telomerase extends telomeres, which are repetitive sequences at the end of eukaryotic chromosomes that exist to cope with the fact that DNA polymerase cannot faithfully replicate the end of the chromosomal sequence. As cells divide, telomeres degrade, and the degradation of telomeres is thought to play a major role in the aging process. Telomerase rebuilds telomeres, and is active in stem cells and cancer cells, but not in most somatic cells (with the exception of cell types that need to divide frequently, such as skin cells). The fact that telomerase is upregulated in cancer cells underscores the fact that limits on cell division are not necessarily a bad thing.

4. Transcription

Recall the central dogma: genetic information flows from DNA to RNA to proteins. The process of going from DNA to RNA—more specifically, messenger RNA (mRNA)—is called transcription. Transcription takes place in the nucleus, and its end result is the creation of an mRNA copy of a gene that can then be transported to the cytosol for translation into a protein.

The DNA helix must be unzipped for transcription to take place, which means that some of the same machinery that we saw in DNA replication has to be engaged, especially enzymes like helicase and topoisomerase. RNA polymerase is the enzyme responsible for RNA synthesis. In eukaryotes, it doesn't just start whenever it sees a start codon; instead, it binds to a promoter region upstream of the start codon with the assistance of transcription factors. The most important promoter in eukaryotes is the TATA box; for more details about promoters, see Chapter 5 on gene expression.

> **MCAT STRATEGY > > >**
>
> Don't be confused by the terms "transcription" and "translation." One way to help remember which is which is to think about how translation involves going from one language to another, like Spanish to English or like nucleic acids to proteins.

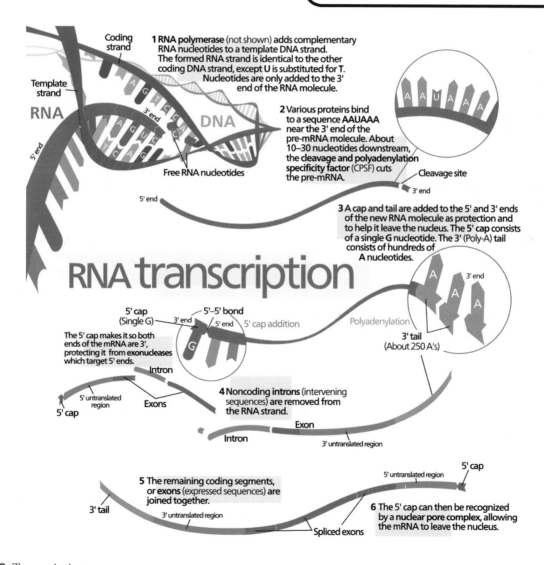

Figure 8. Transcription.

> > **CONNECTIONS** < <

Chapter 5 of Biology

The other important point to consider about RNA polymerase is which strand it uses as a template. There is no need for two RNAs to be synthesized at the same time, so there is no equivalent of the leading/ lagging strand issues that we saw with DNA replication. Similarly to DNA polymerase, RNA polymerase travels along the template strand in the 3'-5' direction, synthesizing an antiparallel complement in the 5'-3' direction. However, the choice of the template strand is far from random. The template strand is known as the antisense strand, and the opposite strand is known as the sense strand, because it corresponds to the codons on the mRNA that is eventually exported to the cytosol for translation.

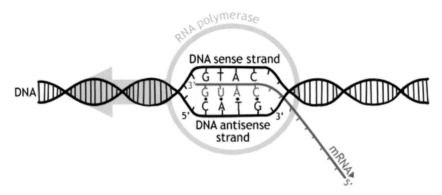

Figure 9. Sense versus antisense strands.

Just as DNA polymerase is not a single enzyme, there are multiple types of RNA polymerase in eukaryotes. Somewhat confusingly, RNA polymerase II is the "default" RNA polymerase that synthesizes hnRNA (the precursor to mRNA) and some small nuclear RNA (snRNA). RNA polymerase I synthesizes ribosomal RNA (rRNA) in the nucleolus, and RNA polymerase III synthesizes transfer RNA (tRNA) and some rRNA.

MCAT STRATEGY > > >

Confusion about the sense versus antisense strands is common, and provides the MCAT with an opportunity to test you on specific content about transcription, base pairing, and directionality of DNA within a single question. Be sure to review this carefully and draw it out a few times until it makes sense. It *is* underlyingly a logical system, but you don't want to be working out its logic on Test Day.

The immediate product of transcription is not mRNA, but heterogeneous nuclear RNA (hnRNA). hnRNA must undergo a set of post-transcriptional modifications to become mRNA. There are three post-transcriptional modifications that you must be familiar with for the MCAT: (1) the 3' poly-A tail, (2) the 5' cap, and (3) splicing. All of these three processes occur only in eukaryotes; in prokaryotes, transcription and translation can occur simultaneously, meaning that there is no room for post-transcriptional modifications.

The 3' poly-A tail is fairly self-explanatory. It is a string of approximately 250 adenine (A) nucleotides added to the 3' end of an hnRNA transcript. It protects the eventual mRNA transcript against rapid degradation in the cytosol. The deadenylation of the poly-A tail by a 3' exonuclease is the first step in mRNA degradation, so the speed with which an mRNA molecule is degraded depends largely on how many A residues are left on it. Why does this matter? Essentially, it's important for the cell to make sure that mRNA sticks around for long enough to do its job, but not for too long, because increasing or decreasing the rate of mRNA transcription is an important part of gene regulation, and it would interfere with this process to keep mRNA transcripts around indefinitely.

The 5' cap is also named intuitively. It refers to a 7-methylguanylate triphosphate cap placed on the 5' end of an hnRNA transcript. Similarly to the 3' poly-A tail, it helps prevent the transcript from being degraded too quickly in the cytosol, but it also prepares the RNA complex for export from the nucleus.

In splicing, noncoding sequences (introns) are removed and coding sequences (exons) are ligated together. Remember that *ex*ons are *ex*pressed. Each gene normally has multiple distinct exons, and they can be ligated in different combinations; that is, if a gene had a set of four introns named A, B, C, and D, possible alternate splicing combinations could include ABCD, ABC, ACD, ABD, BCD, and so on. This dramatically increases the amount of different, but related proteins that can be expressed from a single gene. Splicing explains why there are over 200,000 proteins in the human body, but only approximately 20,000 genes. Splicing is carried out by the spliceosome, a combination of small nuclear RNAs (snRNAs) and protein complexes. When combined, they are known as small nuclear ribonuclear proteins or snRNPs.

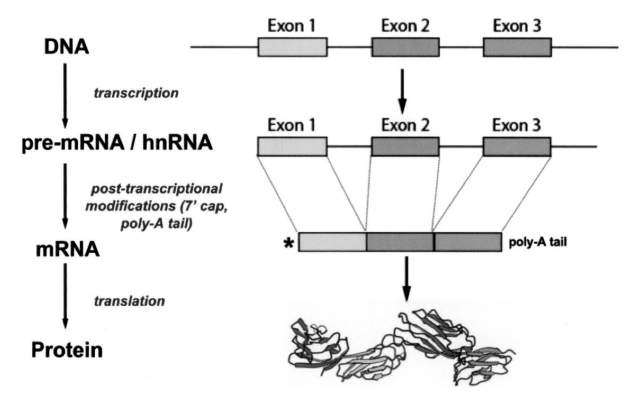

Figure 10. Post-transcriptional modifications.

5. Translation

Translation is the process in which an mRNA sequence is translated into a protein, with each codon corresponding to an amino acid. It takes place in the cytoplasm in both prokaryotes and eukaryotes; in prokaryotes, translation occurs simultaneously with transcription, but the presence of the nuclear membrane in eukaryotes means that these two processes must be separated.

Transfer RNA, or tRNA, is a relatively small RNA molecule characterized by a hairpin structure that is responsible for "translating" between codons and amino acids. At the bottom of the hairpin structure, tRNA molecules contain an anticodon, which is specifically complementary to a certain codon of mRNA. Enzymes known as aminoacyl-tRNA synthetases do the work of "charging" tRNA molecules with the appropriate amino acids by attaching the C-terminus of the amino acid in question to the 3' end of the tRNA molecule. "Charging" the tRNA molecule requires the investment of two ATP bonds, and this energy is then used to power the formation of a peptide bond during translation. This means that translation (i.e., protein synthesis) is an energy-consuming process. On one hand, this fact may not be surprising, but on the other hand, it has implications for the regulation of gene expression because it implies that it is disadvantageous to synthesize proteins that the cell doesn't need.

Figure 11. tRNA.

Ribosomal RNA (rRNA) is the major part of the structure of ribosomes, where translation takes place. Ribosomes contain multiple rRNA strands with associated proteins, and have two major components: the large subunit (50S in prokaryotes and 60S in eukaryotes) and the small subunit (30S in prokaryotes, 40S in eukaryotes), with overall sizes of 70S for the prokaryotic ribosome and 80S for the eukaryotic ribosome (recall that Svedberg units describe sedimentation behavior and do not add linearly). The large subunit catalyzes the formation of the polypeptide chain, while the small unit reads the RNA.

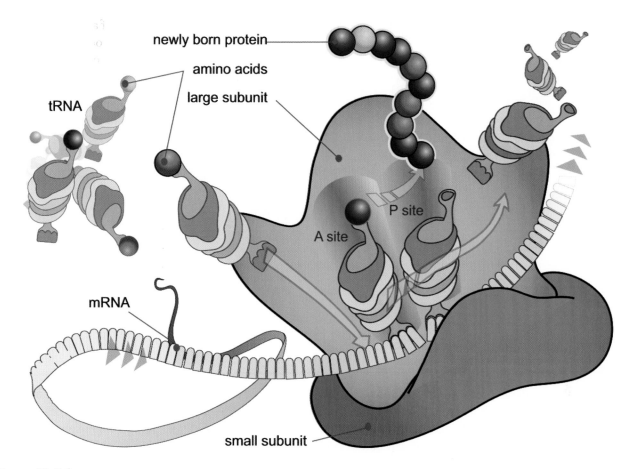

Figure 12. Ribosome structure.

Translation occurs in three steps: initiation, elongation, and termination.

Initiation occurs when the mRNA sequence binds to the small ribosomal subunit, either at a region in the 5' untranslated region known as the Shine-Dalgarno sequence (in prokaryotes) or to the 5' cap in eukaryotes (recall that 5' capping is unique to eukaryotic mRNA). The first tRNA is known as the initiator tRNA, and it binds to the start codon (AUG). The initial amino acid is methionine in eukaryotes, but N-formylmethionine in prokaryotes. Once this happens, initiation factors facilitate the binding of the small ribosomal subunit to the large ribosomal subunit, forming the initiation complex.

Elongation is the next step. During elongation, the ribosome reads the mRNA in the 5' to 3' direction and synthesizes a polypeptide from its N terminus to its C terminus, which is one of the reasons why amino acid sequences are traditionally specified in the N-to-C order. Proteins known as elongation factors help move this process along. The MCAT expects you to be aware of three binding sites that are involved in elongation. The A site contains the next aminoacyl-tRNA complex, and at the P site a peptide bond is formed between the growing polypeptide chain and the incoming amino acid. The tRNA, which is now no longer "charged," briefly pauses at the E site and detaches from the mRNA.

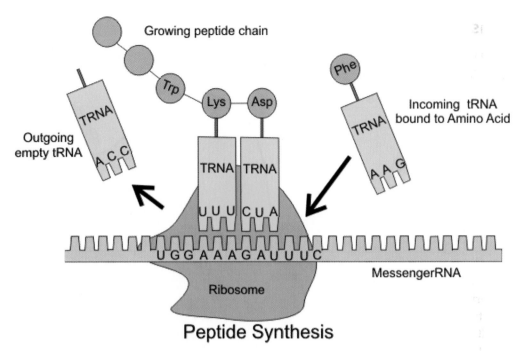

Figure 13. Translation mechanism.

Finally, proteins undergo post-translational modifications. They may be covalently modified by the addition of various functional groups. These modifications can affect the functionality of a protein or play a role in affect signaling pathways. Phosphorylation is the most common example, and describes the addition of phosphates by enzymes known as kinases, which regulates the activity of enzymes. Glycosylation describes the addition of carbohydrates, and the effects of glycosylation include improvements in protein stability, regulatory functions, and structural/functional roles (glycosylated molecules play a major role in cell adhesion and recognition; note that the human ABO blood system is based on glycoproteins). These are the two most common types of covalent modifications you will encounter on the MCAT, although many different moieties can be added to proteins. It is possible that you might encounter another type of post-translational covalent modification in a passage, but if so, you can expect that the passage will provide you with the necessary details.

MCAT STRATEGY >>>

Post-translational modifications are often absolutely essential for the proper functioning of proteins, so be sure not to just skim them over. How would interfering with various types of post-translational modifications affect the ability of a cell to do its job? How could you tell experimentally? This is precisely the kind of material that could be presented in a passage. There's no way you could prepare yourself specifically for all the ways passages could ask about this topic, but you can prepare yourself in general terms by starting to think about hypotheticals.

Protein folding is another important modification, because the eventual function of proteins depends to a great extent on their shape. While protein folding generally does follow some large-scale principles regarding polarity (with nonpolar residues more likely to be found towards the inner structure of the core), the details are very challenging to predict, and proteins known as chaperones help guide this process.

The formation of quaternary structure can also be considered an example of post-translational modification, as can cleavage. Cleavage is a frequent occurrence in the synthesis and processing of peptide hormones; the original transcript is a preprohormone, which is then cleaved to a prohormone, which is finally cleaved to the active form of a hormone immediately before release from the cell. The reason for this is to prevent hormones from inappropriately affecting the cells they are synthesized in.

6. Mutations and Repairs

Errors can happen during DNA replication. In this section, we will discuss those errors, their effects, and how the cell combats them.

Let's start by considering point mutations, which occur when DNA polymerase incorrectly carries out base-pair matching. This means that the corresponding mRNA codon synthesized from that DNA sequence will be off by one base, such as CAG instead of CGG. The effect of this varies depending on the specific location and outcome of the point mutation, as follows:

> > CONNECTIONS < <

Chapter 7 of Biology

> Silent mutations occur if the mutated codon codes for the same amino acid as the original codon. Such mutations have essentially no effect on the physiological function of the organism. An example would be GCU [alanine] → GCA [alanine].

> Conservative point mutations are examples of missense mutations that occur when the mutated codon codes for an amino acid that has similar functional properties (e.g., polarity and size) as the amino acid coded for by the original codon. An example would be GAU [aspartic acid] → GAG [glutamic acid]. Conservative point mutations are expected to have a relatively small effect on the functionality of the protein coded for by the gene, although the word "relatively" is important; protein folding is very tricky to predict and biological functionality can be exquisitely sensitive to small changes, so this is more of a guideline than a rule.

> Non-conservative point mutations are missense mutations that occur when the mutated codon codes for an amino acid with dissimilar functional properties to the amino acid coded for by the original codon. An example would be GCG [alanine] → GAG [glutamic acid]. All things being equal, a non-conservative point mutation could be expected to have a significant impact on the functionality of the protein in question.

> Nonsense mutations occur when the mutated codon is a stop codon. This truncates the translation process early, and is generally associated with significant malfunctioning in the protein product of the gene, especially if a nonsense mutation occurs relatively early in the gene.

One or more nucleotides can be added to or deleted from the genome, in what are known as addition or deletion mutations, respectively. If 3 or a multiple of 3 nucleotides are added or deleted, then one or more amino acids are deleted from or added to the protein, with consequences that would be difficult to predict; on one hand, it may not be catastrophic, but on the other hand, it could be important, depending on the region of the protein and the specific details of the codon in question. However, if the number of nucleotides added or deleted is *not* a multiple of 3 (i.e., 1, 2, 4, 5, 7,…), a frameshift mutation results, and all of the downstream codons can be expected to code for different amino acids. This is likely to have a massive effect (probably deleterious) on the functionality of the eventual protein product.

MCAT STRATEGY > > >

Review the types of mutations carefully, because if you get a question about a type of mutation on Test Day, that should be a relatively straightforward, "gettable" point. Know both what a certain type of mutation is and how likely it is to have a major effect, because you can apply that knowledge to problem-solving.

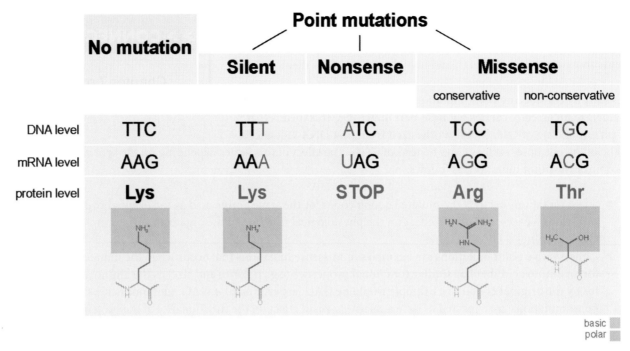

	No mutation	Point mutations			
		Silent	Nonsense	Missense	
				conservative	non-conservative
DNA level	TTC	TTT	ATC	TCC	TGC
mRNA level	AAG	AAA	UAG	AGG	ACG
protein level	**Lys**	Lys	STOP	Arg	Thr

basic
polar

Figure 14. Types of mutations.

Additionally, there are larger-scale mutations that can have a more general effect on the structure of a chromosome. Similarly to what we saw with point mutations, there are three large-scale options for what can happen with larger mutations: you can delete a chromosomal region, add extra copies of a chromosomal region, or move chromosomal regions around. Deletion of large chromosomal regions is known simply as deletion, while adding extra copies of a region is known as duplication. The effect of deletion is straightforward; it removes certain genes from a chromosome, leading either to loss of heterozygosity or a reduction in gene dosage (i.e., the amount that gets transcribed) depending on whether the other copy of the chromosome has a different allele or the same allele. The effect of amplification is generally to increase the gene dosage by leading to more transcription of the genes in question. Inversion can also occur when a mistake takes place in the directionality of a chromosome, in which a segment is reversed from end to end. All things being equal, inversions are generally harmless, although they may lead to an increased risk of miscarriage or infertility due to a higher likelihood of problems arising in gametes.

The terms translocation and insertion are used to describe what happens when chromosomal regions are moved around. Translocation refers to a scenario in which a sequence of genes switches places from one chromosome to another, while insertion describes what happens if a sequence is moved from one chromosome to another (the difference is that translocation involves a reciprocal switch, whereas insertion is a one-way change). In balanced translocations, the exchange of genetic material is even, and nothing is lost or missing, while in unbalanced translocations, the exchange is unequal. Generally speaking, balanced translocations are not usually in and of themselves harmful, although they may increase the likelihood of an individual's offspring having an unbalanced translocation. However, if the origin point of a balanced translocation lies within the middle of a gene, that can potentially have a negative impact. Translocations should be distinguished from transposons, which are generally non-coding genetic elements that can move from chromosome to chromosome. These comprise over 40% of the human genome and are generally not problematic unless they are inserted somewhere that breaks up a coding sequence.

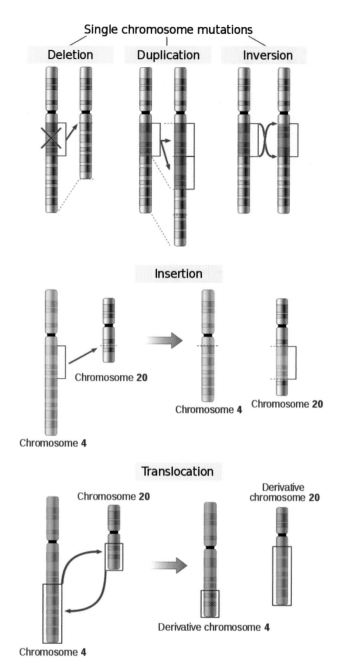

Figure 15. Chromosomal mutations.

Another way to generate a chromosomal abnormality is to have too many or too few copies of a given chromosome. This is known as aneuploidy, and results from nondisjunction during cell division. Having only one copy of a chromosome is known as monosomy, and having three copies is known as trisomy. We commonly think of aneuploidy as occurring in meiosis, and indeed, this is the only way for aneuploidy to be inheritable. For this reason, nondisjunction during meiosis is the cause of aneuploidies such as Down syndrome (trisomy 21) or Turner syndrome (monosomy X). However, nondisjunction during mitosis can also occur, with two particularly relevant examples. First, if nondisjunction takes place during mitotic divisions early in embryogenesis, an aneuploidy may affect large proportions of the body, but not all body cells. When applied to Down syndrome, for instance, this leads to a condition known as mosaic Down syndrome, which is generally somewhat less severe. Second, aneuploidies due to nondisjunction during mitosis are extremely common in cancer cells.

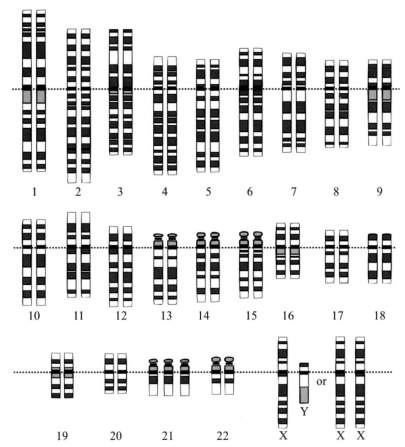

Figure 16. Aneuploidy in Down syndrome.

During DNA replication, DNA polymerase makes errors at approximately the rate of one error per billion bases added. While on one hand, this is a phenomenal rate of success that we may all envy in our personal and professional lives, the fact that the human genome contains approximately six billion base pairs in diploid cells means that we would expect approximately six errors to occur each time a cell undergoes divisions. This could add up to be a real problem. Fortunately, DNA polymerase also has what is often referred to as a "proofreading" ability. When DNA base pairs are mismatched due to errors in copying, the hydrogen-bonding interactions between the base pairs are relatively unstable, which is detected by DNA polymerase. DNA polymerase can excise the base pair in question and reinsert the correct base, a functionality that is referred to as 3'-5' exonuclease activity.

DNA damage can also be caused by external sources, such as reactive oxygen species produced by metabolic pathways within the organism, radiation, mutagenic compounds/toxins, and viruses. These substances are known as mutagens, and most mutagens are also carcinogens, because mutations ultimately can give rise to cancer. Several specialized proteins repair DNA; research into DNA repair won the 2015 Nobel Prize in Chemistry, and as is often the case for areas of intense ongoing research, the MCAT expects you to be aware of the general principles but not to know the cutting-edge details.

There are two mechanisms of DNA repair: base excision repair and nucleotide excision repair. Base excision repair deals with relatively small-scale errors, such as mismatched pairs; oxidized, alkylated, or deaminated bases; and the mistaken inclusion of uracil in DNA. Mismatch repair can be thought of as a subset of base excision repair, and has specific proteins dedicated to that functionality during the G_2 stage of the cell cycle. Nucleotide excision repair targets larger lesions, such as DNA adducts that include thymine dimers, which result from damage by ultraviolet light.

Additionally, the mitotic checkpoint (also known as the spindle checkpoint) takes place in metaphase and is a step that guards against aneuploidy.

7. Must-Knows

> Central dogma: information flows from DNA to RNA to protein.
> Codons: groups of 3 RNA bases that code for amino acids; third position is "wobble"
  — Stop: UGA, UAA, UAG; start: AUG: start (methionine)
> Complementary base pairs: A/T, C/G [A/U in RNA] opposite strand is antiparallel.
> DNA coils around histones: euchromatin is loose and transcriptionally active, while heterochromatin is dense and transcriptionally inactive.
> DNA replication is semiconservative. DNA polymerase reads 3'-5' and synthesizes 5'-3'.
> Replication is uninterrupted on leading strand; Okazaki fragments are synthesized from lagging strand and joined together using ligase.
> In transcription, mRNA is synthesized from the antisense/template strand, and is identical (except for having U instead of T) to sense strand.
> Post-transcriptional modifications of hnRNA → mRNA: 3' poly A tail (anti-degradation in cytoplasm), 5' cap (transport and anti-degradation), splicing (non-coding sequences removed and coding sequences ligated)
> Translation: mRNA → protein in ribosomes through tRNA, which links codon to amino acids.
> Prokaryotic ribosomes: 70S (30S + 50S), eukaryotic ribosomes: 80S (40S + 60S)
> Translation: initiation, elongation, termination; binding sites for elongation are A, P, E.
> Small-scale mutations (point and/or a few nucleotides):
  — Silent point mutations don't affect AA outcome
  — Conservative point mutations: similar AA, non-conservative: AA w/ different properties [missense mutations]
  — Nonsense mutations: premature stop codon
  — Insertions/deletions → frameshift mutations, change all downstream AAs
> Larger-scale mutations:
  — Translocations: swap of genetic material
  — Aneuploidy: due to nondisjunction during division.

Practice Passage

A DNA polymerase is an enzyme that catalyzes the formation of a strand of nucleotides based on a DNA template. During the S phase of the cell cycle, two copies of DNA polymerase act on the existing genetic material to create two new copies. The process of DNA replication however, requires much more than the presence of DNA polymerase. The many enzymes involved and their function are outlined in Figure 1.

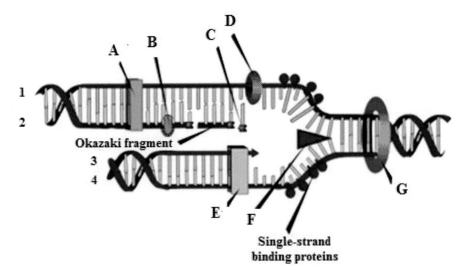

Figure 1. Schematic of DNA replication

DNA polymerase can only add new nucleotides to the 3' end of the strand being synthesized. DNA polymerases make about one mistake per billion nucleotides added. Most DNA polymerases have the built in ability to recognize and correct these mistakes when they occur. When mistakes occur, the offending base is cleaved out of the strand by enzymes and DNA polymerase will add the correct base. After this, DNA ligase connects the loose ends.

DNA ligase catalyzes the joining together of two DNA strands by forming a phosphodiester bond between the two strands. DNA ligase first binds an AMP molecule to a lysine residue in its structure. This AMP is attacked by the 5' phosphate group between the nucleotides, transferring the AMP to the phosphate group. The addition of the AMP to the 5' phosphate makes the phosphorous atom more susceptible to attack by the 3' OH group of the next nucleotide. The attack results in the release of AMP and H_2O and the formation of a phosphodiester bond.

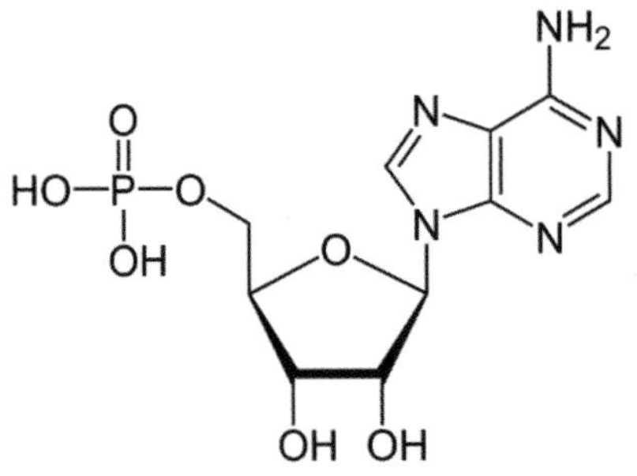

Figure 2. AMP

1. If there are 6 billion base pairs in a diploid cell, how many errors will occur on average during DNA replication in that cell?
   A. 3
   B. 6
   C. 9
   D. 12

2. A segment of the DNA coding for helicase is shown below.

   5' - AGTCTCCGGATTAACGATGC - 3'
   | | | | | | | | | | | | | | | | | | | |
   3' - TCAGAGGCCTAATTGCTACG - 5'

   If the strands are being opened from right to left and replicated, which strand will require DNA ligase to complete its complement?
   A. The top strand because DNA polymerase will be adding nucleotides in the 3' direction from left to right on the top strand.
   B. The top strand because DNA polymerase will be adding nucleotides in the 3' direction from right to left on the top strand.
   C. The bottom strand because DNA polymerase will be adding nucleotides in the 3' direction from left to right on the bottom strand.
   D. The bottom strand because DNA polymerase will be adding nucleotides in the 3' direction from right to left on the bottom strand.

3. Which of the following represents how a bond is formed between adjacent nucleotides being joined by DNA ligase?

A.

B.

C.

D.

4. Which of the following labeled enzymes on Figure 1 is primase?
   A. D
   B. E
   C. F
   D. G

5. Which of the following best describes the effect of addition of AMP to a phosphate group?
   A. AMP is electron donating and contributes to the phosphate's nucleophilic affinity.
   B. AMP is electron donating and contributes to the phosphorus atom's electrophilic nature.
   C. AMP is electron withdrawing.
   D. AMP is electron donating and contributes to the phosphorus atom's electronegativity.

6. What are the correct directionality designations on the template and complementary strands shown in Figure 1?

A.

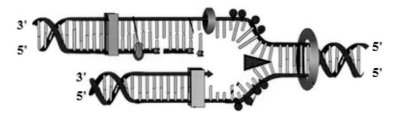

B.

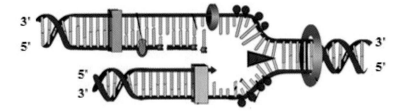

C.

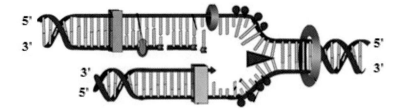

D.

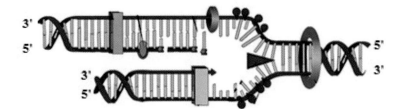

7. Polymerase chain reaction processing and subsequent enzymatic function analysis of the DNA polymerases used in eukaryotic DNA replication would most likely reveal:
   A. enzymes with identical secondary structure and identical replicative functions.
   B. enzymes with different primary structure and identical replicative functions.
   C. enzymes with different secondary structure and different replicative functions.
   D. enzymes with different primary structure and identical tertiary structure.

Practice Passage Explanations

A DNA polymerase is an enzyme that catalyzes the formation of a strand of nucleotides based on a DNA template. During the S phase of the cell cycle, two copies of DNA polymerase act on the existing genetic material to create two new copies. The process of DNA replication however, requires much more than the presence of DNA polymerase. The many enzymes involved and their function are outlined in Figure 1.

Key terms: DNA polymerase, S phase, DNA replication

Cause and effect: S phase = 2 DNA pol copying genome

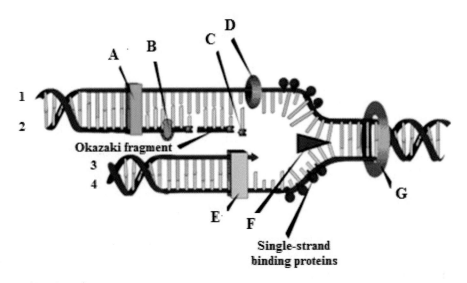

Figure 1. Schematic of DNA replication

Figure 1 shows the enzymes/enzyme locations involved in DNA replication; the unlabeled items suggest possible questions

DNA polymerase can only add new nucleotides to the 3' end of the strand being synthesized. DNA polymerases make about one mistake per billion nucleotides added. Most DNA polymerases have the built in ability to recognize and correct these mistakes when they occur. When mistakes occur, the offending base is cleaved out of the strand by enzymes and DNA polymerase will add the correct base. After this, DNA ligase connects the loose ends.

Key terms: DNA pol, mistake per billion, DNA ligase

Cause and effect: pols have built in corrective mechanisms and a low error rate; 1 error/billion bp → repair → DNA ligase reconnection

DNA ligase catalyzes the joining together of two DNA strands by forming a phosphodiester bond between the two strands. DNA ligase first binds an AMP molecule to a lysine residue in its structure. This AMP is attacked by the 5' phosphate group between the nucleotides, transferring the AMP to the phosphate group. The addition of the AMP to the 5' phosphate makes the phosphorous atom more susceptible to attack by the 3' OH group of the next nucleotide. The attack results in the release of AMP and H2O and the formation of a phosphodiester bond.

Key terms: phosphodiester bond, AMP molecule, lysine, 5' phosphate group, 3' OH.

Cause and effect: We are told about the function of DNA ligase and how it brings about the ligation of two adjacent nucleotides. It uses an AMP intermediate to catalyze the 3' OH attack of the adjacent 5' phosphate group.

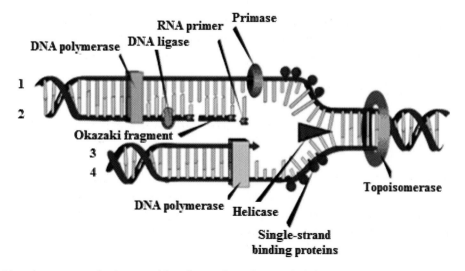

Figure 2. AMP

1. D is correct. Paragraph 2 states that 1 mistake will occur per billion nucleotides added on average. If the genome has 6 billion base pairs and we are making a copy of it, then we will need to add 12 billion bases. At 1 error per billion bps, we can expect 12 errors.

2. C is correct. This question is really asking use to identify the lagging strand (where complementary DNA is made discontinuously and the resulting fragments require stitching together by DNA ligase). We must know that DNA polymerase adds nucleotides on the 3' side of the strand being synthesized. This means that it will synthesize in the direction of the 5' end of the template strand. Thus, if the DNA is opening at the right, the bottom strand will be the lagging strand where Okazaki fragments are formed.

3. D is correct. This question asks us to interpret what is stated in the last paragraph. The paragraph states that the 3' OH group of one nucleotide attacks the 5' phosphorus of the next. Since we are dealing with DNA, the 2 carbon should not have an OH group attached.
   A, C: The phosphate does not attack a carbon.
   B. This is an RNA molecule attacking the phosphate.

4. A is correct. This question requires outside knowledge. DNA primase adds an RNA primer to which DNA polymerase can begin working.

B. E is DNA polymerase, which assembles the nucleotides needed during DNA duplication.
C. F is helicase, which unwinds the DNA during transcription and duplication.
D. G is topoisomerase, which helps prevent DNA supercoiling during transcription and replication.

5. C is correct. This question asks us to interpret what is stated in the last paragraph. The paragraph states that the addition of AMP to the 5' phosphate group makes it susceptible to attack by OH which is a nucleophile. This means that the phosphate group becomes less electron-rich. This can only occur if AMP is withdrawing electron density from the 5' phosphate group. Thus choice C is correct.

    A, B, and D: AMP cannot be adding electron density to the phosphate group because it is being attacked by a nucleophile.

6. B is correct. We must remember for test day that during S phase, one parent strand is the leading strand (where complementary DNA is synthesized continuously) and the other parent strand is the lagging strand (where complementary DNA is synthesized discontinuously). Examining the new strands being made in Figure 1, we can see the one on bottom has its complementary strand being made continuously, while the top strand has its complementary strand being made as small, Okazaki fragments. Since DNA polymerase can only make new DNA in the 5' to 3' direction, the bottom parent strand must be 3' to 5' and its complement 5' to 3' (eliminate choices C and D).

    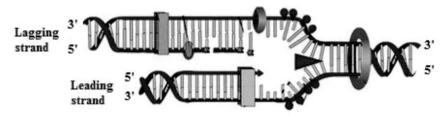

    We can eliminate choice A because strands in the double helix are antiparallel, meaning the 5' end of one strand is lined up with the 3' strand of the other.

7. C is correct. In eukaryotic DNA replication, there are several DNA polymerase isoforms involved. Two isoforms perform the bulk of the processing during DNA replication as shown in Figure 1. DNA pol α is responsible for priming during replication (labeled A in Figure 1), while DNA pol δ is the main DNA replication enzyme (labeled E in Figure 1). These enzymes also vary in their primary, secondary, and tertiary structure.

Independent Questions

1. Which of the following is true of DNA polymerase III (the main polymerase associated with DNA synthesis) in human cells?
   A. It cannot begin extending a new strand until primase synthesizes a DNA primer at the initiation point of extension.
   B. It adds new nucleotides to each preceding 3' hydroxyl group.
   C. It has an innate reverse transcriptase activity.
   D. It reads its DNA template strand in the 5' to 3' direction.

2. A particular enzyme mimics the activity of histone deacetylase. This enzyme most likely:
   A. renders histones less positively charged.
   B. increases the rate of transcription of associated genes.
   C. makes histones interact more closely with associated DNA.
   D. promotes the formation of euchromatin.

3. The mRNA transcribed from a dsDNA molecule has a partial sequence of 5'-AUGAAUC-3'. The corresponding sequence on the sense DNA strand is:
   A. 3'-TACTTAG-5'.
   B. 3'-UACUUAG-5'.
   C. 5'-AUGAAUC-3'.
   D. 5'-ATGAATC-3'.

4. Which of the following is a post-transcriptional modification in eukaryotes?
   A. Glycosylation
   B. Splicing out of exons and rejoining of introns
   C. Addition of a 3' poly-A tail that permanently protects the transcript from degradation
   D. Addition of a 5' 7-methylguanylate cap

5. All of the following are stop codons EXCEPT:
   A. UGA.
   B. AUG.
   C. UAA.
   D. UAG.

6. Select all of the following that constitute differences between prokaryotic and eukaryotic translation.
   I. The initiator tRNA is bound to N-formylmethionine in eukaryotes, but it is bound to methionine in prokaryotes.
   II. Initiation takes place at the Shine-Dalgarno sequence in prokaryotes, while it occurs at the 5' cap in eukaryotes.
   III. Translation takes place on ribosomes in eukaryotes, but prokaryotes lack ribosomes, so they conduct this process in the cytosol.
   A. I only
   B. II only
   C. II and III only
   D. I, II, and III

7. Of the mutations below, which would be expected to have the most deleterious (harmful) effect on the final protein product?
   A. An insertion of 19 nucleotides and a deletion of 1 nucleotide at a neighboring position
   B. A deletion of 14 nucleotides in a coding region
   C. A deletion of 34 nucleotides in an intron region
   D. A conservative point mutation

8. Which of the following enzymes possesses a 3'-to-5' exonuclease activity?
   A. Helicase
   B. RNA polymerase
   C. DNA polymerase
   D. Ligase

Independent Question Explanations

1. B is correct. DNA pol III, which synthesizes new DNA strands complementary to a template, requires an existing 3' hydroxyl (OH) group to "build off of" as it extends its new strand. For this reason, DNA pol III in human cells requires an RNA (not DNA!) primer synthesized by primase. The DNA template strand is read in the 3' to 5' direction, and human DNA polymerase does not have the capacity for reverse transcription (although reverse transcriptase, a separate enzyme, technically is a type of DNA polymerase).

2. C is correct. Acetyl groups on histones make these proteins less positively charged, causing them to associate less tightly with the negatively-charged DNA wrapped around them. Histone *de*acetylase, then, removes these groups, causing the histones to be *more* positively charged and to interact more closely with the DNA surrounding them (choice C). This reduces the transcription of genes on that DNA. Note that a tightly bound state is termed heterochromatin; euchromatin, in contrast, would reflect loose, more transcriptionally active DNA.

3. D is correct. The sense DNA strand should have the same sequence as the mRNA strand produced, except the DNA strand should contain thymine instead of uracil. Here, choices B and C represent mRNA, not DNA, and choice A is the sequence of the antisense DNA strand.

4. D is correct. Post-transcriptional modifications include addition of a 5' cap (specifically, a 7-methylguanylate cap), addition of a 3' poly-A tail, and splicing. However, the poly-A tail does not *permanently* protect the transcript; on the contrary, it is degraded fairly rapidly. Additionally, splicing is a process that removes introns, not exons, and glycosylation is a post-*translational* modification.

5. B is correct. AUG is the start codon, which codes for methionine in eukaryotes and N-formylmethionine in prokaryotes. UGA, UAA, and UAG are all stop codons.

6. B is correct. In prokaryotes, initiation occurs at a position termed the Shine-Dalgarno sequence. In contrast, eukaryotic initiation of transcription happens at the 5' cap (II is correct). Roman numeral I is reversed, and RN III is outright false; while prokaryotes do lack membrane-bound organelles, ribosomes are not bound by a membrane, and prokaryotes certainly contain them.

7. B is correct. Since 14 is not a multiple of 3, this mutation will result in a frameshift. Since frameshifts alter the entire sequence that follows the position of the mutation, they usually have severe effects on the final protein product. Choice A is tempting, but the net result is an insertion of 18 nucleotides, and 18 is a multiple of 3. Thus, the reading frame for the sequence after both mutations will *not* be shifted. Finally, introns are not found in the mature mRNA transcript, so choice C would not affect the protein. Conservative point mutations typically have less severe effects than frameshifts.

8. C is correct. In addition to its main role in synthesizing new DNA strands that are complementary to a template, DNA polymerase is also able to excise mismatched bases and replace them with the correct base at that position. This proofreading mechanism is termed a 3'-5' exonuclease activity.

Genetic Inheritance and Evolution

0. Introduction

Now that we've covered the molecular mechanisms of genetics, let's zoom out a little bit to explore how genetic traits are inherited. Historically these were somewhat different branches of scientific inquiry, which is part of why we still tend to consider them separately. After all, livestock breeding, which depends on manipulating the inheritance of genetic traits, is an ancient part of human history, and it is hardly a new observation that children tend to resemble their parents (albeit imperfectly!).

1. Mendelian Genetics

Gregor Mendel, an Austro-Hungarian monk and scientist of Czech background who lived from 1822 to 1884, is now honored as the founder of genetics, although he had no knowledge of DNA and his findings were largely lost to science for more than three decades before being re-publicized around the turn of the 20th century. Mendel became famous for experiments with breeding pea plants and tracking how various traits were inherited. In doing so, he discovered some classic findings of genetics; for instance, if round and wrinkled peas are crossed, the offspring are all round, but in the next generation, wrinkled peas again appear, with a distribution of 25% wrinkled to 75% round. Mendel himself coined the terms "dominant" and "recessive" to describe the behavior of what we now call genes. Several key concepts are associated with the field known as Mendelian genetics, and are important for the MCAT. We will outline them below.

First, it is fundamental to distinguish between phenotypes and genotypes. The term "phenotype" is sometimes understood as "appearance," but is better thought of as the physical manifestation of a genetic trait. In Mendel's experiments, the phenotypes of interest were characteristics visible to the naked eye, such as the color or shape of peas, but in modern genetic research, phenotypes may not be immediately obvious and may take considerable effort to measure. An example might be the efficiency with which cells carry out a certain metabolic pathway. The genotype, in contrast, describes the combination of genes responsible for that phenotype.

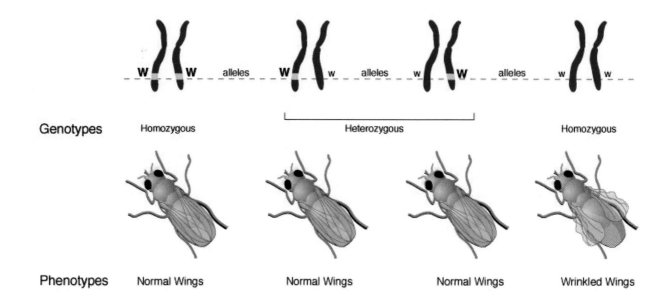

Figure 1. Phenotype versus genotype.

The reason why it is important to distinguish between the phenotype and genotype is that the relationship between the two is not one-to-one. That is, a certain phenotype can correspond to multiple genotypes (the converse does not hold, at least within the realm of classical Mendelian genetics; we do always expect a single genotype to correspond to a single phenotype). This is the essence of Mendel's discovery about the distribution of pea plant phenotypes across generations: the way to explain why wrinkled peas "disappear" but "re-emerge" after a generation of only round peas is to recognize that not all of the round peas have the same underlying genes.

Seed		Flower	Pod		Stem	
Form	**Cotyledons**	**Color**	**Form**	**Color**	**Place**	**Size**
ROUND	YELLOW	WHITE	FULL	YELLOW	AXIAL FLOWERS	TALL
WRINKLED	GREEN	PURPLE	CONSTRICTED	GREEN	TERMINAL FLOWERS	SHORT

Figure 2. Mendelian experiments with peas.

A gene is defined as a sequence of DNA that codes for a given trait, and the term allele is used to refer to variations of that gene. To continue exploring the example of Mendelian pea shape, the gene for pea shape has a round allele and a wrinkled allele. As discussed in previous chapters, in eukaryotes, genes are organized into linear chromosomes, and humans have two copies of each chromosome, one inherited maternally and the other inherited paternally (the exception is for the sex chromosomes; recall that females have two X chromosomes and males have an X chromosome and a Y chromosome that is inherited paternally). The same basic principle holds true for eukaryotes in general, although plants are known for higher-order ploidies, such that they might have three, four, or even more copies of each chromosome. Copies of the same chromosome are referred to as homologues, because they contain the same set of genes, even if they have different alleles. Moreover, each gene occurs at a specific place on a chromosome, known as a locus. This property means that genes can be described in terms of their loci. Combining all of this information, we can conclude that humans inherit two alleles for each gene: one inherited maternally and one inherited paternally (again, with the exception of sex-chromosome genes in males).

Alleles can be described as dominant or recessive. For dominant alleles, only one copy is necessary for its associated phenotype to be expressed, while for recessive alleles, both alleles must be recessive for the phenotype in question to be expressed. Capital letters are usually used to indicate dominant alleles, while lowercase letters are used for recessive alleles. Mutations can also be classified as gain-of-function mutations, in which the mutated protein can do something the original protein couldn't, or loss-of-function mutations, in which the mutated protein can no longer perform the function of the original protein. Loss-of-function mutations tend to be recessive, because the presence of an unmutated allele on the other chromosome allows the cell to compensate, whereas gain-of-function mutations tend to be dominant. Note that "gain of function" does not necessarily mean advantageous! Some dominant mutations, such as the mutation responsible for Huntingon's disease, can be fatal.

Now we can connect these observations with the Mendelian example of round versus wrinkled pea shape. Let's use a capital R to refer to the round allele, which is dominant, and a lowercase r to refer to the wrinkled allele, which is recessive. In the first round of crosses, Mendel crossed purebred round peas (genotype: RR) with purebred wrinkled peas (genotype: rr). Let's illustrate this in a Punnett square, a common technique for illustrating genetic crosses where the parental genotypes are aligned along the top row and left-hand side of the square, and the genotypic outcomes are obtained by combining one allele from each parent:

	R	r
R	Rr	Rr
R	Rr	Rr

Figure 3. Punnett square for first generation (F1) cross of round and wrinkled peas.

As we can see, all of the offspring contain one dominant R allele from one parent and one recessive allele from the other parent. This is an excellent time to introduce the important concepts of homozygosity, heterozygosity, and hemizygosity. Homozygous organisms have two copies of the same allele. Therefore, in the cross illustrated in Figure 1, both sets of parents are homozygous (one set is homozygous dominant and the other set is homozygous recessive). Heterozygous organisms have one copy each of two different alleles, as is the case for all of the offspring in Figure 1. Hemizygous is a somewhat less commonly used term that describes a situation in which only one copy of a given allele is present. This can occur due to nondisjunction in an organism with aneuploidy, or more simply, it can occur with regard to genes on the X and Y chromosomes in male humans.

In the F1 generation, all of the offspring are heterozygotes and manifest the dominant (round) phenotype due to the presence of a single dominant allele.

Next, let's explore what happens when the F1 generation of all-round peas from Figure 1 is crossed with itself:

	R	r
R	RR	Rr
r	rR	rr

Figure 4. Punnett square for second generation (F2) cross of F1 peas.

Let's take a close look at the results shown in Figure 2. The genotypes show a 1:2:1 ratio, with 25% of the offspring homozygous dominant (RR), 50% heterozygous (Rr or rR; both of these are functionally the same and are generally noted just as Rr), and 25% homozygous recessive. However, the phenotypes show a 3:1 ratio in favor of the dominant phenotype, because only homozygous recessives will actually manifest the recessive phenotype.

What happens if we have a phenotypically dominant individual, but need to know its genotype—that is, whether it is homozygous dominant or heterozygous? In such cases, test crosses can be performed. In a test cross, an individual with a dominant phenotype is crossed with an individual with the recessive phenotype. If the phenotypically dominant organism is homozygous, the F1 generation will not have any individuals manifesting the recessive phenotype, whereas if it is heterozygous, approximately 50% of the offspring will manifest the recessive phenotype. This is shown below in Figure 3:

> **MCAT STRATEGY > > >**
>
> Be prepared to work out probabilities for a variety of starting genotypes, and also be aware that the MCAT may ask somewhat tricky questions in which you have to be careful about the wording. Be sure to note whether an inheritance problem is asking about all offspring or just sons or daughters, and to check that the mutation being asked about takes place in a germ cell, because mutations in somatic cells are not hereditable.

Test cross of homozygous dominant + homozygous recessive organisms.

	r	r
R	Rr	Rr
R	Rr	Rr

Test cross of heterozygous + homozygous recessive organisms.

	r	r
R	Rr	Rr
r	rr	rr

Figure 5. Test cross.

Test crossing should be distinguished from backcrossing, which is a technique used in plant cultivation, animal breeding, and cell culture, in which a hybrid is crossed with a parent or with an organism genotypically similar to the parent. The goal of backcrossing to obtain offspring more similar to the parent.

A point of terminology you should also be aware of is the distinction between wild-type and mutated. "Wild-type" doesn't apply well to the example of Mendel's pea experiments, because all of those phenotypes were present in a lineage of plants cultivated by humans. However, it comes up often in fruit fly experiments and in experiments with various cell types. The term wild-type is used to refer to the default phenotype or genotype that is present in most members of a species, in contrast to a mutation. In fruit fly research, this has led to a slightly different pattern of notation than we used above. For example, the wild-type eye color of fruit flies is red, but a mutation exists that results in white eyes. This mutation is known as w, and the wild-type allele is marked with a plus sign, so w corresponds to *having* the mutation, while w^+ means *not having* the mutation. This notation is admittedly confusing, so it's worth taking a moment to familiarize yourself with.

Note that the distinction between wild-type and mutated is *not* the same as the distinction between functional and non-functional. This is a common point of confusion. Wild type refers, strictly speaking, to the variant of an allele that is most prevalent in a population. It is entirely possible, though, that a new mutation could be advantageous from a functional point of view. It is also worth noting briefly that the classical concept of the wild-type variant is somewhat out of date, because modern sequencing techniques have underscored the presence of tremendous genetic diversity within species; it is an oversimplification to say that there is *one* wild-type allele/phenotype, because multiple genotypes can yield functionally equivalent phenotypes. Nonetheless, it is a historically influential concept, the terminology is still used today, and it very well could appear on the MCAT.

Now that we've covered the basics of Mendelian genetics, let's review some ways in which it can get a little bit more complicated than the classical picture of pea plant experiments. From a big-picture perspective, step back and recall that the reality of genetic inheritance *must* be more complicated than we outlined above, because even on an intuitive level, we know that there is more to inheritance than simple dichotomies like tall/short, green/yellow, and round/wrinkled. An especially important point is that the concept of dominance is actually considerably more complex than it first appears.

The type of dominance that we saw in Mendel's experiments—where one copy of the dominant gene is enough to induce the dominant phenotype, and there is no phenotypic difference between homozygous dominant individuals and heterozygotes—is an example of complete dominance. However, other patterns of dominance exist, including codominance and incomplete dominance.

Codominance takes place when two dominant alleles can be expressed at the same time. The classic example of this is the human ABO blood typing system, which refers to the presence of the antigens known as A and B expressed on erythrocytes (O refers to the *absence* of either A or B). Individuals can have the following blood types: A, B, AB, or O (you may also be aware of plus and minus as part of an individual's blood type; this refers to the Rh blood group system, which is a different system biochemically, although it is also quite clinically relevant). The fact that an AB phenotype is possible indicates that these traits are codominant. Another common example involves the appearance of colored spots in an organism's fur, skin, or outer surface; if B is an allele for black fur and W is an allele for white fur, a pattern of black-and-white spots would reflect a codominant relationship.

Incomplete dominance, in contrast, occurs when a heterozygote displays a blended phenotype. The classic example of this is the snapdragon flower. Homozygous snapdragon flowers are red or white, while heterozygotes have a blended phenotype of pink.

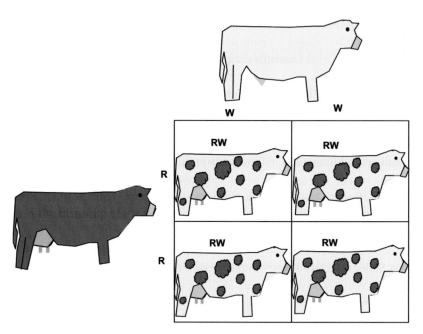

Figure 6A. Codominance.

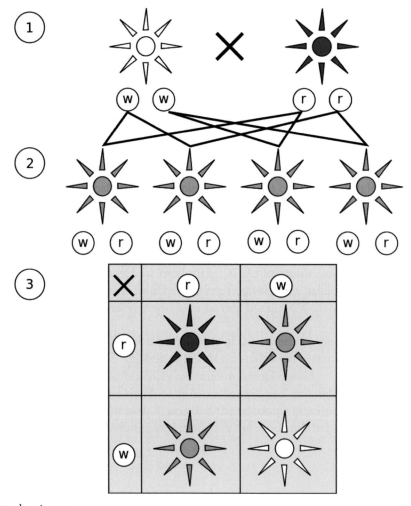

Figure 6B. Incomplete dominance.

Some other concepts complicate the relationship between a genotype and the associated phenotype. Penetrance refers to the likelihood that the carrier of a given genotype (most often associated with a dominant allele) will manifest the corresponding phenotype. An example is the presence of certain mutations in the *BRCA1* gene; a woman with this mutation has an 80% risk of developing breast cancer over the course of her lifetime. This means that the *BRCA1* mutation has 80% penetrance. A logical question would be what causes the gradations in expression that we refer to as penetrance, and the answer (as is often the case in real-world genetics) is complicated. In some cases, such as *BRCA1*, environmental factors most likely account for the 20% of women with *BRCA1* mutations who do not develop breast cancer. Other genes may also affect the penetrance of a mutation, meaning that the overall pattern of presence is polygenic. Additionally, epigenetic modifications can affect gene expression, with potential impacts on penetrance.

Expressivity is a concept that may seem similar to penetrance, but is in fact quite different. While penetrance refers to how often a mutation is phenotypically expressed, expressivity refers to the intensity or extent of variation in the phenotype. Another way of thinking about this is that penetrance is a yes/no question (does an organism express a certain phenotype or not?) while expressivity is a shades-of-gray question (how much of an effect does a mutation have on the phenotype?). For mutations associated with human disease, expressivity can be thought of as the severity of the condition.

Now that we have these basic concepts in our toolkit, let's move on to take a closer look at specific inheritance patterns, on the level of genes, families, and communities.

2. Inheritance Patterns

A principle underlying Mendelian genetics that is easy to skip over is the idea that alleles are randomly distributed among an organism's offspring, and that there is no relationship between genes in terms of which alleles are inherited. Returning to Mendel's peas, let's imagine what happens if we look at a cross in terms of both pea shape (round vs. wrinkled) and color of the flower (purple vs. white), where R and P refer to the dominant traits of round shape and purple color, respectively. In this hypothetical experiment, we will cross heterozygotes for both traits. This is known as a dihybrid cross.

> **MCAT STRATEGY > > >**
>
> Whenever you're studying a topic that's heavy in terminology, do so with an eye towards how that terminology can be tested. In particular, note key words or phenomena that are strongly associated with certain terms. For example, we could simplify the above outline as follows: codominance → both at once; incomplete dominance → blended; penetrance → do you show it or not?; expressivity → how much?. Shorthand like that would not impress your biology professor, but the good news is that you don't have to. You just have to be able to select the right answer on Test Day.

	RP	Rp	rP	rp
RP	RRPP <round, purple>	RRPp <round, purple>	RrPP <round, purple>	RrPp <round, purple>
Rp	RRPp <round, purple>	RRpp <round, white>	RrpP <round, purple>	Rrpp <round, white>
rP	rRPP <round, purple>	rRPp <round, purple>	rrPP <wrinkled, purple>	rrPp <wrinkled, purple>
rp	rRpP <round, purple>	rRpp <round, white>	rrPp <wrinkled, purple>	rrpp <wrinkled, white>

Figure 7. Dihybrid cross of pea plants for shape and flower color.

This leads to a characteristic distribution: 9/16 of the offspring will have the dual dominant phenotype (round, purple), 6/16 of the offspring will have one recessive trait (3/16 will be round and white and 3/16 will be wrinkled and purple), and only 1/16 will show the dual recessive phenotype. The 9:3:3:1 distribution for a dihybrid cross of two heterozygotes is well-known enough to be worth memorizing, but don't forget that performing a dihybrid cross with different genotypes would lead to different results, and you can always create a Punnett square to calculate the probabilities associated with a specific case.

MCAT STRATEGY > > >

Create a few Punnett squares for dihybrid crosses on your own to become familiar with how to set them up. They're not the most likely topic to come up on Test Day, but they are a possibility, and you wouldn't want to waste precious time worrying about how to line stuff up on the axes of the chart.

When calculating the probabilities for the dihybrid cross, note that an unspoken assumption of the Punnett square methodology is that there is no link between inheritance of an allele of the R gene and inheritance of the allele of the P gene. In Mendelian genetics, this is known as the law of independent assortment.

The law of independent assortment is grounded in molecular genetics. First, it is logical that the alleles of genes on different chromosomes will be inherited independently, due to the random orientation of homologous pairs on the metaphase plate in metaphase I of meiosis. Recall what this means in simple terms: you have maternal and paternal copies of all of your autosomal chromosomes, and if you have offspring, it is completely random which copy they will inherit from you. However, independent assortment also applies to genes on the same chromosome due to crossing over during prophase I of meiosis. Sometimes it can seem that genetic recombination is anomalous, but that's not actually the case; recombination among homologous chromosomes during prophase I is actually the rule, not the exception.

However, the formation of chiasmata (points of crossing over) on the chromosome is also essentially random. This means that genes close to each other are less likely to undergo recombination than genes that are further away from each other, and if genes are close enough to each other, this tendency can be strong enough to violate the law of independent assortment. This phenomenon is known as linkage, and the recombination frequency (θ) describes how often a single crossover will occur between two genes during meiosis. If the recombination frequency is greater than 50%, then the genes in question obey the law of independent assortment.

The finding that the recombination frequency is a property of the distance between genes on the chromosome led to the conclusion that recombination frequency can be used to create a map of a given chromosome in terms of physical distance. The distance associated with a 1% increment in the recombination frequency is known as a centimorgan (cM), named after Thomas Hunt Morgan, whose work was fundamental in establishing the concept of linkage.

However, we still have to account for one more complication. So far, we've been talking about a single crossover event separating two genes, but crossover events are common, and it is entirely possible for more than one to occur in the space between two genes. This is known as a double crossover (as compared to single crossovers, which we have been discussing so far). The contrast between single and double crossovers is presented in Figure 8.

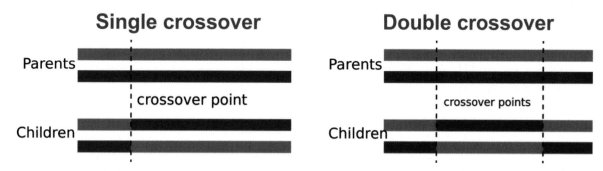

Figure 8. Single and double crossovers.

In humans, autosomal dominant and recessive patterns of inheritance exist, as well as sex-linked patterns of inheritance. While you may remember pedigree analysis from your coursework in biology or genetics, it is not specifically listed as a required topic for the MCAT. However, pedigrees have appeared in some official AAMC materials, so you should be aware of them, as well as knowing the different inheritance patterns observed in humans and what some of their distinctive features are in terms of how they manifest within a family.

Autosomal patterns of inheritance are defined by the absence of a gender bias among offspring. Remember, though, that if you have a small sample size, the even distribution may not be immediately obvious. Just as it wouldn't be *that* remarkable to flip a coin four times and have it come up heads three times instead of two, it wouldn't be particularly unusual for an autosomal mutation to manifest in, say, two out of three females and one out of three males. Recessive mutations are defined by their ability to skip generations, as we saw with the example of round and wrinkled pea shapes in the classic Mendelian example presented in Figure 1. Dominant mutations cannot skip generations.

It should be noted that recessive mutations *can* skip generations, but they do not have to. Imagine a cross between two pea plants with genotypes of Rr and rr: the recessive mutation (r) is present in the parental generation, and we can predict that 50% of the offspring will also have the genotype rr, thereby manifesting the mutation. However, the pattern of recessive mutations skipping generations is typical for genetics as presented on the MCAT, for two reasons. The first reason is practical: the MCAT is a standardized test and the test writers must, to a certain extent, rely on typical distinctions to test your knowledge of content. Second, this pattern is common in the real world, because the alleles coding for recessive mutations are often relatively rare on the population level, making it unlikely (but not impossible) for a homozygous recessive individual to mate with a heterozygote (or carrier).

Sex-linked inheritance takes place for genes located on the X chromosome. Why not the Y chromosome? Over time, evolutionary developments have led the Y chromosome to be stripped down of virtually all content besides what is necessary for sex determination. The absence or near-absence of other genes on the Y chromosome means that Y-linked patterns of inheritance are extremely rare; some textbooks report hairy ears in some populations of India as an example of Y-linked inheritance, but this is no longer thought to be the case. Therefore, for the purposes of the MCAT, sex-linked is X-linked.

X-linked inheritance patterns are characterized by an asymmetry in the sex of affected individuals. Let's work through this with regard to X-linked recessive mutations, because those are much more likely to appear on the MCAT than X-linked dominant inheritance. Let's use the notation X to refer to a normal allele on the X chromosome and X' to refer to a recessive mutation, and review a few possible outcomes of mating: (1) a heterozygote (carrier) female (genotype of XX') mating with an unaffected male (XY), (2) a homozygous dominant (XX) female mating with an affected male (X'Y), and (3) a heterozygous female (XX') mating with an affected male (X'Y). The corresponding Punnett squares are shown below in Figure 9, with the affected offspring shown in red and carriers in blue.

XX' female + XY male

	X	Y
X	XX	XY
X'	X'X	X'Y

XX female + X'Y male

	X'	Y
X	XX'	XY
X	XX'	XY

XX' female + X'Y male

	X'	Y
X	XX'	XY
X'	X'X'	X'Y

Figure 9. X-linked recessive mutations.

The basic principle that you need to be aware of is that females inherit one X chromosome from their mother and one from their father, while males *only* get their single X chromosome from their mother. Since males only have one X chromosome, having a single mutated allele will suffice to manifest a recessive mutation. Therefore, affected male children can be born to a couple where neither parent manifests the recessive phenotype, but it is much rarer for female children to be affected, and it is only possible for that to occur when the father is affected by the condition and the mother is a carrier. This reasoning leads us to an actionable conclusion that we can apply on the MCAT: X-linked mutations are *much* more likely to affect male offspring.

With all of the above in mind, we can create a flow chart for how to distinguish between autosomal dominant, autosomal recessive, and sex-linked patterns of inheritance.

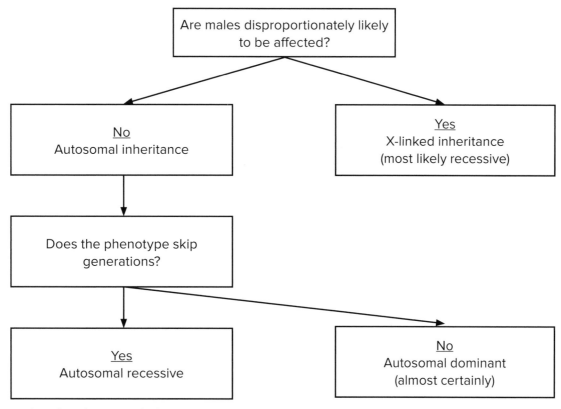

Figure 10. Flow chart for types of inheritance.

3. Population Genetics and Evolution

Next, let's zoom out even more to see how these concepts play out on the level of populations. To do so, we'll need to look at genetics from the perspective of evolution/natural selection, concepts first presented in Darwin's *Origin of Species* in 1859 that have been elaborated on since and currently form the basis for much of modern biology. In the 1973 words of the evolutionary biologist (and, parenthetically, self-described creationist) Theodosius Dobzhansky, "nothing in biology makes sense except in the light of evolution."

Many misconceptions exist about evolution, and many of those misconceptions serve to make studying evolution much more complex than it needs to be. An evolutionary system must have only three structural features: (1) variations in the population, (2) a mechanism for those variations to be reproduced over time, and (3) environmental constraints that allow favorable variations to be reproduced more than others, which is known as differential reproduction. Biological evolution is actually only one example of an evolutionary system; evolutionary systems have been used in computer modeling and applied to other fields of inquiry, such as linguistics. In biology, point (1) is accounted for by genetic and phenotypic variations within the population (we will not concern ourselves here with the origin of life), point (2) is accounted for by sexual and asexual reproduction, and point (3) is accounted for by what is known as natural selection. The key point here is that differential reproduction leads to selection over time.

Natural selection simply refers to the tendency of certain phenotypes to be favored in terms of reproduction. It does not mean the same thing as evolution: natural selection is the mechanism through which evolution takes place. Natural selection is closely linked to the term fitness, which in the evolutionary context *only* refers to the chance of reproduction associated with a certain phenotype compared to baseline. Fitness *must* be defined in terms of specific environmental constraints. This is a common misconception, so it is worth dwelling on. Let's consider two types of bacteria: *Acetobacter aceti*, which grows best in a pH range of 5.4-6.3 and is used industrially to produce vinegar (acetic acid) from the ethanol contained in wine, and *Natronomonas pharaonis*, which likes very salty conditions (3.5

M NaCl) and grows best in alkaline conditions, at a pH of 8.5. We might be inclined to ask which bacterium is more fit—but that question does not even make sense! The answer depends on the environment, because *A. aceti* grows (and reproduces) best in acidic conditions and *N. pharaonis* grows (and reproduces) best in salty, alkaline conditions. Asking which is more "fit" in absolute terms is like asking "which are better, sandals or rain boots?" Rain boots are better for cold rainy days, and sandals are better for a warm day at the beach. Claiming that one is better in absolute terms is at best unhelpful, and doesn't really make much sense.

MCAT STRATEGY > > >

Evolutionary theory is rarely directly tested on the MCAT, but it's worth investing some time in making sure that you have a clear conceptual foundation in order to avoid making mistakes or spending too much time on questions that deal with this topic indirectly. The concepts of evolution and fitness have a way of being relevant in experimental passages that primarily deal with other topics.

The classic formulation of Darwinian principles focuses on individual fitness, but many organisms live in groups. While humans form a truly exceptional case of group dynamics involving the cultural transmission of knowledge through language, it is reasonably common for group dynamics to play a major role in the life cycles of other animals. Therefore, a major problem for evolutionary theorists over the course of the 20th century was to account for group dynamics in evolution. The history of these ideas goes well beyond the scope of the MCAT, so we'll focus on a few takeaway points. The concept of group selection was proposed, arguing that natural selection could act on the level of the group, not the individual. The related concept of inclusive fitness expands the rigorous evolutionary definition of fitness (defined in terms of the differential reproduction of alleles) to account not just for individuals but their relatives, who can be expected to share many of the same alleles. This idea helps to explain altruistic behavior; when the early 20th-century British biologist J. B. S. Haldane was asked whether he would sacrifice his life to save that of his brother, he quipped "No, but I would to save two brothers or eight cousins." This captures the essence of group/kin selection in a nutshell: from the point of view of a gene, it can be advantageous for an individual to engage in altruistic behavior or even self-sacrifice to ensure the survival of more copies of the gene.

Note how we've switched our perspective from focusing on individual organisms to focusing on genes. This is a hallmark of modern genetics. The concept of the gene pool, which can be thought of as the combined set of all genes/alleles in a population, is often used to describe the genetic status of a population. In this framework, evolutionary success can be thought of as an increase in the representation of a certain allele within the gene pool.

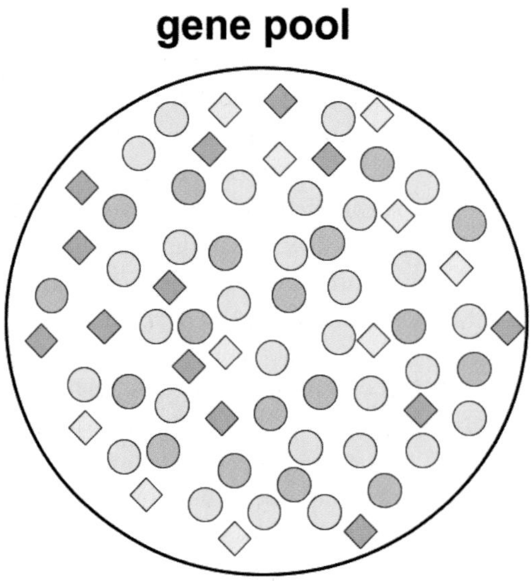

gene pool

Figure 11. Gene pool.

The concept of Hardy-Weinberg equilibrium is used to model stable gene pools. For Hardy-Weinberg equilibrium to apply to a population, it must meet the following criteria:

1. Organisms must be diploid and reproduce sexually.

2. Mating is random.

3. The population size is very large.

4. Alleles are randomly distributed by sex.

5. No mutations occur.

6. There is no migration into or out of the population.

Obviously, it is difficult to find real-world populations that meet these criteria perfectly, so you may ask why we use this model. The answer is that Hardy-Weinberg equilibrium is an example of an analytical simplification that leads to elegant results, much like how we often neglect the effect of air resistance in physics. In particular, the Hardy-Weinberg equations allow us to use allele frequencies to predict the distribution of phenotypes in the population and vice versa. If p and q are the only two alleles of a gene present in the population, then $p + q = 1$. Think of 1 as being like 100% here (similarly to how these numbers are used in probability). This equation is just a way of saying that the two alleles p and q account for the whole population. Where things get interesting is if you square the equation: $(p + q)^2 = 1^2 \rightarrow p^2 + 2pq + q^2 = 1$. This second equation allows us to connect genotypes and phenotypes, because the p^2 and q^2 terms correspond to individuals homozygous for p and q, respectively, while the $2pq$ term gives the frequency of heterozygotes. Let's work through an example problem.

Suppose that 9% of a population obeying Hardy-Weinberg equilibrium manifests a certain recessive mutation. How many people are carriers? We're told that 9% of the population are homozygous recessive; this means that $q^2 = 0.09$, so q is therefore 0.3. We can use the equation $p + q = 1$ to determine p from q. In this case, $p = 0.7$. The frequency of heterozygotes corresponds to $2pq$ or $2(0.7)(0.3)$, which equals 0.42, meaning that 42% of the population are carriers.

However, as mentioned, Hardy-Weinberg equilibrium often fails to apply perfectly to real-world populations, and exploring some exceptions to the Hardy-Weinberg assumptions can help illuminate some important dynamics in evolutionary biology.

First, selection obviously can operate on the population level. Multiple distinct "types" of selection have been identified to describe the different outcomes associated with different types of selective pressures on phenotypes that vary along a spectrum. That is, the discussion below does not apply to binary phenotypes where an organism either has a trait or not, but to categories that can vary, like height or weight. Many such features are polygenic, meaning that multiple genes contribute to them. Let's imagine a phenotype such as height with values distributed on a bell curve throughout a population.

Stabilizing selection occurs if both extremes are selected against: that is, if very short and very tall individuals have lower reproductive fitness, the height of the population will be maintained within a tight range. Directional selection occurs if only one extreme phenotype is selected against and the other extreme is favored. To work with the example of height, if we can imagine that for some reason very tall people are selected against, the population would become shorter. Disruptive selection occurs when the median phenotype is selected against. Darwin's observations of finches on the Galapagos Islands are a classic example of this. He noted that they had either large or small beaks, but not medium-sized beaks, and proposed that this was due to the size of the seeds they used for food, which were either large or small, such that a medium-sized beak would not be particularly useful. These examples also provide helpful illustrations of a crucial conceptual point: selection acts directly on phenotypes, but only indirectly on genotypes.

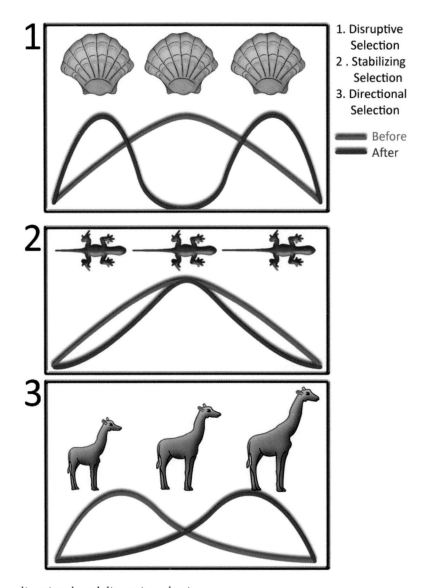

Figure 11. Stabilizing, directional, and disruptive selection.

MCAT STRATEGY > > >

You do need to be aware of all of these details, but don't get bogged down in them. Terms like "directional selection" are really red herrings in a certain sense: there is only one mechanism of selection, natural selection, but it can have different results depending on the external circumstances.

Other mechanisms are associated with changes in the gene pool of a species, such as genetic drift and bottlenecks. Genetic drift refers to the role of chance, in the absence of strong selective pressures, in determining the reproductive fitness of various alleles. In a population at any given time, it may be that no strong pressure exists for a certain allele, so it may randomly happen to be reproduced more or less often. These random effects can add up over the course of evolution. A related, but more specific, concept is that of an evolutionary bottleneck. Bottlenecks occur when some external event dramatically reduces the size of a population in a way that is essentially random with regard to most if not all alleles. An example would be if a sudden flood wipes out 80% of a population—for the most part, survival will be random. It is possible for a non-representative subset of the gene pool to remain after a bottleneck, with implications for the future evolutionary history of the population. A real-world example is provided by the incidence of Tay-Sachs disease in Ashkenazi Jews (the population of Jews who historically lived in northern Europe). It is thought that Ashkenazi Jews experienced a major bottleneck early in their history, and one result of this is the unusually high prevalence in that community of Tay-Sachs disease, an autosomal recessive disorder that is fatal in young children.

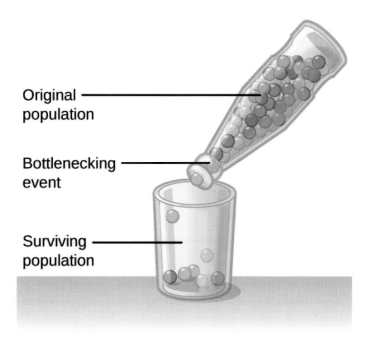

Figure 12. Bottleneck.

These considerations lead us to the topic of speciation, which describes how a new species evolves through evolution. A species is defined as a group of organisms that can successfully breed to form fertile offspring. The presence of different selective pressures over time can lead to the emergence of new species. However, considerable phenotypic variation can exist within a single species. This is known as polymorphism; examples of polymorphism abound throughout biology, but a helpful example to keep in mind is the ABO blood type in humans discussed earlier in this chapter. Organisms in specific environments may undergo processes of adaptation and specialization, in which certain individuals or subpopulations develop evolutionary strategies specific to certain microenvironments, or niches. These processes do not constitute speciation in and of themselves, but they can help set the stage for speciation. Inbreeding and outbreeding can also occur within populations; inbreeding is breeding between genetically closely related individuals and can lead to the increased manifestation of recessive mutations and other deleterious effects, while outbreeding refers to breeding among genetically distant members of a population.

Since differences between species are defined in terms of reproductive isolation, it is helpful to distinguish between prezygotic and postzygotic barriers to reproduction. Prezygotic barriers refer to anything that stops reproduction before the formation of a zygote, such as occupying different ecological niches, having different patterns of breeding, not engaging in reproductive behavior with members of the other species, incompatible reproductive anatomy, or the inability for fertilization to occur after intercourse.

However, sometimes a zygote is formed, and postzygotic barriers describe various forms of reproductive isolation that can occur after a zygote is formed. One simple way is for the zygote to simply be unable to develop to term. However, sometimes members of two different species can produce viable offspring. These offspring are known as hybrids. Mules are a common example: they are the offspring of a horse and a donkey, and are viable themselves but cannot produce offspring. This is known as hybrid sterility. It is also possible for hybrids to be fertile, but for fertility to break down in the second generation, in a process known as hybrid breakdown. On the level of the gene pool, genes can sometimes travel between species, in what is known as leakage.

Life has been present on Earth, and subjected to evolution, for a mind-bogglingly long time. The Earth is slightly over 4.6 billion years old, and the first traces of life date to approximately 3 billion years ago, although life may have existed even earlier. All living organisms on Earth, ranging from ourselves to the bacteria that colonize us, are thought to have derived from a single common ancestor due to the presence of many shared biochemical pathways across all forms of life. Eukaryotes are known to have evolved by approximately 1.5 billion years ago, and the earliest animal fossils are known from about 580 million years ago. Our species, *Homo sapiens sapiens,* is thought to have evolved approximately 200,000 years ago. You do not have to know these details for the MCAT, but it is useful to have a sense of the depth of evolutionary time and the fact that we are relative newcomers to the scene, so to speak.

Since random errors accumulate on the genome at a relatively fixed rate, the extent to which two genomes differ serves as a proxy for how long ago they had a shared common ancestor. Analytical techniques based on this insight have yielded tremendous results in evolutionary history. This so-called "molecular clock" can also be applied to help solve mysteries about emerging disease. Molecular-clock analyses have played a major role, for example, in attempts to determine how the human immunodeficiency virus (HIV; the virus that causes AIDS) originated and spread.

4. Must-Knows

> Phenotype = physical manifestation of a trait; genotype = underlying genes.
> Allele = specific variant of a given gene, such as round/wrinkled shape of peas.
> Dominant alleles only need one copy present for phenotype to occur; recessive alleles manifest the corresponding phenotype if no dominant alleles are present.
> Homozygous = both alleles the same; heterozygous = two different alleles present.
> Phenotype ≠ genotype; dominant phenotype can correspond to either homozygous dominant (RR) or heterozygous (Rr) genotypes.
> Test cross: dominant-phenotype individual crossed with recessive individual to determine phenotype.
> Codominance = two different alleles expressed at the same type (human ABO blood type); incomplete dominance = blended phenotype in heterozygotes (red × white snapdragon flowers → pink offspring)
> Law of independent assortment: inheritance of various genes not correlated with each other.
> Linkage: exception to independent assortment; genes physically close to each other on the same chromosome tend to have their alleles inherited together. Recombination frequency can be used to map location of genes on chromosomes.
> Autosomal inheritance: on non-sex chromosomes; sex-linked inheritance: for genes on X chromosome.
> Recessive inheritance is characterized by skipping generations (dominant mutations cannot) and X-linked recessive traits affect more males than females because males only have one X chromosome.
> Hardy-Weinberg equilibrium: assumptions include (1) diploid sexual reproduction; (2) random mating; (3) large population; (4) random distribution of alleles by sex; (5) no mutations; (6) no migration. Leads to following equations for allele frequency: $p + q = 1$, $p^2 + 2pq + q^2 = 1$.
> Fitness is defined in terms of reproductive success.
> Speciation: formation of new species, defined by reproductive isolation (inability to produce fertile offspring).
> Stabilizing selection: extremes selected against, phenotype maintained within strict range. Directional selection: one extreme selected against, phenotype moves to the other end. Disruptive selection: middle selected against, population swings to favor both extremes.
> Accumulation of random changes in genome over time → "molecular clock" method of dating divergence from last common ancestor.

This page left intentionally blank.

Practice Passage

Huntington's disease (HD) is a severe hereditary neurodegenerative disorder caused by an expansion of CAG repeats at the *HTT* gene on chromosome 4 that codes the Huntington cytoplasmic protein (Htt).

HTT contains multiple repeats of a trinucleotide sequence - CAG. CAG codes for glutamine, and translation of the repeats produces a polyglutamine (polyQ) tract. The length of the segment containing the repeats varies. When the length of this repeated section reaches a certain threshold, it produces an altered form of the protein, mHtt, which is toxic to cells of the striatum.

To further study the association between CAG length and the age of onset (AOO) of HD, a worldwide epidemiological study on HD was conducted. Geneticists studying HD inheritance found that it is rare for HD to be caused by a new mutation. It was also confirmed that the length of the repeated sequence influenced the age of onset and the progression and severity of symptoms experienced by affected individuals and their affected offspring (Table 1).

Table 1. Analysis Results of HD Population

REPEAT COUNT	DISEASE STATUS	AGE OF ONSET (YEARS)	PROBABILITY OF AFFECTED OFFSPRING
<26	Unaffected		0
27–35	Unaffected		<<50%
36–39	May be affected	After 40	50%
≥40	Affected	25–39, earlier with increased count	50%

The functional form of the association between the onset time t and CAG repeat length x has been debated for decades. The data collected in the study yielded a model which captures the relation between the AOO of HD and the CAG length through a logistic link.

Geneticists further examined the role of inheritance in Huntington's disease by interviewing an early-stage Huntington's patient from the study. Their relevant family history is presented below.

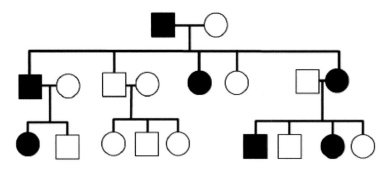

Figure 1. Family history interview results

Adapted from Ma, Y., & Wang, Y. (2014). Nonparametric modeling and analysis of association between Huntington's disease onset and CAG repeats. Statistics in Medicine, 33(8), 1369–1382. under CCBY

1. According to the family history presented in the passage, Huntington's disease displays what pattern of inheritance?
   A. Autosomal recessive
   B. Autosomal dominant
   C. X-linked recessive
   D. Y-linked dominant

2. Given the results of the geneticists' work, what is the maximum number of possible glutamine residues in the polyQ region of Htt in an individual displaying a normal phenotype?
   A. 25
   B. 35
   C. 39
   D. 40

3. Investigation of the role of genetics in HD has shown that mating between homozygotes for the HD producing HTT gene and homozygotes for normal HTT can produce a third phenotype that is neurologically abnormal, but not nearly to the extent required to be classified as HD. This situation is most analogous to:
   A. incomplete dominance.
   B. codominance.
   C. double crossover.
   D. genetic leakage.

4. What is the probability that both of the children of an affected father with two copies of the HTT allele, containing more than 40 CAG repeats, and a mother with fewer than 26 CAG repeats, will express the mHtt protein?
   A. 25%
   B. 50%
   C. 75%
   D. 100%

5. The observation that not all individuals containing 36-39 CAG repeats display clinical symptoms of Huntington's disease can be explained in terms of what property?
   A. Incomplete penetrance
   B. Variable expressivity
   C. Pleiotropy
   D. Genetic anticipation

6. If baldness is an X-linked recessive disorder, who could NOT also have been a carrier of the baldness gene found in a bald man?
   A. The bald male's mother
   B. The bald male's maternal grandmother
   C. The bald male's paternal grandfather
   D. The bald male's maternal grandfather

7. A biometry expert is hired by the lab to decide on the proper test to evaluate HD data. If all samples used in the test are to be random samples from populations that are normally distributed with equal variance, what test are they most likely to use?
   A. Mann-Whitney U test
   B. Linear regression analysis
   C. ANOVA
   D. Paired t-test

Practice Passage Explanations

Huntington's disease (HD) is a severe hereditary neurodegenerative disorder caused by an expansion of CAG repeats at the *HTT* gene on chromosome 4 that codes the Huntington cytoplasmic protein (Htt).

Key terms: HD, chromosome 4

Cause and effect: CAG repeat expansion on HTT → HD

HTT contains multiple repeats of a trinucleotide sequence - CAG. CAG codes for glutamine, and translation of the repeats produces a polyglutamine (polyQ) tract. The length of the segment containing the repeats varies. When the length of this repeated section reaches a certain threshold, it produces an altered form of the protein, mHtt, which is toxic to cells of the striatum.

Key terms: HD, Huntingtin protein, trinucleotide repeat, polyQ tract, mutant Htt

Cause and effect: CAG repeat threshold met → mutated Htt → striatal neuron loss → HD

To further study the association between CAG length and the age of onset (AOO) of HD, a worldwide epidemiological study on HD was conducted. Geneticists studying HD inheritance found that it is rare for HD to be caused by a new mutation. It was also confirmed that the length of the repeated sequence influenced the age of onset and the progression and severity of symptoms experienced by affected individuals and their affected offspring (Table 1).

Key terms: rare for new mutation, length of sequence

Cause and effect: HD rarely caused by a new mutation; repeat length influences several factors of HD, including inheritance

Table 1. Analysis Results of HD Population

REPEAT COUNT	DISEASE STATUS	AGE OF ONSET (YEARS)	PROBABILITY OF AFFECTED OFFSPRING
<26	Unaffected		0
27–35	Unaffected		<<50%
36–39	May be affected	After 40	50%
≥40	Affected	25–39, earlier with increased count	50%

Table 1 shows the relationship between repeat count and onset/severity of disease; 40+ repeats guarantees symptoms and accelerates the disease significantly; however there is no change in inheritance as a result

The functional form of the association between the onset time *t* and CAG repeat length *x* has been debated for decades. The data collected in the study yielded a model which captures the relation between the AOO of HD and the CAG length through a logistic link.

Key terms: model, functional association

Cause and effect: model can be used to describe relationship between AOO, repeat length and disease

Geneticists further examined the role of inheritance in Huntington's disease by interviewing an early-stage Huntington's patient from the study. Their relevant family history is presented below.

Key terms: role of inheritance

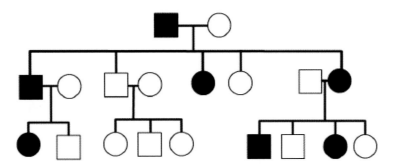

Figure 1. Family history interview results

Figure 1 suggests autosomal dominant inheritance since we have both genders equally affected, and we see no cases where unaffected parents have an affected child

Adapted from Ma, Y., & Wang, Y. (2014). Nonparametric modeling and analysis of association between Huntington's disease onset and CAG repeats. Statistics in Medicine, 33(8), 1369–1382. under CCBY

1. B is correct. This pedigree strongly suggests an autosomal dominant mode of inheritance. No generations are skipped and approximately half of the children with an unaffected and affected parent are affected. No affected children have two unaffected parents. Additionally, all three children of the unaffected mother and father in the second generation are unaffected. These facts all suggest a dominant disease. Male-to-male transmission occurs and not all daughters of affected males and unaffected females are affected. Together, these show an autosomal dominant pattern of inheritance. You may also have been able to answer this question based on outside knowledge, because Huntington's disease is often used as an example of autosomal dominant inheritance in biology coursework. Nonetheless, it is always good practice to check that your outside knowledge is consistent with passage information.

2. C is correct. Start by examining the data in Table 1. Individuals with fewer than 35 repeats will not show symptoms. Those with 36-39 may not be affected. Thus the maximum number of glutamine residues in Htt in a phenotypically normal individual is 39.

A, B: Individuals with as many as 35 glutamine repeats will remain unaffected, while those with between 36-39 repeats may or may not affected.

    D. Individuals with 40 or more repeats will be affected by the disease.

3. A is correct. With incomplete dominance, a cross between organisms with two different phenotypes produces offspring with a third phenotype that is a blending of the parental traits (e.g. white flowers crossed with red flowers yield pink flowers). This is most analogous to the situation in the question stem.

    B. In codominance, a cross between organisms with two different phenotypes produces offspring with a third phenotype in which both of the parental traits appear together. For example, crossing red flowers with white flowers and getting red and white spotted flowers.

    C. In double crossovers, chromatids from two homologous chromosomes come in contact at two points. This would not explain the blending of the two traits into a third phenotype in between the two others (normal vs. HD).

    D. Genetic leakage is when genes flow from one species to another. This is a concern for things like genetically modified foods, antibiotic resistance, avian flu, anywhere genes are able to cross species.

4. D is correct. Table 1 provides the probability that the offspring of an individual with one expanded HTT allele containing 40 or more repeats and an individual with a repeat count < 26 on either HTT allele is 50%. This probability reflects the fact that the affected offspring is affected because the allele they received from their affected parent was the parent's mutant copy of the HTT allele containing the expanded trinucleotide region. Given HD's autosomal dominant pattern of inheritance, if a parent contained two such alleles, they MUST pass a mutant copy of that allele to all offspring, all of whom would be affected.

5. A is correct. Incomplete penetrance means that clinical symptoms (phenotype) are not always present in individuals who have the disease-causing mutation (genotype). This is consistent with the situation presented in the question stem.

    B. Expressivity refers to variations in a phenotype among individuals carrying a particular genotype. This differs from penetrance, which refers to the likelihood of the gene generating any associated phenotype. Variable expressivity occurs when a phenotype is expressed differently among individuals with the same genotype.

    C. Pleiotropy occurs when a single gene influences multiple, seemingly unrelated phenotypic traits. For example phenylketonuria is a disease that affects multiple systems but is caused by a single gene defect.

    D. Anticipation is a phenomenon whereby the symptoms of a genetic disorder become apparent at an earlier age and with increasing severity over succeeding generations.

6. C is correct. X-linked diseases cannot pass from male to male, while they can pass from a female parent to male or female offspring. The bald male must have received his X' chromosome from his mother. She in turn could have received that same X' chromosome from her father or mother. The paternal side gave the bald male his Y chromosome so no one on the paternal side will have carried the same X chromosome as the affected male.

7. C correct. The proper test is not just one that meets some of the criteria in the question stem, but one that satisfies all the assumptions provided. The best fit here is an analysis of variance (ANOVA) test.

    A. A Mann-Whitney U test only assumes there are random samples used.

    B. Linear regression analysis assumes that for a random sample of Y values for each X, that Y is normally distributed with equal variance for each X, and that the relationship is linear.

    D. The paired t-test assumes that random samples of pairs are used and that the differences are normally distributed.

Independent Questions

1. A test cross is often performed to identify the genotype of an organism that exhibits a dominant phenotype. In the case of a test cross concerning two traits, the organism with the dominant phenotype might be crossed with an organism with which of the following genotypes?
   A. AaBb
   B. aabb
   C. AABB
   D. AABb

2. A disease that exhibits high penetrance is most likely to have what pattern in a population?
   A. Individuals with the mutated genotype exhibit the disease phenotype.
   B. Individuals with the mutation rarely exhibit the disease and do so at variable severity.
   C. Individuals with the wild-type genotype exhibit the disease.
   D. Individuals with the mutated genotype cannot have viable offspring.

3. A certain genetic condition is often inherited mother-to-son, but virtually never appears to be inherited by sons from their fathers. This information is most consistent with:
   A. an autosomal dominant inheritance pattern.
   B. an autosomal recessive inheritance pattern.
   C. an X-linked recessive inheritance pattern.
   D. none of the above are consistent with this information.

4. Crossing red with white flowers can result in an intermediate phenotype of pink flowers. This pattern of inheritance is most consistent with:
   A. incomplete dominance.
   B. codominance.
   C. expressivity.
   D. epigenetics.

5. On his final exam, a biology student must use limited information to discern the inheritance pattern of a genetic liver disease. The student knows that at least one individual in each generation of a four-generation family displayed the disease phenotype. He also knows that a homozygous, healthy woman in the family had a son who carried at least one allele for the disease. The biology student can conclude that:
   A. the disease is not recessive.
   B. the disease is X-linked.
   C. the disease is not X-linked.
   D. the disease has high penetrance.

6. What is the relationship between genetic linkage and the physical locations of two genes on the same chromosome?
   A. Genes that are physically close together are less likely to be linked.
   B. Genes that are physically far apart are less likely to be linked.
   C. Genes that are separated by many other genes are less likely to be linked, regardless of the physical distance between the two genes.
   D. Genes that are separated by many other genes are more likely to be linked, regardless of the physical distance between the two genes.

7. Bacterial models are often used to study disease inheritance and transmission. What is unique about bacterial genomes or DNA transmission that makes these useful models?
   A. Bacteria proliferate quickly, allowing constant analysis of their genomes.
   B. Bacteria are haploid organisms.
   C. Bacterial plasmids are the exclusive tool used for DNA transmission.
   D. Conjugative pili are easy to manipulate for specific DNA insertions.

8. Disease A is an autosomal recessive condition that affects the lungs and digestive system. Interestingly, the allele for disease A appears in the population with the same frequency as the wild-type (non-disease) allele, and those are the only two alleles known to exist at that locus. If a healthy male of unknown genotype has a child with a female who is a carrier for this disease, what is the probability that their child will have Disease A?
   A. 0%
   B. 12.5%
   C. 25%
   D. 33%

Independent Question Explanations

1. B is correct. A test cross crosses the organism in question with an organism that is homozygous for the recessive trait. If any offspring display the recessive phenotype, then the unknown parent must be a heterozygote, rather than being homozygous dominant. Here, we are dealing with two traits, so we want to cross our unknown organism with an individual who is homozygous recessive for both.

2. A is correct. Diseases with high penetrance show a high correlation between individuals that have the disease genotype and individuals who exhibit the signs and symptoms of the disease. In other words, those with the mutated genotype should also display the disease phenotype. Choice B is characteristic of diseases with low penetrance and variable expressivity.

3. C is correct. X-linked recessive diseases are often transmitted via carrier mothers. Since males have only one X chromosome, inheriting one faulty allele from the mother will lead to the disease phenotype. In contrast, since males inherit their Y chromosome from their fathers, X-linked conditions are not passed down father-to-son.

4. A is correct. Incomplete dominance is a form of inheritance in which neither allele is completely expressed over the other. This results in an intermediate phenotype for heterozygotes. Choice B, codominance, refers to a pattern in which both alleles are fully expressed (for example, the A and B alleles in the ABO blood typing system).

5. C is correct. The son referenced in the question stem must have inherited a disease allele from his father, since his mother was homozygous for the non-disease allele. Males inherit their Y, not their X, chromosome from their fathers, so this disease cannot be X-linked. Do not fall for choice A— just because this disease did not happen to skip

generations in this case does not mean that we can conclude for certain that it is not recessive!

6. B is correct. Genetic linkage is the tendency of DNA sequences to be inherited together. If crossing over did not occur during meiosis, then genes on the same chromosome would always be inherited together. However, crossing over can separate genes, which is more likely to occur if the physical distance between them is large. For this reason, we can say that genes separated by a large physical distance are less likely to be linked. The number of other genes between the two genes in question does not directly impact linkage.

7. B is correct. Bacteria are haploid organisms, which not only improves their division times, but also allows for simple genetic analysis. Because they only have one allele per gene, the presence of a mutated allele and its corresponding phenotype is easily observable and analyzed. Bacteria do proliferate quickly, but so do some eukaryotes, so choice A does not qualify as a "unique" characteristic.

8. B is correct. Note that the question stem indicates that the male is healthy, so he cannot be homozygous recessive with respect to Disease A. Thus, he can only be heterozygous (Aa) or homozygous dominant (AA). Since the question stem states that the A and a alleles appear in the population with the same frequency, we must assume that these two possible genotypes are equally likely. From this information, we see that the father has a 25%, or ¼, chance of passing on a diseased allele to the child, while the mother has a 50%, or ½, chance of passing on a diseased allele. Multiplying ¼ by ½ gives 1/8, or, 12.5%.

Gene Expression, Biotechnology, and Laboratory Techniques

CHAPTER 5

0. Introduction

In this chapter, we discuss gene expression, biotechnology, and laboratory techniques: three topics that are often treated separately, but actually form a coherent whole within modern biological research.

Although they are sometimes treated as an afterthought in biology textbooks, these topics are important for the MCAT for two main reasons. First, they are a predictable source of a few questions, usually in the Biological and Biochemical Foundations section. Second, and perhaps more importantly, these topics are regularly incorporated into modern biological research, so understanding them thoroughly yields major dividends in terms of improving your ability to understand passages about biological research quickly and accurately, which can contribute to an overall improvement of a point or two in the Biological and Biochemical Foundations section.

Fundamentally, gene expression refers to all the ways in which cells can regulate the transcription and translation of genes to produce more of certain products and less of others. It lies at the foundation of how organisms develop, how physiological systems respond to stimuli, and how systematic disorders emerge.

1. Gene Expression and Development

With regard to development, gene expression explains why virtually all cells within the body contain the same genetic code (with the notable exception of erythrocytes, which do not contain a nucleus, and rare conditions such as chimerism that go beyond the scope of the MCAT), but have drastically different morphology and functionality. Complex signaling patterns throughout development induce cell differentiation, which describes how embryonic stem cells first differentiate into the ectoderm, mesoderm, and endoderm, and then into the diverse range of specialized cells present in the mature body.

Stem cells—relatively undifferentiated cells that can differentiate into more specialized cells and reproduce through mitosis—are also present in adults. These are known as somatic stem cells, and come in a variety of types, with the following notable examples: hematopoietic stem cells, which differentiate into various types of blood cells; intestinal stem cells, which provide the basis for the constant renewal of the cells lining the surface of the intestines; and mesenchymal stem cells, which are capable of differentiating into a wide range of cell types, including adipocytes (fat cells), osteoblasts, and hepatocytes (liver cells). For the MCAT, you don't need to memorize the different somatic stem cell types, but it is useful to be aware of their existence and general function.

Stem cells can be classified along a scale of potency, which refers to the range of cell types that they can differentiate into. Totipotent cells are able to differentiate into any type of cell; in humans, this applies only to the zygote through the stage of the morula. Pluripotent cells are able to differentiate into any of the germ layers (ectoderm, mesoderm, and endoderm), and can be obtained from the internal cell mass of the blastocyst. Adult stem cells are multipotent, which refers to the ability to differentiate into several types of cells within a relatively limited functional scope. You may also encounter the term oligopotent, which refers to a stem cell that can only derive into a few types of cells (Greek *oligo-* = "few"), although oligopotency forms a continuum with multipotency that does not have clear boundaries.

Much research is currently being conducted into the clinical application of stem cells as treatment for various conditions. Totipotent and pluripotent stem cells have attracted particular interest due to their ability to differentiate into the broadest range of cell types, but ethical dilemmas have arisen from the fact that such stem cells are only found in embryos. For this reason, interest has emerged in the possibility of converting multipotent stem cells found in adults into pluripotent or totipotent cells. The 2012 Nobel Prize in Physiology or Medicine was awarded to Shinya Yamanaka and Sir John Gurdon for their work on induced pluripotent stem cells—that is, reprogramming adult multipotent stem cells to become pluripotent. Research has also been conducted into inducing totipotency. However, the clinical applicability of these techniques remains to be established. Regardless, stem cell research is a fascinating and promising domain of potential future therapeutic strategies.

A final important point regarding gene expression and development is the importance of properly regulated apoptosis in development. Although apoptosis (programmed cell death) may sound like a negative phenomenon, when properly regulated, it actually plays a fundamental role in proper development as well as in maintaining health. In embryonic development, apoptosis plays a major role in defining the boundaries of organs and tissues. A common example of this is the fact that in the developing human embryo, fingers and toes are initially linked by webbed structures, and apoptosis of the cells in those structures is what allows fingers and toes to become separate by the time of birth. The pathways regulating apoptosis are very complicated, but you should be aware that common causes of apoptosis include failure for a cell to pass the appropriate mitotic checkpoints, cell-internal signaling after mitochondrial dysfunction, lysosomes bursting (autolysis), and as a response to external signaling pathways that may be misregulated in various disease processes.

MCAT STRATEGY > > >

On one hand, stem cells are likely to be tested by relatively simple questions on their basic definition, degrees of potency, or embryonic versus adult stem cells. On the other hand, though, it's helpful to be aware of the bigger picture regarding stem cells because they could be discussed in a passage, at which point already having a general familiarity with the topic can save you valuable time and mental energy that you can apply directly to the questions.

2. Gene Expression in Prokaryotes

For the purposes of the MCAT, gene expression in prokaryotes is synonymous with the concept of the operon; the Jacob-Monod model of the operon won the 1965 Nobel Prize in Physiology or Medicine, and the MCAT expects you to be familiar with its workings. If necessary, take some time to review basic facts about prokaryotes (Chapter 2) and the molecular machinery of gene expression (Chapter 3).

Operons are important because they are relatively simple and mechanistic systems that allow a bacterium to respond to changes in its environment by increasing or decreasing the expression of certain genes as appropriate. Operons can be under positive or negative control. In negative control, a repressor prevents transcription by binding to the operator (a sequence upstream of the first protein-coding region), while in positive control, an activator stimulates transcription. The classic examples that the MCAT is likely to test you on, the *lac* operon and the *trp* operon, both involve negative control, but differ in that the *lac* operon is inducible and the *trp* operon is repressible. In a negative inducible operon, the repressor is normally present and the genes are not expressed except under specific conditions. In a negative repressible operon, the genes are usually transcribed, but transcription can be halted by binding of the repressor in appropriate conditions.

> > CONNECTIONS < <

Chapter 2 and Chapter 3
of Biology

The *lac* operon was discovered in *Escherichia coli,* but its principles have been subsequently found to be present more broadly in prokaryotes. The basic idea is that *E. coli* has the ability to metabolize glucose, while the *lac* operon gives *E. coli* the ability to metabolize lactose if it is present. However, expressing the proteins necessary to metabolize lactose is energetically somewhat expensive, so it is advantageous for *E. coli* to express that cellular machinery only when lactose is present, and even more so, when lactose is present but glucose is absent. The *lac* operon allows *E. coli* to do just that.

The *lac* operon is presented below in Figure 1. The sequences *lacZ, lacY,* and *lacA* are protein-encoding regions necessary for lactose metabolism. The operator region is located upstream of those coding sequences, and the promoter region is located upstream of the operator. The catabolite activator protein (CAP) binding sequence is located upstream of the promoter. When no lactose is present, the repressor is bound to the operator and prevents RNA polymerase from transcribing the structural genes.

The *lac* Operon and its Control Elements

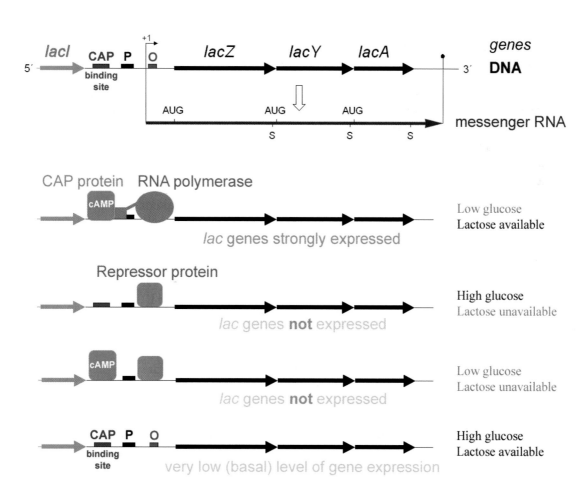

Figure 1. The *lac* operon.

When lactose is present, its isomer, allolactose binds with the repressor, dissociating it from the operator. This allows RNA polymerase to transcribe the structural genes: at this point, *E. coli* now has the ability to metabolize lactose. However, in prokaryotic metabolism just as in life, just because you can doesn't mean that you should! As we mentioned above, there is an energetic cost involved in metabolizing lactose, so it is not advantageous to metabolize lactose if ample glucose is present. This is where CAP comes in. If glucose is low, cellular levels of cyclic adenosine monophosphate (cAMP) are high. cAMP binds to CAP, inducing it to bind to the aptly-named CAP binding sequence. When it does so, CAP promotes elevated transcription of the *lac* structural genes. This is an example of positive control; thus, the *lac* operon is in fact under both negative and positive control.

Table 1 below summarizes the structure and function of the *lac* operon in various environmental conditions.

> > CONNECTIONS < <

Chapter 10 of Biology

LACTOSE?	GLUCOSE?	REPRESSOR	CAP	OUTCOME
N	Y	Bound to operator	Absent	No lactose metabolism
Y	Y	Released from operator	Absent	Weak lactose metabolism
Y	N	Released from operator	Binds to CAP binding sequence	Strong lactose metabolism

MCAT STRATEGY > > >

Operons involve a lot of detail, especially for a relatively isolated topic. When studying operons, focus first on the outcomes in various situations, because you can leverage the logic of how the organism responds to various situations to help remember what mechanisms must be in place to ensure that functionality.

The *lac* operon is the most famous example of an operon, but you should also be aware of the *trp* operon, which contains genes for the synthesis of tryptophan. However, it is energetically unfavorable for these genes to be expressed if tryptophan is present, so the *trp* operon allows these genes to be expressed in the absence of tryptophan, but not when it is present. When tryptophan is absent, the repressor does not bind to the operator, and tryptophan synthesis proceeds. However, when tryptophan is present, it binds to the repressor protein and causes it to bind to the operator, thereby inhibiting synthesis. Since transcription is not repressed by default (as in the case of the *lac* operon), but can be induced by environmental conditions, the *trp* operon is considered to be an example of an repressible negative operon.

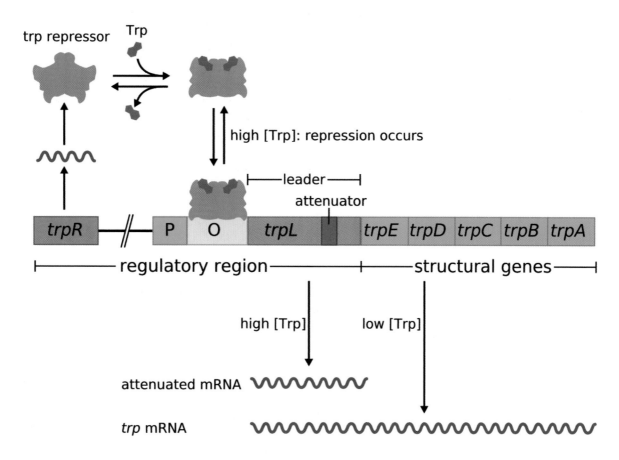

Figure 2. The *trp* operon.

3. Gene Expression in Eukaryotes

The regulation of gene expression in eukaryotes is much more complicated than in prokaryotes. For prokaryotes, the MCAT expects you to be able to use the operon model to explain how organisms react to specific stimuli (e.g., the presence or absence of lactose or tryptophan). In contrast, for eukaryotes it is necessary to be aware of diverse mechanisms that play a role in gene expression regulation in response to diverse stimuli and signaling cascades.

First, let's look at regions upstream of the protein-coding elements of a given gene. The basic problem to be solved here is for the transcriptional machinery to identify the right place to start transcription, and to do so in a way that can be regulated. The first step in this functionality involves sequences of base pairs present in the genome. Upstream regions of DNA that initiate transcription are known as promoters. In eukaryotes, many promoters are characterized by specific highly-conserved gene sequences. The TATA box is located approximately 30 base pairs upstream of the coding sequence, while the GC box and CAAT box are located roughly 10-150 base pairs upstream of the TATA box. These sequences are named for their characteristic base pair sequences (5'-TATAAA-3', 5'-GGGCGG-3', and 5'-GGCCAATCT-3' for the TATA, GC, and CAAT boxes respectively), and their function is to bind to proteins that help recruit RNA polymerase to initiate transcription. For example, the TATA box binds the TATA-binding protein (TBP), which, in association with some other proteins, comprises a transcription factor that contributes to the binding of RNA polymerase.

In general, transcription factors are proteins that regulate expression by binding to a specific DNA sequence through what is termed a DNA-binding domain. Once bound to a sequence of DNA, transcription factors can recruit other regulatory proteins; for example, proteins that play a role in acetylation or methylation, which are discussed below.

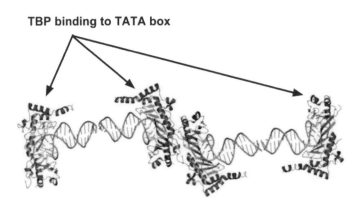

Figure 3. Promoter region with TBP bound to TATA box.

In addition to promoters, the eukaryotic genome contains enhancers, which allow gene expression at even higher levels than usual in response to the appropriate stimuli. Unlike promoters, enhancers do not have to be located in close proximity to the coding region of the gene. Typically, they may be considerably further upstream than promoters, but enhancers have been found both upstream and downstream of the coding region, as well as quite far away. Given the tremendous diversity of enhancers, how do they upregulate expression? To answer this question, think three-dimensionally! Enhancers bind transcription factors that twist DNA into a hairpin loop, bringing distant regions into close proximity to each other. These transcription factors may be very specific with regard to certain signaling elements. For example, estrogen (like other steroid hormones) binds with a nuclear estrogen receptor (ERα or ERβ), which then binds with enhancers known as estrogen response elements on the genome to modify transcription.

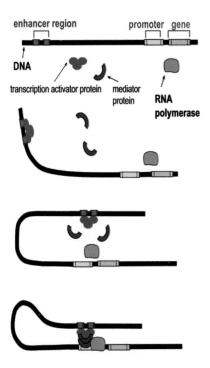

Figure 4. Enhancer region.

Silencers are the opposite of enhancers in eukaryotic cells; they are regions of DNA to which transcription factors known as repressors bind. As the name indicates, repressors inhibit the transcription of the gene that they target. However, silencers have been discovered more recently than enhancers, and their function has not been characterized in as much detail as that of enhancers.

Another mechanism of increasing the expression of a gene is to duplicate it on the chromosome. Across generations, this can result from sequential mutations, with potential long-term effects on the genome. Within a single generation, the duplication of oncogenes is frequently observed in cancer cells, a phenomenon that is linked to the dysregulation of repair mechanisms in cancer cells.

MCAT STRATEGY > > >

Gene expression in eukaryotes involves a tremendously detailed regulatory apparatus. Focus on the essentials to help you memorize the details. Recall that a cell *must* be able to respond to stimuli by producing more or less of the product of various genes, and then work backwards to figure out the general kinds of functionality (e.g., promoters and enhancers) necessary to do that.

In order for transcription factors to function, and for transcription to take place, the relevant molecules must be able to access the DNA. DNA is packaged around histones, which are then packaged either relatively densely to form heterochromatin or relatively loosely (in what is commonly termed a "beads on a string") structure to form euchromatin. Heterochromatin appears dark under the microscope and is associated with transcriptional inactivity, because the DNA is packaged too densely for transcription to take place. In contrast, the less dense structure of euchromatin appears light under the microscope and is associated with transcriptional activity.

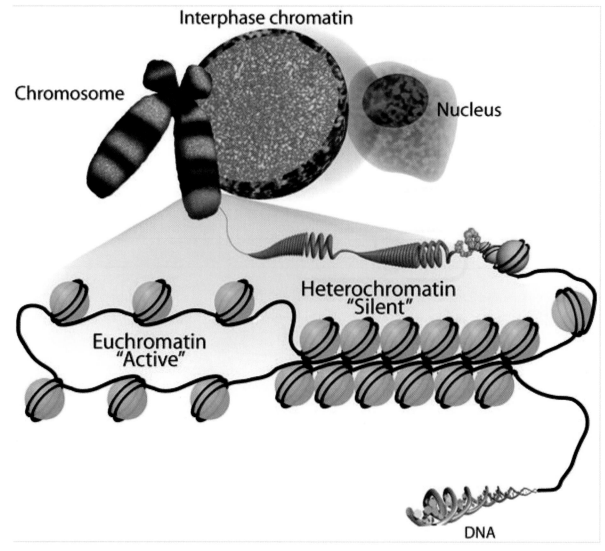

Figure 5. Euchromatin and heterochromatin.

MCAT STRATEGY > > >

It's worth taking some time to slowly and carefully walk through why acetylation has the effect of increasing transcription, because this is an instance where a very low-level property (intermolecular attractions between oppositely-charged molecules) has very high-level effects. Connections like that are MCAT favorites.

Certain transcription factors, known as histone acetyltransferases, can modify histone structure. As the name implies, histone acetyltransferases transfer acetyl groups from acetyl-CoA to lysine residues on histones. This makes histones less positively charged, weakening their ability to interact with the highly negatively-charged phosphate groups on DNA, which in turns results in a looser wrapping pattern that allows other transcription factors to access the genome more easily. For this reason, acetylation generally has the effect of increasing transcription.

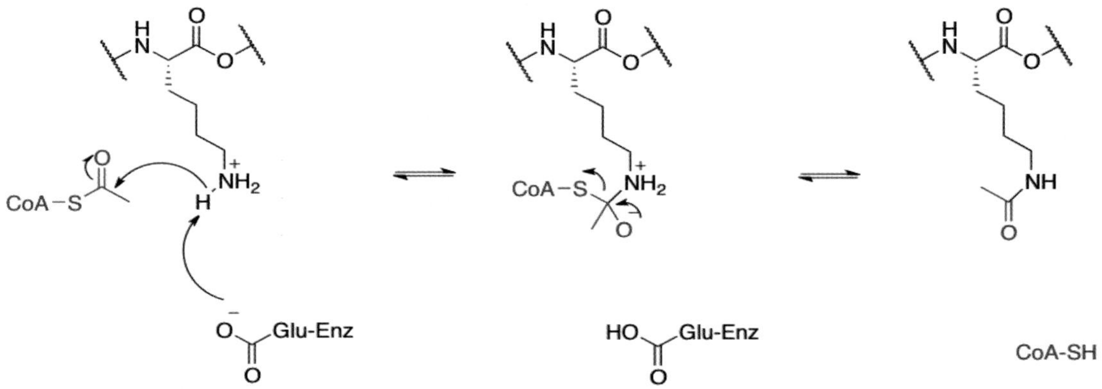

Figure 6. Acetylation of lysine.

Figure 6 shows the acetylation of a lysine residue, which is a typical part of histone acetylation. In the context of this chapter, don't worry too much about the mechanism (although it may make sense to revisit this once you have studied organic chemistry mechanisms), but note that the positive charge in lysine is lost.

Gene expression is also affected by DNA methylation, in which a methyl group is added to cytosine or adenine. Methylation is currently the focus of intense ongoing research because its function is not fully understood; however, it is thought to play a role in processes as diverse as embryonic development, aging, and cancer. For the MCAT, you should be aware that methylation is generally thought to deactivate genes. As shown in Figure 7, methylation can also be the trigger for processes such as the deamination of 5-methyl cytosine to result in thymidine, which would constitute a point mutation in the DNA code.

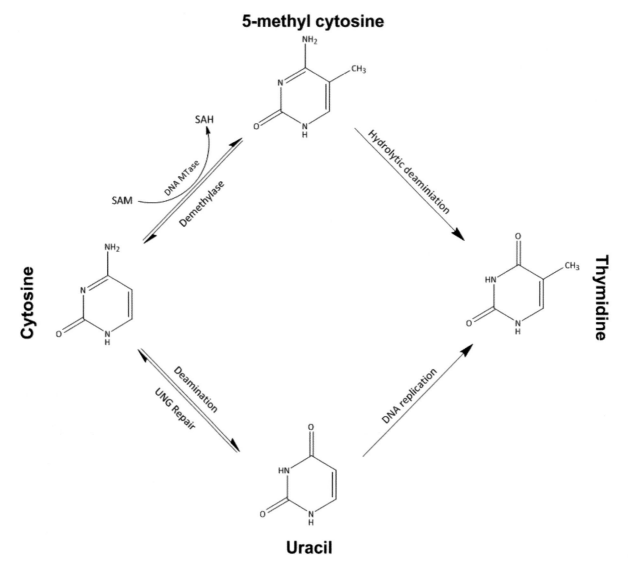

5-methyl cytosine

Cytosine

Thymidine

Uracil

Figure 7. DNA methylation.

Methylation also plays a major role in the phenomenon known as epigenetics, which refers to inheritable phenotypic changes involving mechanisms other than the alteration of the genome itself. For example, a 2011 study found altered methylation patterns in the glucocorticoid receptor in adolescents whose mothers experienced intimate partner violence during pregnancy. A 2014 study found that prediabetes in fathers increased the susceptibility of their offspring to diabetes due to methylation changes in gametes. This is an area of ongoing research that the MCAT will not expect you to be responsible for in any detail, but it could potentially appear in passages, so a very general familiarity with the concept may pay off on Test Day.

In addition to regulatory proteins and the covalent modification of histones and DNA through acetylation and methylation, non-coding RNA plays a role in gene expression. The category of non-coding RNA refers to any RNA that is not translated into a protein, with a familiar example being transfer RNA (tRNA). An exciting line of research in the last 20 years has identified a role for non-coding RNA in the suppression of gene expression through the degradation of mRNA sequences before translation. Two categories of such non-coding RNA are small interfering RNA (siRNA) and microRNA (miRNA), which differ in terms of structure: miRNA strands are single-nucleotide strands incorporated into an RNA structure with a characteristic hairpin loop, while siRNA molecules are short and double-stranded. Both tend to be approximately 22 nucleotides in length. The crucial point to remember for the

MCAT, though, is that miRNA and siRNA both silence genes by interrupting expression between transcription and translation. Enhancer RNA (eRNA) has also been identified; eRNA sequences are transcribed from enhancer regions of the DNA and appear to be associated with increased transcriptional activity. However, this is a very new area of research and the physiological function of eRNA has not been conclusively determined yet.

Although the MCAT in general does not expect you to be aware of the details regarding the pathogenesis of various diseases, there are a few exceptions to this rule of thumb, corresponding to diseases where it is important for you to be familiar with the basic mechanisms underlying the disorder. Cancer is one of those diseases, and in particular you should be aware of cancer as a disease in which gene expression is abnormal. To make sense of that assertion, let's step back and review the steps involved in oncogenesis, or the development of cancer.

A tumor describes any abnormal proliferation of cells; benign tumors remain localized, whereas malignant tumors, which are what the term "cancer" properly refers to, can invade other organs and tissues in the body, in a process called metastasis. The first step in oncogenesis, tumor initiation, involves changes that allow a single cell to proliferate abnormally. This means that the cell must develop the ability to bypass regulatory steps of the cell cycle that normally help to restrain mitotic proliferation. Tumor progression occurs as a cell develops the ability to proliferate even more aggressively, such that its descendants are preferentially selected for and come to predominate the growing tumor. In addition, malignant cells often undergo mutations allowing them to secrete growth factors to stimulate their own growth, proteases that digest components of the extracellular matrix and favor metastasis, and growth factors that promote the formation of new blood vessels to feed the growing tumor (angiogenesis).

Most typically, oncogenesis is associated with mutations that occur by random chance (and elude the normal DNA repair machinery in the cell) or as a result of mutagenic compounds known as carcinogens. These mutations alter the functionality of crucial genes in the cell. However, oncogenesis is also associated with dysregulation of gene expression, as abnormally elevated expression of genes involved in growth and proliferation can help contribute to the development of a tumor. Additionally, miRNA activity is abnormal in cancerous cells, further pointing to the importance of gene expression in oncogenesis. Moreover, compounds known as tumor promoters help induce the growth of proliferative cells by stimulating the activity of proteins involved in growth and division.

The genes involved in oncogenesis can be divided into oncogenes and tumor suppressor genes. The basic difference between them is that oncogenes function to promote abnormal growth and proliferation, leading to cancer, while tumor suppressor genes function to prevent tumorigenic properties.

Oncogenes were first identified based on studies of cancer-causing viruses, known as tumor viruses. Examples affecting humans include the hepatitis B and C viruses, which cause liver cancer; papillomaviruses, which cause cervical and other anogenital cancers; Epstein-Barr virus, which causes Burkitt's lymphoma and nasopharyngeal carcinoma; Kaposi's sarcoma-associated herpesvirus, which causes Kaposi's sarcoma; and human T- cell lymphotropic virus, which causes adult T-cell leukemia. Many tumor viruses contain retroviral oncogenes, which are reverse-transcribed into the DNA of infected cells; these oncogenes (such as *ras, raf,* and *src*) often encode proteins that are key components of signaling pathways that stimulate cell proliferation.

However, oncogenes also play a role in driving tumorigenesis in cells that have not been infected with a tumor virus. Genes that function as oncogenes after mutation or inappropriately elevated expression are known as proto-oncogenes. Broadly speaking, oncogenes

> **MCAT STRATEGY > > >**
>
> You won't have to give a lecture on oncogenesis off the top of your head on Test Day, but you may have to synthesize information presented to you in a passage and make predictions about the effects of upregulating or downregulating different genes on the likelihood of cancer to form or metastasize. Therefore, investing some time into carefully working through these fundamentals is likely to pay off.

can be classified as genes coding for growth factors, receptor tyrosine kinases (examples include epidermal growth factor receptor [EGFR] and platelet-derived growth factor receptor [PDGFR]), cytoplasmic protein kinases (examples include the Src family and the Raf family), transcription factors (Myc), and regulatory GTPases (the Ras family). Kinases are crucially involved in transducing signals involved in activating cell growth and differentiation, while regulatory GTPases such as the Ras family are likewise involved in signaling in a major growth/differentiation pathway.

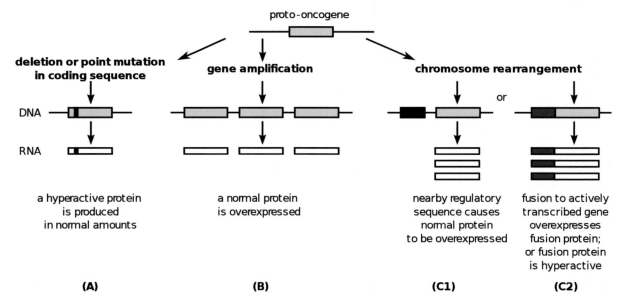

Figure 8. Proto-oncogene → oncogene diagram.

As the name suggests, tumor suppressor genes inhibit oncogenesis when properly functioning. Mutation-induced dysfunction in these genes means that a cell will not be able to protect itself against oncogenesis as effectively. The major functions of tumor suppressor genes include repressing the expression of genes that are essential for the cell cycle to progress, ensuring that the cell responds appropriately to DNA damage detected at cell cycle checkpoints (stopping the cell cycle for repair or inducing apoptosis, as necessary), repairing DNA damage, and preventing the changes in adhesion and proliferation involved in metastasis. An important oncogene to be aware of is the *TP53* gene that encodes the p53 protein involved in responding appropriately to cell damage, because it is implicated in more than half of all human cancers. Additionally, mutations in the *BRCA* genes, which are responsible for repairing and responding to DNA damage, are associated with dramatically increased risks of breast and ovarian cancer. In many families, these mutations are inherited, which has led to *BRCA* testing becoming one of the best-known examples of the potential of genetic screening. Famously, the well-known actress Angelina Jolie underwent a preventive double mastectomy and removal of her ovaries and fallopian tubes after learning that she was affected by hereditary *BRCA* mutations that had contributed to a devastating family history of cancer.

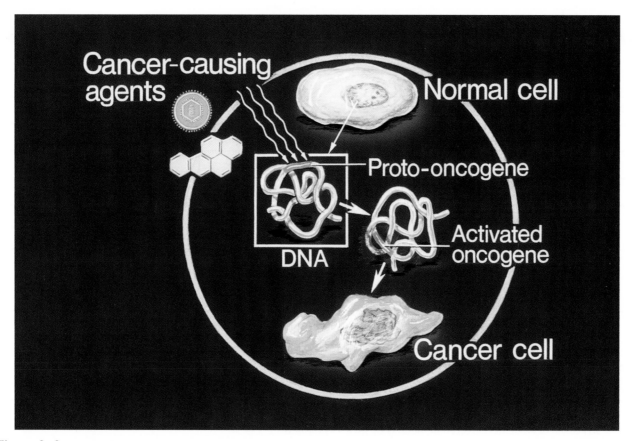

Figure 9. Oncogenesis.

The range of mechanisms involved in eukaryotic gene expression is complicated, but for the MCAT it is often only necessary to be able to associate a given regulatory element with a simple response of "on" (upregulation through increased expression) or "off" (downregulation through decreased regulation). Table 2 summarizes the components of eukaryotic gene regulation that we have discussed in terms of whether they lead to an "on" or "off" response.

ELEMENT	WHAT IS IT?	ON OR OFF?
Enhancer	DNA sequence	On
Silencer	DNA sequence	Off
Transcription factors	Regulatory proteins	On
Acetylation	Covalent modification of histones	On
Methylation	Covalent modification of nucleotides	Off
siRNA, miRNA	Non-coding RNA sequences	Off
Oncogenes	Abnormal genes promoting improper growth/proliferation	On (to an abnormal extent)
Proto-oncogenes	Normal genes regulating growth that become oncogenes when mutated or abnormally expressed	On (to a normal extent)
Tumor suppressor genes	Genes regulating cell cycle, response to damaged DNA, adhesion, transcription	Off (when functioning properly)
		On (when mutated)

Table 2. Effects of elements involved in eukaryotic gene expression.

4. Recombinant DNA

The creation and application of recombinant DNA is one of the most significant accomplishments in biotechnology over the last 40 years, and for the MCAT, you are expected to be aware of the basic mechanisms involved in such research.

The discovery of restriction enzymes, also known as restriction endonucleases, paved the way for the development of recombinant DNA technologies. In nature, they occur in prokaryotes and archaea, where they act as a defense system against invading viruses by cleaving DNA in response to specific recognition sites, corresponding to sequences of 4 to 8 bases. These recognition sites usually involve some degree of symmetry, as reflected by palindromic sequences. These palindromic sequences often involve inverted repeats, in which the palindrome is reflected diagonally across the plane of symmetry created by drawing a vertical line through the middle of the recognition site. When a restriction enzyme cleaves a DNA sequence vertically across the recognition site, the resulting fragments have "blunt" ends, whereas "sticky" ends result from restriction enzymes that cleave a DNA sequence in a zig-zag fashion. Restriction enzymes can cleave DNA either within the recognition site or at some distance from it.

EcoRI restriction enzyme: sticky ends

SmaI restriction enzyme: blunt ends

GAATTC
CTTAAG

CCCGGG
GGGCCC

Figure 10. Restriction enzymes and blunt/sticky ends.

The basic reason why restriction enzymes are so important is that they generate fragments that can be "tied" back together by DNA ligase without necessarily respecting the original location of the sequences. In other words, if you put a sequence of human DNA and a sequence of pig DNA in a Petri dish, digest the sequences with a restriction enzyme, and then treat the fragments with DNA ligase, you will get sequences of human + human DNA, pig + pig DNA, and human + pig DNA. This process is known as recombination.

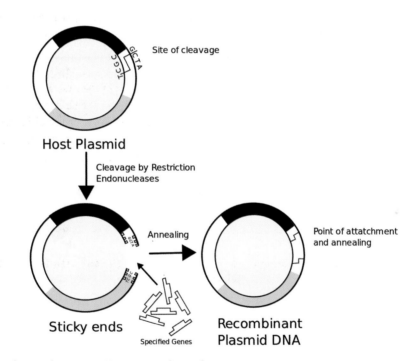

Figure 11. Generation of recombinant DNA using sticky ends.

However, for recombinant DNA to be useful, it is essential to be able to replicate novel DNA sequences in significant quantities. To do this, researchers use vectors, which are DNA molecules used to carry genetic material into a cell where it can be replicated or expressed. Two main types of vectors are used: plasmids and bacteriophages (viruses that infect bacteria).

Plasmids are short circular DNA molecules that can replicate independently in bacteria. Recombinant plasmids carrying human DNA inserts can be introduced into *E. coli*, where they replicate along with the bacteria to yield millions of copies of plasmid DNA. The DNA of these plasmids can then be isolated, generating large quantities of recombinant molecules containing a single fragment of human DNA. The fragment can then be easily isolated from the rest of the vector DNA by restriction endonuclease digestion and gel electrophoresis, allowing a pure fragment of human DNA to be analyzed and further manipulated. In order to generate recombinant plasmids, human DNA and plasmid DNA are digested with the appropriate restriction enzymes, and then DNA ligase is used for re-sealing. Some human DNA strands re-link together, as do some plasmid DNA strands, but some novel human-plasmid recombinant DNA strands emerge from this process as well.

The next step in the process is to treat *E. coli* cells with the plasmid/DNA mixture. This generates a diverse set of bacteria: some do not take up any plasmids, some take up non-recombinant plasmids, and some take up recombinant plasmids. How do we distinguish between these outcomes? Scientists take advantage of two main techniques to do so. First, plasmids used for genetic engineering generally contain antibiotic resistance genes, such that treatment with an antibiotic can kill off *E. coli* cells that did not take up any plasmids and select for those that did. The next step is to distinguish between non-recombinant and recombinant plasmids. This can be done through what is known as a reporter gene. A reporter gene codes for a product leading to an obvious phenotypic change (such as a change in color) and contains recognition sites for the restriction enzyme that is used in the restriction. This means that *E. coli* cells with non-recombinant plasmids will express the reporter gene normally, while *E. coli* cells with recombinant plasmids will not, allowing them to be distinguished and sub-cultured.

MCAT STRATEGY > > >

Recombinant DNA is very commonly used in modern experimental protocols, and can therefore show up in experimentally focused passages on the MCAT. The real payoff for studying this section thoroughly is not so much because you will be directly tested on it (although that's certainly possible) but because a solid understanding of this material will help you read and process passages more quickly and effectively.

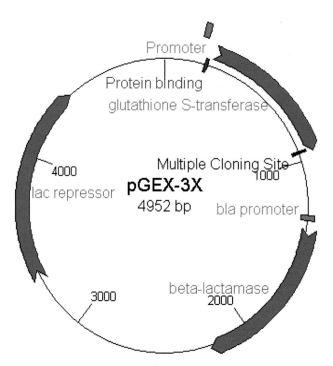

Figure 12. Recombinant DNA in a plasmid vector.

The key features of plasmids used in genetic engineering are presented in Table 3.

FEATURE	FUNCTION
Origin of replication	Tells host cell DNA polymerase to initiate replication
Restriction site	Recognition site for a restriction enzyme to cleave DNA
Antibiotic resistance gene	Allows selection of bacteria that have taken up the plasmid
Reporter gene	Distinguishes bacteria with recombinant plasmids from those with non-recombinant plasmids

Table 3. Key elements of plasmids and their functions.

Plasmids are not the only vector used for cloning DNA sequences. One limitation of standard *E. coli* plasmids is size, as these plasmids generally contain 2-4 kb of DNA. Bacteriophage λ vectors can be used for sequences as large as 15 kb. Additionally, even larger sequences can be transferred using bacteriophage P1 vectors. The principle of bacteriophage vectors is similar to that of plasmid vectors; the major difference of note is that bacteriophage vectors work by stripping out non-essential genes to carry recombinant sequences.

RNA sequences can also be cloned, through the generation of complementary DNA (cDNA). The first step is to synthesize a DNA copy of the RNA using the enzyme reverse transcriptase. The DNA product is called cDNA because it is complementary to the template RNA. cDNA can then be ligated to vector DNA in the manner previously discussed. Since eukaryotic genes are usually interrupted by noncoding sequences, which are removed from mRNA by splicing, the ability to clone cDNA as well as genomic DNA has been critical for understanding gene structure and function. Additionally, cDNA cloning allows the mRNA corresponding to a single gene to be isolated as a molecular clone. DNA libraries, both of genomic DNA and cDNA, have been developed to allow researchers access to the DNA fragments that interest them in their research.

Plasmid vectors are useful both for amplifying DNA sequences for subsequent analysis and for generating large amounts of the products of the genes of interest. For instance, for approximately the last 30 years, insulin for the treatment of diabetics has been synthesized using recombinant bacterial plasmids. Incorporating recombinant DNA for insulin into colonies of bacteria allow tremendous amounts of insulin to be generated in a cost-efficient and scalable manner.

Recombinant DNA technology is also widely used in modern research to help elucidate the function of various genes. One common way of doing this is to use transgenic or knockout organisms. In general, transgenic is a term that refers to any organism whose genome has been modified; this can be done for practical purposes, as in the case of genetically engineered organisms in agriculture, or to elucidate the function of genes. Knockout organisms are those in which one or more genes have been disabled. The goal of such research is to compare the functionality of organisms without a functioning copy of a given gene with that of wild-type organisms, in order to obtain more information about the function of a gene. The MCAT will not expect you to be aware of the extended process involved in generating lineages of knockout organisms, but you may be presented with a passage presenting the results of research conducted into knockout organisms. Knockout models of thousands of human diseases have been created, and are a fundamental component of modern biomedical research.

5. Biotechnology: Applications and Ethics

Advances in biotechnology have been applied in several fields, ranging from medicine to pharmacology, forensics, remediation of pollution, and agriculture. The medical applications of DNA technology include the development of relatively widespread and cheap DNA screening techniques, allowing individuals to undergo genetic screening to assess their risk of certain disorders. Gene therapy is another promising subject of ongoing research; the idea is to splice in a functional copy of a gene in the cells of a patient with a nonfunctional allele. This would theoretically allow the effective treatment of currently devastating genetic disorders, but has yet to emerge beyond the stage of research. DNA technology has also been widely applied in pharmacology; of particular note, many substances crucial for medical treatment are now produced by recombinant bacteria, such as insulin, tumor necrosis factor, interferons, and components of vaccines. To give a sense of how dramatic of a transformation this was, consider that until the 1980s, insulin used to treat diabetics was harvested from pig pancreases!

Biotechnology has also been used in the field of forensics, with DNA analysis used to identify the perpetrators of various crimes, as well as victims. Additionally, DNA technology revolutionized agriculture, with the development of genetically engineered strains of crops that have the ability to be pesticide-resistant, grow in a wider range of conditions, and even contain nutrients that are otherwise unavailable (an example of this is golden rice, which was engineered to contain beta-carotene). However, the use of genetically engineered crops has also been the source of considerable controversy, with concerns being raised about issues including the impact of genetic engineering on food security, the loss of biodiversity, food allergies, consumer safety, and other unintended effects. In fact, bans on genetically engineered crops have been passed in five counties in California, two in Oregon, and one apiece in Washington and Hawaii.

> **MCAT STRATEGY > > >**
>
> Considerations regarding the ethics and applications of DNA technology may seem peripheral, but they have explicitly been identified as testable content by the AAMC, so be sure to have a general sense of the issues.

Ethical concerns have also been raised regarding stem cell therapy, particularly regarding the use of embryonic stem cells, which must be obtained from embryos. In 2001, President George W. Bush implemented a policy restricting federal funding to research on pre-existing human embryonic stem cell lines, although some of those restrictions were removed by President Barack Obama in 2009 via an executive order. Complicated state laws exist regarding stem cells as well. These ethical and legal concerns are part of the reason why so much excitement has accompanied the research into reprogramming adult stem cells to become pluripotent, as discussed in section 1.

6. Laboratory Techniques

Underlying the spectacular range of applications of biotechnology is a set of important laboratory techniques that you must be aware of for the MCAT. As we saw with recombinant DNA technology, these techniques may be the topic of specific questions, but they are especially likely to occur in passages, such that it is necessary to understand these techniques in order to understand the data presented in a passage.

Gel electrophoresis is a technique used to analyze nucleic acids (DNA and RNA) by size. The principle of gel electrophoresis is to suspend charged macromolecules in an agarose gel and apply an electric field by applying a positive charge (anode) at one end and a negative charge (cathode) at another end. Note that the anode is positively charged and the cathode is negatively charged in an electrophoresis apparatus because this is an electrolytic cell, not a galvanic cell. Macromolecules will move in response to the charge, but their movement through the gel is affected by size, with smaller molecules moving more quickly and larger molecules moving more slowly. Nucleic acids have a high degree of negative charge due to the presence of many phosphate groups, and such that they will migrate away from the negatively charged cathode and towards the positively charged anode. Following electrophoresis, the DNA is stained with a fluorescent dye and photographed. Molecular-weight size markers, also known as ladders, are fragments with known sizes that can be run parallel to the DNA of interest in an electrophoresis experiment to identify the approximate size of the DNA fragments being analyzed.

> > CONNECTIONS < <

Chapter 5 of Biochemistry

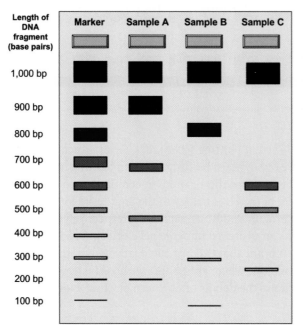

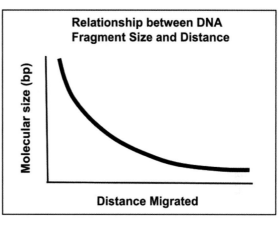

Figure 13. Gel electrophoresis of DNA, with a ladder.

Another key technique in genetics research is hybridization, which refers to the ability of single-strand DNA (or RNA) to form base pairs with a complementary sequence. The fact that DNA strands can be split ("melted") at elevated temperatures means that single-strand DNA can be generated easily under laboratory conditions, at which point the principle of hybridization can be used in several different ways. As discussed below, hybridization is an important step in polymerase chain reaction (PCR). It can also be used to identify target sequences by using a hybridization probe, which is a specific DNA or RNA fragment-that is, one known to the researchers-that can be labeled radioactively. If it is added to a sample of DNA or RNA being studied and the sample is heated to generate single-strand DNA or RNA, then the single-stranded radiolabeled probes will anneal with complementary sequences. Analysis of the radiolabeling can then determine the presence of the sequence of interest in the DNA that is tested.

MCAT STRATEGY > > >

If you have ever worked in a lab and performed this technique as part of real-world molecular biology research, you will be aware that the actual processes involved in performing hybridization—or many other of the techniques discussed in this chapter—are more complicated than presented here. However, the MCAT only expects you to be aware of the basic principles of these techniques: what they use, the basic mechanisms involved, and what kind of results they give.

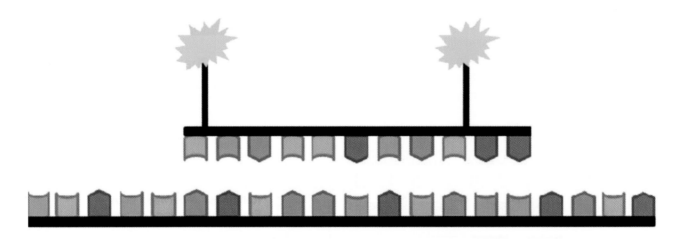

Figure 14. DNA hybridization and a DNA probe.

The principles of electrophoresis and hybridization are combined in blotting techniques. Several such techniques have been developed, but for the MCAT, you should be aware of Southern blotting, western blotting, and northern blotting. Southern blotting was developed by the researcher Edwin Southern, and is a technique used to identify specific DNA sequences. The western and northern blots were named by analogy to the Southern blot (and are therefore often not capitalized), and are used to identify protein and RNA sequences, respectively. In these sequences, the molecules of interest (DNA or RNA fragments, or proteins) undergo gel electrophoresis to separate them by size, and then are transferred to a nitrocellulose membrane that can be heated, at which point probe analysis can be performed (the process is slightly different for western blots, where antibodies are used instead of DNA/RNA probes). This process is outlined below in Figure 15, which shows the details of northern blotting. Nonetheless, the basic principles apply for all types of blotting.

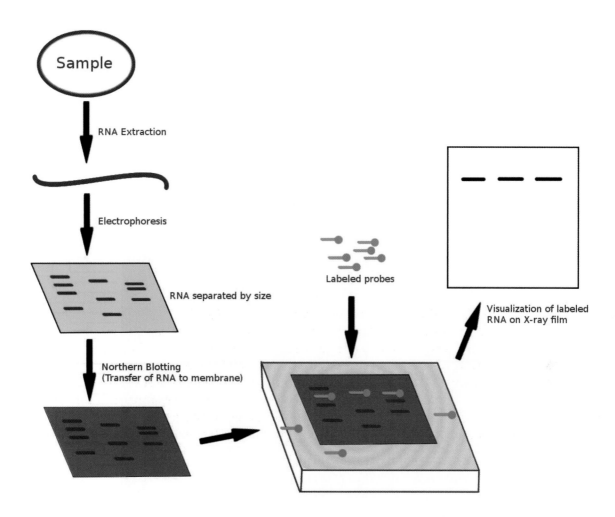

Figure 15. Northern blotting.

DNA microarrays have been developed to leverage hybridization on a larger scale than is possible using Southern blotting, with the possibility of analyzing tens of thousands of genes simultaneously. As the complete sequences of eukaryotic genomes have become available, DNA microarrays, which operate on the basic principle of hybridization, have enabled researchers to undertake global analyses of sequences present in either cellular DNA or RNA samples.

A DNA microarray consists of a glass slide or membrane filter on which oligonucleotides or fragments of cDNA are printed by a robotic system in small spots at high density.

MCAT STRATEGY > > >

For many MCAT questions on blotting techniques, all you have to know is which blotting technique goes with which macromolecule. A common mnemonic for this is SNoW DRoP: Southern, northern, and western (SNoW) blotting analyze DNA, RNA, and protein (DRoP), respectively.

Each spot on an array consists of a single oligonucleotide or cDNA. More than 10,000 unique DNA sequences can be printed onto a typical glass microscope slide, so it is readily possible to produce DNA microarrays containing sequences representing all the genes in cellular genomes. One widespread application of DNA microarrays is in the study of gene expression; for example, it can be used to compare the genes expressed by two different cell types. In an experiment of this type, cDNA probes are synthesized from the mRNAs expressed in each of the two cell types (e.g. cancer cells and normal cells). The two cDNA sequences are labeled with different fluorescent dyes (typically red and green) and a mixture of the cDNA is hybridized to a DNA microarray in which 10,000 or more human genes are represented as single spots. The array is then analyzed using a high-resolution laser scanner, and the relative extent of transcription of each gene in the cancer cells compared to the normal cells is indicated by the ratio of red to green fluorescence at the a given position on the array.

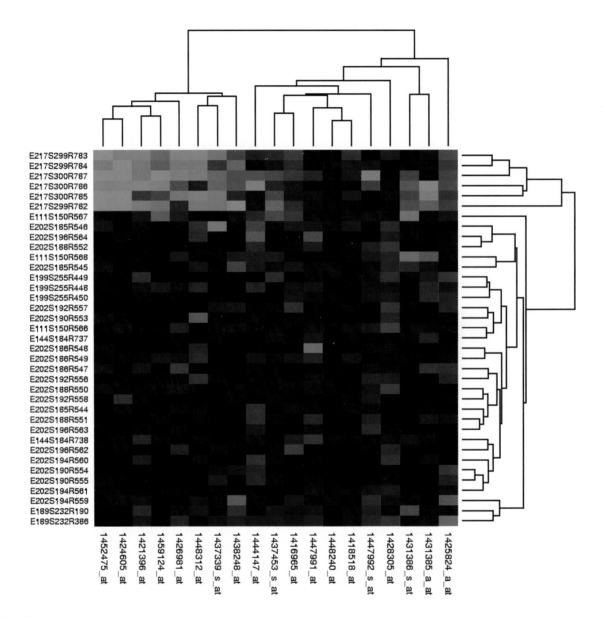

Figure 16. DNA microarray.

Various techniques have been used to determine the sequence of DNA. This is a field that has been revolutionized in the last 20-30 years. The human genome was first mapped under the auspices of the Human Genome Project, which started in 1990, took 13 years (and came in ahead of schedule!), and cost nearly 3 billion dollars. In 2001, the cost to sequence a human genome was approximately 100 million dollars, which dropped to under 1,000 dollars by 2015. There are very few, if any, parallels to a decrease in the cost of such a basic procedure by a factor of 10^5, or 100,000, over the course of less than 15 years, and it is difficult to overstate how dramatic the impact of this has been on research into genetics and personalized medicine (although these issues go beyond the scope of the MCAT).

Novel sequencing techniques have been developed, but the MCAT expects you to be aware of a classic technique, known as the Sanger method or the dideoxy chain termination method. This was the method of choice from the 1980s through the mid-2000s, and was used in the Human Genome Project, before being supplanted by next-generation methods.

The Sanger method of DNA sequencing is based on premature termination of DNA synthesis resulting from the inclusion of chain-terminating dideoxynucleotides, which do not contain the 3' hydroxyl group, in DNA polymerase reactions. DNA synthesis is initiated at a unique site on the cloned DNA from a synthetic primer. The DNA synthesis reaction includes each of four dideoxynucleotides (A, C, G, and T) in addition to their normal counterparts. Each of the four dideoxynucleotides is labeled with a different fluorescent dye, so their incorporation into DNA can be monitored. Incorporation of these dideoxynucleotides stops further DNA synthesis because no 3' hydroxyl group is available as a site for the addition of the next nucleotide. Thus, a series of labeled DNA molecules is generated, each terminating at the base represented by a specific dideoxynucleotide. Those fragments of DNA are then separated according to size by gel electrophoresis. As the newly synthesized DNA strands are electrophoresed through the gel, they pass through a laser that excites the fluorescent labels. The resulting emitted light is then detected by a photomultiplier, and a computer collects and analyzes the resultant data. The size of each fragment is determined by its terminal dideoxynucleotide, marked by a specific color fluorescence, so the DNA sequence can be read from the order of fluorescent-labeled fragments as they migrate through the gel. High-throughput automated DNA sequencing of this type has enabled large-scale analysis required for determination of the sequences of completed genomes, including that of humans.

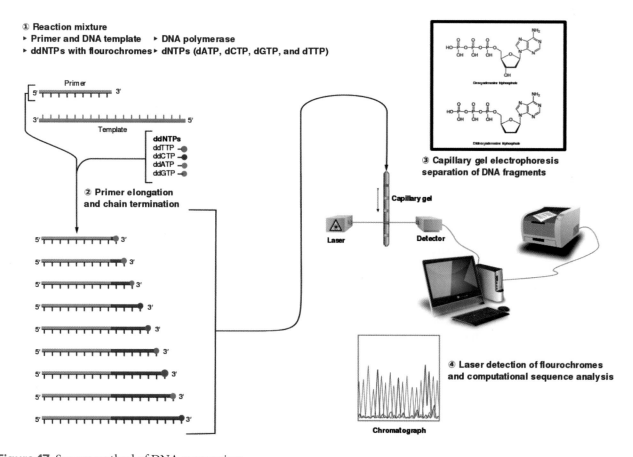

Figure 17. Sanger method of DNA sequencing.

DNA sequencing, genetic engineering, and many other applications depend on the ability to produce large quantities of specific DNA sequences. Cloning can be used to do this, but the development of the polymerase chain reaction

(PCR), the research for which won the Nobel Prize in 1993, allowed this to be carried out on an unprecedented level. Essentially, DNA polymerase is used for repeated replications of a defined segment of DNA. Provided that some sequence of the DNA molecule of interest is known, PCR can achieve a striking amplification of DNA content via reactions carried out entirely in vitro. The number of DNA molecules increases exponentially, doubling with each round of replication, so a substantial quantity of DNA can be obtained from a relatively small initial sample of template copies. For example, a single DNA molecule amplified through 30 cycles of replication would theoretically yield 2^{30}, or more than a billion, progeny molecules. Single DNA molecules can thus be amplified to yield readily detectable quantities of DNA that can be isolated by molecular cloning or further analyzed directly by restriction endonuclease digestion or nucleotide sequencing. The general procedure for PCR amplification is shown in Figure 15.

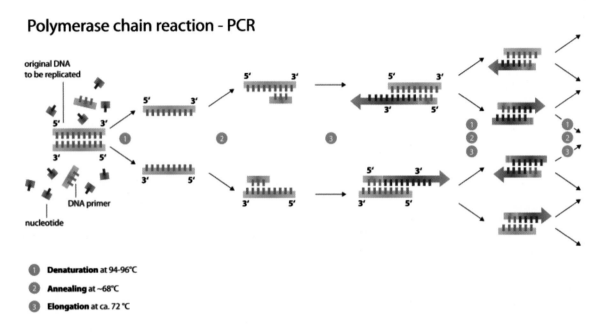

Figure 18. PCR.

The starting material in PCR amplification of DNA can be either a cloned fragment of DNA or a mixture of DNA molecules; for example, total DNA from human cells. A specific region of DNA can be amplified from such a mixture, provided that the nucleotide sequence surrounding the region is known so that primers can be designed to initiate DNA synthesis at the desired point. Such primers are usually chemically synthesized oligonucleotides containing 15-20 bases of DNA. Two primers are used to initiate DNA synthesis in opposite directions from complementary DNA strands. The reaction is started by heating the template DNA to a high temperature, typically 95°C, to separate the two strands. The temperature is then lowered to allow the primers to pair with their complementary sequences on the template strands. DNA polymerase then uses the primers to synthesize a new strand complementary to each template. Thus, through a single cycle of amplification, two new DNA molecules are synthesized from one template molecule. This process can be repeated multiple times, with a twofold increase in the number of DNA molecules following each round of replication.

The multiple cycles of heating and cooling involved in PCR are performed by programmable heating blocks called thermocyclers. The DNA polymerases used in these reactions are heat-stable enzymes from bacteria such as *Thermus aquaticus*, which reside in hot springs where temperatures can exceed 75°C. (DNA polymerase derived from *T. aquaticus* is called *Taq* polymerase.) Because these polymerases remain stable even at high temperatures, they are used to replicate the strands of DNA, so PCR amplification can be performed rapidly and automatically. RNA sequences can also be amplified by this method if reverse transcriptase is used to synthesize a cDNA copy prior to PCR amplification.

If the sequence of a target gene is known sufficiently well, a primer for it can be specified. Given this, PCR amplification provides a powerful tool for detecting small amounts of specific DNA or RNA molecules in a complex mixture of other molecules. In such a situation, the only DNA molecules that will be amplified by PCR are those containing sequences complementary to the primers used in the reaction. Therefore, PCR can selectively amplify a specific template from heterogeneous mixtures, such as total cell DNA or RNA. This extraordinary sensitivity has made PCR an important method for a variety of applications, including analysis of gene expression in cells where target DNA is available in only small quantities. The DNA segments amplified by PCR can also be directly sequenced or ligated to vectors and propagated as molecular clones. PCR thus allows the amplification and cloning of any segment of DNA for which primers can be designed. Since the complete genome sequences of many organisms are now known, PCR can be used to amplify and clone a wide array of desired DNA fragments.

7. Must-Knows

> Gene expression: explains how cells with same DNA become different in development.
> Stem cells are capable of differentiation, and can be totipotent (can differentiate into anything), pluripotent (can differentiate into any of the germ layers), or multipotent (a more limited range). Only embryonic stem cells are totipotent/pluripotent in nature; adult stem cells are multipotent.
> Operons are features of prokaryotes
  - Positive vs. negative control: in negative control, a repressor prevents transcription; in positive control, an activator stimulates transcription.
  - *Lac* operon: negative inducible. In absence of lactose, repressor blocks transcription. When lactose is present, allolactose disengages repressor, allowing transcription. Low glucose levels upregulate transcription through CAP (positive control).
  - *Trp* operon: negative repressible. Tryptophan usually synthesized, but when already present, tryptophan causes repressor to bind to operator sequence and block transcription.
> Eukaryotes:
  - Promoters: upstream DNA sequences that initiate transcription
  - Enhancers: DNA sequences that allow higher than usual transcription
  - Transcription factors: proteins that regulate expression by binding to a specific DNA sequence
  - Heterochromatin: dense, associated with transcriptional inactivity
  - Euchromatin: less dense, associated with transcriptional activity
  - Histone acetylation: ↑ transcription
  - DNA methylation: ↓ transcription
  - siRNA and miRNA: ↓ transcription
> Cancer: associated with mutations and altered gene expression patterns leading to uncontrolled proliferation.
  - Oncogenes: when turned on via mutations, promote division and cancer.
  - Tumor suppressor genes: normally restrict division; when inactivated, cancer is more likely to develop.
> Recombinant DNA and laboratory techniques:
  - Restriction enzymes cut DNA at specific points, leading to blunt and sticky ends that can be recombined.
  - Plasmid and bacteriophage vectors are used to transfer/amplify recombinant DNA.
  - Electrophoresis: separates DNA/RNA molecules by size.
  - Hybridization: used in Southern, northern, and western blotting to detect specific DNA, RNA, and protein sequences, respectively.
  - Sanger sequencing method uses dideoxynucleotides to terminate synthesis and electrophoresis to analyze fragment size.
  - PCR: used to make exponentially large numbers of copies of DNA in short amount of time; uses primers.

Practice Passage

Recombination is the exchange of genes between homologous chromosomes. This commonly occurs as a result of crossing over during meiosis. The likelihood of crossing over appears to be correlated with the size of the chromosome. Crossing over results from the formation of Holliday junctions: a junction between four strands of DNA.

Two common forms of genetic recombination involving Holliday junctions occur during prophase and metaphase of meiosis I. The first occurs when corresponding strands on each chromosome are broken. A single strand break on each homolog will result in a Holliday junction. There are two ways to resolve the Holliday junction - the first is for enzymes to cut the strands at points A and C as shown in Figure 1.

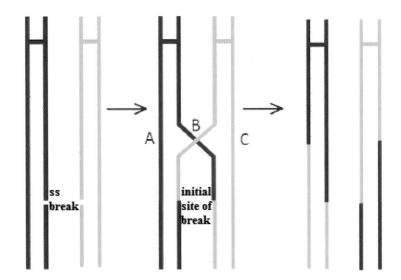

Figure 1. Holliday junction location and repair

A second form of Holliday junction recombination occurs during meiosis I and can be seen in Figure 2. This form occurs when there is a double strand break in one chromosome. The nucleus may attempt enzymatic repairs, which result in the chromosomes ending up with two Holliday junctions.

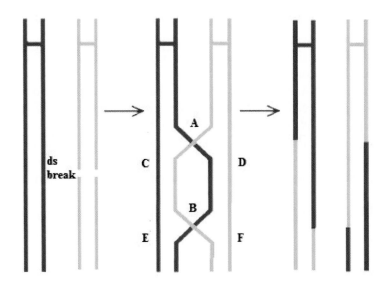

Figure 2. Double Holliday junction

T4 endonuclease and *T7 endonuclease I* are well characterized junction resolvases. They interact specifically with the junction and cleave these four way junctions by introducing nicks at asymmetrically related positions across the junction. There are two ways of doing this. The first is to cleave the DNA at A and B, in a mechanism similar to that of restriction endonucleases. This cleavage produces nonrecombinant chromosomes. The second option is to cleave first at A or B and second at C and D together or E and F together. When this happens we will get two recombinant chromosomes that have exchanged a significant amount of genetic material.

Adapted from Brázda, V., & Coufal, J. (2017). Recognition of Local DNA Structures by p53 Protein. International Journal of Molecular Sciences, 18(2), 375. Under CCBY 4.0

1. What best explains why cleaving at A and B in Figure 2 results in nonrecombinant chromosomes?
   A. There would be no interchange of genetic material.
   B. The segment of DNA that is interchanged will not likely contain any significant number of genes.
   C. The cleavage would result in the exchange of the whole sister chromatids.
   D. The cleavage would result in two free-floating segments of DNA.

2. Which of the following strands are the most likely result if the Holliday junction in Figure 1 is cleaved at point B?

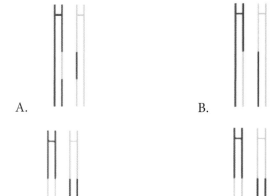

A.

B.

C.

D.

3. Which chromosome is most likely to be manipulated by the synaptonemal complex and show crossing over?
   A. 1 (2000 genes)
   B. 18 (200 genes)
   C. X (800 genes)
   D. Y (50 genes)

4. One of the scientists studying Holliday junctions proposes in an article that it is possible for genetic recombination to occur during meiosis II. Will their proposal be accepted?
   A. Yes, sister chromatids on one chromosome can exchange genetic material.
   B. Yes, slight overlap of adjacent chromosomal arms makes it possible for crossing over to occur between two nonhomologous chromosomes.
   C. No, recombination requires two homologous but distinct chromosomes.
   D. No, sister chromatids cannot get close enough during metaphase II.

5. Which of the following combinations of DNA cuts will result in the greatest amount of base pairs exchanged between the two chromosomes in figure 2?
   A. Cleaving at A, E, and F
   B. Cleaving at A, C, and D
   C. Cleaving at B, E, and F
   D. Cleaving at B, C, and D

6. Some labs have attempted to replicate the Holliday junction repair mechanism using artificial resolvases. Which of the following sequences found at a Holliday junction will NOT be targeted by this mechanism?
   A. 5'-GGCC-3'
      3'-CCGG-5'
   B. 5'-GGATCC-3'
      3'-CCTAGG-5'
   C. 5'-GAAT-3'
      3'-TAAG-5'
   D. 5'-GTAGAC-3'
      3'-CATCTG-5'

7. A new study aimed at treating X-linked severe combined immunodeficiency (X-SCID) with a retroviral vector resulted in many patients developing lung cancer. What is the best explanation for this outcome?
   A. Vector insertion inactivated a latent oncogene near the target site.
   B. Decreased expression of interleukin-7 as a result of vector insertion
   C. Proliferation of an epithelial cell's clones due to vector insertion on chromosome 11
   D. DNA insertion into the host genome increased the expression of p53 proteins

Practice Passage Explanations

Recombination is the exchange of genes between homologous chromosomes. This commonly occurs as a result of crossing over during meiosis. The likelihood of crossing over appears to be correlated with the size of the chromosome. Crossing over results from the formation of Holliday junctions: a junction between four strands of DNA.

Key terms: recombination, meiosis, Holliday junctions

Two common forms of genetic recombination involving Holliday junctions occur during prophase and metaphase of meiosis I. The first occurs when corresponding strands on each chromosome are broken. A single strand break on each homolog will result in a Holliday junction. There are two ways to resolve the Holliday junction - the first is for enzymes to cut the strands at points A and C as shown in Figure 1.

Key terms: single strand cleavage, resolve

Cause and effect: ssb → Holliday junction; repair mechanism involves separation

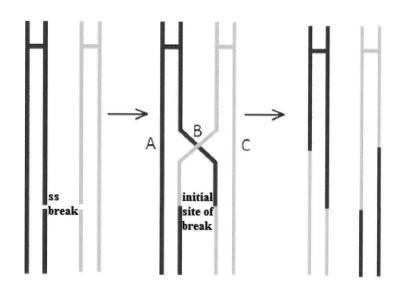

Figure 1. Holliday junction location and repair

Figure 1 shows the formation of the heteroduplex region during HJ repair; the result when the strands are cut at A and C is shown

A second form of Holliday junction recombination occurs during meiosis I and can be seen in Figure 2. This form occurs when there is a double strand break in one chromosome. The nucleus may attempt enzymatic repairs, which result in the chromosomes ending up with two Holliday junctions.

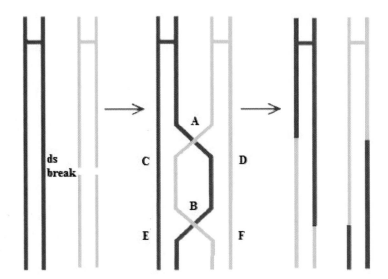

Figure 2. Double Holliday junction

Figure 2 shows a possible scenario where a double Holliday junction may form between chromosomes. One way of resolving it is illustrated here.

T4 endonuclease and T7 endonuclease I are well characterized junction resolvases. They interact specifically with the junction and cleave these four way junctions by introducing nicks at asymmetrically related positions across the junction. There are two ways of doing this. The first is to cleave the DNA at A and B, in a mechanism similar to that of restriction endonucleases. This cleavage produces nonrecombinant chromosomes. The second option is to cleave first at A or B and second at C and D together or E and F together. When this happens we will get two recombinant chromosomes that have exchanged a significant amount of genetic material.

Key terms: nonrecombinant

Contrast: two ways to repair 2-Holliday junction: HJ → nonrecombinant OR HJ → recombinants

Adapted from Brázda, V., & Coufal, J. (2017). Recognition of Local DNA Structures by p53 Protein. International Journal of Molecular Sciences, 18(2), 375. Under CCBY 4.0

1. B is correct. Paragraph 4 tells us that the cleavage in Figure 2 results in nonrecombinat chromosomes. If cleaved at points A and B, the homologous chromosomes would simply exchange that short segment of DNA between A and B to get something like this:

   There will be some exchange of DNA but the chromosomes will not be recombinant because there will be no exchange of genes.
   A. There will be a small interchange.
   C. This is not true, the Holliday junctions are nowhere near the centromeres of the chromosomes.
   D. Cleavage at this site will not result in completely separate DNA strands.

2. A is correct. This question requires us to consider Figure 1 and what change will occur given the circumstance in the stem. If cleaved at point B, the strands will rectify themselves by joining their original chromosomes and there will be a small segment of DNA that has transferred between chromosomes. The result is two non-recombinant chromosomes.

3. A is correct. The synaptonemal complex is the highly organized filament structure that is built during prophase I and is designed to carry out the process of crossing over. That means this questions simply wants us to determine which chromosome is most likely to experience crossing over. Paragraph 1 informs you that crossing over has a certain probability of occurring based on the size of the chromosomes in question. Since chromosome 1 is significantly larger than the other three options, it will be most likely to undergo crossing over.
   B. Chromosome 18 is smaller than chromosome 1 and thus is not as likely to experience crossing over during meiosis I.
   C. Chromosome X is smaller than chromosome 1 and thus is not as likely to experience crossing over during meiosis I.
   D. Chromosome Y is smaller than chromosome 1 and thus is not as likely to experience crossing over during meiosis I.

4. C is correct. This question requires us to know what recombination entails. Recombination is the exchange of genetic material to create new genetic possibilities. Exchange of genetic material between sister chromatids, if possible, would have no effect on genetic variance because sister chromatids are identical.
   A. It is not possible to recombine two perfectly identical chromosomal arms.
   B. Genetic machinery cannot recombine chromosomes unless they are homologous.
   D. This statement is false. Sister chromatids are attached to each other and arranged along the metaphase plate in metaphase II.

5. B is correct. This question requires us to visualize and compare the results of the four possible cuts on the two Holliday junctions in Figure 2.

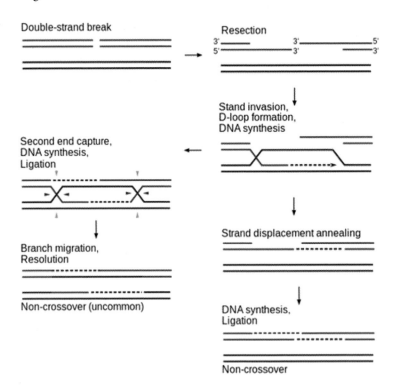

6. D is correct. Paragraph 4 tells us that the resolvases are endonucleases. Restriction enzymes, also known as restriction endonucleases, are enzymes that cut a DNA molecule at a particular place. They are essential tools for recombinant DNA technology. The enzyme "scans" a DNA molecule looking for a particular sequence typically four to six nucleotides in length. Once it finds this recognition sequence, it stops and cuts the strands. This is known as enzyme digestion. On double stranded DNA the recognition sequence is on both strands, but runs in opposite directions. This allows the enzyme to cut both strands. The targets for these enzymes are most commonly palindromic. Only choice D fails to meet this criteria.

7. C is correct. Most of the approaches to gene therapy involve the use of vectors to introduce a functioning gene into damaged cells. Typically these vectors are retroviruses or adeno-associated viruses. A major challenge with these approaches is that when foreign DNA is inserted into the host genome, it can and often does disturb normal gene function at the insertion site. In this case we want insertion to explain overproduction or over-proliferation of cells (i.e. cancer).
    A. Oncogenes are genes that can cause cells to turn cancerous. Inactivating one would not cause cancer.
    B. IL-7 is a cytokine that acts as a hematopoietic growth factor and is secreted by cells in the bone marrow and thymus. Under-expression is the opposite of what would be expected in an immunodeficiency disease treatment. However, even if it were under-expressed, this molecule would likely affect B and T cell development, not cause cancer in the lungs.
    D. Tumor protein 53, aka p53, is one of the most famous and potent anti-tumor proteins in humans.

Independent Questions

1. In an *E. coli* cell with abundant lactose present:
   A. the repressor is bound to the operator.
   B. gene transcription of the structural *lac* genes does not take place.
   C. allolactose is bound to the operator.
   D. allolactose is bound to the repressor.

2. Which of the following are classified as noncoding RNAs?
   I. tRNA
   II. siRNA
   III. mRNA
   IV. miRNA
   A. I only
   B. I and II only
   C. I, II, and IV only
   D. I, II, III, and IV

3. Restriction enzymes are classified as what type of enzyme?
   A. Exonucleases
   B. Ribonucleases
   C. Endonucleases
   D. Kinases

4. cDNA differs from the DNA coding for the same gene in which of the following ways?
   A. The cDNA sequence for the gene is typically shorter.
   B. cDNA contains introns.
   C. The cDNA sequence is complementary to the DNA that codes for the gene in question.
   D. The cDNA sequence was created from an mRNA template, so it contains uracil instead of thymine.

5. In gel electrophoresis, DNA molecules are:
   A. negatively charged, so they move toward the anode.
   B. negatively charged, so they move toward the cathode.
   C. positively charged, so they move toward the cathode.
   D. The sign of the net charge on a DNA molecule depends on the nitrogenous bases that comprise the DNA sequence.

6. Northern blotting, western blotting, and Southern blotting are used to identify molecules of which type, respectively?
   A. RNA, protein, DNA
   B. DNA, protein, RNA
   C. RNA, DNA, protein
   D. Protein, RNA, DNA

7. The molecule below is utilized as part of a Sanger sequencing procedure.

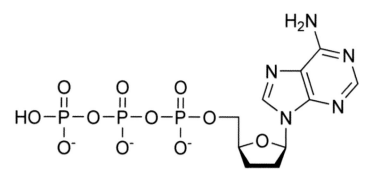

   The identity of this molecule is most likely which of the following?
   A. dCTP
   B. ddCTP
   C. dATP
   D. ddATP

8. Polymerase chain reaction (PCR) requires use of a thermostable DNA polymerase. The use of such a polymerase is especially important due to which step of the PCR cycle?
   A. Extension
   B. Annealing
   C. Denaturation
   D. Amplification

Independent Question Explanations

1. D is correct. When lactose is present, transcription of structural *lac* genes takes place so the bacterium can metabolize the lactose sugar. Allolactose (an isomer of lactose) binds to the repressor, causing it to dissociate from the operator region. With the operator now available, transcription can take place.

2. C is correct. Of the choices listed, tRNA (transfer RNA), siRNA (short interfering RNA), and miRNA (microRNA) are noncoding RNAs, which are not translated into protein. Messenger RNA (mRNA) is translated, so it is considered coding RNA.

3. C is correct. Restriction enzymes are alternatively known as restriction endonucleases. Endonucleases are enzymes that cleave within a nucleic acid sequence (as opposed to exonucleases, which cleave nucleotides from the ends of a nucleic acid chain). Ribonucleases degrade RNA, which is not accurate in this case, because restriction enzymes cleave DNA. Kinases catalyze the phosphorylation of proteins.

4. A is correct. cDNA, or complementary DNA, is DNA that is reverse transcribed from the associated mRNA molecule. The result is a cDNA sequence that is very similar to the regular DNA sequence, but that lacks introns (since mature mRNA does not contain introns). For this reason, a cDNA sequence will be shorter than the associated DNA sequence, assuming that the DNA sequence does include at least one intron. Choice C is incorrect because cDNA is named for being complementary to mRNA, not DNA, and choice D is incorrect because all forms of DNA contain thymine.

5. A is correct. DNA molecules contain a uniform negative charge-to-mass ratio due to the presence of anionic phosphate groups along their backbones. In gel electrophoresis, the apparatus functions like an electrolytic cell, in which the anode is positive and the cathode is negative. Since opposite charges attract, the negative DNA molecules will migrate toward the positive anode.

6. A is correct. Northern blotting is used to identify RNA. Southern blotting was developed first of the three procedures and identifies specific DNA sequences. Finally, western blotting identifies proteins.

7. D is correct. You should remember from your reading of the chapter that Sanger sequencing involves the use of dideoxynucleotides, or nucleotides that lack an -OH group on both the 2' and 3' carbons. The given diagram depicts such a structure, so the answer must be either choice B (ddCTP) or choice D (ddATP). The structure shown contains two fused rings in its nitrogenous base, which is characteristic of purines; the answer thus must be choice D (ddATP, or dideoxyadenosine triphosphate).

8. C is correct. The highest-temperature step of a PCR reaction is the denaturation step, in which the reaction mixture is heated to around 95°C. This heat is required to separate the two parent DNA strands. Since the DNA polymerase used in PCR is present throughout the cycle, it must be able to withstand such high temperatures without a significant loss of function.

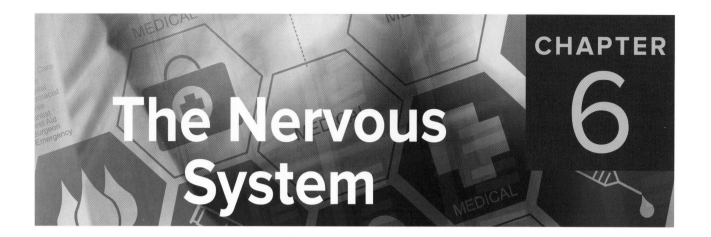

The Nervous System

The nervous system is the body's means of taking in information, integrating that information, and then controlling and coordinating much of the body's activity through other physiological systems.

> > CONNECTIONS < <

Psychology chapter 1

0. Introduction

In this chapter, we will start with a brief discussion of some general features of the nervous system before moving on to an in-depth discussion neurons, the functional unit in the nervous system. Neurons transmit information through action potentials and send that information to other neurons or to effector cells across synapses. After discussing the mechanisms behind signal transmission, we will briefly discuss some concepts related to electrochemistry and physics, as the MCAT is fond of asking cross-disciplinary questions that tie neurons into these other concept areas. Finally, we'll wrap up the chapter by reviewing the divisions of the peripheral and central nervous systems.

1. General Function of the Nervous System

The core function of the nervous system is simple: communication. In this regard, it functions very similarly to the endocrine system, which will be discussed in more detail in a later chapter. The key contrast between nervous and endocrine coordination comes in the speed with which these systems can react to input. Nerves can fire off action potentials in mere fractions of a second, whereas endocrine responses tend to be slower and more long-lasting. For example, in the case of the development of sex characteristics, the body's response to endocrine communication can be life-long.

MCAT STRATEGY > > >

Mastering MCAT content involves spaced repetition. Even if you've already gone through the nervous system chapter in the psychology book, take this opportunity to review the information again.

This communication sifts through the vast data from the environment, and from internal senses (e.g. stretch receptors in the bladder to let you know you need to pee), which lets the body react, both with conscious behaviors and unconscious reflexes to help maintain homeostasis. Neurons and sense receptors in the peripheral nervous system (PNS) take in information and bring it to the brain or spinal cord, which comprise the central nervous system (CNS).

That information is then integrated and the body can respond. Some responses can be so simple they don't even involve the brain. The knee jerk response (patellar tendon reflex) is an example of such a response. In other cases, the information undergoes highly complex processing which may involve conscious reflection and higher judgment or decision-making processes.

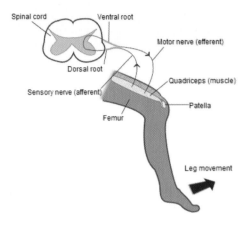

Figure 1. Patellar Tendon Reflex

2. Neurons and Glia

The basic functional unit of the nervous system is the neuron. A neuron is a very highly specialized cell designed to integrate inputs and output a signal in the form of an action potential. This level of specialization means that neurons no longer undergo the normal cell cycle and are, like skeletal muscle cells, in the G_0 resting phase and no longer dividing.

The neuron is built out of several components which you should know for the test. The main body of the cell, the soma, houses the cell's nucleus and other large organelles. The cell takes input through dendrites, projections off the cell body which can connect to input from other nerves or other specialized sense organs. A single neuron may have a handful of dendrites or even hundreds or thousands. By contrast, each neuron only has a single axon. The axon is a single, long projection from the soma and is the structure through which a neuron outputs its action potentials. Just before the axon, the cell body tapers into a region called the axon hillock, where a neuron integrates the various input signals it receives and decides whether to send a signal down the axon.

The axon itself can be coated with an insulating sheath of material called myelin. Not all cells are myelinated. Myelin acts as an insulator that allows for much more rapid conduction of action potentials. Breaks in the myelin sheath, called nodes of Ranvier are dotted along the myelinated axon. The axon ends in the nerve terminal where the cell can synapse with (communicate with) either another nerve cell, a muscle, or a gland.

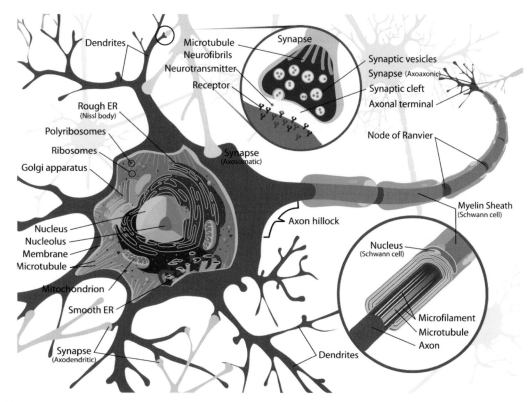

Figure 2. Neuron

There are six different types of glial cells that provide support to neurons in both the CNS and PNS. While the function of the nervous system was first thought to depend almost entirely on neurons, with glial cells seen as being of secondary importance, more recent research has shown that by managing the microenvironments around neurons and performing other support functions, glial cells are of critical importance in the smooth functioning of the nervous system. The table below provides a brief description of the functions of the glial cells you will be expected to recognize on the exam. After that is a short description of the four types of neurons.

GLIAL CELLS	
Oligodendrocytes	Provide myelination in the CNS
Schwann cells	Provide myelination in the PNS
Astrocytes	Provide various support functions to neurons in the CNS
Ependymal cells	Produce and circulate cerebrospinal fluid in the CNS
Satellite cells	Control the microenvironment around cell bodies in ganglia in the PNS
Microglia	Macrophages that clean out microbes and debris in the CNS

Table 1. Glial cells.

NEURON TYPES	
Unipolar	A single dendrite that splits into dendrioles but no axon. Found in cerebellum and associated with balance. More commonly found in insects than humans.
Bipolar	Sensory neuron for smell, sight, taste, hearing, and balance.
Pseudounipolar	Sensory neuron in PNS. One axon splits with one part running to the spinal cord and one running to the periphery. Found in the dorsal root ganglia.
Multipolar	Has a single axon and multiple dendrites. The classic image of a neuron. Includes motor neurons and interneurons.

Table 2. Neuron types.

3. Membrane Potentials, Action Potentials and Synapses

All of the body's cells maintain a potential difference across their membranes. That is, the area on the inside of the cell membrane maintains a negative voltage potential relative to the area on the outside of the plasma membrane. This potential allows the cell to carry out a number of different functions, and in some cells—neurons and muscle cells—this potential can be manipulated quickly across large portions of the cell to achieve a particular effect (sending an action potential or twitching a muscle fiber).

Neural Membrane and Resting Potential

The nerve cell maintains a resting potential of -70 mV. When the inside of the cell loses this negative potential, the cell is said to be depolarized, and when it drops to a more negative potential (after peaking at +40 mV in an action potential) it is said to be hyperpolarized. This resting potential is maintained by the constant action of the sodium-potassium ATPase (the Na^+/K^+ pump) which pushes three sodium ions out of the cell for every two potassium ions it brings in. This electrochemical gradient is also maintained by the fact that the hydrophobic core of the plasma membrane doesn't allow ions to easily diffuse back across.

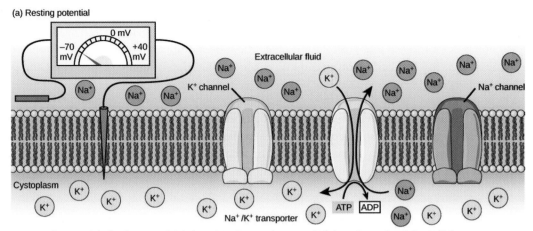

(a) Resting potential

At the resting potential, all voltage-gated Na⁺ channels and most voltage-gated K⁺ channels are closed. The Na⁺/K⁺ transporter pumps K⁺ ions into the cell and Na⁺ ions out.

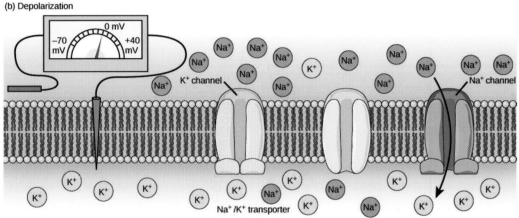

(b) Depolarization

In response to a depolarization, some Na⁺ channels open, allowing Na⁺ ions to enter the cell. The membrane starts to depolarize (the charge across the membrane lessens). If the threshold of excitation is reached, all the Na⁺ channels open.

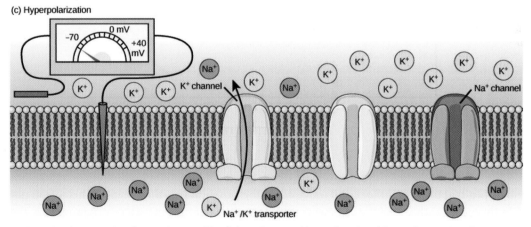

(c) Hyperpolarization

At the peak action potential, Na⁺ channels close while K⁺ channels open. K⁺ leaves the cell, and the membrane eventually becomes hyperpolarized.

Figure 3. Membrane Potential

During the resting state, channels that permit sodium or potassium to rush through are closed (although potassium leak channels are open which permit slow diffusion of K⁺). When an excitatory stimulus hits the neuron (typically inputs from dendrites), the cell's potential is brought from -70 mV to a more positive state. It is possible for such signals to fail to bring the neuron up to the threshold potential of -55 mV, however. These are shown in the figure below as "failed initiations."

If the excitatory stimulus is strong enough, and the cell's resting potential is brought up to -55 mV, the cell will undergo an action potential (shown below). In the first phase of the action potential, depolarization, the sodium voltage-gated channels open and Na⁺ ions rush into the cell. The sudden influx of positive charges continues until the cell membrane reaches full depolarization at +40 mV, at which point the sodium channels close and potassium voltage-gated channels open.

Now that the interior of the cell is positive, the potassium is pushed by both electrical potential and by its own concentration gradient to rush out, causing repolarization. Repolarization continues until the cell overshoots the -70 mV level, making the cell temporarily hyperpolarized, during what is called the refractory period. Then, the sodium potassium pumps get back to work to re-establish the resting state of the cell.

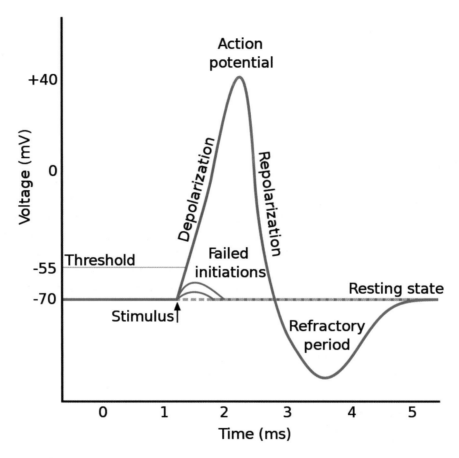

Figure 4. Action Potential

Action potentials begin at the axon hillock and move down the axon towards the synapse. This action potential can either move slowly and smoothly long the cell membrane if the cell is unmyelinated, or can jump very rapidly down the axon from one node of Ranvier to the next if the cell is myelinated.

Remember that for a section of nerve membrane to undergo an action potential, it must have its membrane brought from -70 mV up to -55 mV. The action potential is transmitted from one node of Ranvier to the next because the +40 mV potential of a depolarized section of nerve membrane can transmit some of that positive potential (in the form of sodium ions) towards the next node. This positive potential need only contribute to a 15 mV increase (remember, from -70 to -55 mV) in the next node to get it to experience an action potential and send the signal further down the axon.

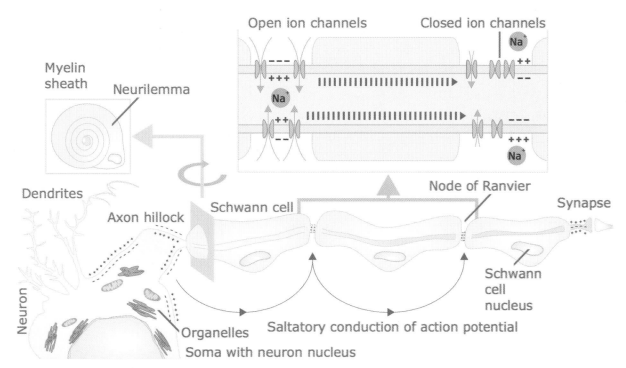

Figure 5. Action Potential Propagation

When the action potential reaches the end of the axon, it transmits a signal via the nerve's synapse with one of three things—another nerve, a muscle cell, or a gland. Neurotransmitters are stored in vesicles in the axon terminal. When the action potential arrives, calcium voltage-gated channels are triggered, allowing Ca^{2+} to rush into the axon terminal. These calcium ions serve as the signal for the cell to use exocytosis to push the neurotransmitters into the synaptic cleft—the space that exists between the axon and the post-synaptic membrane. The space of the cleft is exceptionally small, such that simple diffusion is enough to very quickly carry the neurotransmitters across the cleft to the post-synaptic membrane. There, the neurotransmitters can act as ligands binding to their receptors.

Neurotransmitters must be cleared out of the synaptic cleft quickly. This allows the body to tightly regulate the strength and timing of the signals sent by nerves. Neurotransmitters can either be broken down by enzymes in the cleft (the classic example being acetylcholinesterase, which breaks down acetylcholine) or taken back up by the axon for re-use later. A clinical example of the importance of this re-uptake is seen in the class of antidepressants called selective serotonin reuptake inhibitors (SSRIs), which can selectively block reuptake and enhance the activity of serotonin in certain synapses in the brain.

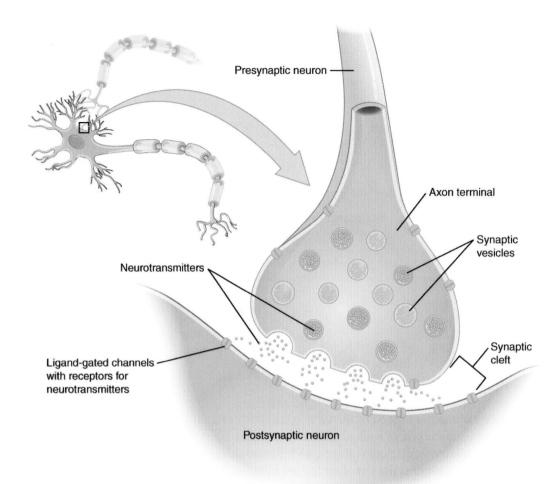

Figure 6. Synapse

4. Neurons and Electrochemistry

A neuron maintains a resting potential of -70 mV by maintaining gradients of ions across the membrane. Because it relies on differences in ion concentrations to generate and use voltage, a neuron can be thought of as a particular kind of galvanic cell—a concentration cell.

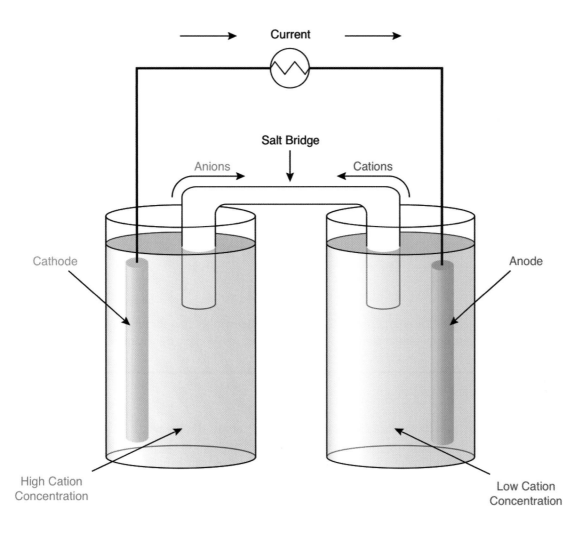

Figure 7. A concentration cell.

In a concentration cell, the same ion is used for both the anode and cathode half-cells. The difference is the concentration of the ions in solution. For example, in the cell shown in Figure 7, the half-cell on the left has a very low cation concentration whereas the beaker on the right has a very high cation concentration. The electrodes in both cases are made of the solid metal of the cation in questions. In the cell on the right, the metal atoms making up the electrode are spontaneously oxidized, releasing cations into the solution (which initially has low cation concentration). At the same time, the cations in the left chamber spontaneously deposit onto the electrode, getting reduced with the electrons produced in the anode half-reaction.

In a neuron, the impermeability of the cell membrane to most ions and large, charged proteins prevents the system from simply coming to equilibrium and losing all of its voltage. The resting voltage for a neuron is largely determined by potassium, as the neural membrane is much more permeable to potassium than sodium, or large negatively-charged proteins.

> **MCAT STRATEGY > > >**
>
> You will almost certainly not have to do any heavy-duty calculations with the Nernst equation. Instead, you'll be expected to do some reasoning with the equation—will your answer be positive or negative?

The MCAT may ask you to apply some physics and chemistry concepts to neurons, specifically in the form of the Nernst equation and the equations for capacitors. In the Nernst equation, we can disregard E° for neurons, as the standard cell potential for a concentration cell is zero. Thus the equation reduces to:

$$E = -\frac{RT}{nr}\ln\left(\frac{K^+in}{K^+out}\right)$$

Note that due to the action of the sodium-potassium pump, the cell maintains a much larger concentration of K^+ inside the cell. Thus the fraction in the equation is greater than one and the log of that number will be positive. But the negative sign in the Nernst equation then gives us a negative number for the voltage (which we know is -70 mV!).

Neural membranes can also be modeled as capacitors, with the ion channels serving as a parallel circuit. While the presentation of this information may seem a little odd, the key to solving any questions the MCAT gives you is to simply apply the equations you already know for capacitors and parallel circuits. Simply plug in whatever information is provided in the passage or question stem:

$$C = \frac{Q}{V}$$

Where C is the capacitance, Q is the charge, and V is the voltage. Remember that for neurons, these are going to be very small numbers. The resting potential is measured in millivolts, so the capacitance and charge are also going to be very small.

$$C = \frac{\varepsilon A}{d}$$

Where C is the capacitance, A is the surface area of the neural membrane, d is the width across the neural membrane, and epsilon is the permittivity of the membrane (would be given in the passage if they actually wanted you to calculate this). When thinking of a neural membrane as a parallel-plate capacitor, remember that the same relationships apply to neural membranes as to any other capacitor—more surface area means more capacitance, and a thinner separation between the plates (very thin for a cell membrane!) means a higher capacitance. Finally, if asked to treat the membrane like a circuit, each ion channel could be seen as a resistor in parallel, and you would simply use the parallel circuit equation:

$$\frac{1}{R_{eq}} = \frac{1}{R_1} + \frac{1}{R_2} \ldots$$

5. Peripheral and Central Nervous Systems

The nervous system can be understand by looking at its different functional components. First, the system is divided into the central (CNS) and peripheral nervous systems (PNS). The central nervous system includes both the brain and the spinal cord. Everything else is the peripheral nervous system—all of the nerves that carry information into the CNS (afferent fibers) or bring signals out of the CNS to the PNS (efferent fibers). While most cell bodies (somas) are found in the central nervous system, there are clusters of cell bodies outside the CNS. These are called ganglia and are found along the sides of the spinal cord, in the digestive system, and elsewhere in the body.

Nerves, or clusters of axons held together by connective tissue, can be defined as afferent or efferent and also as motor or sensory. Sensory nerves are afferent and bring sensory data into the CNS, carrying information about the environment or about the body's own internal state. Motor neurons are effectors and signal muscle cells to contract.

These sensory and motor nerves either connect to the spinal cord, in which case they are called spinal nerves, or directly enter the skull, in which case they are cranial nerves. Nerves can be further classified functionally as either autonomic, somatic, or visceral. Visceral nerves connect to the digestive system to modulate its functioning. Somatic nerves connect to skeletal muscle to allow for voluntary movement. The autonomic nervous system connects to various involuntary responses in the body, including things like sweating, blushing, pupil dilation, and so on.

Finally, the autonomic nervous system can be further divided. It is crucial to recognize the difference between the sympathetic and parasympathetic systems. The sympathetic nervous system stimulates the body in the classic "fight or flight" response. If the body needs to get ready for action, it will do things like dilate the pupils, raise the heart rate, and increase blood flow to skeletal muscles to prepare for sudden action. By contrast, the parasympathetic nervous system is the "rest and digest" system that increases blood flow to the digestive system, slows the heart rate, and so on.

> **MCAT STRATEGY > > >**
>
> Remember the word SAME: sensory afferent, motor efferent.

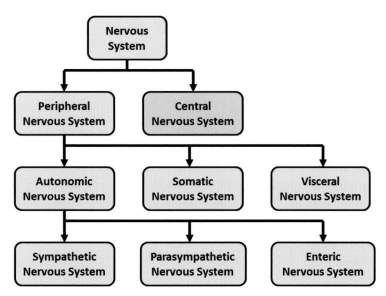

Figure 8. Components of the Nervous System

The central nervous system—brain and spinal cord—are protected by bones (skull and vertebral column, respectively) and tough membranes called meninges, and are cushioned by cerebrospinal fluid (CSF). CSF is secreted by specialized glial cells called ependymal cells and circulates across the brain and down the spinal cord.

The Central Nervous System

The brainstem (consisting of the midbrain, pons, and medulla oblongata), provides the connection from the brain to the spinal cord. It serves to regulate crucial functions basic to the survival of the organism—things like heart rate, respiration, sleep, and overall activation of the rest of the CNS. The cerebellum, found just underneath the occipital lobe, serves to direct complex coordinated movement, such as walking or playing the piano. The basal ganglia are located just under the cortex and connect to both the brainstem and the cortical lobes. The basal ganglia are involved in a number of different functions, including voluntary movement, habitual behaviors, learning, and emotion.

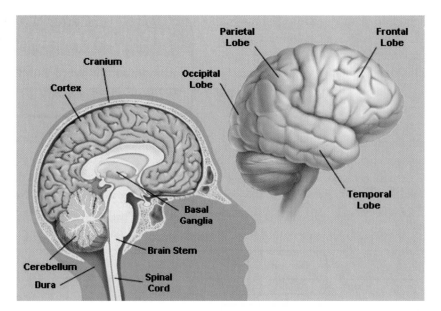

Figure 9. The Brain.

The cerebral cortices overlay the rest of the brain's structures and are responsible for many of the higher functions seen in humans. The cortices can be divided into four lobes: frontal, parietal, occipital, and temporal. Each lobe is associated with a wide variety of functions related to sensation, motor activity, and cognition. In particular, the frontal lobe is associated with making judgments and regulating behavior as a part of executive functioning. The occipital lobe is most closely related to visual processing, as data from the optic nerves are sent directly there. The parietal lobe is associated with integrating various sensory input, and both the parietal and temporal lobes are important for language.

TABLE 3 PARTS OF THE BRAIN		
Hindbrain	Cerebellum	Coordinated movement
	Medulla oblongata	Autonomic functions such as breathing, heart rate, blood pressure
	Pons	Relays signals between the cerebellum, medulla and the rest of the brain. Involved in sleep, respiration, swallowing, taste, bladder control, and balance.
Midbrain	Inferior colliculus	Processes auditory signals and sends them to the medial geniculate nucleus in the thalamus.
	Superior colliculus	Processes visual signals and participates in control of eye movements.
Forebrain	Amygdala	Processes memory, emotions, and decision-making.
	Basal ganglia	Participate in motivation, in controlling eye movements, and modulate decision-making.
	Frontal lobe	Involved in voluntary movement, memory processing, planning, motivation, and attention
	Hippocampus	Consolidation of short-term memory into long-term memory
	Hypothalamus	Links the nervous system to the endocrine system via the pituitary gland.
	Occipital lobe	Visual processing
	Parietal lobe	Sensory processing
	Pineal gland	Modulates sleep through melatonin production.
	Posterior pituitary	Projection through which the hypothalamus secretes oxytocin and vasopressin
	Septal nuclei	Part of the reward pathway.
	Temporal lobe	Involved in processing sense information to help form memory and attach meaning to information. Includes Wernicke's area.
	Thalamus	Relays sense and motor signals and regulates sleep and alertness

Neurons in both the central and peripheral nervous systems must communicate with each other via neurotransmitters. Make sure you're familiar with the following neurotransmitters for Test Day.

TABLE 4 NEUROTRANSMITTERS	
Acetylcholine	Activates muscle contraction at the neuromuscular junction. Used in all autonomic outputs from the brain to autonomic ganglia. Used in the parasympathetic nervous system for post-ganglionic connections.
Dopamine	Used in reward pathways and motor pathways. Particularly associated with Parkinson's disease and the loss of dopaminergic neurons in the substantia nigra.
Endorphin	Pain suppression and can produce euphoria
Epinephrine	Stimulates fight-or-flight response
GABA	Main inhibitory neurotransmitter of the CNS that hyperpolarizes cells to reduce action potential firing. Associated with many of the physiological effects of alcohol intoxication.
Glutamate	Excitatory neurotransmitter and most common neurotransmitter (90% of brain cells are glutaminergic).
Glycine	Inhibitory neurotransmitter of the spinal cord and brainstem. Can work in conjunction with GABA.
Norepinephrine	Used in post-ganglionic connections in the sympathetic division of the autonomic nervous system. Increases arousal, alertness, and focuses attention.
Serotonin	Regulates intestinal movement in the GI tract and regulates mood, appetite, and sleep in the brain. Low levels particularly associated with depressive mood disorders.

Studying the Brain

Scientists have been examining the brain for well over a century, using a variety of techniques. At first, such explorations were limited to crude anatomical manipulations—destroying chunks of the brain in animals and studying the effects.

Throughout the early 20th century, doctors began carefully studying human patients who had suffered brain trauma. By meticulously cataloguing the patient's various abilities and deficiencies, doctors could then associate such deficiencies with areas of the brain that showed trauma by performing an extensive autopsy of the brain.

This process provided a wealth of information about which areas of the brain were associated with certain functions, and allowed scientists to take the next step—surgically opening the skull and stimulating regions of the brain with small electrodes. By keeping the patient awake and lucid throughout the process, doctors could have the patient report what subjective experience was associated with such stimulation.

In the latter part of the 20th century and moving into the 21st century, scientists have been able to study the brain in even more detail through imaging techniques that don't require any surgical intervention.

An EEG measures electrical impulses in the brain by covering the scalp with small sensors. Researchers can then present the subject with various stimuli and record which areas of the brain demonstrate increased electrical activity.

Instead of measuring electrical activity, scientists can watch the level of blood flow in parts of the brain. By injecting a tracer molecule, scientists are able to image which parts of the brain are more active in response to certain stimuli. More active brain areas will see an increase in blood flow, and thus an increase in the tracer molecule.

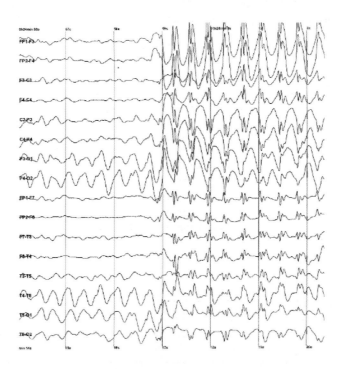

Figure 10. EEG.

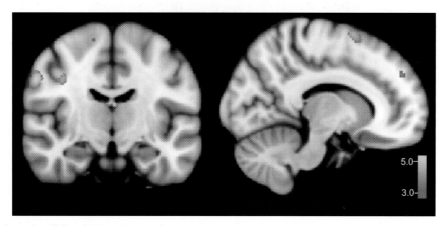

Figure 11. Regional cerebral blood flow.

Brains can also be imaged using MRI, PET, and CT scans. MRI scans use magnetic fields and radio waves to image parts of the brain while avoiding the dangers of bombarding the body with ionizing radiation such as X-rays. Functional MRI, or fMRI trades spatial resolution for temporal resolution and allows scientists to map active parts of the brain. It does so by analyzing the differences in oxyhemoglobin and deoxyhemoglobin concentration in parts of the brain. PET scans work by injecting the patient with a radioactive analogue of glucose, and then

MCAT STRATEGY > > >

Focus on exactly what's measured in various techniques. EEG: electrical activity; PET: metabolic activity through glucose uptake; fMRI: metabolic activity through oxygen utilization (hemoglobin in the blood)

measuring the radioactive emissions from the body. Much like MRI and fMRI, PET scans work on the principle that more active areas of the brain will show increased metabolism, and thus increase uptake of glucose. Such uptake can then be converted into a false-color "heat map" of the brain to show areas of increased or decreased activity. Finally, CT scans use X-rays, but unlike a typical single two-dimensional X-ray film, CT machines use computer processing to take many X-ray measurements from multiple different angles, generating images that can be used for diagnosis.

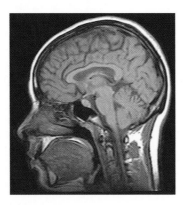

Figure 12. Brain MRI.

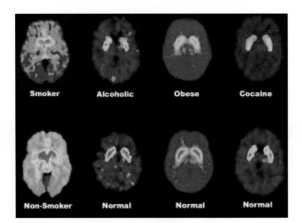

Figure 13. PET scan comparing brains of addicts and non-addicts.

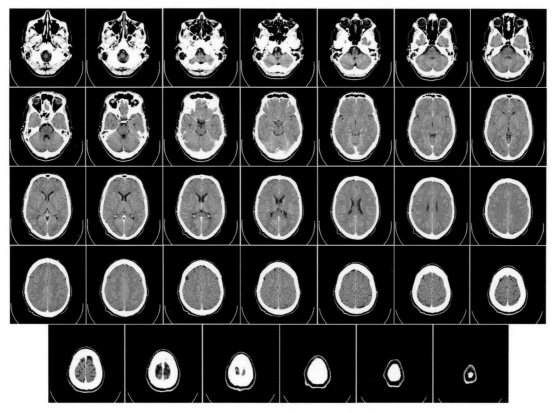

Figure 14. CT scan of the head.

6. Must-Knows

> The nervous system serves to take in and integrate information from the environment, and then allow the organism to respond appropriately.

> The functional unit of the nervous system is the neuron, and all neurons require supporting glial cells to function correctly.
  - Glial cells include oligodendrocytes, Schwann cells, ependymal cells, satellite cells, and microglia.
  - Neurons come in several types, including sensory cells that are bipolar and pseudounipolar, and motor and interneurons that are multipolar.

> Neurons maintain a resting potential of -70 mV by pumping sodium out and potassium in to the cell, and maintain selective permeability that does not allow sodium cells or proteins bearing negatively charged residues to pass through the membrane.

> Neurons transmit information via action potentials.
  - An action potential begins with a depolarization phase during which sodium rushes into the cell.
  - After peaking at +40 mV, the cell closes sodium channels and opens potassium channels. Potassium rushes out of the cell, repolarizing it.
  - The cell briefly hyperpolarizes with a potential below -70 mV. During this phase, it is much more difficult to stimulate a new action potential.
  - The sodium-potassium pump slowly re-establishes the resting state.

> When the action potential reaches the end of the axon, the signal is transmitted to the post-synaptic membrane via a neurotransmitter.
  - Calcium rushes in to the pre-synaptic axon terminal, which sends vesicles containing neurotransmitter into the synaptic cleft. The neurotransmitter binds to the post-synaptic membrane and causes its effect.

> Neurons can be modeled both as concentration cells and as capacitors. The MCAT will want you to be familiar with these concepts from chemistry and physics and be able to apply them even if you're working through a biology passage.
> The peripheral nervous system is divided into the autonomic and somatic nervous systems.
  - The somatic nervous system controls voluntary responses via skeletal muscle.
  - The autonomic nervous system controls involuntary responses through the sympathetic (fight or flight) and the parasympathetic (rest and digest) systems.
> The central nervous system includes both the brain and the spinal cord. The various components of the brain are associated with key functions.
> The brain can be studied using a number of different imaging techniques, such as EEG, PET, fMRI, and CT scans.

This page left intentionally blank.

Practice Passage

Alzheimer's disease is a neurodegenerative disorder that predominantly affects individuals over the age of 65. As the disease progresses, patients lose much of their long-term memory, and short-term memory loss can often cause them to become irritable and withdrawn. Many researchers believe that disease symptoms are attributed to one of two proteins: amyloid-beta (Aβ) and tau (τ).

The Aβ theory suggests that the Aβ peptide (40 amino acids long) aggregates to form extracellular clumps called "plaques" in brain tissue. Mouse models that overexpress the Aβ gene demonstrate behaviors and memory loss similar to that of Alzheimer's patients. The natural function of Aβ is weakly implicated in oxidative stress protection and kinase activation. Aβ becomes dangerous when improper folding in its tertiary structure leads to accumulation of the protein at neurotoxic levels, particularly in neuroglia.

The τ theory posits that symptoms are due to hyperphosphorylation of the τ protein (up to 440 amino acids long), whose normal function is to stabilize microtubules. Hyperphosphorylation causes τ tangles inside neuronal soma and triggers microtubule collapse. Recent clinical drug research has focused on this mechanism (Table 1).

Table 1. Tau-related Treatment Mechanisms

Approach	Mechanism of action
Tideglusib	Inhibitor of GSK 3β (in Phase IIb)
	Completed but results not yet reported
TauRx	Inhibits tau aggregation (in Phase II)
LMTX	Reduces the level of aggregated and misfolded tau (in Phase III)
AADvac1	Peptide targeting pathological tau (in Phase I)

A third hypothesis centers on proline, an amino acid whose structure prevents typical protein geometry. It remains possible that it is not necessarily one microbiological entity that is responsible for the disease, but rather multiple genes or proteins gone awry.

Adapted from Boutajangout, A., & Wisniewski, T. (2014). Tau Based Therapeutic Approaches for Alzheimer's disease. Gerontology, 60(5), 381-385. under CCBY

1. The τ protein is likely to cause disruptions in which cellular processes?
    I. Mitosis
    II. Translation
    III. Intracellular transport
    A. I only
    B. I and III only
    C. II and III only
    D. I, II, and III

2. Which organelle in the hippocampal soma will exhibit the most increased activity as a direct result of overproduction of Aβ in Alzheimer's patients?
   A. Ribosome
   B. Smooth endoplasmic rleticulum
   C. Mitochondrion
   D. Nucleus

3. Microscopic analysis of Alzheimer's patient brains reveal that the plaques are abnormal clusters of "sticky" proteins that build up in the synapse. The memory problems discussed in the passage are likely due to:
   A. small clumps of proteins that block cell-to-cell signaling.
   B. plaques that activate acute immune system inflammation.
   C. disintegration of the nutrient transport system within neurons.
   D. blockage of supraspinal pathways in the CNS.

4. Suppose researchers have implicated another protein in causing Alzheimer's disease. This protein is found to be made up of 35 amino acids, including 18 proline residues. The secondary structure will most likely have a(n):
   A. large number of alpha helices.
   B. large number of beta sheets.
   C. an alternative secondary structure.
   D. even numbers of alpha helices and beta sheets.

5. When creating a clone library, why is an antibiotic resistance gene included on the plasmid to be used?
   A. Antibiotic resistance is needed in case of contamination of the media that the clones will grow on.
   B. Bacteria only take up plasmids that confer a selective advantage to them.
   C. The clones will be plated on media containing antibiotics and only successfully transformed clones will grow.
   D. Antibiotic resistance differentiates plasmids that have inserts from those that do not.

6. According to the Aβ theory, which of the following cells is most adversely affected by the progression of the disease?
   A. Enteric glia
   B. Astrocytes
   C. Schwann cells
   D. Satellite cells

7. What sense is most strongly associated with the memory functions that are adversely impacted by Alzheimer's disease?
   A. Gustation
   B. Audioreception
   C. Tactioception
   D. Olfaction

Practice Passage Explanations

Alzheimer's disease is a neurodegenerative disorder that predominantly affects individuals over the age of 65. As the disease progresses, patients lose much of their long-term memory, and short-term memory loss can often cause them to become irritable and withdrawn. Many researchers believe that disease symptoms are attributed to one of two proteins: amyloid-beta (Aβ) and tau (τ).

Key terms: Alzheimer's, Aβ, τ

Cause and effect: Aβ and τ → brain changes → Alzheimer's symptoms (memory)

The Aβ theory suggests that the Aβ peptide (40 amino acids long) aggregates to form extracellular clumps called "plaques" in brain tissue. Mouse models that overexpress the Aβ gene demonstrate behaviors and memory loss similar to that of Alzheimer's patients. The natural function of Aβ is weakly implicated in oxidative stress protection and kinase activation. Aβ becomes dangerous when improper folding in its tertiary structure leads to accumulation of the protein at neurotoxic levels, particularly in neuroglia.

Key terms: Aβ theory, oxidative stress, kinase activation, tertiary structure

Contrast: Aβ protein involved in oxidative stress protection and kinase activity; misfolding of 3° structure → neurotoxic accumulations of protein

The τ theory posits that symptoms are due to hyperphosphorylation of the τ protein (up to 440 amino acids long), whose normal function is to stabilize microtubules. Hyperphosphorylation causes τ tangles inside neuronal soma and triggers microtubule collapse. Recent clinical drug research has focused on this mechanism (Table 1).

Key terms: τ theory, hyperphosphorylation, microtubules

Cause and effect: τ tangles caused by protein hyperphosphorylation → microtubule collapse → cell death (no toxicity like Aβ theory)

Table 1. Tau-related Treatment Mechanisms

Approach	Mechanism of action
Tideglusib	Inhibitor of GSK 3β (in Phase IIb)
	Completed but results not yet reported
TauRx	Inhibits tau aggregation (in Phase II)
LMTX	Reduces the level of aggregated and misfolded tau (in Phase III)
AADvac1	Peptide targeting pathological tau (in Phase I)

A third hypothesis centers on proline, an amino acid whose structure prevents typical protein geometry. It remains possible that it is not necessarily one microbiological entity that is responsible for the disease, but rather multiple genes or proteins gone awry.

Key terms: proline, protein geometry

Cause and effect: proline ring structure → rigidity → disruption of protein geometry

Adapted from Boutajangout, A., & Wisniewski, T. (2014). Tau Based Therapeutic Approaches for Alzheimer's disease. Gerontology, 60(5), 381-385. under CCBY

1. B is correct. In paragraph 3 we are told the tau protein plays a crucial role in stabilizing microtubules. Any process that relies on proper microtubule function is likely to be affected.
    I: The τ protein disrupts microtubule stabilization, and leads to microtubule collapse. Microtubules are involved in mitosis because they are the fundamental component of the mitotic spindles.
    II: Microtubules are not involved in translation, and so this process would likely be unaffected.
    III: Microtubules are also used heavily in intracellular transport through the motor proteins dynein and kinesin. Transport would be affected by microtubule collapse.

2. A is correct. The Aβ theory states that Alzheimer's is a result of overexpression of the *Aβ* gene and Aβ protein. The most direct cause of this is protein production. The ribosome is the site of protein synthesis (i.e. translation) in the cell soma (cell body).
    B. The ribosomes are located on the rough endoplasmic reticulum, not the smooth endoplasmic reticulum. The smooth endoplasmic reticulum is responsible for synthesizing lipids and steroids, not proteins.
    C. The mitochondrion is not involved in protein synthesis. Mitochondria generate most of the cell's energy supply in the form of ATP.
    D. The nucleus is where transcription occurs, not translation.

3. A is correct. We want a disruption that would best explain memory changes in the brain. There are several mechanisms involved in memory (e.g. long-term potentiation), but all hinge on the fact that neurons need to be able to effectively communicate in order for memories to form and be recalled.
    B, C, D: These would not sufficiently explain memory problems in the patients. In fact, C is what explains the neurotoxicity in the τ theory. Tangles form inside dying cells. In areas where tangles form, the twisted strands of tau disintegrate the transport system so that nutrients and other supplies cannot move through the cells, which die. Supraspinal pathways are those that descend from the CNS out to the PNS and help control spinal reflexes (e.g. patellar tendon reflex in the knee).

4. C is correct. As stated in the final paragraph, proline may be involved in Alzheimer's. We should know that proline is a unique amino acid that has a distinctive cyclic structure that prevents standard geometry.

    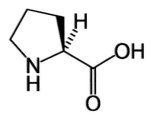

    This forces proteins to adopt secondary structures that are not alpha helices or beta sheets. It is commonly found in turns, an alternative secondary structure.
    A, B, D: Due to proline's unique nature, it will not give rise to alpha helices or beta sheets.

5. C is correct. This is the first level of selection to make sure the clones have been transformed with the correct plasmid.
    A. The clones are grown on media containing antibiotics.
    B. This is not true. Bacteria cannot "know" if a plasmid will give them an advantage.
    D. This only differentiates clones that have plasmids from those that don't.

6. B is correct. The Aβ theory is outlined in paragraph 2, which tells us that neuroglia are particularly affected by the accumulation of plaques. Neuroglia, aka glial cells, are non-neuronal cells that maintain homeostasis, form myelin, and provide support and protection for neurons in the central (oligodendrocytes, astrocytes, radial glia) and peripheral nervous systems (Schwann cells, satellite cells, enteric glial cells).

A, C, D: These are glial cells, but are found then the PNS, not the brain/CNS, which is what is affected in Alzheimer's.

7. D is correct. The sense of smell is closely linked with memory, more so than any of the other senses. Those with full olfactory function can often think of smells that evoke specific memories. For example, the scent of cut grass can conjure up recollections of a childhood spent outside playing with friends.

A, B, C: These are taste, hearing and touch, respectively.

Independent Questions

1. At the peak of an action potential, which of the following statements describes the flow of ions across the neuronal cell membrane?
   A. Sodium is flowing in, potassium is flowing out
   B. Sodium is flowing out, potassium is flowing in
   C. Sodium is not flowing, potassium is flowing out
   D. Sodium is flowing out, potassium is not flowing

2. Which term refers to the specialized part of a neuron in which action potentials are summated before propagating down the axon?
   A. Dendrite
   B. Soma
   C. Axon hillock
   D. Synaptic cleft

3. Electrical synapses, which operate through gap junctions, are composed of which protein subunit?
   A. Actin
   B. Connexin
   C. Claudins
   D. Integrins

4. Myelin is critical for the fast transmission of action potentials. In demyelinating diseases such as multiple sclerosis, the principal myelinating cells in the CNS are damaged. What are these cells, and what are the equivalent cells in the PNS?
   A. Oligodendrocytes, Schwann cells
   B. Glial cells, oligodendrocytes
   C. Schwann cells, oligodendrocytes
   D. Oligodendrocytes, glial cells

5. A researcher is using a voltage-clamp technique to analyze an axon. He notes that the axon membrane was originally at a resting potential of –70 mV, but later became slightly hyperpolarized. What may have occurred to cause this change?
   A. Voltage-gated sodium channels opened.
   B. Voltage-gated potassium channels closed.
   C. Calcium ions entered the cell.
   D. Potassium ions exited the cell.

6. The patellar reflex is elicited by striking the patellar ligament, which then activates spindle fibers in the muscle. Efferent nerves are responsible for which part of this reflex?
   A. Sensing the stretching of the patellar ligament
   B. Top-down processing of the stimulus
   C. Extension of the leg
   D. Contraction of the leg

7. The resident macrophages of the central nervous system are termed:
   A. microglia.
   B. ependymal cells.
   C. astrocytes.
   D. satellite glial cells.

8. The carotid sinus contains baroreceptors that are responsible for detecting changes in blood pressure. Which organ in the central nervous system is most responsible for responding to changes in pressure?
   A. Posterior pituitary gland
   B. Pineal gland
   C. Purkinje fibers
   D. Inferior colliculus

Independent Question Explanations

1. C is correct. At the peak of an action potential, the membrane potential of the neuron is approximately +40 mV. At this positive voltage, sodium ceases to flow into the cell (sodium channels close), while voltage-gated potassium channels open to allow potassium to flow out of the cell.

2. C is correct. The axon hillock is the specialized part of the cell body that connects to the axon. It is here that action potentials are summated before traveling down the axon.

3. B is correct. Six connexin subunits form the hemichannel that connects the cytoplasms of adjacent neurons. Claudins comprise tight junctions, while actin is involved in the formation of the cytoskeleton. Integrins form transmembrane channels involved in adhesion to the extracellular matrix.

4. A is correct. Oligodendrocytes are responsible for myelinating nerve axons in the CNS, while Schwann cells perform similar functions in the PNS.

5. D is correct. Hyperpolarization refers to a state in which the membrane potential is more negative than its resting value. As such, the "change" referenced in the question stem is the neuron becoming more negative. The only answer choice that would lead to a more negative potential is choice D, as potassium ions are positive, so their exit from the cell would make its interior more negative. The other three options would all be more likely to make the cell more positive.

6. C is correct. Efferent nerves are responsible for carrying out the reflexive action. In this case, this action is extension of the leg following activation of muscle spindle fibers in the quadricep.

7. A is correct. Microglia are a type of glial cell that function as macrophages in the central nervous system. As such, they provide an active immune defense by clearing out pathogens from the brain. Ependymal cells produce cerebrospinal fluid, astrocytes perform various support functions, and satellite glial cells regulate the microenvironment of the cell.

8. A is correct. The pituitary gland—specifically the neurohypophysis—stores antidiuretic hormone. If baroreceptors detect low blood pressure, the pituitary gland can release ADH to conserve water and thus raise the blood pressure. The pineal gland produces melatonin, while the inferior colliculus is important in auditory processing. Purkinje fibers are found in the heart.

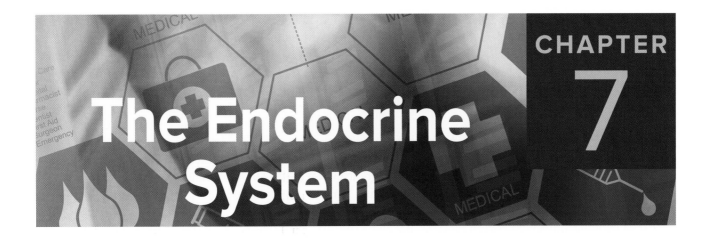

The Endocrine System

CHAPTER 7

0. Introduction

The endocrine system refers to the organs that secrete hormones, which are signal molecules secreted into the bloodstream that are used for communication and the regulation of physiological parameters.

The endocrine system is a very high-yield topic, and a thorough knowledge of it absolutely will pay off on Test Day. There are a few reasons for this that go above and beyond the basic fact that it is involved in essential physiological functions, which is true for other organ systems as well. First, the revised 2015 MCAT places a major focus on information flow and regulation, and this is precisely the function of the endocrine system, meaning that the endocrine system is a rich source of questions about these broader, more abstract topics. Second, a solid understanding of the endocrine system is important for understanding how other organ systems function, and also has implications for psychology. Third, as we will discuss in more depth later in this chapter, the chemical concept of polarity is crucial for understanding how different hormones work. Whenever you see an intersection between a biological system and a core concept from chemistry or physics, pay close attention! Such intersections are very likely to come up on Test Day. Fourth, remember that the single largest category of MCAT questions is Skill 2 (Scientific Reasoning and Problem-Solving), and the communicative and regulatory functions of the endocrine system make it a very promising target for passage-based questions testing this skill.

As you're studying, it's important for you to learn how to approach the endocrine system through multiple conceptual lenses, because this chapter contains a tremendous amount of information that can be organized and approached in many different ways. On Test Day, you will have to apply information about the endocrine system in the context of a specific passage or question, and you must know the material from multiple different angles in order to do so efficiently and accurately—just like, as a future physician, you will have to apply your knowledge of the endocrine system to the medical conditions of individual patients. At a minimum, you should understand (1) how the chemical structure of hormones influences their effects on the body, (2) the physiological effects of hormones and how they are regulated, and (3) the organs that make up the endocrine system and which hormones they secrete. These goals are reflected in this chapter, which starts with a discussion of the

> **> > CONNECTIONS < <**
>
> **Psychology Chapter 1 and Biology Chapter 10**

mechanisms and regulatory principles of the endocrine system, then moves to an overview of the physiological effects of hormones, and concludes with a review of the organs involved in the endocrine system.

1. Mechanisms and Regulation

Terminology

A reasonable first question about the endocrine system would be "why do they call it that?" In fact, a crucial first step in studying the endocrine system is to be able to give a good answer to this question, and in particular, to be able to define what it means to say that something is an endocrine gland.

Let's start with the difference between exocrine and endocrine glands, because this contrast is key to understanding the definition of an endocrine gland. The basic difference is that exocrine glands secrete their products into ducts, whereas endocrine glands secrete hormones directly into the circulatory system. Exocrine glands are found in the digestive system, and in general, are responsible for secreting bodily fluids, such as sweat (sweat glands), skin oil (sebaceous glands), earwax (ceruminous glands), breastmilk (mammary glands), saliva (salivary glands), tears (lacrimal glands), and mucus (mucous glands). The most important endocrine glands, discussed in more detail later in the chapter, are the hypothalamus, pituitary gland, thyroid gland, parathyroid, adrenal cortex and medulla, pancreas, and gonads. An organ can have both exocrine and endocrine glands. The best-known example of this is the pancreas, which releases digestive enzymes through ducts (exocrine function) and releases key hormones such as insulin and glucagon (endocrine function). The liver is also an example of this, as it secretes bile through the bile duct (exocrine function) and also secretes hormones such as angiotensinogen.

MCAT STRATEGY > > >

These terms can be difficult to keep separate, but a careful study of their prefixes can help with these and other medical terms. For exocrine, think of the same "ex-" as in "external"—exocrine glands secrete something *out* through ducts. The prefix "endo-" means "inside," so think of endocrine glands as secreting things into your bloodstream, which runs *inside* of you. "Para" means "close to or next to," so paracrine signaling is signaling to nearby cells. "Auto-" means "self-," so autocrine signaling is when a cell affects itself. "Juxta-" is less common, but you can think of words like *juxtaposition* or even being *just next to* something.

Although the definition of an endocrine gland is the single most important aspect of this discussion of terminology, it's helpful to have an understanding of all the other terms describing signaling and secretion that end in "-crine," in order to eliminate potential sources of confusion.

One set of "-crine" terms refers to the physical scope of a signaling pattern. Paracrine signaling occurs when a cell secretes a signaling molecule that acts on nearby cells, and is heavily involved in differentiation in embryonic development. The crucial point of contrast with endocrine signaling is that endocrine signaling has long-distance effects throughout the entire organism. Autocrine signaling takes place when a cell releases a molecule that acts on itself, and is thought to play a role in the development of cancer. Less commonly, you may encounter juxtacine signaling, which refers to signaling that requires cells to be in close contact with each other—that is, juxtacrine signaling is even more local than paracrine signaling.

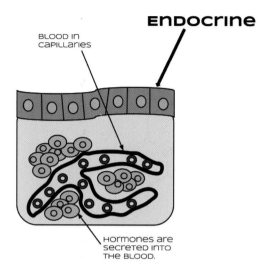
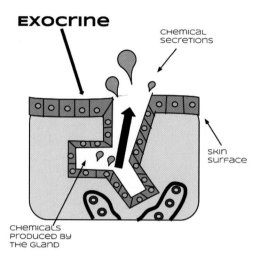

Figure 1. Endocrine versus exocrine signaling.

Another set of "-crine" terms is used to classify ways in which exocrine glands release substances. These terms are relatively low-yield for the MCAT, and are very unlikely to be the primary focus of a question, but are worth being able to recognize if they appear among the answer choices. If a cell releases its secretions through exocytosis, it is known as a merocrine cell; the term eccrine refers more specifically to merocrine cells in the sweat glands. Apocrine cells release their secretions through membrane-bound vesicles, and some examples include the cells of the mammary gland and certain sweat glands in the human body. Be sure not to confuse "apocrine" with "autocrine!" Finally, holocrine secretion results from rupture of the plasma membrane, destroying the cell and releasing its product from the cytoplasm into the lumen. Examples include the sebaceous glands of the skin.

Structure and Mechanisms of Action

Hormones can be classified according to their chemical structure as peptide hormones, steroid hormones, or amino acid derivatives. The distinction between peptide and steroid hormones is especially important because this difference in chemical structure, reflecting two high-yield classes of molecules you should be aware of from biochemistry, causes peptide and steroid hormones to function differently.

So, what's the difference? As the name implies, peptide hormones are composed of a polypeptide chain—that is, a chain of amino acids. Steroid hormones are derivatives of the lipid cholesterol, and have a characteristic four-ring structure. This leads us to the most fundamental distinction between these two classes of hormones: peptide hormones are hydrophilic, and steroid hormones are hydrophobic. This is the key to understanding why peptide and steroid hormones have different mechanisms of action and tend to have different physiological effects.

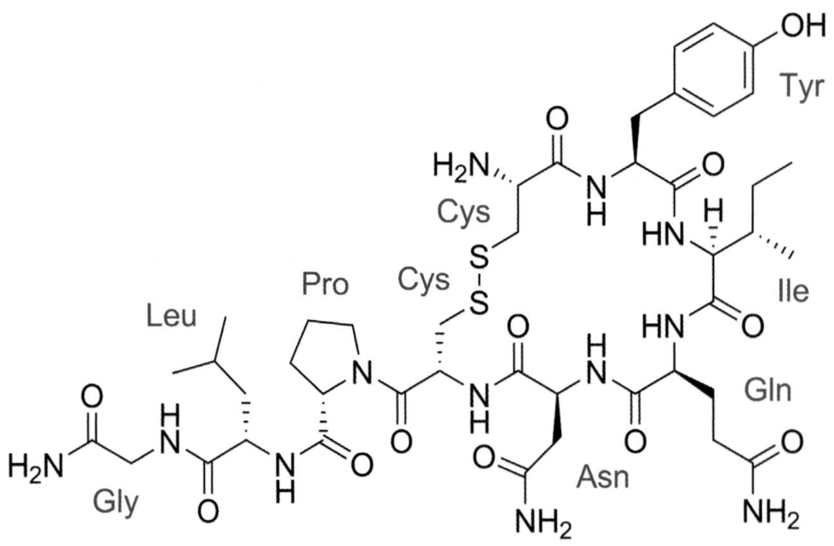

Figure 2. Structure of oxytocin, a peptide hormone.

> > CONNECTIONS < <

Chapter 1 of Biology

First, let's explore the consequences of peptide hormones being hydrophilic. Since they're hydrophilic, they diffuse freely in the blood, but cannot freely cross the lipid bilayer membrane of their target cells. This means that they have to exert their effects through receptors embedded on the outer surface of the plasma membrane, which then change their conformation to produce an effect in the target cell (also known as the effector), often through a second messenger, such as cyclic AMP (cAMP), cyclic GMP (cGMP), or inositol triphosphate (IP_3). Second messenger systems (the hormone itself is referred to as the first messenger) result in a signal cascade that allows the signal to undergo rapid amplification within the cell, which can cause a rapid and intense impact on cellular function. Therefore, peptide hormones are typically associated with rapid, short-term changes in physiological function. We will see several examples of this below when we discuss the endocrine control of blood chemistry.

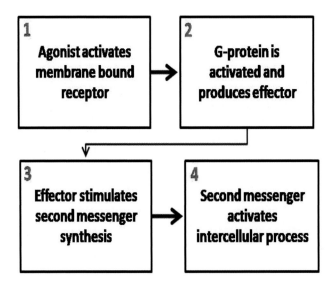

Figure 3. Second messenger systems.

How does this picture change for steroid hormones, which are hydrophobic and therefore have a solubility profile opposite that of peptide hormones? First, steroid hormones are not soluble in the bloodstream, and therefore require transport proteins to reach their targets. These transport hormones may be relatively specific (for example, sex hormone-binding globulin transports estradiol and testosterone) or relatively non-specific (for example, albumin). Once steroid hormones reach their target cells, their small size and hydrophobicity allow them to diffuse directly through the lipid bilayer membrane and enter the cell. Once in the cytosol, they bind with nuclear receptors. The nuclear receptor-hormone complex undergoes a conformational change (one noteworthy type is dimerization, in which two receptor-hormone complexes are paired) and is translocated to the nucleus. In the nucleus, the receptor-hormone complex binds directly to DNA and affects gene transcription. Since steroid hormones work by modulating gene transcription, they are associated with slower-onset and longer-lasting physiological effects.

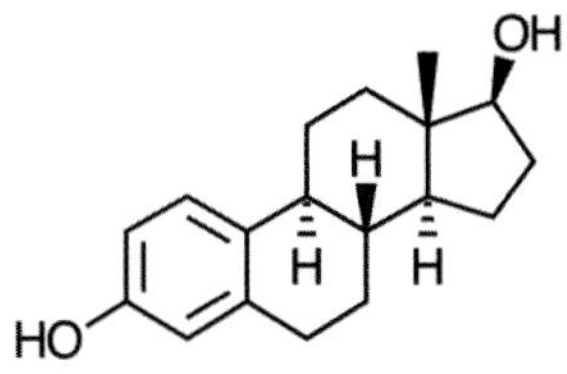

estradiol (a form of estrogen)

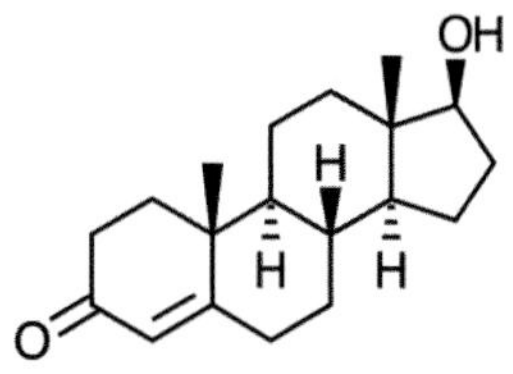

testosterone

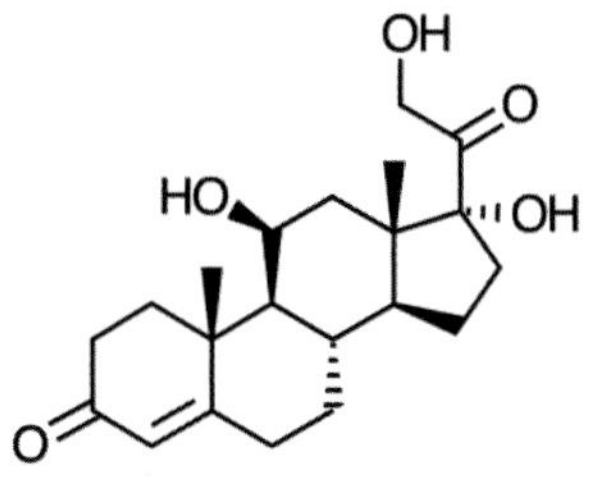

cortisol

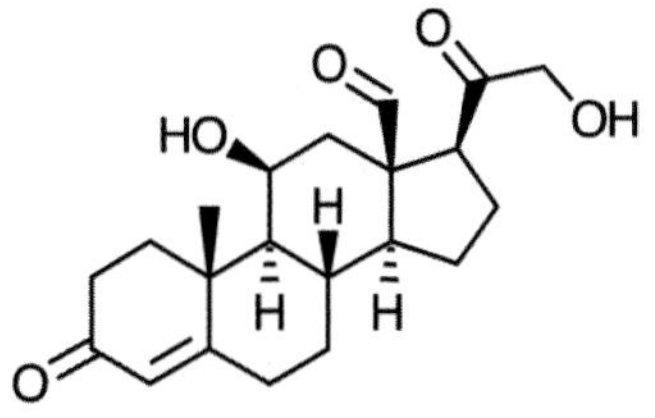

aldosterone

Figure 4. Structure of steroid hormones.

Another important distinction between peptide hormones and steroid hormones is how they are synthesized and released into circulation. Peptide hormones are produced in stages; they are first translated as preprohormones, which are early precursors that are transferred to the rough ER and modified into prohormones, which are inactive immediate precursors of the hormones. Prohormones are processed in the Golgi apparatus, where they are cleaved by endopeptidases and may be modified by the addition of carbohydrates to generate the final, active form of the hormone. The hormones are then packaged into vesicles to be released through exocytosis. In contrast, steroid hormones are synthesized from cholesterol in the smooth ER and diffuse directly through the cell membrane.

MCAT STRATEGY > > >

The connection between hormone structure and function is a prototypical example of how the MCAT likes to test the interplay between biochemical structures and physiological outcomes. Walk through this line of reasoning a couple of times and then be alert to other instances where it could be applied, both while studying and eventually on Test Day itself.

These points, as well as some other distinctions between peptide and steroid hormones, are summarized below in Table 1.

Table 1. Key differences between peptide and steroid hormones.

	PEPTIDE HORMONES	STEROID HORMONES
Biochemical precursor	Amino acids	Cholesterol (lipid)
Size	Relatively large but variable	Small
Polarity	Polar	Nonpolar
Hydrophilic or hydrophobic?	Hydrophilic	Hydrophobic
Location of synthesis	Rough ER → Golgi → vesicles → exocytosis	Smooth ER
Intermediate stages?	Yes (preprohormones, prohormones, hormones)	No
Solubility in blood	Soluble; freely diffuse	Insoluble; require transport protein
Type of receptor	Membrane-bound receptor	Nuclear receptor
Interaction with lipid membrane of target cell	Cannot diffuse	Diffuse through membrane
Mechanism of effect	Second messenger system in cytosol	DNA transcription in nucleus
Physiological effects	Fast onset, short-term	Slow onset, longer-term
Typical functions	Regulation of other hormones, short-term responses	Sex, sugar [glucocorticoids], and salt [mineralocorticoids] (the three S's)
Examples	Thyroid-stimulating hormone, oxytocin, insulin, calcitonin	Estrogen, testosterone, cortisol, aldosterone

MCAT STRATEGY > > >

Most of the hormones you have to know for the MCAT are peptide hormones. Learn the steroid hormones and amino acid-derived hormones separately, and assume that anything else is a peptide hormone unless a passage or question stem tells you differently.

Finally, amino acid-derived hormones are small hormones derived from individual amino acids. The thyroid hormones (T_3, triiodothyronine and T_4, thyroxine) are tyrosine derivatives that are lipid-soluble and behave much like steroid hormones, with powerful and long-lasting effects on metabolism. In contrast, the catecholamines epinephrine and norepinephrine are also derived from tyrosine, but are water-soluble and act similarly to peptide hormones, exerting powerful short-term effects in response to stress. Melatonin, which plays a major role in regulating wakefulness cycles, is both lipid-soluble and water-soluble and is derived from tryptophan.

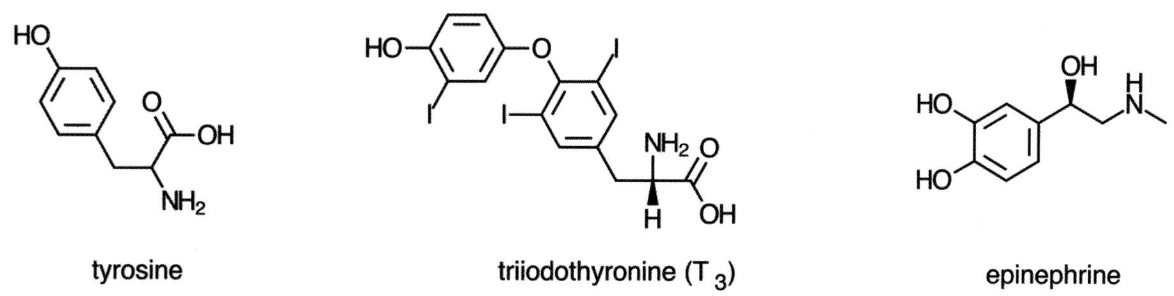

tyrosine   triiodothyronine (T $_3$)   epinephrine

Figure 5. Structures of tyrosine, T$_3$, and epinephrine.

Regulation

So far, we've been talking about hormones in terms of their physiological effects, but it's also possible for hormones to affect the release of other hormones. Such hormones are known as tropic hormones. Nontropic hormones target other cell types and directly induce physiological effects.

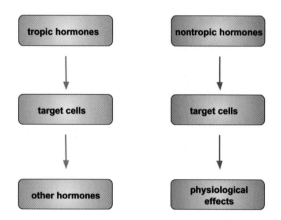

Figure 6. Tropic vs. nontropic hormones.

On Test Day, it is absolutely crucial for you to understand the broad principles underlying endocrine regulation, and in particular the distinction between negative and positive feedback. Negative feedback loops are by far the most common regulatory mechanism in the endocrine system, and can be thought of in several ways. From a functional point of view, negative feedback systems serve to maintain homeostasis—that is, to maintain a relatively constant value of a physiological parameter despite external stimuli. From a technical point of view, negative feedback refers to a phenomenon in which a "downstream" product of a pathway inhibits the pathway itself.

A classic example of a negative feedback loop is the hypothalamus-anterior pituitary-adrenal cortex (HPA) axis. The hypothalamus secretes a tropic hormone known as corticotropin-releasing hormone (CRH), which acts on the anterior pituitary gland and stimulates the release of another tropic hormone known as adrenocorticotropic hormone (ACTH). ACTH then acts on the adrenal cortex, causing the release of cortisol, a steroid hormone that plays a role in long-term responses to stress. Elevated levels of cortisol then inhibit the release of both CRH and ACTH. As always, when studying a synthetic or regulatory pathway, the first question we should ask is: what's the point of this from a physiological point of view? In this case, the negative feedback exerted by cortisol on CRH and ACTH inhibits further cortisol production, which prevents levels of cortisol from skyrocketing out of control and inducing an overly intense long-term stress response.

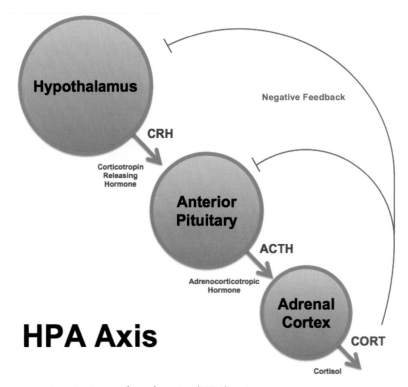

Figure 7. Hypothalamus-anterior pituitary-adrenal cortex (HPA) axis.

Positive feedback loops in the endocrine system are much rarer. From a functional perspective, a positive feedback loop works to push a system out of its normal limits, and from a technical point of view it means that the "downstream" product of a pathway stimulates its own production. A common example of a positive feedback system involves oxytocin, a small peptide hormone secreted by the posterior pituitary gland. Oxytocin has several effects, as we'll discuss in more detail later in this chapter, but one of its most important effects is that it stimulates contractions of the uterus at the end of pregnancy. Uterine contractions stimulate the release of more oxytocin, which stimulates stronger uterine contractions, and the process continues to amplify itself through labor and childbirth (also known as parturition). Note that this process has a well-defined external physiological endpoint. Without such an endpoint, positive feedback loops would tend to spiral out of control, resulting in dangerously extreme physiological states.

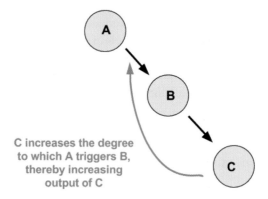

negative feedback

C prevents A from triggering B, thereby reducing output of C

positive feedback

C increases the degree to which A triggers B, thereby increasing output of C

Figure 8. Negative vs. positive feedback loops.

A concept related to regulation that you should be aware of for Test Day is that of neuroendocrinology, a term that basically refers to the fact that the nervous and endocrine systems "talk to" each other. From a big picture point of view, this is necessary because the nervous and the endocrine systems can be thought of as the two communication networks of the body, and they have to interact to make sure that the body responds appropriately to stimuli. An example of how this plays out is provided by the HPA axis, which we presented above as starting with the release of CRH by the hypothalamus to stimulate ACTH secretion in the anterior pituitary. A natural follow-up question would be: why does the hypothalamus release CRH? The answer is that it does so in response to signaling from the nervous system regarding stressful stimuli. Neuronal signaling allows the body to quickly integrate information about external stimuli and new developments in the body, which then needs to be relayed to the endocrine system. For this reason, the hypothalamus is often considered the bridge between the nervous and endocrine systems.

> **MCAT STRATEGY >>>**
>
> You should be very, very careful about choosing "positive feedback" as the answer to any question on the MCAT. A passage may point you in that direction, but in general, when thinking about endocrine regulation (and, for that matter, the regulation of biochemical pathways), your default assumption should always be negative feedback.

2. Physiological Effects of Hormones

Now that we've covered the basic principles governing the endocrine system, let's move on to discuss the specific physiological effects of various hormones.

Glucose Levels

Glucose can be thought of as the body's main source of fuel under most circumstances, and the regulation of blood glucose levels is therefore critically important in maintaining overall metabolic function. The two main hormones associated with glucose regulation are insulin and glucagon, although growth hormone (GH), epinephrine, and cortisol also affect glucose levels.

Insulin is a peptide hormone released by the beta cells of the pancreas in response to high blood glucose levels, and its basic function is to reduce blood glucose levels by promoting the transport of glucose into cells via insulin receptors, which activate membrane-bound glucose transporters and increase the transport of amino acids into the cell. Let's work through the consequences of increased glucose uptake in cells. First, the cells have to do something with all of this glucose, and there are three basic options: cells can use the glucose immediately through glycolysis, muscle and liver cells can store the glucose as glycogen, and adipocytes (fat cells) can mobilize fatty acids to store downstream byproducts of glucose metabolism in the form of triglycerides. Insulin upregulates all of those processes, as well as protein synthesis. A consequence of all of these effects is that insulin reduces the rate of glycogenolysis, lipolysis, fatty acid oxidation in the muscle and liver, and protein breakdown in the muscles. The effects of insulin are numerous, but they are all logically linked in that they reflect the presence of excess available energy in the form of glucose.

Glucagon is a peptide hormone released by the alpha cells of the pancreas and is essentially the opposite of insulin. It is released in response to low glucose levels and has the effect of increasing blood glucose levels by promoting glycogenolysis and gluconeogenesis in liver cells.

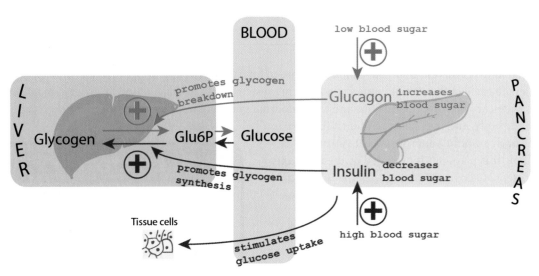

Figure 9. Regulation of insulin and glucagon.

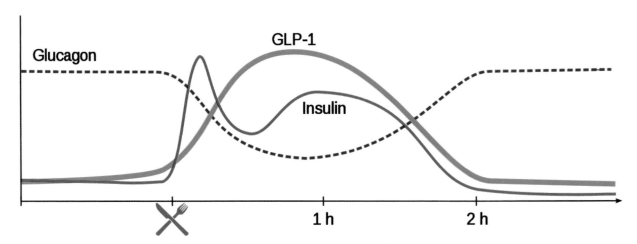

Figure 10. Effects of insulin and glucagon over time in response to a meal.

As important as insulin and glucagon are, they are not the only hormones that increase blood glucose levels. Cortisol (the main example of a class of hormones known as glucocorticoids) is released by the adrenal cortex. It is associated with long-term responses to stress and increases blood glucose levels. Epinephrine, which is released by the adrenal medulla and plays a major role in the fight-or-flight response to immediate stress, also raises blood glucose levels. In addition, under conditions of intense physical stress, as well as during periods of physical growth, growth hormone

(GH) can be released. GH has many functions, including increasing blood glucose levels due to its antagonistic effects on insulin. Nonetheless, on Test Day, if you see a question about blood glucose levels, you should immediately think of the insulin-glucagon pair, unless the passage or question points you specifically in the direction of other hormones that may affect blood glucose levels.

Calcium Levels

Calcium plays a key role in multiple physiological functions, most notably in bones, neurotransmitter release, muscle contractions, and as a second messenger within the cell. The body must maintain serum Ca^{2+} levels within very tight ranges, and the primary hormones that do so are parathyroid hormone (PTH) and calcitonin.

PTH is secreted from the parathyroid in response to low blood calcium levels and elevates blood calcium levels by stimulating increased activity in osteoclasts, which are cells that break down bone, releasing calcium into the blood. Calcitonin has the opposite effect; it is released by the C cells of the thyroid and inhibits osteoclast activity. Just as a review, osteoblasts are cells that help build bone—and therefore reduce blood calcium levels by "storing" calcium in bone tissue—whereas osteoclasts are cells that break down bone, releasing calcium into the bloodstream.

CLINICAL CONNECTIONS > > >

Diabetes mellitus (DM) is one of the most important diseases to be aware of for the MCAT. Diabetes is commonly associated with elevated glucose levels (hyperglycemia), but underlyingly is a disorder of insulin metabolism. Type 1 DM is an autoimmune disorder in which the beta cells of the pancreas are destroyed; as a result, insulin is not produced. Patients with type 1 DM require treatment in the form of insulin injections. Type 2 DM involves insulin resistance that develops as a result of chronically elevated blood sugar levels. In its initial stages, type 2 DM can be treated with drugs that improve insulin response, such as metformin, but patients with type 2 DM may also eventually require insulin injections.

MCAT STRATEGY > > >

You can remember what glucagon does by recalling that it kicks in when *glucose* is *gone*.

> > CONNECTIONS < <

Chapter 12 of Biology

Modeling

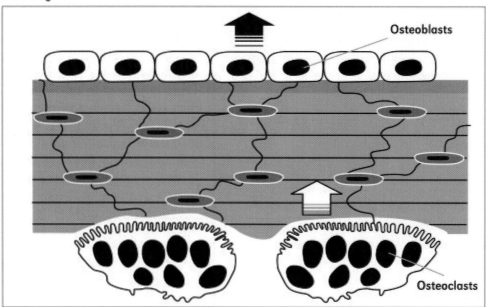

Remodeling

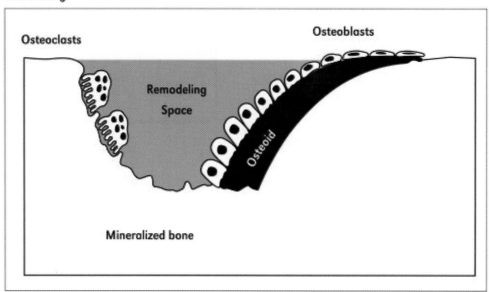

Figure 11. Osteoblasts and osteoclasts.

Although it is not always considered a hormone, vitamin D plays a crucial role in the regulation of serum calcium and phosphate levels, and is definitely worth being aware of on Test Day. Vitamin D exists in multiple forms, not all of which are relevant for calcium regulation. Cholecalciferol is the inactive form of vitamin D_3, which is processed to form calcitriol, which is the biologically active form that affects calcium and phosphate levels. Calcitriol has a similar function to PTH in that it increases serum calcium levels, but it does so primarily through a different mechanism: it promotes the absorption of Ca^{2+} from the gastrointestinal tract.

> > **CONNECTIONS** < <

Chapter 10 of Biology

Fluid Regulation

Another crucial task performed by the endocrine system is the regulation of fluid levels in the body—which you can think of in terms of blood volume for the purposes of the MCAT—and the optimal osmolarity of the blood. There are two basic scenarios that the body can encounter: too little fluid and too much fluid. Let's first think through how these conditions manifest in terms of physiological markers, because this is a prerequisite to correctly applying the information described in this section on Test Day. Having too little fluid in one's system manifests in three important ways: reduced blood volume (because relatively little water is present in the blood plasma), reduced blood pressure (a consequence of reduced blood volume—less liquid is present to exert pressure against the walls of the blood vessels), and increased blood osmolarity (the same solutes are present, but less solvent is available). Correspondingly, increases in the amount of fluid present in the system manifest as increased blood volume (because more water is present in the blood plasma), increased blood pressure (more blood volume means more pressure against the walls of the blood vessels), and decreased blood osmolarity (the same solutes are present, but more solvent is available).

> **MCAT STRATEGY > > >**
>
> Practice working through these causal relationships until they become second nature. If given information about relative levels of fluid, you should immediately be able to predict the consequences for blood volume, pressure, and osmolarity.

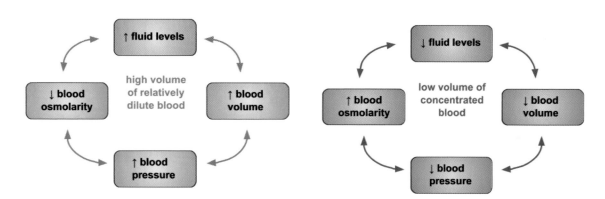

Figure 12. Relationships between fluid levels, blood volume, blood pressure, and blood osmolarity.

Two major hormones respond to low fluid levels by increasing fluid retention: aldosterone (the main example of a class of steroid hormones known as mineralocorticoids) and anti-diuretic hormone (ADH), a peptide hormone that is also known as vasopressin. However, these two hormones have different mechanisms. Aldosterone works by increasing sodium absorption in the distal convoluted tubule and collecting duct of the nephron, which drives water absorption. Aldosterone also increases excretion of potassium and hydrogen ions in the urine. In contrast to aldosterone, the effects of which focus

> **MCAT STRATEGY > > >**
>
> The presence of an *s* in aldosterone can help you remember that its mechanism involves *s*odium reabsorption.

on solutes, ADH increases the permeability of the collecting duct to water, thereby increasing water absorption. A consequence of this is that ADH acts to reduce the osmolarity of blood by increasing the amount of water present without changing the solute levels, whereas aldosterone does not affect osmolarity because sodium reabsorption drives water absorption.

ADH is released by the posterior pituitary gland in response to low blood pressure and high plasma osmolarity (remember that these are two indicators of the same basic problem of dehydration!). Aldosterone is released by the adrenal cortex in response to low blood pressure, but is regulated by the renin-angiotensin-aldosterone system, as illustrated in Figure 13. In response to low blood pressure, the juxtaglomerular cells of the kidney release an enzyme known as renin. Renin converts angiotensinogen, which is an inactive plasma protein (analogous to a prohormone), into angiotensin I. In the lungs, angiotensin-converting enzyme converts angiotensin I to angiotensin II, which is the immediate stimulus of aldosterone release. Aldosterone restores blood pressure, which in turn inhibits the release of renin, in another example of a negative feedback loop.

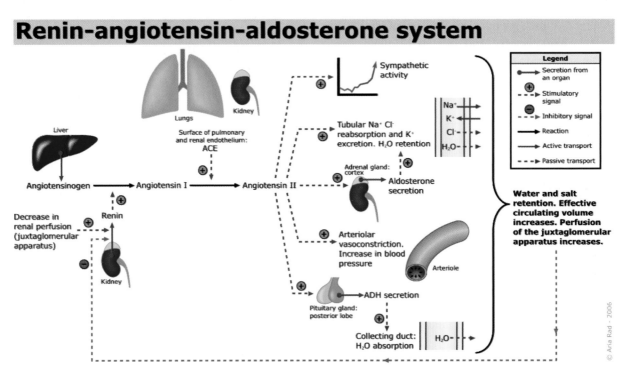

Figure 13. Renin-angiotensin-aldosterone system.

Although less high-yield for the MCAT, it is worth being aware of atrial natriuretic peptide (ANP; also known as atrial natriuretic factor [ANF]), which is a hormone that the endocrine system uses to deal with the problem of excess blood volume. Essentially, it is the opposite of aldosterone. It is released in response to high blood volume and decreases sodium reabsorption in the distal convoluted tubule and the collecting duct, as well as increasing the glomerular filtration rate and inhibiting aldosterone release.

Stress

We've already discussed stress to some extent in the section on blood glucose regulation, since the elevation of blood glucose levels is one element of the body's response to stress. The most important differentiation for the MCAT is between long-term and short-term responses to stress.

The steroid hormone cortisol is associated with long-term responses to stress. Cortisol is released from the adrenal cortex and is a member of the class of hormones known as glucocorticoids (other examples include cortisone and prednisone, but cortisol is by far the most important for Test Day). Cortisol has two main effects that you should be aware of. First, it increases blood glucose levels by stimulating gluconeogenesis and acting as an insulin antagonist, facilitating insulin resistance. Second, it reduces inflammation by inhibiting certain inflammatory immune responses.

Short-term responses to stress (the "fight or flight" response) are associated with epinephrine and norepinephrine, which are hormones (although norepinephrine also functions as a neurotransmitter) derived from tyrosine. Epinephrine and norepinephrine belong to a family of hormones known as catecholamines and are released from the adrenal medulla. They increase blood glucose levels through a variety of mechanisms, including glycogenolysis, gluconeogenesis, and glucagon release. These hormones also lead to a broad range of systematic responses, including an increased heart rate, respiratory rate, lipolysis, and vasodilation of the blood vessels supplying skeletal muscles combined with vasoconstriction of the blood vessels supplying the digestive system.

The effects of epinephrine and norepinephrine presented here are very similar to those of the sympathetic nervous system, as discussed in Chapter 6. Some terminological clarification is in order to understand why this topic needs to be discussed in the context of the endocrine system as well. We briefly mentioned that norepinephrine is both a neurotransmitter and a hormone—how can this be? Norepinephrine is a neurotransmitter when it is used to relay signals between neurons in the sympathetic nervous system, but when it is released into the blood to induce systemic effects in other organ systems, it functions as a hormone. Analogously, sympathetic nervous system signaling (together with adrenocorticotropic hormone [ACTH]) triggers the release of epinephrine into the blood, at which point it functions as a hormone to exert its downstream effects. Another way of thinking about this might involve a division of labor between the nervous system and the endocrine system in response to stress. The sympathetic nervous system has the job of recognizing immediate stressors and telling the body to respond accordingly, and then the endocrine system is involved in making the stress response itself happen in all of the various organs whose functions are altered as part of this process.

CLINICAL CONNECTIONS > > >

Anti-hypertensive medications are a mainstay of the everyday practice of medicine, and physicians must understand the different mechanisms of blood pressure medications in order to prescribe them appropriately. The renin-angiotensin-aldosterone system is an area that scientists have targeted with this goal in mind. Inhibitors of angiotensin-converting enzyme (ACE inhibitors) prevent the formation of angiotensin II, which reduces blood pressure by inhibiting aldosterone secretion and counteracting the tendency of angiotensin II itself to raise blood pressure.

MCAT STRATEGY > > >

Information about the function of a substance is often reflected in its nomenclature. Imagine you had never before heard of atrial natriuretic peptide and wanted to know what it does. Well, "atrial" tells you that it's secreted from the heart muscles, and "peptide" tells you that it's a peptide. For the "natriuretic" part of the name, think of the chemical symbol for sodium (Na), and "uretic" might point you towards thinking about urine! This doesn't give you the whole story about its function, but it at least gives you somewhere to start reasoning about it. Leveraging information like this can be very helpful in tackling passages.

CLINICAL CONNECTIONS > > >

Cortisone is a glucocorticoid with anti-inflammatory effects that is often directly injected to treat inflamed muscles or joints.

> > CONNECTIONS < <

Chapter 6 of Biology

Metabolic Rate

The thyroid hormones triiodothyronine (T_3) and thyroxine (T_4) regulate the body's general metabolic rate. T_4 contains four iodine atoms and is the prohormone, or precursor, of T_3, which contains three iodine atoms; beyond this structural difference, T_3 and T_4 can be thought of as synonymous for the purposes of the MCAT. They are released in response to thyroid-stimulating hormone (TSH). Insufficient levels of thyroid hormones, often caused by an iodine deficiency, leads to hypothyroidism, which is a clinical condition characterized by fatigue, cold intolerance, weight gain, and reductions in body temperature, heart rate, and respiratory rate. Hyperthyroidism, which may be caused by a tumor, results in the opposite set of symptoms.

Reproduction and Secondary Sex Characteristics

These topics are discussed in greater detail in Chapter 8, which focuses on the reproductive system, but it is nonetheless useful to briefly review the hormonal regulation of reproduction and secondary sex characteristics in the context of the endocrine system as a whole, in order to gain an appreciation of how high-level themes such as the contrast between peptide and steroid hormones and the concepts of negative and positive feedback can be applied.

Estrogen and testosterone, which are steroid hormones secreted by the ovaries and testes, respectively, are the two most important hormones involved in reproduction and the development of secondary sex characteristics. For the MCAT, you should be aware that estrogen is involved in the regulation of the menstrual cycle and contributes to the development of female secondary sex characteristics, while testosterone contributes to the development of male secondary sex characteristics. In reality, both hormones have a complex profile of systemic effects, but a full discussion of the effects of these hormones can wait for medical school. Another steroid hormone involved in the reproductive system that you should be aware of is progesterone, which prepares the uterus for implantation and maintains it throughout pregnancy. Note how all three of these hormones have relatively long-term effects, as is typical for steroid hormones!

The release of estrogen and testosterone is stimulated by luteinizing hormone (LH), which is a peptide hormone secreted in response to low levels of these hormones. LH also stimulates estrogen release during the luteal surge of the menstrual cycle, leading to ovulation, and in response to the release of gonadotropin-releasing hormone (GnRH). Another peptide hormone released in response to GnRH that plays an important role in reproduction is follicle-stimulating hormone (FSH), which, as the name suggests, promotes the growth of ovarian follicles in females. It also has the effect of promoting spermatogenesis in males. During pregnancy, human chorionic gonadotropin (hCG) maintains the corpus luteum and induces it to secrete progesterone during the first trimester.

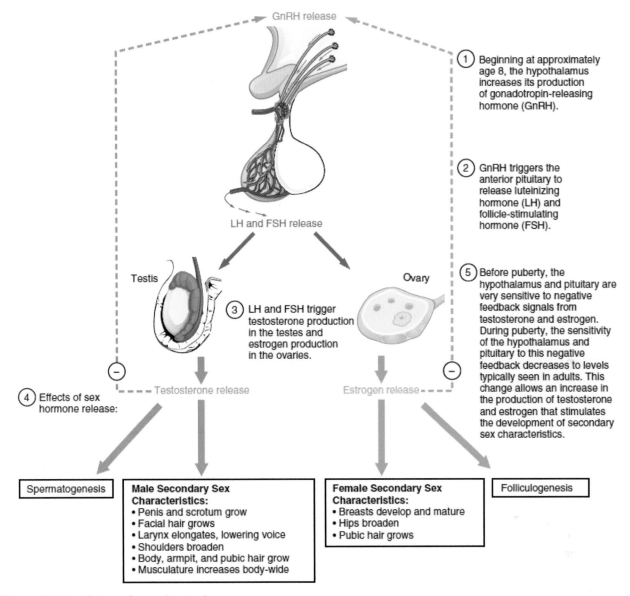

Figure 14. Regulation of reproductive hormones.

A final hormone related to reproduction that you should be aware of is prolactin, which acts on the mammary glands to enable milk production. Prolactin is released in response to the reduced levels of dopamine that occur after the placenta is expelled during childbirth. Dopamine secretion from the hypothalamus is also reduced in response to an infant latching onto the breast, thereby facilitating milk production.

Regulation of Other Hormones (Tropic Hormones)

Finally, tropic hormones have the function of regulating other hormones, thereby contributing to the exquisitely fine-tuned ability of the endocrine system to respond to various stimuli.

Several crucial tropic hormones are released by the anterior pituitary gland. Thyroid-stimulating hormone (TSH) promotes the release of the thyroid hormones T_3 and T_4, while adrenocorticotropic hormone (ACTH) stimulates the adrenal cortex to release mineralocorticoids and glucocorticoids (which belong to the class of hormones known as corticosteroids). Luteinizing hormone (LH) is a tropic hormone that stimulates the release of estrogen and testosterone, as discussed in the section dealing with reproduction, and follicle-stimulating hormone (FSH) activates further signaling pathways to promote the development of ovarian follicles and spermatogenesis.

Although the above tropic hormones are the most important for the MCAT, it is worth being aware that tropic hormones can themselves be regulated by other tropic hormones. Many such hormones are secreted from the hypothalamus, which can be thought of as the bridge between the nervous and endocrine system. Examples of tropic hormones secreted from the hypothalamus include gonadotropin-releasing hormone (GnRH), which stimulates the release of LH and FSH; thyrotropin-releasing hormone (TRH), which stimulates the release of TSH; corticotropin-releasing factor (CRF), which stimulates the release of ACTH; and growth hormone-releasing hormone (GHRH), which stimulates the release of growth hormone.

A final tropic hormone to be aware of is human chorionic gonadotropin (hCG), which stimulates the release of progesterone to maintain the uterus throughout the first trimester of pregnancy.

The following table summarizes the hormones essential for the MCAT according to function. Since some hormones are involved in multiple functions, this table contains some duplication of hormones.

Table 2. Hormones involved in crucial functions of the endocrine system.

FUNCTION	HORMONE	STRUCTURAL TYPE	STIMULUS	EFFECT	LOCATION OF SECRETION
Glucose levels	Insulin	Peptide	↑ Glucose	↓ Glucose	Pancreas (beta cells)
	Glucagon	Peptide	↓ Glucose	↑ Glucose	Pancreas (alpha cells)
	Cortisol	Steroid	Stress	↑ Glucose (& other systemic effects)	Adrenal cortex
	Epinephrine	AA-derived (polar)			Adrenal medulla
	Growth hormone (GH)	Peptide	Stress (and growth)	↑ Glucose	Anterior pituitary
Calcium levels	Parathyroid hormone (PTH)	Peptide	↓ Ca^{2+}	↑ Ca^{2+}	Parathyroid
	Calcitonin	Peptide	↑ Ca^{2+}	↓ Ca^{2+}	Thyroid
Fluid regulation	Aldosterone	Steroid	↓ BP, ↑ osmolarity, angiotensin II	↑ Na^+ reabsorption in DCT, ↑ fluid levels	Adrenal cortex
	Anti-diuretic hormone (ADH, vasopressin)	Peptide	↓ BP, ↑ osmolarity	↑ H_2O reabsorption in collecting duct	Posterior pituitary
	Atrial natriuretic peptide (ANP)	Peptide	↑ Blood volume	↓ Na^+ reabsorption in DCT, ↓ fluid levels	Heart muscle cells

Stress	Cortisol	Steroid	Stress (long-term)	↑ Glucose, ↓ inflammation	Adrenal cortex
	Epinephrine	Amino acid-derived (polar)	Stress (short-term)	↑ Glucose, sympathetic nervous system/ fight-or-flight response	Adrenal medulla
	Norepinephrine	Amino acid-derived (polar)			
Metabolic rate	T$_3$ and T$_4$	Amino acid-derived (nonpolar)	TSH	↑ Basal metabolic rate	Thyroid
Reproduction and development	Estrogen	Steroid	LH	Female secondary sex characteristics, menstrual cycle regulation	Ovaries
	Testosterone	Steroid		Male secondary sex characteristics	Testes
	Progesterone	Steroid	hCG	Prepares and maintains uterus for pregnancy	Ovaries, placenta
	Luteinizing hormone (LH)	Peptide	GnRH, ↓ estrogen or testosterone	↑ Estrogen or testosterone	Anterior pituitary
	Follicle-stimulating hormone (FSH)	Peptide	GnRH	Follicle development, spermatogenesis	Anterior pituitary
	Human chorionic gonadotropin (hCG)	Peptide	Implantation	↑ Progesterone	Placenta
	Prolactin	Peptide	↓ Dopamine	Milk production	Anterior pituitary
	Oxytocin	Peptide	Neural signaling (uterine stretching, nipple stimulation)	Smooth muscle contraction (uterine contractions in labor, milk release in breastfeeding)	Posterior pituitary

Tropic hormones	Thyroid-stimulating hormone (TSH)	Peptide	TRH	↑ Thyroid hormones	Anterior pituitary
	Adreno-corticotropic hormone (ACTH)	Peptide	CRF	↑ Adrenal cortex activity (↑ corticosteroids)	Anterior pituitary
	Luteinizing hormone (LH)	Peptide	GnRH, ↓ estrogen or testosterone	↑ Estrogen or testosterone	Anterior pituitary
	Follicle-stimulating hormone (FSH)	Peptide	GnRH	Follicle development, spermatogenesis	Anterior pituitary
	Human chorionic gonadotropin (hCG)	Peptide	Implantation	↑ Progesterone	Placenta
	Gonadotropin-releasing hormone (GnRH)	Peptide	Neural signaling	↑ LH, ↑ FSH	Hypothalamus
	Thyrotropin-releasing hormone (TRH)	Peptide	Neural signaling	↑ TSH	Hypothalamus
	Corticotropin-releasing factor (CRF)	Peptide	Neural signaling in response to stress	↑ ACTH	Hypothalamus
	Growth hormone-releasing hormone (GHRH)	Peptide	Neural signaling	↑ GH	Hypothalamus

3. Organs of the Endocrine System

Although MCAT passages are likely to focus on the physiological and systemic effects of hormones, it is also necessary to understand the function of each organ of the endocrine system and to know which hormones they release. This section breaks down hormones according to their associated organ and provides information about those organs. Some information is repeated from the previous section that focused on key endocrine functions; in such cases, a more detailed discussion is presented in the previous section. However, this section also presents some other hormones that have isolated effects less closely linked to crucial general functions of the endocrine system. A complete list of MCAT-relevant hormones is presented in Table 3.

Hypothalamus

As we've discussed, the endocrine system ultimately relies on signaling from the nervous system in order to properly respond to external stimuli. The hypothalamus plays a crucial role in this process and can be thought of as the bridge between the nervous system and the endocrine system. It is located in the forebrain, directly above the pituitary gland, and receives input from several sources elsewhere in the brain. It then secretes several tropic hormones into the hypophyseal portal system, which connects the hypothalamus to the anterior pituitary. The interlocking capillary beds of the hypophyseal portal system allow the hormones secreted by the hypothalamus to be conveyed quickly and directly to the anterior pituitary, facilitating the fine-tuned control of downstream endocrine responses. The other portal system in the body is the hepatic portal system, discussed in Chapter 10.

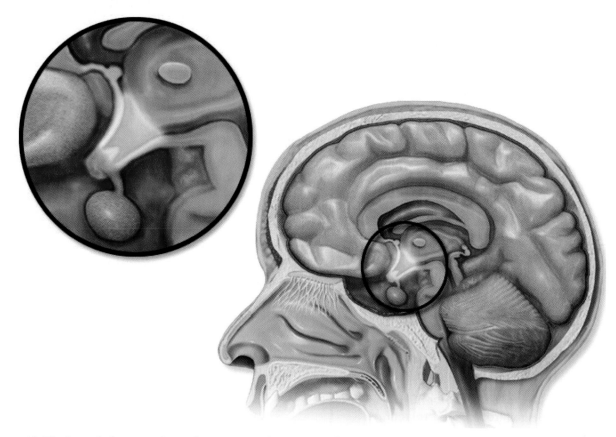

Figure 16. The hypothalamus and its role in neuroendocrine signaling.

For the most part, the tropic hormones secreted by the hypothalamus regulate the secretion of other tropic hormones. This is the case for gonadotropin-releasing hormone (GnRH), which promotes the secretion of luteinizing hormone (LH) and follicle-stimulating hormone (FSH) from the anterior pituitary, thyrotropin-releasing hormone (TRH), which stimulates the anterior pituitary to release thyroid-stimulating hormone (TSH), and corticotropin-releasing factor (CRF), which promotes the secretion of adrenocorticotropic hormone (ACTH) from the anterior pituitary. The hypothalamus also secretes growth hormone-releasing hormone (GHRH), which stimulates the secretion of growth hormone, which is a nontropic hormone released from the anterior pituitary gland.

Pituitary (Anterior and Posterior)

The pituitary gland is divided into two parts: the anterior and posterior pituitary gland, which have drastically different functions, to the point that you should approach them as two distinct endocrine organs. One point of commonality, however, is that all of the hormones secreted by the pituitary are peptide hormones.

As discussed above, the anterior pituitary receives input from the hypothalamus via the hypophyseal portal system, and secretes both tropic and direct hormones.

The tropic hormones released by the anterior pituitary include luteinizing hormone (LH) and follicle-stimulating hormone (FSH), which are released in response to gonadotropin-releasing hormone (GnRH) release from the hypothalamus. In males, LH stimulates Leydig cells to release testosterone, and in females LH stimulates the release of estrogen and is involved in the luteal surge in the menstrual cycle. In females, FSH stimulates the growth of ovarian follicles and in males promotes spermatogenesis. The anterior pituitary releases adrenocorticotropic hormone (ACTH), which acts on the adrenal cortex to induce the secretion of corticosteroids, most notably cortisol and aldosterone. Thyroid-stimulating hormone (TSH) is released by the anterior pituitary and acts on the thyroid to stimulate the release of the thyroid hormones.

> ## MCAT STRATEGY > > >
>
> It can be difficult to remember all of the multi-step signaling pathways that the MCAT expects you to be aware of. One general principle that can help you organize these processes is that signaling works in a top-down manner—that is, the closer you are to the head, the more likely a hormone is to have a general regulatory function, while hormones secreted below the head are more likely to exert specific direct physiological effects. This is not a 100% rule, but may prove helpful in organizing this information conceptually and in making an educated guess if necessary on Test Day.

The direct hormones released by the anterior pituitary are prolactin, endorphin, and growth hormones. Prolactin acts on the mammary glands to stimulate milk production in response to reduced dopamine levels. Endorphins are a family of hormones that reduce the perception of pain. Growth hormone is released both in response to stress and when the body is undergoing periods of accelerated growth. It exerts a range of systemic effects associated with growth, and also, when released in response to stress, has the effect of raising blood glucose levels.

> ## MCAT STRATEGY > > >
>
> Mnemonic: FLAT PEG stands for FSH, LH, ACTH, and TSH (all tropic) and prolactin, endorphin, and growth hormones (all nontropic).

The posterior pituitary gland releases hormones in direct response to signaling from the hypothalamus. It is responsible for the release of two hormones: anti-diuretic hormone (ADH), also known as vasopressin, and oxytocin. ADH plays a major role in regulating fluid balance in the body, and is released in response to low blood volume and high blood osmolarity, both of which are signals of dehydration. It promotes water reabsorption directly by increasing the permeability of the collecting duct, resulting in increased blood pressure, increased blood volume, and decreased blood osmolarity. Oxytocin has two main functions that you should be aware of: it promotes uterine contractions leading up to childbirth and milk ejection, which results from the contraction of smooth muscle tissues in the milk ducts. The role of oxytocin in promoting uterine contractions is a well-known example of a positive feedback loop, as discussed earlier in the chapter. In addition to this, oxytocin plays an important role in promoting social bonding.

Parathyroid and Thyroid

The thyroid is located on the anterior (front) surface of the trachea, and the parathyroid glands are four small glands, roughly the size of peas, located on the posterior (back) of the thyroid. The thyroid produces T_3 and T_4, often referred to simply as thyroid hormone, which act to increase an individual's basal metabolic rate, as well as calcitonin, which decreases plasma Ca^{2+} levels by decreasing Ca^{2+} absorption from the intestines, increasing Ca^{2+} storage in the bones (if Ca^{2+} is locked up in bone tissue, it's not in the blood), and increasing Ca^{2+} excretion from the body.

The parathyroids release parathyroid hormone (PTH), which has the opposite effect of calcitonin. PTH increases Ca^{2+} levels by exerting opposite effects to those of calcitonin: it increases Ca^{2+} absorption from the intestine, decreases Ca^{2+} storage in the bones, and promotes Ca^{2+} retention instead of excretion.

Adrenal Cortex and Medulla

The adrenal glands sit on top of the kidney, and each adrenal gland consists of two anatomically and functionally distinct areas: the cortex and the medulla.

The adrenal cortex secretes steroid hormones known as corticosteroids, which are further subclassified into glucocorticoids (the main example of which is cortisol), mineralocorticoids (the main example of which is aldosterone), and the cortical sex hormones. Cortisol is involved in long-term responses to stress and has the effect of increasing blood glucose and decreasing inflammatory immune responses. Aldosterone promotes fluid retention by increasing Na$^+$ reabsorption in the distal convoluted tubule. Cortical sex hormones are a category of hormones including various androgens and estrogens, such as testosterone. Generally speaking, cortical sex hormones do not play a major role in the regulation of secondary sex characteristics due to the larger quantity of sex hormones produced in the gonads, but they are worth being aware of.

The adrenal medulla secretes the amino-acid derived hormones epinephrine and norepinephrine, which are involved in short-term stress responses. They are members of a larger class of compounds known as catecholamines; practically speaking, all this means is that you should be able to associate the term "catecholamine" with these hormones if it comes up on Test Day. They have the effect of increasing blood glucose levels and mediating many of the responses involved in the fight-or-flight stress response induced by the sympathetic nervous system.

> **MCAT STRATEGY >>>**
>
> This is a good example of the various ways the body can handle an excess of something: absorb less of it, do something with it to avoid the negative effects of having it in excess, and/or get rid of it.

> **MCAT STRATEGY >>>**
>
> PTH is an excellent example to contrast with calcitonin, in that it illustrates strategies the body can use to hang on to something when it needs it: absorb more of it, mobilize it from elsewhere in the body, and/or avoid excreting it.

> **MCAT STRATEGY >>>**
>
> Associate the adrenal *cortex* with *cort*isol and other steroids.

Pancreas

The pancreas is located behind the stomach in the abdominal cavity, and is noteworthy because it plays an important role in both the endocrine and digestive systems. The endocrine cells of the pancreas you have to be aware of for the MCAT are referred to using Greek letters: alpha cells, beta cells, and delta cells.

The alpha cells of the pancreas secrete glucagon, which is secreted in response to low blood glucose levels and has the effect of increasing blood glucose levels. The beta cells of the pancreas secrete insulin, which has the opposite effect: it is released in response to high blood glucose levels and reduces blood glucose levels by promoting the uptake of glucose into cells. The delta cells of the pancreas secrete somatostatin, which slows down the rate of digestive hormone secretion in response to high levels of glucose and amino acids (i.e., it tells the body to be less efficient about processing food when plenty of nutrients are already present).

Gonads

The reproductive system and its anatomy are discussed in more detail in Chapter 8. For the endocrine system, it is most important to be aware that both the ovaries (in females) and testes (in males) respond to the gonadotropins luteinizing hormone (LH) and follicle-stimulating hormone (FSH), and release estrogen and testosterone, respectively. These steroid hormones have a range of effects; for the purposes of the MCAT, their most important effect is stimulating the development of secondary sex characteristics.

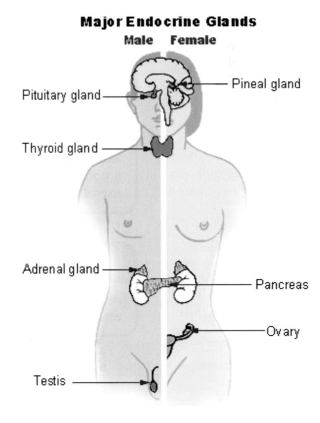

Major Endocrine Glands

Male   Female

Pituitary gland ——
Pineal gland ——
Thyroid gland ——
Adrenal gland ——
Pancreas ——
Ovary ——
Testis ——

Figure 17. Key endocrine organs of the body.

Others

Not all endocrine cells are located in the major endocrine organs or are deeply interwoven into the major physiological functions of the endocrine system discussed in Section 2. This section briefly presents select other hormones to be aware of for the MCAT.

In the brain, the pineal gland secretes an amino-acid derived hormone known as melatonin, which has a variety of functions, including the regulation of circadian rhythms.

Muscle cells of the heart release atrial natriuretic peptide (ANP), which has effects opposite to those of aldosterone: that is, it is released in response to high blood volume and has the net effect of decreasing blood volume by promoting fluid excretion. Its mechanisms are discussed in more depth above, in Section 2.

The thymus is an immune organ where T cells mature, and it secretes thymosin, which is a hormone important for the development and maturation of T cells.

The digestive system includes endocrine cells involved in the release of digestive hormones, such as gastrin, secretin, and cholecystokinin. These are discussed in more detail in Chapter 10 on the digestive system, and are not usually included in discussions of the endocrine system because they do not exert systemic effects.

> > **CONNECTIONS** < <

Chapter 10 of Biology

Table 3 summarizes all MCAT-relevant hormones sorted by the organ they are secreted from. Be sure to study both this and Table 2, which sorts the hormones by important physiological functions. Being able to approach the hormones through both lenses will prove very advantageous on the MCAT.

Table 3. Important hormones for the MCAT by organ of secretion.

ORGAN	HORMONE	STRUCTURAL TYPE	STIMULUS	EFFECT	NOTES
Hypothalamus	Gonadotropin-releasing hormone (GnRH)	Peptide	Neural signaling	↑ LH, ↑ FSH	Not highest-yield for the MCAT; be aware of these hormones but they should not be your highest priority
	Thyrotropin-releasing hormone (TRH)	Peptide	Neural signaling	↑ TSH	
	Corticotropin-releasing factor (CRF)	Peptide	Neural signaling in response to stress	↑ ACTH	
	Growth hormone-releasing hormone (GHRH)	Peptide	Neural signaling	↑ GH	

Anterior pituitary	Thyroid-stimulating hormone (TSH)	Peptide	TRH	↑ Thyroid hormones	
	Adrenocorticotropic hormone (ACTH)	Peptide	CRF	↑ Adrenal cortex activity (↑ corticosteroids)	
	Luteinizing hormone (LH)	Peptide	GnRH, ↓ estrogen or testosterone	↑ Estrogen or testosterone	
	Follicle-stimulating hormone (FSH)	Peptide	GnRH	Follicle development, spermatogenesis	
	Prolactin	Peptide	↓ Dopamine	Milk production	
	Endorphins	Peptide	Pain, exercise	↓ Pain	
	Growth hormone (GH)	Peptide	Stress (and growth)	↑ Glucose	
Posterior pituitary	Oxytocin	Peptide	Neural signaling (uterine stretching, nipple stimulation)	Smooth muscle contraction (uterine contractions in labor, milk release in breastfeeding)	Example of positive feedback
	Anti-diuretic hormone (ADH, vasopressin)	Peptide	↓ BP, ↑ osmolarity	↑ H_2O reabsorption in collecting duct	
Parathyroid	Parathyroid hormone (PTH)	Peptide	↓ Ca^{2+}	↑ Ca^{2+}	
Thyroid	T_3 and T_4	Amino acid-derived (nonpolar)	TSH	↑ Basal metabolic rate	Contain 3 and 4 iodine atoms, respectively
	Calcitonin	Peptide	↑ Ca^{2+}	↓ Ca^{2+}	
Adrenal cortex	Cortisol	Steroid	Stress (long-term)	↑ Glucose, ↓ inflammation	Most important glucocorticoid; also classified as corticosteroid
	Aldosterone	Steroid	↓ BP, ↑ osmolarity, angiotensin II	↑ Na^+ reabsorption in DCT, ↑ fluid levels	Most important mineralo-corticoid; also classified as a corticosteroid

Adrenal medulla	Epinephrine	Amino acid-derived (polar)	Stress (short-term)	↑ Glucose, sympathetic nervous system/ fight-or-flight response	
	Norepinephrine	Amino acid-derived (polar)			Also a neurotransmitter with major role in sympathetic nervous response
Pancreas	Insulin	Peptide	↑ Glucose	↓ Glucose	Secreted in beta cells of pancreas
	Glucagon	Peptide	↓ Glucose	↑ Glucose	Secreted in alpha cells of pancreas
	Somatostatin	Peptide	Neural signaling, ↑ glucose, ↑ amino acids	Inhibits digestive hormones, slows digestion	Secreted in delta cells of pancreas
Reproductive organs	Estrogen	Steroid	LH	Female secondary sex characteristics, menstrual cycle regulation	Secreted in ovaries
	Testosterone	Steroid		Male secondary sex characteristics	Secreted in testes
	Progesterone	Steroid	hCG	Prepares and maintains uterus for pregnancy	Secreted in ovaries, placenta
	Human chorionic gonadotropin (hCG)	Peptide	Implantation	↑ Progesterone	Secreted in placenta
Others	Melatonin	Amino acid-derived	Neural signaling	Circadian rhythms	Pineal gland
	Atrial natriuretic peptide (ANP)	Peptide	↑ Blood volume	↓ Na^+ reabsorption in DCT, ↓ fluid levels	Heart muscle cells
	Digestive hormones	Peptides	Various (see Chapter 10)	Various (see Chapter 10)	Endocrine cells in the digestive system
	Thymosin	Peptide	Various	T-cell development	Thymus

4. Must-Knows

> High-level points about the endocrine system:
> - "Endocrine" refers specifically to ductless glands that release signaling molecules (hormones) into circulation
> - Its role is communication among organ systems
> - Endocrine signaling is slower than neural signaling, and many endocrine functions are ultimately controlled by the nervous system (through intermediaries)
>
> The structural differences between peptide hormones, steroid hormones, and amino acid hormones, and how they contribute to the function of these hormone types
> - Peptide hormones are made up from amino acid chains, and are hydrophilic and (relatively) large. Steroid hormones are derived from cholesterol, have a four-ring structure, and are lipophilic.
> - Peptide hormones cannot diffuse through the plasma membranes of their target cells, so they interact with transmembrane receptors that activate second messenger signaling systems in the cytosol.
> - Steroid hormones can and do diffuse through the plasma membranes of their target cells, bind with nuclear receptors, and influence gene expression in their target cells
> - Peptide hormones typically have quick-onset, short-acting effects. Steroid hormones typically have a delayed onset and long-lasting effects.
> - Steroid hormones affect sex (estrogen, testosterone, progesterone), salt (aldosterone, a mineralocorticoid), and sugar (cortisol, a glucocorticoid). Amino acid-derived hormones include T_3/T_4 and (nor)epinephrine. All other high-yield hormones are peptides.
>
> Negative feedback: common in the body; downstream product inhibits upstream steps; maintains homeostasis.
>
> Positive feedback: unusual in body; downstream product upregulates upstream steps; pushes the body towards an extreme state; example is oxytocin in labor/childbirth.
>
> Major functions of the endocrine system:
> - Glucose: Insulin ↓ glucose, glucagon ↑ glucose
> - Serum calcium concentration: PTH & vitamin D_3 ↑ Ca^{2+}, Calcitonin ↓ Ca^{2+}
> - Fluids: Aldosterone & ADH ↑ fluid retention, ANP ↑ fluid excretion
> - Stress: Cortisol: ↑ glucose, long-term stress, epinephrine ↑ glucose and sympathetic response, short-term stress
> - Metabolic rate: T_3 and T_4 ↑ basal metabolic rate
> - Reproduction and development: Estrogen & testosterone → secondary sex characteristics
> - Tropic hormones play role in multi-step signaling pathways

This page left intentionally blank.

Practice Passage

The hypophysis is a major hub in the human endocrine system. The gland is split into two parts called the anterior and posterior pituitary glands which differ in the hormones they release. The anterior pituitary contains five types of cells: corticotropes, thyrotropes, prolactins, gonadotropes, and somatotropes. Each cell type secretes a different hormone.

The anterior pituitary's secretion of hormones is regulated by hormones released by the hypothalamus. This is possible because the hypothalamus and anterior pituitary are connected through the hypophyseal portal system: a system of blood vessels connecting the two glands (Figure 1).

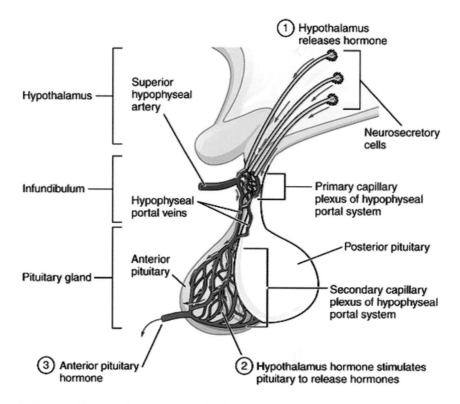

Figure 1. Anterior pituitary and hypothalamic communication

Pituitary regulating hormones secreted by the hypothalamus include gonadotropin-releasing hormone, corticotropin-releasing hormone, prolactin-releasing hormone, and growth hormone-releasing hormone.

Hormone secretion from the anterior pituitary can also be regulated by other body systems. The molecule gamma-aminobutyric acid (GABA) can stimulate the secretion of growth hormone (GH), luteinizing hormone (LH), and thyroid-stimulating hormone (TSH).

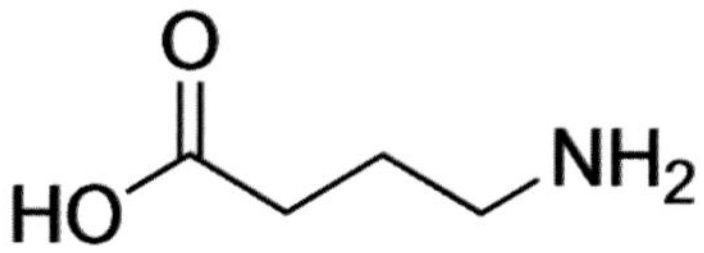

Figure 2. Gamma aminobutyric acid

Prostaglandins are a class of lipids that inhibit ACTH release and stimulate TSH, GH, and LH release. Prostaglandins always contain 20 carbons and have a 5-carbon ring.

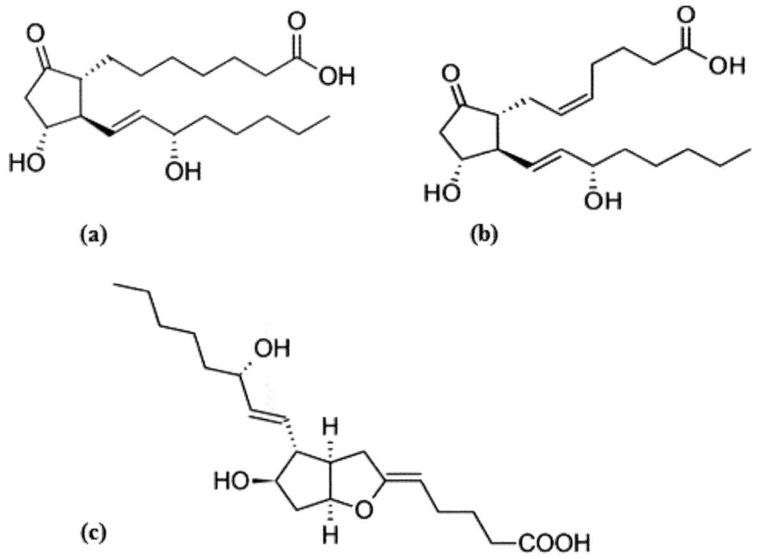

Figure 3. Prostaglandins E₁ (a), E₂ (b), and I₂ (c)

Figure 1 image adapted from OpenStax College via Wikipedia under CCBY 3.0

1. What is the IUPAC name for GABA?
   A. Amino-4-butyric acid
   B. 4-carboxybutanamine
   C. 4-aminobutanoic acid
   D. 1-hydroxy 4-aminobutanone

2. Which of the following is the LEAST likely to be observed in a patient with the following hormone panel results?

HORMONE	SECRETION
GH	Above normal
Vasopressin	Below normal
Gastrin	Normal
PTH	Below normal
Testosterone	Normal

   A. Increased bone growth
   B. Increased secretion of GHRH
   C. Decreased secretion of calcitonin
   D. Decreased activity of prostaglandins on somatotropes

3. Which type of cell most likely releases LH and FSH from the anterior pituitary?
   A. Gonadotropes
   B. Somatotropes
   C. Corticotropes
   D. Thyrotropes

4. What is the significance of the subscripts in the names of the prostaglandins shown in figure 3?
   A. They indicate the number of ring structures in the molecule.
   B. They indicate the relative size of the prostaglandin.
   C. They indicate the number of carbon-carbon π bonds in the molecule.
   D. They indicate the number of acidic functional groups.

5. Which of the following are likely to trigger an increase in triiodothyronine production?
   I. A tumor in the thyrotropes of the anterior pituitary
   II. A decrease in TRH production
   III. A decrease in gamma-aminobutyric acid production
   A. I only
   B. I and II only
   C. II and III only
   D. I and III only

6. Which of the following is NOT a primary classification of hormones?
   A. Amino acid-derived
   B. Peptide
   C. Exocrine
   D. Steroid

7. Giantism is a condition characterized by height in the top 0.01% off the population, and excessive growth of the hands, face, and feet. This condition is most likely a result of:
   A. excess hGH before blastulation.
   B. excess hGH before puberty.
   C. insufficient hGH after puberty.
   D. insufficient hGH before puberty.

Practice Passage Explanations

The hypophysis is a major hub in the human endocrine system. The gland is split into two parts called the anterior and posterior pituitary glands which differ in the hormones they release. The anterior pituitary contains five types of cells: corticotropes, thyrotropes, prolactins, gonadotropes, and somatotropes. Each cell type secretes a different hormone.

Key terms: hypophysis, anterior/posterior pituitary, 5 cell types

Cause and effect: cell names imply hormone types released; corticotropes = ACTH, thyrotropes = TSH, prolactins = prolactin, gonadotropes = FSH and LH, somatotropes = GH

The anterior pituitary's secretion of hormones is regulated by hormones released by the hypothalamus. This is possible because the hypothalamus and anterior pituitary are connected through the hypophyseal portal system: a system of blood vessels connecting the two glands (Figure 1).

Key terms: anterior pituitary, hypophyseal portal system.

Cause and effect: hypothalamus regulates the anterior pituitary and the hypophyseal portal system allows for communication/feedback

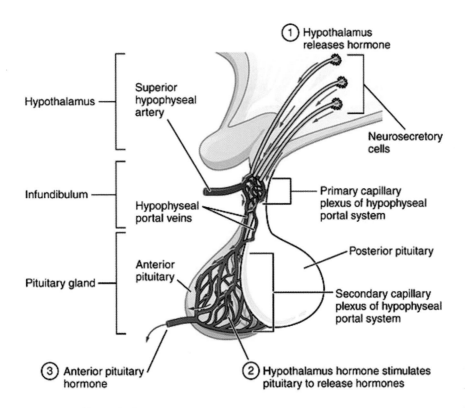

Figure 1. Anterior pituitary and hypothalamic communication

Figure 1 shows a schematic of the function of the anterior pituitary in conjunction with the hypothalamus

Pituitary regulating hormones secreted by the hypothalamus include gonadotropin-releasing hormone, corticotropin-releasing hormone, prolactin-releasing hormone, and growth hormone-releasing hormone.

Key terms: pituitary regulating hormones, hypothalamus

Cause and effect: GnRH, CRH, PRH, GHRH regulate anterior pituitary hormones

Hormone secretion from the anterior pituitary can also be regulated by other body systems. The molecule gamma-aminobutyric acid (GABA) can stimulate the secretion of growth hormone (GH), luteinizing hormone (LH), and thyroid-stimulating hormone (TSH).

Key terms: GABA

Cause and effect: GABA → increased GH/LH/TSH

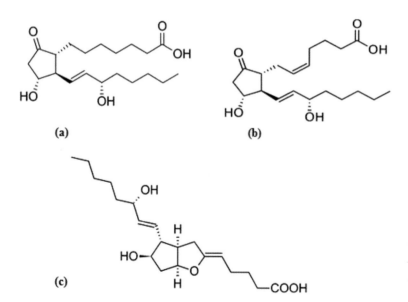

Figure 2. Gamma aminobutyric acid

Figure 2 shows the amino group on the "gamma" carbon (third C from the carbonyl C)

Prostaglandins are a class of lipids that inhibit ACTH release and stimulate TSH, GH, and LH release. Prostaglandins always contain 20 carbons and have a 5-carbon ring.

Key terms: prostaglandins

Cause and effect: gamma aminobutyric acid down-regulates GH, LH, TSH while prostaglandins down-regulate ACTH but stimulate TSH, GH, and LH

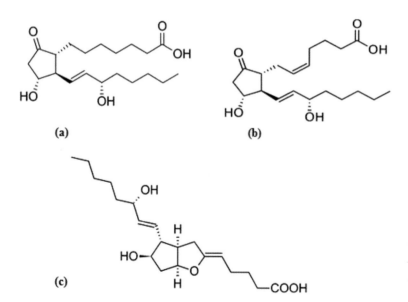

(a)

(b)

(c)

Figure 3. Prostaglandins E_1 (a), E_2 (b), and I_2 (c)

Figure 3 shows the structure of 3 prostaglandins, so anticipate questions on functional groups, precrsors or derivatives

Figure 1 image adapted from OpenStax College via Wikipedia under CCBY 3.0

1. C is correct. In GABA we have a 4 carbon chain (but-) and a carboxylic acid group, which takes priority. Thus, our answer must contain 4-amino, a but- prefix, and –oic acid as its suffix. 4-aminobutanoic acid is correct.
   A: The 4 is placed incorrectly, and butyric acid is the common name, not the systematic IUPAC name.
   B: The carboxylic acid functional group has priority, not the amine group.
   D. There is no ketone group on GABA (-one).

2. B is correct. This question effectively asks us to determine the effects of increased GH secretion. It is not likely that this would stimulate more GHRH production because GHRH acts to stimulate GH secretion. This type of positive feedback loop is not a common biological process.
   A. GH stimulates growth.
   C. Calcitonin would not likely be directly affected at first, but it is more likely to occur than choice B because GH takes calcium from the blood.
   D. Somatotropes secrete GH. It is likely that there will be less activity of prostaglandins on somatotropes because prostaglandins stimulate GH secretion.

3. A is correct. This question asks us to reason which cell likely produces the gonadotropins LH and FSH.
   B. Somatotropes secrete GH.
   C. Corticotropes secrete ACTH.
   D. Thyrotropes secrete TSH.

4. C is correct. This question asks us to reason from Figure 3 why the prostaglandins have the classification of 1 or 2 as in E_1, E_2, and I_2. The structures of the molecules would suggest that the number has to do with the number of double bonds in the structure.
   A. Prostaglandin E_2 has one ring.
   B. The sizes of the prostaglandins are all the same. They have 20 carbons each.
   D. The prostaglandins all have one carboxylic acid and two hydroxyl groups.

5. A is correct. Triiodothyronine is the formal name of T_3. This question asks us to determine the plausible causes of an increase in T_3 production. Since T_3 is a thyroid hormone, an increase in TSH would do it. RN I corresponds to an increased secretion of the thyrotropic hormone, TSH.
   II: A decrease in TRH production would only decrease TSH and T_3 production.
   III: A decrease in GABA production would only decrease TSH secretion.

6. C is correct. Hormones can be grouped into 3 main types: amino acid-derived (e.g. T_3, T_4), protein/peptide (e.g. ADH, GH) and steroid (cholesterol derived, e.g. cortisol, progesterone). Exocrine does not refer to a class of hormones, but rather to the mechanism of release. Exocrine hormones are secreted via a duct into the blood and usually effect a distant organ or tissue, while endocrine hormones are secreted within the tissue and enter the blood stream via capillaries.

7. B is correct. In order for the excessive growth described in the question stem to occur, the overstimulation of growth process must have occurred prior to the fusing of bone growth (i.e. epiphyseal) plates, which occurs after puberty.

Independent Questions

1. A hormone that acts on neighboring cells is best described as which of the following?
   A. Autocrine
   B. Paracrine
   C. Endocrine
   D. Exocrine

2. Tropic hormones are vital for proper hormonal responses. If the anterior pituitary gland was surgically removed, which of the following effects would most clearly be demonstrated?
   A. A reduction in basal metabolic rate
   B. An increased stress response to exercise
   C. A decreased ability to fall asleep
   D. An oversecretion of digestive enzymes

3. Which of the following glands or structures plays the largest role in the regulation of circadian rhythm?
   A. The adrenal glands
   B. The pituitary gland
   C. Enteroendocrine cells
   D. The pineal gland

4. The adrenal gland is heavily involved in the regulation of water retention by the kidneys, largely through the release of a particular hormone. Increased secretion of this mineralocorticoid leads to which of the following?
   A. Sodium retention, potassium retention, water retention
   B. Calcium secretion, phosphate retention, water retention
   C. Sodium retention, potassium secretion, water retention
   D. Bicarbonate secretion, hydrogen retention, water retention

5. All of the following act as second messengers EXCEPT:
   A. cyclic AMP (cAMP).
   B. cyclic GMP (cGMP).
   C. adenosine triphosphate (ATP).
   D. calcium ions.

6. Steroid hormones:
   A. are characterized by a structure containing five fused rings.
   B. include insulin and glucagon.
   C. affect gene translation in the nucleus.
   D. generally exert longer-lasting effects than peptide hormones.

7. Recent research advances for the treatment of type 1 diabetes mellitus have investigated the use of stem cell therapies. One treatment first takes the patient's stem cells, differentiates them into mature cells, and finally transplants them back into the patient's pancreas. Which cell type should these cells differentiate into?
   A. Alpha cells
   B. Beta cells
   C. Delta cells
   D. Epsilon cells

8. An important pathway in the human body begins with the secretion of CRH, which then promotes the secretion of ACTH. In turn, ACTH promotes the secretion of cortisol. List the glands or structures that produce these three hormones, beginning with that which produces CRH.
   A. Hypothalamus, posterior pituitary, adrenal medulla
   B. Hypothalamus, anterior pituitary, adrenal medulla
   C. Hypothalamus, anterior pituitary, adrenal cortex
   D. Hypothalamus, posterior pituitary, adrenal cortex

Independent Question Explanations

1. B is correct. A paracrine hormone acts on nearby cells. Autocrine hormones act on the cell that secreted them, while endocrine hormones travel and act on distant sites. Exocrine activity involves the secretion of products through ducts, not into the bloodstream.

2. A is correct. The anterior pituitary gland secretes a number of vital tropic hormones, one of which is thyroid-stimulating hormone (TSH). This hormone acts on the thyroid gland to promote the secretion of thyroxine (T_4) and triiodothyronine (T_3). These thyroid hormones increase the metabolic rate of nearly every cell in the body.

3. D is correct. The pineal gland secretes melatonin, the principal function of which is to regulate sleep patterns. Melatonin secretion is stimulated by darkness and inhibited by light.

4. C is correct. The adrenal mineralocorticoid referenced by the question stem is aldosterone. This steroid hormone acts on the distal tubules and collecting ducts of the kidney nephron and stimulates sodium retention—and thus, water retention—along with potassium secretion.

5. C is correct. Calcium ions, cAMP, and cGMP are all common second messengers. Adenosine triphosphate (ATP) is the cell's main source of energy; while cells do respond to signals of energy abundance or insufficiency, it is not considered a second messenger.

6. D is correct. Steroid hormones pass directly through the plasma membrane and eventually make it to the nucleus, where they affect gene transcription (not translation). This typically results in longer-lasting physiological effects than those of peptide hormones, which act through more rapid second messenger pathways. Steroids are derived from cholesterol, the structure of which contains four fused rings. Insulin and glucagon are peptides, not steroids.

7. B is correct. In Type 1 diabetes mellitus, the patient's immune system destroys his or her pancreatic beta cells, resulting in an inability to produce insulin. This proposed stem cell therapy involves regenerating the beta cells. The alpha cells in the pancreas produce glucagon, delta cells produce somatostatin, and epsilon cells produce a hormone known as ghrelin.

8. C is correct. CRH is corticotropin-releasing hormone, which is secreted by the hypothalamus. ACTH, or adrenocorticotropic hormone, is released by the anterior pituitary gland and acts on the adrenal cortex to release cortisol.

This page left intentionally blank.

Reproduction and Development

CHAPTER 8

0. Introduction

Reproductive health is a tremendously diverse and important domain of medicine, which you will explore in more depth in medical school. The MCAT does not expect you to be aware of everything there is to know regarding reproductive health, but you are expected to have a grounding in the anatomical and physiological basics that will provide a scaffold for you to expand upon later. As always for the MCAT, it is important to focus on areas where anatomical/physiological information can be approached with an eye towards building connections with signaling systems, interactions with the environment, and other areas of testable content, and the reproductive system has abundant examples of such intersections. In this chapter, we will start by presenting the basic anatomy and physiology of the male and female reproductive systems, including spermatogenesis and oogenesis, then proceed to discuss embryogenesis, development, and pregnancy, and conclude with an overview of the hormonal control of reproduction that builds upon the material presented in Chapter 7 on the endocrine system.

1. Male Reproductive System

For both the female and male reproductive systems, it is helpful to distinguish between the terms "genitalia" and "gonads." Gonads are specifically the organs in which gametes are made: that is, the testes in males and the ovaries in females. The term "genitalia" refers more broadly to the reproductive organs, and in particular the external organs, which can be further specified as the external genitalia. In the male reproductive system, the external genitalia are the penis and scrotum.

The scrotum is a pouch that hangs behind the penis. Its main function is to contain the testes. The testes (singular = testis) are where sperm is produced, but also secrete hormones, most notably testosterone. An interesting aspect of spermatogenesis is that it operates best a few degrees below body temperature, and the scrotum therefore contains musculature to regulate the temperature of the testes. When the external temperature is cold, the testes should be closer to the body to keep them at the correct temperature; to do so, the Cremaster muscle pulls the scrotum up and closer to the body, while the Dartos muscle contracts and makes the scrotum wrinkly, which has the effect of reducing the surface area through which heat can be lost. The opposite changes happen in hot environments where the testes need to be cooled instead of warmed.

The core of the testis is made up by seminiferous tubules that are separated by septa (singular = septum; "septum" is the anatomical term for a barrier or partition between two spaces, and is used in many different contexts in anatomy). The seminiferous tubules are where meiosis and spermatogenesis take place. Germ cells are present within the seminiferous tubules, and Sertoli cells, which constitute the epithelium of the seminiferous tubules, help germ cells to develop into spermatozoa. Additionally, Leydig cells are found adjacent to the seminiferous tubules; these cells are linked to the endocrine function of the testes and secrete androgens (male sex hormones) such as testosterone.

Immature spermatozoa made in the seminiferous tubules move to the epididymis, a structure attached to the rear of the testes that is used for the storage and further maturation of spermatozoa. When spermatozoa enter the epididymis, they are non-motile (unable to move independently), but they gain this ability over the period of 2-3 months that they are stored in the epididymis. The life cycle of spermatozoa splits at the epididymis: either spermatozoa proceed through ejaculation or are broken down and reabsorbed.

MCAT STRATEGY > > >

A well-known mnemonic for the path taken by spermatozoa is SEVEN UP: <u>s</u>eminiferous tubules, <u>e</u>pididymis, <u>v</u>as deferens, <u>e</u>jaculatory ducts, <u>n</u>othing (this is a placeholder to make the mnemonic work), <u>u</u>rethra, <u>p</u>enis.

In the event of ejaculation, spermatozoa move from the epididymis to the vas deferens, a tube that connects the epididymis to the ejaculatory ducts. The ejaculatory ducts are formed by a fusion of the vas deferens with the seminal vesicles, which are glands located below the urinary bladder that generate the majority of the liquid component of semen. In particular, the seminal vesicles secrete fructose, vitamins, enzymes, and other proteins necessary for spermatozoa to stay alive after ejaculation. The ejaculatory ducts run through the prostate glands, and then join with the urethra. Secretions from the bulbourethral glands (also referred to as the Cowper's glands) known as pre-ejaculate lubricate the urethra before ejaculation and neutralize any remaining acidic urine that is present. The semen then travels through the urethra and is released from the penis upon ejaculation.

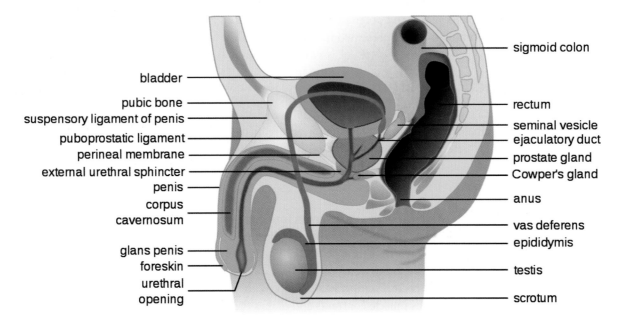

Figure 1. Male reproductive system.

An important point to remember is the distinction between sperm (or spermatozoa) and semen. Sperm are the haploid gametes with flagella that can fertilize an egg, while semen is the alkaline liquid containing nutrients that they are carried in. Semen is alkaline (weakly basic) because the female reproductive tract is acidic; the vaginal pH normally ranges between 3.8 and 4.5. (For reference, the skin maintains a pH of approximately 4.7-5.2, many fruits have a pH between 3 and 5, and wine tends to have a pH of 3-4). It is entirely possible for ejaculated semen not to contain any sperm; this condition is known as azoospermia, is associated with male-factor infertility, can have multiple causes, and affects approximately 1% of the population.

2. Female Reproductive System

The female reproductive system can also be subdivided into internal and external genitalia. The internal genitalia include the ovaries, fallopian tubes, uterus, cervix, and vagina, while the external genitalia are collectively known as the vulva; some important structures of the vulva include the labia majora, labia minora, clitoris, and vaginal opening.

The ovaries are the female gonads, and are where oogenesis takes place, resulting in mature egg cells. The interior of the ovaries contains many follicles; at the beginning of puberty, approximately 400,000 follicles are present. Each follicle contains an oocyte (immature egg cell), which is supported by various other cells that provide nutrients and hormonal support to the oocytes. During each menstrual cycle, one follicle releases a mature ovum (egg) into the Fallopian tube (also known as the oviduct), in a process known as ovulation. The ovaries are also endocrine organs, and secrete estrogen and progesterone.

The Fallopian tubes connect the ovaries to the uterus. They have a smooth muscle layer that carries out peristalsis (patterns of automatic muscle contraction that push contents through a tube; see Chapter 10) and an abundance of ciliated cells; both of these anatomical structures help move ova from the ovaries to the uterus.

> **> > CONNECTIONS < <**
>
> **Chapter 10 of Biology**

The uterus is where a fetus develops during pregnancy. Its innermost layer, composed of epithelial cells and a mucous membrane, is known as the endometrium. Its middle layer consists of smooth muscle, and is known as the myometrium (the prefix "myo-" is often used for structures involving muscles). The lower part of the uterus is known as the cervix (from a Latin term meaning "neck"; etymologically, the name of this structure means "neck of the uterus"). The cervix is cylindrical, and the cervical canal connects the uterine cavity with the vaginal canal. Sperm deposited in the vagina during intercourse must travel through the cervical canal for fertilization to take place; for this reason, mechanically blocking the cervical canal has historically been one approach to contraception. The vagina runs from the cervix to the vaginal opening. The vaginal canal is elastic and muscular, and can stretch to accommodate a fetus during childbirth. The vagina also is home to a rich population of bacteria, and the maintenance of healthy vaginal microbiota is an important aspect of reproductive health.

As mentioned above, the external female genitalia are collectively known as the vulva. The urethral opening is located anterior (front) to the vaginal opening, and both structures are flanked by the labia minora, or inner lips. The labia minora are in turn located between the labia majora, or outer lips. The labia minora in particular help protect the sensitive areas of the urethral opening and vaginal opening from irritations and infections. The clitoris is a complex, highly innervated sex organ; the visible area of the clitoris is located anterior to the urethral opening, with the clitoral hood formed by the junction of the labia minora and the clitoral glans located underneath.

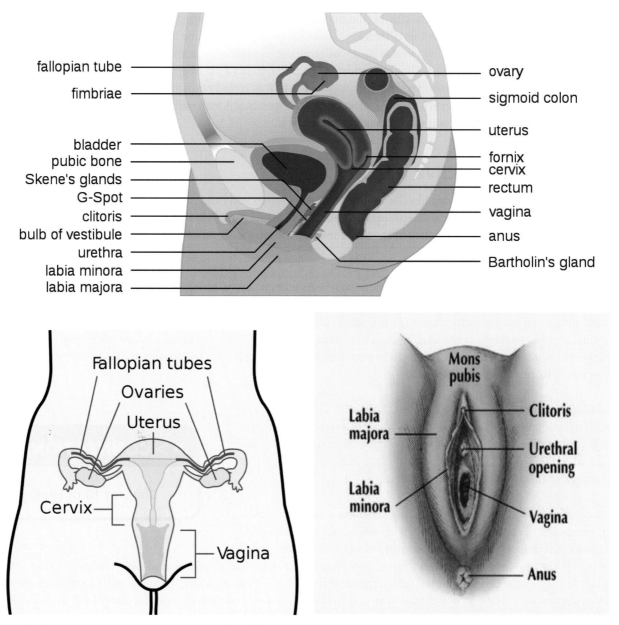

Figure 2. Female reproductive system, sagittal and frontal views.

3. Spermatogenesis and Oogenesis

Spermatogenesis and oogenesis refer to the processes through which gametes (spermatozoa and ova, respectively) are generated. They are similar in that both involve meiosis, but have several important differences.

Spermatogenesis begins with spermatogonial stem cells and ends with mature spermatozoa, but there are several intermediate stages that you should be familiar with. First, spermatogonial stem cells can either divide into descendent spermatogonial stem cells (thereby maintaining the supply) or differentiate into spermatogonia. Spermatogonia divide through mitosis into two primary spermatocytes. Primary spermatocytes go through meiosis I and divide into two secondary spermatocytes. This is where the transition from diploid (2n) to haploid (n) happens. Secondary spermatocytes then go through meiosis II, forming spermatids. A total of four spermatids are formed from each primary spermatocyte. This process corresponds fairly closely with how meiosis is generally shown in textbook chapters on cell biology.

Spermatids initially lack some of the most important features of the mature sperm cells that are released during ejaculation, and they gain those features in a process known as spermiogenesis. The main events of spermiogenesis are as follows: (1) formation of the acrosomal cap, which facilitates the ability of a sperm to fertilize an egg; (2) formation of a tail; and (3) loss of excess cytoplasm. Spermiogenesis results in non-mature spermatozoa that are incapable of independent movement, and are transferred to the epididymis to undergo maturation.

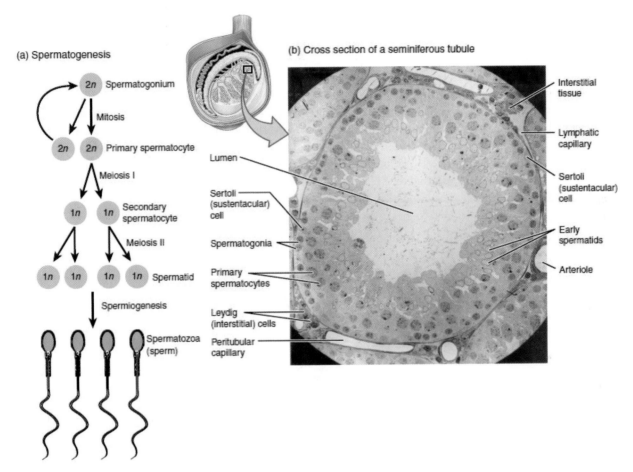

Figure 3. Spermatogenesis.

As suggested by the fact that spermatids must lose excess cytoplasm, mature sperm cells are very compact, and contain more or less the bare minimum of structures necessary for their functionality. A mature sperm cell has a head, a mid-piece, and a tail. The head contains the cell's DNA and is surrounded by the acrosomal cap. The mid-piece contains abundant mitochondria, which are necessary because sperm cells require quite a bit of energy throughout their life cycle, and the tail provides motility.

Spermatogenesis is initiated during puberty and continues throughout the lifespan. The process of spermatogenesis takes approximately 3 months, and approximately 100 million viable sperm are produced daily. As mentioned above in section 1, spermatogenesis is highly sensitive to temperature; in particular, it is most effective a few degrees Celsius below the body temperature, which is reflected in the ability of the scrotum to retract and contract in order to regulate its temperature. Spermatogenesis is actually a very sensitive process in general, and it can be adversely affected by factors as diverse as hormones, vitamin deficiencies, oxidative stress, and exposure to toxins.

Oogenesis begins with oogonia, which are formed from primordial germ cells in a process known as gametogenesis. At least some oogonia are present by approximately weeks 4-5 of fetal development, and they continue to be developed through the first five months of development. Oogonia differentiate into primary oocytes. The next stage of development is for primary oocytes to undergo meiosis I and become secondary oocytes, but this process is halted in fetuses in prophase I. Thus, female babies are born with the full set of oocytes necessary for their lifetime: approximately 1-2 million are present at birth, which is decreased to 300,000 at the time of puberty.

Once primary oocytes are frozen at prophase I, oogenesis is essentially halted until puberty. Menarche, or the first menstrual cycle, marks the resumption of oogenesis, but only in a few cells at a time. The ovum that is released during ovulation completes meiosis I, but instead of resulting in two identical secondary oocytes, one secondary oocyte is generated, along with one polar body. Meiosis I in oogenesis is an unequal division: the secondary oocyte gets the vast majority of the cytoplasm from the primary oocyte, while the polar body essentially just withers away. Similarly to what we saw with primary oocytes, secondary oocytes start undergoing meiosis II, but are frozen at prophase II until fertilization. Since fertilization is involved in the next step, we will cover it in more detail in the next section, but the essential point is that the secondary oocyte completes meiosis II, generating a mature ovum and another polar body.

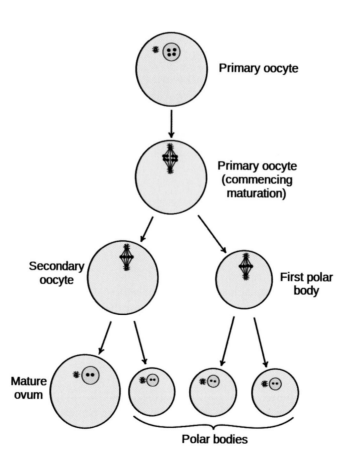

Figure 4. Oogenesis.

4. Embryogenesis, Development, and Pregnancy

Fertilization takes place in the Fallopian tube, and the first step is for a sperm cell to encounter a secondary oocyte. To understand what happens next, we need to take a closer look at the anatomy of the secondary oocyte, and to keep in mind the big-picture goal here: a mechanism needs to be in place to ensure that *one, and only one* sperm cell can fertilize an egg. If this process fails, and more than one sperm cell fertilizes an egg (known as polyspermy), a viable zygote will not be created.

As the sperm cell approaches the secondary oocyte, it passes through area known as the corona radiata, which comprises a layer of follicular cells surrounding the oocyte. Next, it passes through the zona pellucida, which is a layer of glycoproteins between the corona radiata and the oocyte. One of the glycoproteins in the zona pellucida binds with the sperm head and triggers the acrosome reaction, in which digestive enzymes are released that allow the nucleus of the sperm cell to enter the egg.

CLINICAL CONNECTIONS > > >

In an interesting side note, researchers in 2007 reported a pair of viable twins that appear to have developed through this mechanism, but for the purposes of the MCAT, polyspermy can be assumed to lead to no pregnancy or a non-viable pregnancy.

At this point, two major events occur. The glycoproteins in the zona pellucida form cross-linked structures that prevent another sperm cell from fertilizing the egg; the steps leading to this outcome are known as the cortical reaction. Additionally, the secondary oocyte completes meiosis II, creating a second polar body and a mature ovum. Then, the haploid nuclei of the sperm cell and the ovum merge, creating a diploid one-cell zygote.

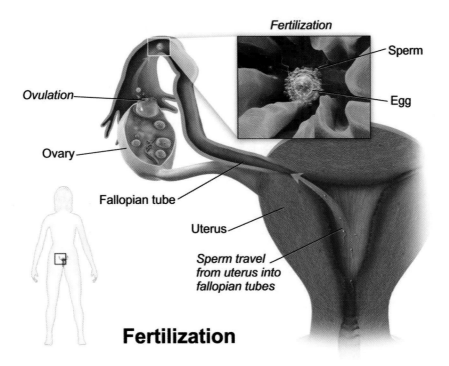

Figure 5. Fertilization.

The zygote must now travel from the Fallopian tubes to the uterus for future development. If this does not happen, the result is known as an ectopic pregnancy (more specifically, a tubal pregnancy occurs if development occurs in the Fallopian tube, but the broader category of ectopic pregnancy also includes zygotic/embryonic development within the abdomen, in the cervix, or in the ovaries). Ectopic pregnancies almost never lead to viable fetuses, and are associated with poor maternal outcomes if not properly treated.

As the zygote travels to the uterus, it undergoes a series of mitotic cell divisions known cleavage. Since the zygote is defined by unicellularity, as soon as cleavage takes place, the zygote is considered to be transformed into an embryo. Also, note that we have now left meiosis behind: the zygote (and embryo) is diploid, and all subsequent cell divisions that take place during embryonic development are mitotic (this holds true for the entire life cycle of the embryo, with the exception of meiotic divisions in the next generation of gametogenesis). During cleavage, the overall size of the embryo does not change: more and more cells are being created, but they are contained within the same space, meaning that the cells are smaller than the original zygote and that the nuclear-to-cytoplasmic (N:C) ratio increases.

Once the zygote has cleaved into a mass of 16 cells by three to four days after fertilization, it is known as the morula (Latin for "little mulberry")—the idea is that the zygote looks like a compact ball at this point. By three to five days after fertilization, the morula develops some degree of internal structure and becomes a blastocyst ("blastula" is the more general term for multicellular organisms; blastulas in mammals are known as blastocysts). The blastocyst is characterized by a fluid-filled cavity in the middle that is known as the blastocoel. As you can see in Figure 7, the blastocoel is not perfectly round. A U-shaped protrusion pokes into part of the blastocoel. This is known as the inner cell mass (ICM), and the ICM is what will eventually develop into the fetus. The other cells surrounding the blastocoel are known as the trophoblast, and eventually generate the placenta.

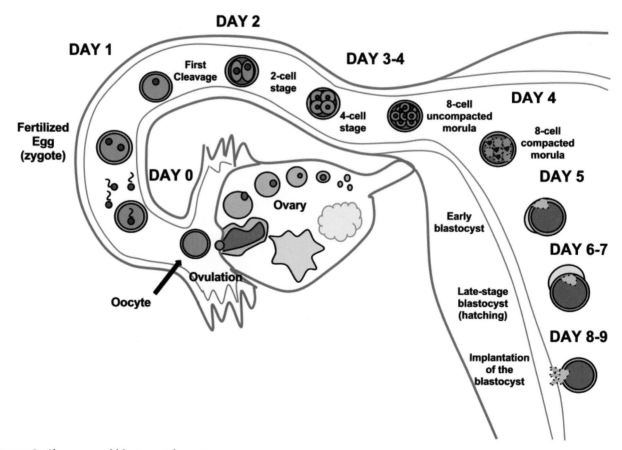

Figure 6. Cleavage and blastocyst formation.

The blastocyst then implants in the uterine endometrium. Implantation is a multi-stage process that involves close communication and adaptation between the embryo and the uterine tissue. In particular, the placenta begins to form from the trophoblast and the chorion and amnion begin to form from parts of the internal cell mass. The chorion and amnion go on to form the amniotic sac, which envelops the embryo/fetus throughout pregnancy.

Once implanted, the embryo further differentiates into the gastrula. The gastrula has three layers: the ectoderm, the mesoderm, and the endoderm. These layers eventually go on to form specific organs and components in the body.

The ectoderm primarily gives rise to the nervous system and epidermis (skin), as well as related structures like hair, nails, and sweat glands. It is also worth noting that the linings of the mouth, anus, and nostrils are also derived from the ectoderm, although the MCAT tends to primarily focus on the nervous system and the skin. The process through which the nervous system is formed from the ectoderm is known as neurulation. The first step in neurulation is the formation of a rod of mesodermal cells known as the notochord, which induces the formation of the neural plate in the ectodermal tissue located above it. The neural plate folds upward, with the neural folds on the side and the neural groove in the middle. The folding process continues, and the neural folds eventually meet, at which point they form the neural tube. The neural tube goes on to form the central nervous system, while neural crest cells initially located on the neural folds form the peripheral nervous system. At the end of this process, the surface ectoderm surrounds the neural tube, such that the central nervous system can develop within the body.

> **MCAT STRATEGY > > >**
>
> You can remember the stages of embryonic development using the following mnemonic: Zach's mother is a big giant nerd, for zygote → morula → blastula/blastocyst → gastrula → neurulation.

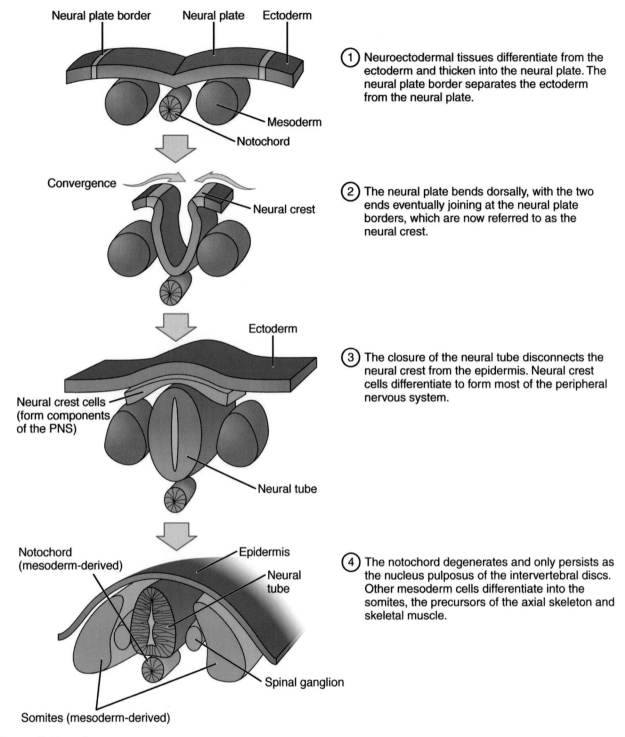

Figure 7. Neurulation.

The mesoderm generates many of the structures present within the body, including the musculature, connective tissue (including blood, bone, and cartilage), the gonads, the kidneys, and the adrenal cortex. The endoderm is basically responsible for interior linings of the body, including the linings of the gastrointestinal system, the pancreas and part of the liver, the urinary bladder and part of the urethra, and the lungs.

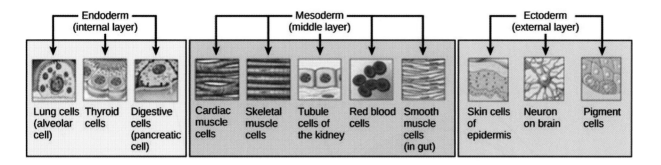

Figure 8. Germ cell layers and their respective developmental paths.

Throughout the first trimester of pregnancy, the major organs develop in a process known as organogenesis, and then in the second and third trimesters, the fetus grows larger and develops further; however, the details of fetal development are beyond the scope of the MCAT. Throughout pregnancy, the fetus obtains nutrients via the placenta, which is an organ that allows nutrient and gas exchange between the mother and the fetus. Maternal blood and fetal blood do not co-mingle, however; instead, maternal blood comes extremely close to the fetal circulation so that nutrients, gases, and waste products can be exchanged through a combination of passive and active transport. The placenta is also an endocrine organ; early in pregnancy, it secretes human chorionic gonadotropin (hCG), and later in pregnancy it secretes progesterone and estrogen. Both hCG and progesterone have the effect of maintaining the pregnancy. One interesting fact to be aware of for the MCAT is that fetal hemoglobin has a higher affinity for oxygen than adult hemoglobin; this fact allows oxygen to be "passed" more efficiently from the maternal circulation to the fetal circulation. The fetus is connected to the placenta through the umbilical cord.

MCAT STRATEGY > > >

The ectoderm basically describes the external layer of organs, the mesoderm describes what's in the middle, and the endoderm develops into the most internal layer (internal linings).

> > CONNECTIONS < <

Chapter 9 of Biology

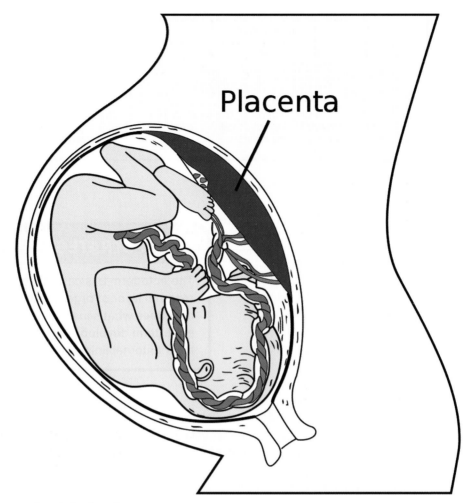

Figure 9. Placenta and umbilical cord.

Sexual differentiation takes place before birth in fetuses. This process is complex, and the MCAT does not expect you to be familiar with all of its details. However, you should know that the female developmental pattern can be thought of as more or less the default, whereas the development of male sex organs is induced by genes on the Y chromosome, in particular the sex-determining region of the Y chromosome (*SRY*). *SRY* causes the development of testes, which secrete hormones that cause the precursor structures of the Wolffian duct and Müllerian duct to differentiate accordingly. In male fetuses, the Wolffian duct differentiates into accessory organs of the male reproductive system, such as the epididymis and vas deferens, while the Müllerian duct is lost. In contrast, in females, the Wolffian duct regresses and the Müllerian duct develops into the uterus, cervix, and upper third of the vagina.

Pregnancy most commonly lasts between 37 and 41 weeks, and comes to an end with labor and childbirth (also known as parturition in medical language). The details of labor and delivery will be covered in medical school, but for the MCAT you should be aware that uterine contractions play a major role in labor, and that they are driven by the hormone oxytocin in a rare example of a physiological positive feedback loop; oxytocin causes uterine contractions, which stimulate more oxytocin release, which stimulates more and stronger uterine contractions, and so on until the fetus is delivered through the vaginal canal.

5. Hormonal Control of Reproduction

Many aspects of the reproductive system are controlled by hormones. We will start by reviewing reproductive development, and then discuss the menstrual cycle.

As discussed above, the sexual differentiation of fetuses takes place before birth. Throughout childhood, little of note happens in this regard until puberty, when wide-ranging hormonal changes take place, facilitating the development of children into sexually mature adults capable of reproduction. Pulses of gonadotropin-releasing hormone (GnRH) set puberty in motion. GnRH stimulates the release of luteinizing hormone (LH) and follicle-stimulating hormone (FSH). It's at this point that we see differences emerge between males and females. LH and FSH affect the ovaries in females and the testes in males, and trigger the release of other downstream hormones. In males, LH causes the Leydig cells of the testes to produce testosterone, while FSH affects Sertoli cells, causing them to produce factors necessary for sperm maturation. In females, FSH causes the production of estrogen, and LH causes the production of progesterone.

Estrogen and testosterone are the main sex hormones in females and males, respectively. Their release during puberty stimulates the development of the reproductive tract as well as secondary sexual characteristics, which are typical markers of biological sex that are not directly involved in reproductive function. For females, secondary sexual characteristics include changes in the pattern of fat distribution, wider hips, the growth of body hair, and the growth of breasts, while for males, they include the development of facial and body hair, a deeper voice, and so on.

Estrogen and progesterone are also involved in the menstrual cycle, which is a regular hormonal cycle in women of reproductive age, repeating at an average interval of 28 days, although considerable variability exists in the timing of menstruation. The menstrual cycle starts at puberty, and continues through menopause, which usually takes place between 45 and 55 years of age and marks the end of the reproductively active period of a woman's life (however, advances in assisted reproductive technology, especially the use of donor eggs, have allowed some women to conceive later in life).

The terms "ovarian cycle" and "uterine cycle" are used to reflect the fact that we can focus either on how the menstrual cycle plays out in the ovaries or in the uterus. We'll focus first on the ovarian cycle and then analyze the uterine cycle, because doing so better reflects the underlying logic of the biological processes at hand. Keeping careful track of which terminology applies to the ovarian cycle and the uterine cycle will also help avoid some common sources of terminological confusion.

MCAT STRATEGY > > >

The MCAT likes to ask about the menstrual cycle because it is a complex, multi-staged physiological process with important real-world implications.

The ovarian cycle begins with the follicular phase, followed by ovulation, which is in turn followed by the luteal phase. As discussed earlier, one ovum is released every menstrual cycle, and the ovarian phase simply reflects the logic of what this process entails. A follicle matures in the follicular phase and releases the egg at ovulation. The luteal phase refers to what happens after the ovum is released; the follicle is transformed into a structure known as the corpus luteum, which secretes progesterone, helping to maintain the uterine lining. The corpus luteum decays towards the end of this period, and another cycle begins.

The uterine cycle begins with menstruation, which overlaps with the first part of the follicular phase of the ovarian cycle. During menstruation, the uterine lining built up in the previous cycle is sloughed off. Menstruation typically lasts from three to five days, although variation within the range of two to seven days is also common (as mentioned above, considerable variability exists among individuals regarding the timing of the menstrual cycle). Once menstruation is complete, the uterine endometrium is built up again during the proliferative phase. The final phase of the uterine cycle is known as the secretory phase, and this overlaps with the luteal phase of the ovarian cycle. During the secretory phase, the uterine endometrium continues to build up and undergoes various changes to make it more receptive for implantation, under the influence of the progesterone secreted by the corpus luteum.

Given a solid understanding of the anatomical steps involved in ovulation and implantation, the stages of the ovarian and uterine cycle are quite logical, because you can think of them as simply reflecting the steps that must happen for this system to work. The next step is to understand how hormonal regulation shapes the various steps of the menstrual cycle. Since hormones can affect both the ovaries and uterus, it is difficult to firmly separate the ovarian and uterine cycles when discussing the hormonal regulation of the menstrual cycle, which underscores the importance of mastering the basic anatomical processes involved.

MCAT STRATEGY > > >

A systematic approach is key for successfully studying the menstrual cycle (and many other topics!) for the MCAT, so be sure that you have a solid grasp of the basic anatomical changes involved in the menstrual cycle before moving on to its hormonal regulation—otherwise, you run the risk of memorizing without understanding, which makes you prone to errors if asked to apply your knowledge in a new context.

At the beginning of the follicular phase, there is a moderate rise in follicle-stimulating hormone (FSH), which induces follicular development before gradually dropping off. Throughout most of the follicular phase, estrogen levels gradually increase, stimulating the development of the uterine endometrium. After estrogen levels reach a certain threshold close to ovulation, they stimulate a brief surge in luteinizing hormone (LH) and FSH levels; the spike in LH levels is particularly notable and is what triggers ovulation. As a side note, this is essentially why LH is called *luteinizing* hormone: by inducing ovulation, it induces the transformation of the follicle into the corpus *luteum*. The luteal phase is characterized by high levels of progesterone, which help maintain the readiness of the uterine endometrium for implantation.

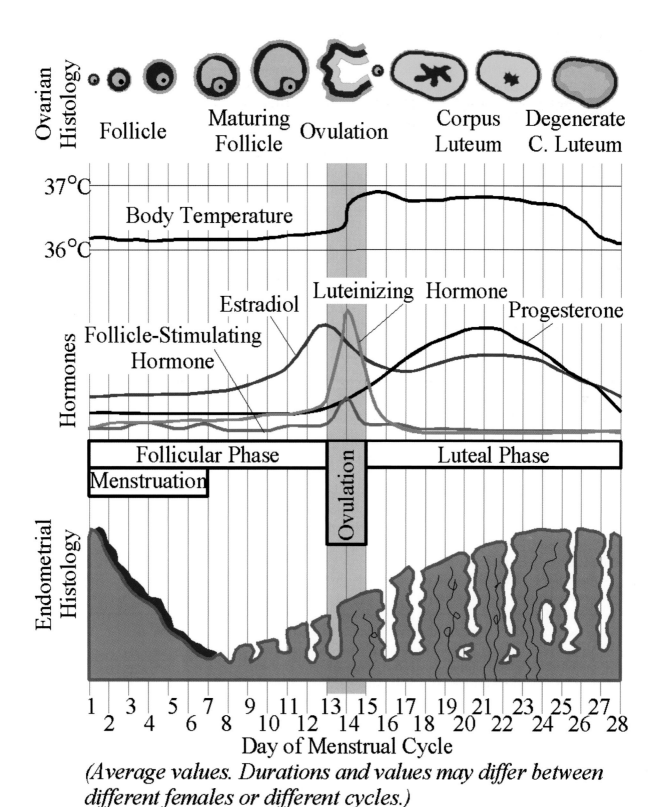

(Average values. Durations and values may differ between different females or different cycles.)

Figure 10. The menstrual cycle

Finally, it's worth taking a brief look at how the body "knows" whether or not implantation has taken place, and therefore whether to transition into another menstrual cycle or into pregnancy. In the absence of implantation, successive negative feedback loops keep the cycle moving. Progesterone exerts negative feedback on LH, and eventually, as LH declines, the corpus luteum will degenerate (remember the close connection between LH and the corpus luteum that is implied by the fact that they essentially share the same name!). As the corpus luteum degenerates, it no longer secretes progesterone. Recall that progesterone keeps the endometrium ready for implantation. If progesterone declines, then so does the ability of the endometrium to undergo implantation, and the stage is set for menstruation and for the next menstrual cycle to happen.

In contrast, if implantation *does* happen, the body has to have some way of preventing the endometrium from being sloughed away. The key here is that the embryo itself secretes a hormone known as human chorionic gonadotropin (hCG), which allows the corpus luteum to be maintained and for progesterone levels to be sustained. By the second trimester, hCG levels drop because they are no longer necessary; by this point, the placenta can function as an endocrine organ and independently secrete progesterone (as well as estrogen).

6. Must-Knows

> Path of sperm through the male reproductive tract: seminiferous tubules → epididymis → vas deferens → ejaculatory duct → urethra → penis (SEVEN UP, where "N" stands for "nothing")
> Path of eggs through female reproductive tract: ovaries → Fallopian tube, then:
>> – If fertilization → zygote/embryo goes to uterus → pregnancy; childbirth through vaginal canal
>> – If no fertilization → uterine lining shed during menstruation
> Spermatogenesis:
>> – Takes place in testes, which are maintained a few degrees Celsius cooler than body temperature.
>> – Spermatogonial stem cells → spermatogonia (2n) → primary spermatocytes (2n) → secondary spermatocytes (n) → spermatids → spermatozoa.
>> – Sperm mature and gain motility in epididymis.
>> – Spermatogenesis is a constant process from puberty throughout rest of lifespan.
> Oogenesis:
>> – Oogonia → primary oocyte + polar body → secondary oocyte + polar body → ovum.
>> – Oogenesis is *not* a constant process; primary oocytes are halted at prophase I at birth, meiosis I completed at ovulation to form secondary oocyte, which is then arrested at prophase II; meiosis II is completed at fertilization.
> Fertilization: takes place in Fallopian tube
>> – Acrosome reaction allows sperm cell to enter egg; results in cortical reaction that prevents polyspermy.
> Stages of embryonic development:
>> – Morula (16-cell ball) → blastocyst (fluid-filled sac in middle) → gastrula (three germ cell layers present)
>> – Ectoderm → skin, nervous system, sweat glands, hair, nails
>> – Mesoderm → connective tissue (including blood and bone), muscles, gonads
>> – Endoderm → internal linings of GI tract, lungs, urinary bladder.
> Menstrual cycle: takes place every ~28 days in reproductive-age women
>> – Ovarian cycle: follicular phase (follicle develops), ovulation (egg is released), luteal phase (follicle → corpus luteum)
>> – Uterine cycle: menstruation (uterine endometrium from previous cycle is shed), proliferative phase (endometrium develops again), secretory phase (endometrium is ready for implantation)
>> – Estrogen gradually rises throughout follicular phase, triggering LH surge, which causes ovulation. Progesterone, secreted by corpus luteum, maintains uterine endometrium for implantation.
>> – If implantation happens, human chorionic gonadotropin (hCG) maintains corpus luteum, thereby maintaining progesterone and maintaining pregnancy.

This page left intentionally blank.

Practice Passage

Hensen's node is a structure at the tip of the primitive streak in the human embryo. The node is a control center that instructs cells in the epiblast to change their fate from non-neural to neural in a process called neural induction. The primitive streak forms on day 15 of development and signals the inner cell mass to be converted into the tri-layered embryonic disc.

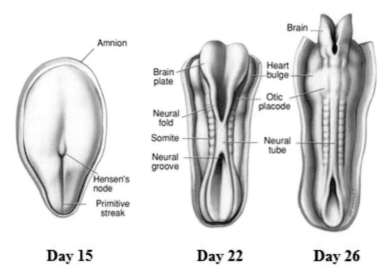

Figure 1. Timeline of neural induction

It is known that bone morphogenetic proteins (BMPs) are expressed by the neural tube and surrounding tissues, but other signals may also be required for proper neurulation. Researchers wished to investigate if the protein calreticulin is involved. Calreticulin is a Ca^{2+}-binding protein which can also inhibit the binding of an androgen receptor to its hormone-responsive DNA element. The *CALR* translation product can also inhibit androgen receptor and retinoic acid receptor transcriptional activities *in vivo*.

To test for cellular secretion of calreticulin, COS cells were transfected with *CALR-Myc* and the supernatant and a lysate of the cells was later collected and tested for the presence of CALR-Myc by western blotting. As a positive control, Chordin-Myc presence was also tested.

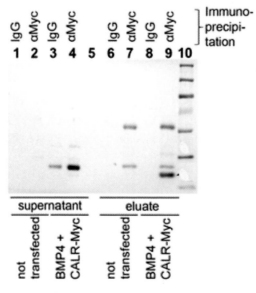

Figure 2. Calreticulin-BMP4 interaction test (Note: Lane 10 contains molecular weight markers)

Next, researchers explored whether calreticulin can bind directly to BMP4. HEK-293T cells were co-transfected with expression constructs encoding BMP4 and Myc-tagged calreticulin (Figure 2). After immunoprecipitation with anti-Myc antibody or mouse IgG (control), the supernatant not bound to the Myc-beads and the eluate from the Myc-beads were analyzed by western blotting, probed with an antibody to BMP4. Lane 10 contains molecular weight markers.

It is believed these results will assist in the growing field of reproductive technology, particularly technology used to monitor fetal development *in utero*.

Adapted from De Almeida, I & Stern, C. (2016). Calreticulin expressed in Hensen's node during neural induction. Developmental Biology, 421(2): 161–170 under CCBY 4.0

1. According to the passage, the primitive streak most likely arrives immediately prior to which process?
   A. Neurulation
   B. Gastrulation
   C. Fertilization
   D. Implantation

2. During fertilization, attachment of the sperm to the ovum gives rise to a Ca^{2+} signal that raises intracellular calcium concentration from 200 nM to a peak of 6 μM in a period of 20 seconds or less, and the wave signal spreads rapidly across the egg from the attachment site. All of the following could explain the generation of this calcium wave EXCEPT:
   A. the reorganization of the endoplasmic reticulum into dense, stacked lamellar clusters during oocyte maturation.
   B. a decease in the sensitivity to IP_3 of the sarcoplasmic reticula in the oocyte during maturation.
   C. seminal fluid near the attachment site contains a calcium concentration as high as 13 M.
   D. the oocyte endoplasmic reticulum is sensitized to calcium release during oocyte maturation.

3. Which of the following results would most strongly support the conclusion that the COS cells tested express calreticulin?
   A. CALR-Myc, but not Chordin-Myc was detected in the supernatant of transfected cells.
   B. Chordin-Myc, but not CALR-Myc was detected in the supernatant of transfected cells.
   C. Both Chordin-Myc and CALR-Myc was detected in the supernatant of transfected cells.
   D. Neither CALR-Myc nor Chordin-Myc was detected in the supernatant of transfected cells.

4. Which of the following events would indicate a normal menstrual cycle has occurred?
   A. A primary oocyte matures into a secondary oocyte
   B. A secondary oocyte completes maturation
   C. A primary oocyte matures into an oogonium
   D. A secondary oocyte matures into a primary oocyte

5. Which of the following serves a reproductive or sexual purpose in males only?
   A. Estradiol
   B. Müllerian ducts
   C. Testosterone
   D. Urethra

6. The anticonvulsant phenytoin is contraindicated in pregnant women, due to its destructive effect on Hensen's node.

Which germ layer in the developing fetus is likely to be directly impacted by the administration of phenytoin to a pregnant woman?
A. Endoderm
B. Mesoderm
C. Ectoderm
D. Amnion

7. According to the results in Figure 2, calreticulin most likely:
A. acts as a BMP4 agonist.
B. acts a BMP4 antagonist.
C. is unable to bind to BMP4 *in vivo*.
D. physically interacts with BMP4.

Practice Passage Explanations

Hensen's node is a structure at the tip of the primitive streak in the human embryo. The node is a control center that instructs cells in the epiblast to change their fate from non-neural to neural in a process called neural induction. The primitive streak forms on day 15 of development and signals the inner cell mass to be converted into the tri-layered embryonic disc.

Key terms: Hensen's node, primitive streak, neural induction

Cause and effect: primitive streak formation → formation of 3 layered disc

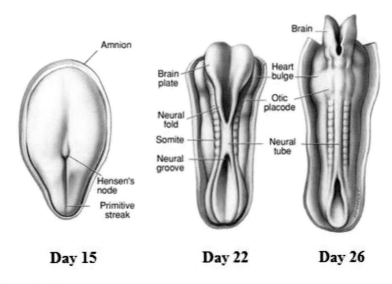

Figure 1. Timeline of neural induction

It is known that bone morphogenetic proteins (BMPs) are expressed by the neural tube and surrounding tissues, but other signals may also be required for proper neurulation. Researchers wished to investigate if the protein calreticulin is involved. Calreticulin is a Ca^{2+}-binding protein which can also inhibit the binding of an androgen receptor to its hormone-responsive DNA element. The *CALR* translation product can also inhibit androgen receptor and retinoic acid receptor transcriptional activities *in vivo*.

Key terms: BMPs, Calreticulin, CALR

Contrast: BMPs are known to affect neurulation, but role of Calreticulin unknown

Cause and effect: CALR protein can inhibit response to testosterone/estrogen

To test for cellular secretion of calreticulin, COS cells were transfected with *CALR-Myc* and the supernatant and a lysate of the cells was later collected and tested for the presence of CALR-Myc by western blotting. As a positive control, Chordin-Myc presence was also tested.

Key terms: transfected, supernatant, lysate, CALR-Myc, positive control

Cause and effect: test to see if introduction of CALR gene → Calreticulin production

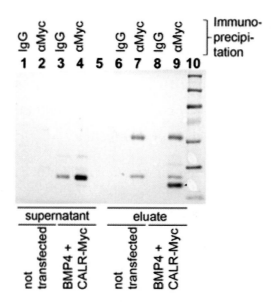

Figure 2. Calreticulin-BMP4 interaction test (Note: Lane 10 contains molecular weight markers)

Figure 2 contains many lanes, so let's group them (supernatant is the liquid lying above a solid residue after precipitation, centrifugation, or other processes: the eluate is the liquid pulled out after elution (washing) to remove captured molecules):

Immunoprecipitation with anti-Myc antibody (lanes 2, 4, 7, 9); with mouse IgG (lanes 1, 3, 6, 8); supernatant not bound to the Myc-beads (lanes 1–4); eluate from the Myc-beads (lanes 6–9); there is a unique band precipitated from the co-transfected cells (experimental lane, lane 9), smaller than what is seen in the control lanes or supernatant lanes; this band likely corresponds to BMP4-CALR binding being identified by the antibody probe

Next, researchers explored whether calreticulin can bind directly to BMP4. HEK-293T cells were co-transfected with expression constructs encoding BMP4 and Myc-tagged calreticulin (Figure 2). After immunoprecipitation with anti-Myc antibody or mouse IgG (control), the supernatant not bound to the Myc-beads and the eluate from the Myc-beads were analyzed by western blotting, probed with an antibody to BMP4. Lane 10 contains molecular weight markers.

Key terms: BMP4, immunoprecipitation, western blotting, BMP4 antibody

Cause and effect: Immunoprecipitation enables the purification of a protein. An antibody for the protein of interest is incubated with a cell extract enabling the antibody to bind to the protein in solution. The antibody/antigen complex is then pulled out of the sample using protein A/G-coupled agarose beads. This isolates the protein of interest from the rest of the sample.

It is believed these results will assist in the growing field of reproductive technology, particularly technology used to monitor fetal development in utero.

Key terms: monitor fetal development

Adapted from De Almeida, I & Stern, C. (2016). Calreticulin expressed in Hensen's node during neural induction. Developmental Biology, 421(2): 161–170 under CCBY 4.0

1. B is correct. According to paragraph 1, the primitive streak arrives on day 15 and marks the onset of ICM development into a tri-layered structure. We should know that this description, along with the time of onset (day 15), indicates the process known as gastrulation. Gastrulation is the process whereby the inner cell mass in converted into the trilaminar embryonic disc comprised of the three primary germ layers (ectoderm, mesoderm and endoderm).

   A. The passage does say that the Hensen's node is directly related to neurulation, but the question is asking about the primitive streak, which paragraph 1 tells us causes the formation of the 3 primary germ layers. Neurulation typically begins around Day 20.

   C. Fertilization, the meeting of sperm and egg, is the incipient event that starts embryonic development. Thus, this event would be Day 0, not Day 15.

   D. Implantation is the early stage of pregnancy at which the fertilized ovum adheres to the wall of the uterus, typically between days 6 and 12. At this stage of prenatal development, the structure is called the blastocyst.

2. B is correct. We are looking for the odd man out here. Three of the answers will help explain the rapid increase in calcium, and one will not. The most common signaling pathway that increases cytoplasmic calcium concentration is the phospholipase C pathway. In this pathway, the IP_3 receptor serves as a Ca^{2+} channel and releases Ca^{2+} from the endoplasmic reticulum. The Ca^{2+} ions bind to protein kinase C (PKC) thereby activating it. Depletion of calcium from the endoplasmic reticulum will lead to Ca^{2+} entry from outside the cell. If the oocyte is less sensitive to IP_3 signaling, the movement of calcium cannot be triggered as easily and thus, would NOT explain such a rapid and quick influx of calcium.

   A. The endoplasmic reticulum is responsible for storage of calcium. A tightly packed, dense organization of the ER within the cells would allow for a large, rapid increase of intracellular calcium.

   C. The seminal fluid travels with the sperm into the vagina and allows for its movement inside the acidic environment. While up to 200 million sperm enter the vagina, only a few hundred will travel past the cervix, uterus and fallopian tube isthmus to meet the oocyte. If some of the fluid is able to travel there as well, and contains such a high concentration of calcium, it could explain a source of extracellular calcium which can enter the cell.

   D. If the oocyte ER becomes more sensitive to calcium release, it will result in a larger calcium release in response to a given stimulus.

3. C is correct. Paragraph 3 states that the Chordin-Myc is used as a positive control to test for CALR secretion. A positive control receives a treatment with a known response (in this case, calreticulin production) so that this positive response can be compared to the unknown response of the treatment. For a positive result, both trials should have similar results. The presence of BOTH Chordin and CALR would indicate that calreticulin is present in both supernatants. If the CALR transfection was successful, the transfected cells should also be detected in the supernatant. This dual result would confirm that calreticulin is present and being expressed by the COS cells.

   A, B, D: As a positive control, the Chordin-Myc indicates the desired result, and the CALR-Myc transfected cell trials should also yield the same results if they also express the calreticulin protein.

4. A is correct. The normal maturation pathway of ova is as follows:
Oogonia (2n) → Primary oocyte (occurs via mitosis, 2n) → Secondary oocyte (completion of meiosis I, n) → Mature ovum (completion of meiosis II, this process requires sperm (n))
Each month (between puberty and menopause) one primary oocyte comes out of its arrest (in prophase I) and develops into a secondary oocyte, which then ruptures from the follicle and is released into the fallopian tube. This complex, neuroendocrine-coordinated process is the menstrual cycle.
   B. Meiosis II is arrested in the processes of spindle formation during metaphase II. Meiosis II is arrested here (the cell is still a secondary oocyte) until the final steps of the maturation, namely the freeing for the second meiosis which is completed only after the spermatozoon has penetrated the secondary oocyte. This would not have to be the case in normal menstruation, which does not require fertilization (sperm meets egg) to occur.
   C, D: These are the opposite of what normally occurs during the menstrual cycle. The oogonium is less mature/developed than the primary oocyte and the primary oocyte is less mature/developed than the secondary oocyte.

5. D is correct. The urethra is the duct connecting the bladder to the outside world, and allows for the elimination of liquid waste (urine). In females, the urethra carries urine from the bladder to a narrow opening in front of the vaginal aperture which is separate from the vagina itself. In males, the urethra opens out at the tip of the penis and is responsible for carrying urine and semen outside the body.
   A. Estradiol, the predominant form of estrogen, plays a critical role in both male and female sexual function. Estradiol in men is essential for modulating libido, erectile function, and spermatogenesis. Estrogen in females helps regulate the menstrual cycle, controlling the growth of the uterine lining during the first part of the cycle.
   B. The Müllerian ducts are the primordial anlage of the female reproductive tract. They differentiate to form the fallopian tubes, uterus, the uterine cervix, and the superior aspect of the vagina.
   C. Both men and women secrete testosterone (though males have far more). In females, the adrenal glands and ovaries produce small amounts of testosterone, which is linked to female sex drive. Specifically, testosterone in women is responsible for the sensitivity of the nipples and clitoris associated with sexual satisfaction.

6. C is correct. The passage states that Hensen's node is responsible for proper neural induction. The ectoderm layer is where neurulation takes place. Neurulation leads to the formation of the neural tube, neural crest cells and the epidermis. The neural tube cells will become the CNS, neural crest cells will become the PNS and enteric nervous system, and the epidermal cells develop into skin, hair, nails, and the eyes.
   A. The portions of the body that develop from the endoderm germ layer include parts of the digestive tract, the respiratory tract, the urinary tract, and several internal organs. This also includes the internal linings of these systems and organs.
   B. The mesoderm gives rise to connective tissues such as cartilage, bone, blood, blood vessel endothelium, in addition to muscle (cardiac, skeletal, smooth).
   D. The *amnion* is a membrane that covers the developing embryo. The amniotic sac eventually fills with fluid, expanding the volume of the amnion and provides a protective environment for the developing embryo.

7. D is correct. The experimental details behind Figure 2 are in paragraph 4. Examining Figure 2 closely, we can see a unique band was precipitated from the co-transfected cells in lane 9, and most likely corresponds to BMP4 (arrow).

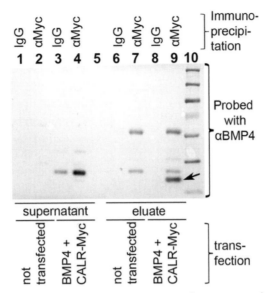

How can we know? This band is absent from controls: supernatant from untransfected cells (lanes 1–2) or from transfected cells (lanes 3–4), eluate from untransfected cells (lanes 6–7), precipitated with control IgG antibody (lanes 1, 3, 6) or with anti-Myc antibody (lanes 2, 4, 7). It is also absent from the eluate of transfected cells precipitated with control antibody (lane 8). These results show that calreticulin secreted from the cells can and does bind to BMP4.

A, B: While the results of the immunoprecipitation and western blotting tell us that calreticulin can bind to BMP4, we do not know the result of this binding. Physiological agonists typically bind to the receptor of the molecule, not the molecule itself. Antagonists may bind to either the target molecule, or the receptor (a receptor antagonist). With the data given, we cannot state for sure what physiological response the protein binding causes.

C. While the test being run were *in vitro*, we have no direct evidence that calreticulin cannot also bind to BMP4 *in vivo* as well.

Independent Questions

1. Which of the following is the correct ejaculatory pathway of sperm?
   A. Epididymis, seminiferous tubules, vas deferens, ejaculatory ducts, urethra, penis
   B. Seminiferous tubules, epididymis, vas deferens, ejaculatory ducts, urethra, penis
   C. Seminiferous tubules, epididymis, ejaculatory ducts, vas deferens, urethra, penis
   D. Epididymis, seminiferous tubules, ejaculatory ducts, vas deferens, urethra, penis

2. Select the statement about oogenesis that is accurate in reference to a healthy female.
   A. Before birth, diploid primary oocytes mature into haploid secondary oocytes.
   B. Before birth, diploid primary oocytes mature into diploid secondary oocytes.
   C. After puberty, diploid primary oocytes mature into haploid secondary oocytes.
   D. After puberty, diploid primary oocytes mature into diploid secondary oocytes.

3. Which of the following is NOT an important role played by the hypothalamic-pituitary axis in ovarian function?
   A. Stimulation of Leydig cell activity
   B. Stimulation of folliculogenesis
   C. Secretion of progesterone
   D. Secretion of estrogen

4. Kallmann's syndrome is a congenital hypogonadotropic hypogonadism. In the developing brain, GnRH-producing neurons fail to migrate to the correct location and instead remain in the cribriform plate, disrupting the olfactory bulbs. A male patient with Kallmann's syndrome would be expected to display:
   A. an increase in LH and FSH levels and an increase in testosterone levels and sperm count.
   B. an increase in LH and FSH levels and a decrease in testosterone levels and sperm count.
   C. a decrease in LH and FSH levels and an increase in testosterone levels and sperm count.
   D. a decrease in LH and FSH levels and a decrease in testosterone levels and sperm count.

5. A patient visits her gynecologist with concerns about her menstrual cycle. She has heard that a typical menstrual cycle lasts 28 days, but hers regularly lasts 35 days. Her doctor assures her that this is very common and that the variation in cycle length is due to:
   A. variability in the luteal phase.
   B. variability in the follicular phase.
   C. variability in the secretory phase.
   D. variation between individuals in their Sertoli cell function.

6. Patricia, a 56-year-old female, has not had her period in the past 5 months and has been experiencing hot flashes. You suspect that she may have begun menopause, so you perform laboratory diagnostic work. Which of the following findings would most strongly support that Patricia is undergoing menopause?
   A. A decrease in estrogen levels along with an increase in FSH and LH levels
   B. A decrease in estrogen, FSH, and LH levels
   C. An increase in estrogen and FSH levels along with a decrease in LH levels
   D. An increase in estrogen, FSH, and LH levels

7. Following childbirth, women undergo dramatic hormonal changes to allow for lactation. When these changes do not occur properly, hormone therapy may be required to breastfeed. Which of the following treatments would be appropriate to induce lactation?
   A. A medication to trigger the production of progesterone
   B. A medication to trigger the production of oxytocin
   C. A medication to trigger the production of estrogen
   D. A medication to trigger the production of prolactin

8. Following fertilization, the implanted embryo releases a hormone that mimics LH and maintains the corpus luteum. This hormone, which can be detected in the urine and blood with high levels of accuracy, is:
   A. human chorionic gonadotropin, a peptide hormone.
   B. human chorionic gonadotropin, a steroid hormone.
   C. estradiol, a peptide hormone.
   D. estradiol, a steroid hormone.

Independent Question Explanations

1. B is correct. Sperm are produced in the seminiferous tubules, then move to the epididymis to mature. Next, they pass through the vas deferens, ejaculatory ducts, and urethra, then exit the body through the penis. This pathway can be remembered using the mnemonic "SEVE(n) UP."

2. C is correct. Females are born with large numbers of primary oocytes arrested in prophase of meiosis I. After puberty, ovulation begins to occur, and with each ovulation event, one primary oocyte completes meiosis I to become a secondary oocyte. Primary oocytes are diploid, but secondary oocytes are haploid, since homologous chromosomes separate during anaphase of meiosis I.

3. A is correct. The hypothalamic-pituitary axis is closely involved in ovarian activity, in particular through the release of FSH and LH from the anterior pituitary. These hormones stimulate folliculogenesis and promote the secretion of progesterone and estrogen. Leydig cells are found in the testicles of males, not in the ovaries of females.

4. D is correct. GnRH, or gonadotropin-releasing hormone, is a tropic peptide hormone produced by the hypothalamus. It is responsible for the release of LH and FSH and the eventual regulation of testosterone levels and sperm count. Disruption of GnRH-producing cells would result in dramatically reduced GnRH production. This would disrupt the hypothalamic-pituitary-gonadal axis, resulting in the downstream decrease of LH and FSH levels. In turn, lowered levels of these peptides would decrease testosterone levels and sperm count.

5. B is correct. Menstrual cycles average 28 days, but they can be as long as 35 days. The variability is due to the follicular, or proliferative phase. The luteal, or secretory, phase is generally constant and lasts 14 days. Note that even if you did not know this, you could eliminate choices A and C because they refer to the same phase, and you could eliminate choice D because Sertoli cells are found in males, not females.

6. A is correct. Menopause begins with the progressive loss of ovarian follicle units, known as atresia. This results in a decrease in ovarian production of estrogen. This reduces the negative feedback to the anterior pituitary, ultimately increasing the levels of FSH and LH.

7. D is correct. Prolactin is the predominant hormone that promotes and maintains lactation. Following childbirth, progesterone and estrogen levels drop, and prolactin levels increase. Oxytocin is involved in the contraction of myoepithelial cells, or "milk letdown."

8. A is correct. Human chorionic gonadotropin, or hCG, is released by the embryo shortly after implantation. This hormone mimics LH and maintains the corpus luteum, thus also maintaining estrogen and progesterone levels. hCG is a peptide hormone; even if you did not know this, you could infer that hCG and LH (a pituitary peptide) likely have some structural similarities.

This page left intentionally blank.

Respiratory and Circulatory Systems

0. Introduction

This chapter deals with the nuts-and-bolts aspects of our physiology that sustain life on a minute-to-minute basis; namely, how we get oxygen from the atmosphere to the tissues that need it for metabolism, and then how we get some of the waste products out of our body. The closely interwoven respiratory and circulatory systems are responsible for this task, although the excretory system also plays a major role in getting rid of waste. As you may have seen already in work or volunteering experiences, and will continue to see in medical school and as a physician, acute problems with the respiratory and circulatory systems can cause major medical emergencies, while chronic respiratory and circulatory problems also have major impacts on quality of life and mortality.

From the point of view of the MCAT, as you study these topics, you should always have gas exchange at the back of your mind. How does oxygen enter the body? Once it enters the body, how does it get to the tissues where it is needed? When carbon dioxide is generated, how does it leave the body? The MCAT places a major emphasis on the general patterns of how biological systems function, and in a certain sense, the story of oxygen is the story of eukaryotic life. This is also underscored by how important oxidative respiration is for the MCAT as a biochemistry topic, although what happens to oxygen within a cell is outside of the scope of this chapter. You will find that focusing on this unifying theme will help you make sense of the details of these physiological systems and to apply them successfully on Test Day.

1. Mechanisms of Breathing

In this section, we'll attempt to answer what may initially seem to be a simple question: how do we breathe? The mechanism of breathing is elegant but intricate, as outlined below.

First, let's review some anatomy. As air enters our body, it travels either through the nostrils (also known as the nares) or the oral cavity. The nasal cavity is located behind the external nostrils, and contains mucous membranes and hairs known as vibrissae that filter out particulate matter. The air then travels down through the pharynx, which is located at the back of the mouth, and is also part of the digestive system because food passes through it as well as air. The next structure of the respiratory tract, the epiglottis, can be thought of as a switch-point that separates the respiratory and digestive systems. The epiglottis is a cartilaginous tissue that covers the larynx during the act of swallowing, shunting food into the esophagus. Otherwise, air continues into the larynx. The larynx contains the

Damage to the alveoli can be devastating. It is a major mechanism of chronic obstructive pulmonary disease, which is primarily caused by tobacco smoking and exposure to air pollution, and results in millions of deaths worldwide each year.

MCAT STRATEGY > > >

A mnemonic you can use for the structures of the respiratory tract is "not many people like to be alone" for nose/mouth → pharynx → larynx → trachea → bronchi → alveoli.

vocal cords, which vibrate to produce sounds when air is pushed through them and are consciously controlled during speaking.

The air then moves down through the trachea (also known as the windpipe). The epithelium of the trachea is lined with goblet cells, which produce mucus, and the epithelial cells themselves are ciliated. Particulate matter and microbes that are still present in the air are trapped in the mucus, and then the cilia push the mucus upwards, where it becomes phlegm that can either be expelled or swallowed. The bronchi (singular = bronchus) then split off from the bottom of the trachea. The transition from the trachea to the bronchi is where the respiratory system becomes bilateral (i.e., has both left and right sides). The epithelium of the bronchi is also lined with goblet cells and ciliated epithelial cells, much like the trachea. The bronchi then divide again into successively smaller segments, known as secondary bronchi, tertiary bronchi, and bronchioles. This process ends in the formation of very small structures known as alveoli, which are where gas exchange occurs. Alveoli are sacs coated with surfactant, a film that reduces surface tension, allowing the alveoli to remain inflated when the lung is compressed during exhalation. Each alveolus is surrounded by tiny capillaries. An average pair of lungs contains something on the order of 600 million alveoli, resulting in a collectively tremendous surface area for gas exchange.

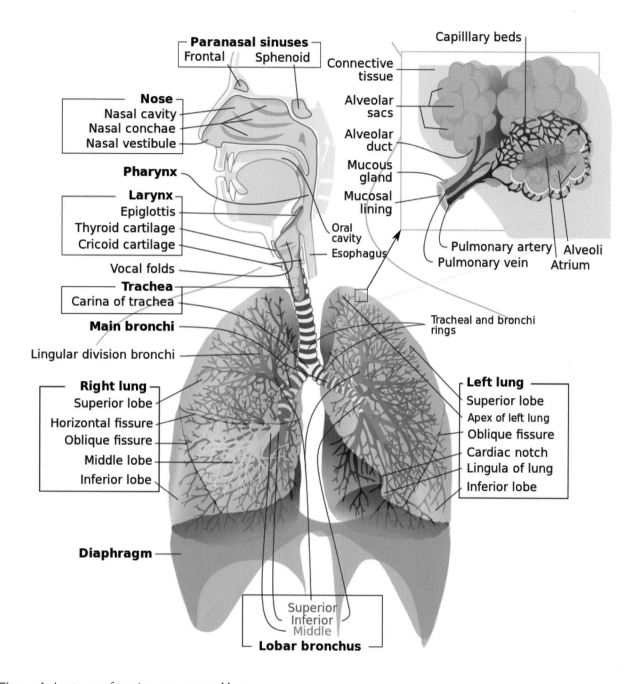

Figure 1. Anatomy of respiratory tract and lungs.

The thoracic cavity contains the lungs as well as the heart, and is protected by the rib cage. However, the lungs do not adhere directly to the thoracic cavity. Instead, the lung is covered by a serous membrane known as the pulmonary pleura, while an outer membrane, known as the parietal pleura, is what adheres to the thoracic cavity. Between the two pleurae is the pleural cavity, which under normal conditions contains just a very thin layer of liquid that lubricates movements between the two pleurae. As a result of certain pathological conditions, fluid can accumulate in the pleural space, resulting in pleural effusion. If air enters the pleural space, the resulting condition is known as pneumothorax. Both pleural effusion and pneumothorax are serious medical conditions that can result in emergencies.

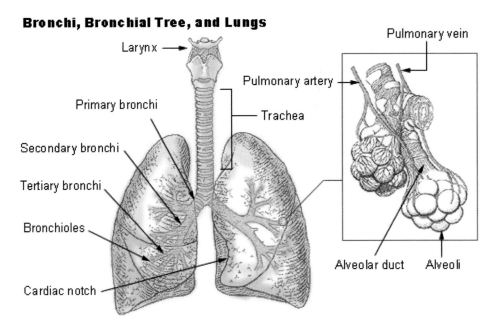

Figure 2. Structure of lungs and alveoli.

Now that we've covered the basic anatomy of the respiratory system, we can make sense of the mechanism of breathing. The main driver of breathing is the diaphragm, the muscle at the bottom of the thoracic cavity that separates it from the abdominal cavity below. When the diaphragm contracts, the thoracic cavity expands. This causes the parietal pleura to expand, causing a pressure gradient that in turn causes the pulmonary pleura and the lungs to expand. When the lungs expand, the pressure within them decreases (remember Boyle's law from general chemistry: pressure and volume are inversely related at a constant temperature). The decreased pressure compared to the external environment causes air to rush into the respiratory tract. This mechanism is known as negative-pressure respiration.

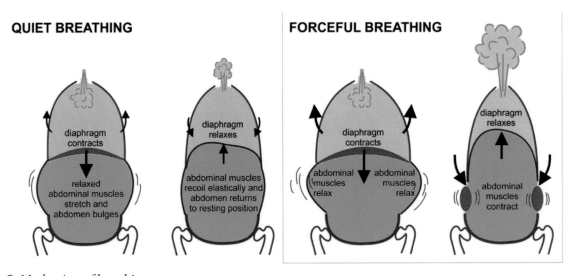

Figure 3. Mechanism of breathing.

Exhalation can be either passive or active. In passive exhalation, the simple relaxation of the diaphragm is enough to cause the lungs to contract, increasing the pressure and expelling air. However, the muscles between the ribs (internal intercostal muscles) and abdominal muscles can be used to force air out more intensely and quickly. This frequently occurs during exercise, but increased reliance on active exhalation even at rest can be a sign of respiratory disease.

The final part of breathing is gas exchange. The mechanism of gas exchange is actually fairly simple. Blood runs through the alveolar capillaries and is separated by a wall only one cell thick from the air that is being breathed in. The deoxygenated blood being returned to the lungs is rich in carbon dioxide (see Sections 2 and 6 for more details regarding this point) and poor in oxygen, while the air being breathed in is rich in oxygen and relatively poor in carbon dioxide. Therefore, oxygen and carbon dioxide can simply diffuse down their respective concentration gradients. Oxygen is carried by hemoglobin, which is described in more detail in Section 6.

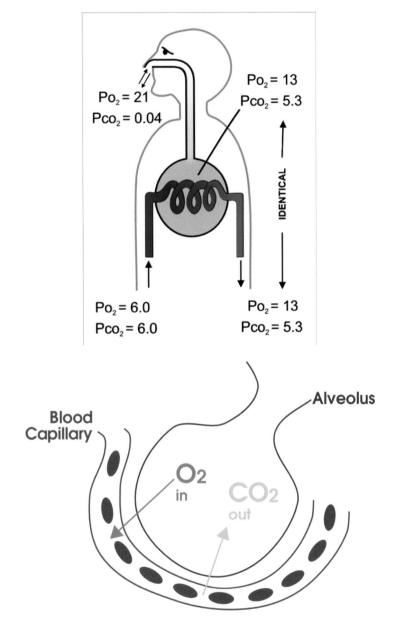

Figure 4. Gas exchange.

Several measures of lung capacity are used in clinical practice. They are not as important as the fundamental physiology of respiration for the MCAT, but they may be worth being aware of. Tidal volume (TV) is the volume of air contained in a normal breath, and then the amount of additional air that can be exhaled after a normal exhalation is known as the expiratory reserve volume (ERV), and the amount of additional air that can be inhaled after a normal inhalation is the inspiratory reserve volume (IRV). There are three other measures not linked to a normal breath. Total lung capacity (TLC), as the name implies, is the most air that can possibly be present in the lungs after inhaling as deeply as possible. The residual volume (RV) is the air that remains in the lungs after breathing out as much as possible, and the vital capacity (VC) is the difference between the TLC and the RV.

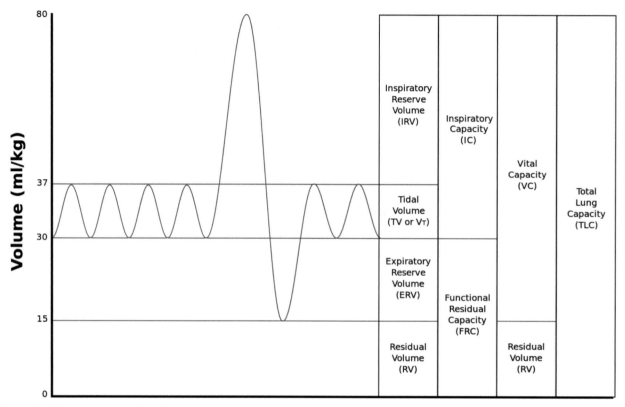

Figure 5. Measurements of respiratory volume.

2. Physiology of Respiration

While it is important to be aware of the basic anatomy of the respiratory tract and the mechanism of breathing, it is even more important to understand the physiology of respiration, because the MCAT loves to focus on how physiological systems work on a basic level, interact with each other, and respond to external stimuli.

> > CONNECTIONS < <

Chapter 11 of Biology

As already mentioned, the ciliated cells and mucus produced throughout the respiratory tract help trap particulate matter and pathogens. Additionally, antibiotic proteins known as defensins are secreted in the respiratory tract. As such, the respiratory system plays a role in the innate immune system.

The respiratory system also plays a role in thermoregulation, although in humans sweating and shivering are the main physiological responses to hyperthermia and hypothermia, respectively. Extensive capillary beds are present in the nasal cavity and the trachea, and they can either expand or contract to allow more or less blood to pass through them. When more blood passes through vessels close to an interface with the external environment (i.e., the skin or the nasal/tracheal epithelium), more heat can be radiated, while when less blood is circulated through such vessels, heat is conserved. These processes are known as vasodilation and vasoconstriction, respectively, and their role in thermoregulation is not limited to the respiratory system; they are discussed more below in section 4. Although the respiratory system does not play a major role in thermoregulation in humans, it does in many mammals that cannot sweat (or can only sweat to a limited extent) and therefore rely on the respiratory system to disperse surplus heat through a pattern of rapid breathing known as panting. In panting, evaporation from the moist surfaces of the tongue and the lungs cools the body.

Of course, the most fundamental function of the respiratory system is gas exchange. Recall that oxygen is used as the final electron acceptor in aerobic respiration, and that carbon dioxide is produced as part of the Krebs cycle and during lactic acid fermentation in anaerobic respiration. This means that you can loosely think of oxygen as providing energy and carbon dioxide as a waste product, the buildup of which indicates that the body needs more energy. Moreover, this dynamic means that blood pH can be used as a rough indicator of the body's energetic state, because carbon dioxide participates in an equilibrium with carbonic acid and the bicarbonate ion, as shown below:

$$CO_2 + H_2O \rightleftharpoons H_2CO_3 \rightleftharpoons HCO_3^- + H^+$$

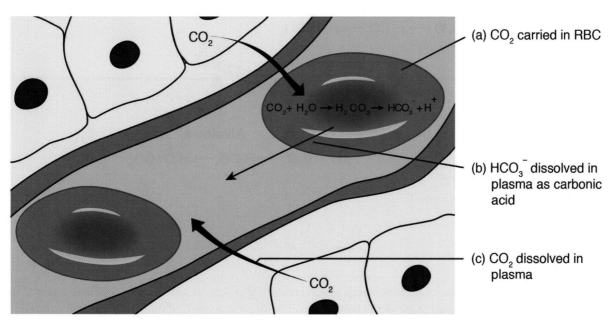

Figure 6. Bicarbonate equilibrium.

This equilibrium is a buffer system that maintains the pH of the blood between 7.35 and 7.45. If the pH of the blood leaves this relatively narrow range, the resulting conditions of acidemia/acidosis (if the pH goes below 7.35) or alkalemia/alkalosis (if the pH goes above 7.45) can have catastrophic consequences. Therefore, too much carbon dioxide in the blood both indicates that the body needs more oxygen to power aerobic respiration and makes the blood too acidic. The nervous system detects this through chemoreceptors that detect acidic conditions; when these chemoreceptors are stimulated, they cause the respiratory rate to increase. As the respiratory rate increases, more carbon dioxide is expelled from the body and more oxygen is brought in. This shifts the balance of the bicarbonate

MCAT STRATEGY > > >

The bicarbonate equilibrium equation is an absolute must for the MCAT. Don't just memorize it, though—also work to understand how Le Châtelier's principle means that the various components of this equation are essentially synonymous in biological processes. For example, all things being equal, more H^+ means more CO_2, and vice versa. Similarly, removing H^+ from the blood is a way to reduce CO_2 concentration in the blood by pushing this reaction to the right.

equilibrium away from H$^+$, and thereby increases the pH of the blood. Similarly, if the pH of the blood is too high (alkalemia), reducing the rate of respiration allows carbon dioxide to build up, thereby re-acidifying the blood.

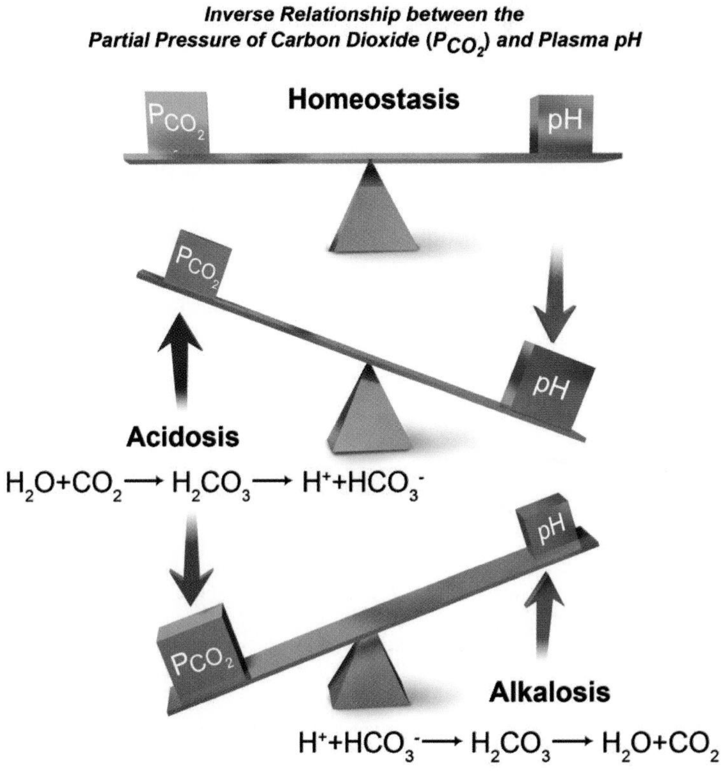

Figure 7. Carbon dioxide and pH control.

3. Blood

The human body contains four to six liters of blood, which consists of two parts: cellular material and plasma. The cellular components of blood are all made in the bone marrow before being released into the circulatory system, while the plasma is the aqueous solution in which these cells are found. Although textbooks tend to focus on the cellular components of blood, plasma is essential to life. Blood plasma is composed of water, nutrients, hormones, proteins, salts, gases, and amino acids. Plasma is so complex that it is near impossible to create in a laboratory, and many college students can therefore make money by selling their plasma to blood banks. When clotting proteins are removed from the plasma, as is common when laboratory tests are performed, the resulting material is known as the serum. The concentration of various substances within the body is often given in terms of serum concentrations; from the point of view of the MCAT, you can think of this as being equivalent to the level of a substance in the bloodstream.

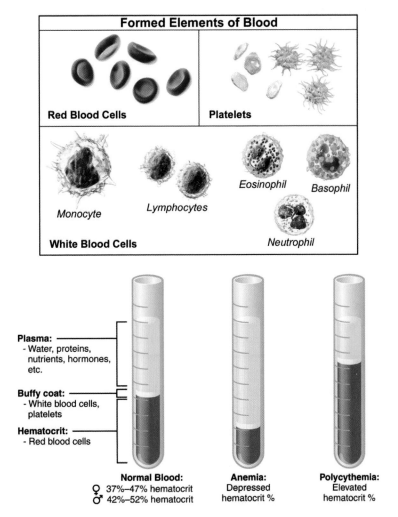

Figure 8. Blood composition.

Plasma is also important because plasma volume is connected both to hydration and blood pressure. Greater plasma volume is correlated with higher blood pressure levels, which makes sense on an intuitive level: all things being equal, if more liquid is contained by the vessel walls, it will exert more pressure. Correspondingly, less plasma volume means lower blood pressure. Since fluctuations in the amount of water present in plasma can cause plasma volume to vary, hydration status is linked to plasma volume; in particular, dehydration is associated with low plasma volume and low blood pressure.

> **MCAT STRATEGY > > >**
>
> Review the material in this paragraph until it becomes a reflex. If a question stem or a passage tells you that an individual has (for instance) less plasma volume, can you predict the consequences for blood pressure? Hydration status? Osmolarity? You want to invest time in developing this reflex now, rather than on Test Day.

Plasma volume is regulated by the endocrine system, jointly with the excretory system. Aldosterone and anti-diuretic hormone (ADH) are two hormones that increase fluid retention. Aldosterone increases sodium absorption in the distal convoluted tubule and collecting duct of the nephron, which drives water reabsorption through osmosis. ADH acts directly on the collecting duct in the nephron to increase water absorption. In contrast, atrial natriuretic peptide (ANP) is essentially the opposite of aldosterone; it decreases plasma volume by decreasing sodium absorption. For more details about these hormones,

> > CONNECTIONS < <

Chapter 7 of Biology

> > CONNECTIONS < <

Chapter 10 of Biology

> > CONNECTIONS < <

Chapter 11 of Biology

see Chapter 7 on the endocrine system, and if you need a review of the nephron, see Chapter 10.

The cellular component of blood is divided into three categories: leukocytes, platelets, and erythrocytes. Leukocytes are also known as white blood cells, and are a major component of the immune system. They are covered in depth in Chapter 11 on the immune system.

Although they are considered to be a cellular component of blood, platelets are not actually whole cells; instead, they are fragments of cells that allow blood to clot. If a blood vessel ruptures, the platelets will react with collagen, thrombin, vitamin K, and calcium to produce a blood clot, preventing blood from continuously leaking out of the vessel. The chain of events leading to clotting, known as the clotting cascade, is quite complicated. The details of the full pathway go beyond what the MCAT requires, but you should be generally aware that the clotting cascade must be tightly regulated in order to strike a balance between forming clots when appropriate to avoid excessive blood loss and overgenerating clots, which can become dislodged and get stuck in a blood vessel, causing a serious medical condition known as thrombosis. Some of the major events of the clotting cascade include the conversion of prothrombin into thrombin, which then converts fibrinogen to fibrin. As the name implies, fibrin forms a fibrous structure that can be thought of as the skeleton of the clot.

Erythrocytes (also known as red blood cells or RBCs) are responsible for carrying oxygen to the different tissues of the body, and aid in carrying carbon dioxide to the lungs, where it can be exhaled. Erythrocytes can do this because they are packed full of hemoglobin, a polymer of 4 proteins and iron that binds oxygen. Erythrocytes are created in the bone marrow in response to erythropoietin, a hormone that is released from the kidney whenever erythrocyte levels are low. During development in the bone marrow, erythrocytes lose their membrane-bound organelles, including their mitochondria and nucleus. As such, they only engage in anaerobic metabolism and have a limited lifespan of only about 100 days. Their lack of internal organelles contributes to their characteristic biconcave shape, which helps them travel more efficiently through capillaries and maximizes their surface area, which assists in gas exchange. Erythrocytes are degraded by the spleen, which is located in the left upper quadrant of the abdomen. In a clinical context, hematocrit refers to the percentage of a blood sample that is composed by red blood cells.

Figure 9. Erythrocytes.

Erythrocytes also express a variety of glycoproteins on their surface, some of which are antigens that play a role in blood typing. A surprising amount of blood typing systems exist, but the most relevant ones for the MCAT are the ABO blood type system and the Rh factor system.

The ABO blood type system is especially important for the MCAT because it is a real-world example of codominance—that is, a system in which more than one dominant phenotype can be manifested at the same time. In an individual with type A blood, the erythrocytes express the A antigen on their surface, in an individual with type B blood, the erythrocytes express the B antigen, and in someone with type AB blood, both the A antigen and the B antigen are present on the surface of the erythrocyte. The recessive phenotype, in which neither the A antigen nor the B antigen is present, is referred to as O. By convention, the gene responsible for the ABO system is referred to using the letter "I": the dominant alleles are denoted as I^A and I^B, while the recessive allele is indicated with a lowercase "i."

> ## CLINICAL CONNECTIONS > > >
>
> The hemoglobin present in erythrocytes undergoes a slow but predictable process of glycation by glucose present in the blood stream. Therefore, the fraction of glycosylated hemoglobin molecules (HbA1c) can be used as a proxy indicator for blood glucose levels on average over approximately the last three months (three months being the average life span of erythrocytes). HbA1c levels, in addition to fasting blood glucose readings, are commonly used to monitor the status of patients with diabetes.

The practical importance of blood typing stems from the fact that individuals develop antibodies against the antigens that they *do not* have, and the body then attacks blood cells that have the antigens that the body considers as foreign. This can be very dangerous, so when a blood transfusion is performed, an individual must receive blood that he or she will not produce antibodies to. This is why blood typing is so important from a medical point of view; in fact, as an interesting historical sidebar, the discovery of blood typing was crucial (along with antiseptic techniques and antibiotics) for routine surgery to become practicable. Table 1 below summarizes the ABO system and its implications for blood donation.

GENOTYPE	BLOOD TYPE	ANTIBODIES PRODUCED	CAN RECEIVE BLOOD FROM:	CAN DONATE BLOOD TO:
$I^A i$	A	Anti-B	A, O	A, AB
$I^A I^A$				
$I^B i$	B	Anti-A	B, O	B, AB
$I^B I^B$				
$I^A I^B$	AB	None	A, B, AB, O	AB
ii	O	Anti-A Anti-B	O	A, B, AB, O

Table 1. ABO blood types and blood donation.

The Rh factor (named because it was discovered in rhesus monkeys) works according to the same basic principle, but it is found on a different gene and does not exhibit codominance; instead, it involves a single antigen that is either present (+) or absent (-). The Rh factor is completely independent from the ABO typing system, so an individual's blood type is characterized both by their ABO status and by their Rh status: for example, someone's blood type could be A^+ or AB^- or O^+. Combining information from both of these systems, we can observe that someone with AB^+

blood is a universal acceptor, because they will not produce anti-A, anti-B, or anti-Rh antibodies, and therefore can accept any type of blood. In contrast, people with type O⁻ blood are universal donors, because their blood contains none of the relevant antigens.

4. Cardiovascular Anatomy

The heart provides the driving force for the blood within the body. It has four chambers: the left and right atria are found at the top of the heart, and the left and right ventricles are found below. Let's review the path of blood as it moves through the heart. Deoxygenated blood returns to the right atrium via the superior and inferior venae cavae and the coronary sinus, which drains the coronary veins. From there, it is pumped into the right ventricle through the tricuspid valve. From the right ventricle, it goes to the pulmonary arteries through the pulmonary semilunar valves. After becoming oxygenated, it is returned to the heart via the pulmonary veins, and enters the left atrium. It is pumped through the bicuspid valve from the left atrium to the left ventricle, and then the left ventricle pushes the blood into circulation (more specifically, through the aortic semilunar valves into the ascending aorta).

MCAT STRATEGY > > >

A mnemonic you can use to help remember the AV valves is LAB RAT: left atrium = bicuspid, right atrium = tricuspid.

The valves in the heart function to ensure that blood only flows in one direction. They can be subdivided into the atrioventricular (AV) valves and the semilunar valves. As the name suggests, the AV valves are found between the atria and ventricles. The bicuspid valve, which regulates blood flow from the left atrium to the left ventricle, is also known as the mitral valve because it was thought to be shaped like a bishop's hat, known as a "mitre." However, the names "bicuspid" and "tricuspid" are arguably more useful, because this helps reinforce the distinction that the bicuspid valve has two leaves, while the tricuspid valve has three. The semilunar (SL) valves are located between the ventricles and the circulation: the pulmonary SL valve helps shunt blood flow into the pulmonary circulation, while the aortic SL valve shunts blood flow into the ascending aorta. Both the pulmonary and aortic SL valves have three leafs. The valves are responsible for the heart sounds: the closure of the AV valves produces the first heart sound ("lub") and the closure of the SL valves produces the second heart sound ("dub").

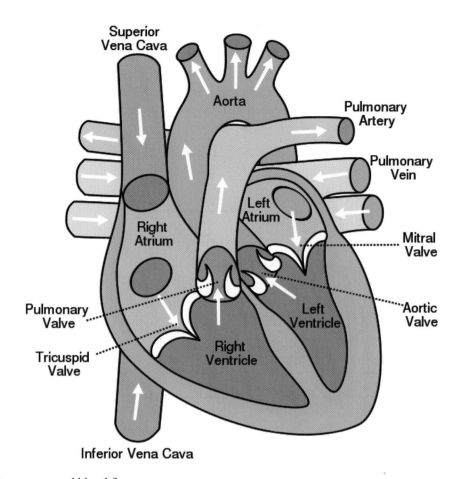

Figure 10. Heart anatomy and blood flow.

The atria have thinner walls and are much less muscular than the ventricles, because their job is to pump the blood into the ventricles, whereas the ventricles are very muscular because they pump blood away from the heart throughout the various vessels. In particular, the left ventricle is the most muscular, as it must pump blood throughout the body, whereas the right ventricle must only pump blood through the lungs and back to the heart. The term "systole" is used to refer to when the heart is contracting, pushing blood into circulation, and the term "diastole" is used to refer to when the heart is relaxed, in between heartbeats. The corresponding blood pressure readings are known as systolic and diastolic, respectively; they are measured in units of mmHg (although this is frequently omitted in clinical contexts) and the systolic blood pressure reading is used first. A normal blood pressure reading is generally considered to be 120/80 mmHg; readings below 90/60 mmHg indicate low blood pressure (hypotension), which can be a sign of shock or other serious medical problems, while readings above 140/90 mmHg are considered to be indicative of high blood pressure (hypertension), which can be a transient response to stress or a chronic condition.

Next, let's move on to track how blood moves throughout the body. There are three types of blood vessels: arteries, capillaries, and veins. Arteries are defined by moving blood *away* from the heart, capillaries are tiny blood vessels where gas exchange takes place, and veins

CLINICAL CONNECTIONS > > >

Hypertension affects almost one in three adults in the United States, making it a mainstay of everyday clinical practice. Hypotension, in contrast, is a common problem encountered in patients who are in shock or undergo trauma. One way or the other, you will become very familiar with blood pressure in the future as you enter into the practice of medicine!

move blood back towards the heart. Students often learn that arteries carry oxygenated blood, while veins carry deoxygenated blood, but this is an oversimplification. In reality, arteries are defined by carrying blood away from the heart (which you can remember by associating "arteries" with "away"), while veins carry blood back to the heart. In the systemic circulation, which supplies blood to the tissues of the body, arteries do indeed supply oxygenated blood; however, in the pulmonary circulation, which specializes in gas exchange, the pulmonary artery carries deoxygenated blood away from the heart to get reloaded with oxygen in the lungs, and then the pulmonary vein returns the newly oxygenated blood to the body.

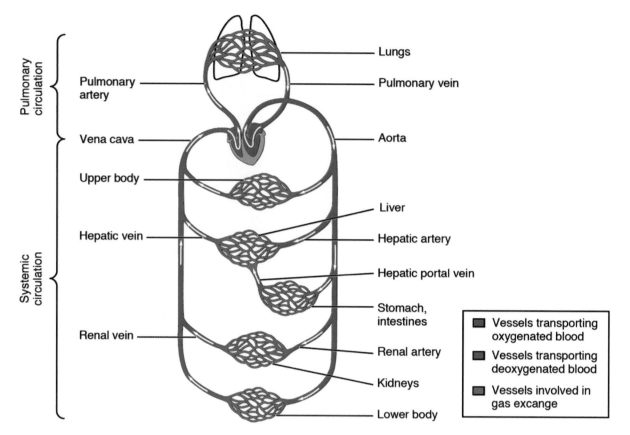

Figure 11. Pulmonary and systemic circulation.

Arteries carry high-pressure blood and therefore have thick muscular walls. They can also constrict and dilate, depending on the needs of the body. As discussed above, this can be used in thermoregulation, in which vasoconstriction of the arteries near the skin is used to conserve heat in a cold environment while vasodilation of those arteries is used to dissipate excess heat. Vasodilation can also be used to supply more oxygenated blood (and more energy) to specific body tissues in response to neurological control. For example, the sympathetic nervous system response ("fight or flight") causes the vessels supplying the muscles to dilate, allowing an influx of oxygenated blood to these tissues, while constricting the vessels that supply the digestive tract. This essentially allows the body to shunt metabolic resources towards a quick response, while postponing functions that are

MCAT STRATEGY > > >

Knowing that arteries and veins are defined by directionality, not oxygenation, and that the pulmonary arteries carry deoxygenated blood while the pulmonary veins carry oxygenated blood, can help answer trick questions and/or eliminate tricky answer choices on Test Day, so make sure it becomes a familiar fact!

essential but can wait until the immediate danger has passed. The parasympathetic nervous system ("rest and digest") has the opposite effect.

As arteries branch off from each other, they develop into smaller, more numerous arterioles. The blood pressure drops quickly between the arterioles and capillaries. Capillaries are tiny, thin vessels through which erythrocytes move one at a time. They are where the main work of gas exchange happens. After moving through the capillaries, deoxygenated blood (in the systemic circulation) moves into venules, which drain into veins, which then gather into the venae cavae before returning to the heart.

Veins, in contrast, carry low-pressure blood and therefore have much thinner walls. However, they have an interesting anatomical quirk of their own, due to the fact that they need to get blood back to the heart without the heart being able to provide a push. This is especially difficult in the lower limbs, where the veins must counteract the downward-pulling effects of gravity. This problem is solved by the presence of valves that allow blood to flow in only one direction.

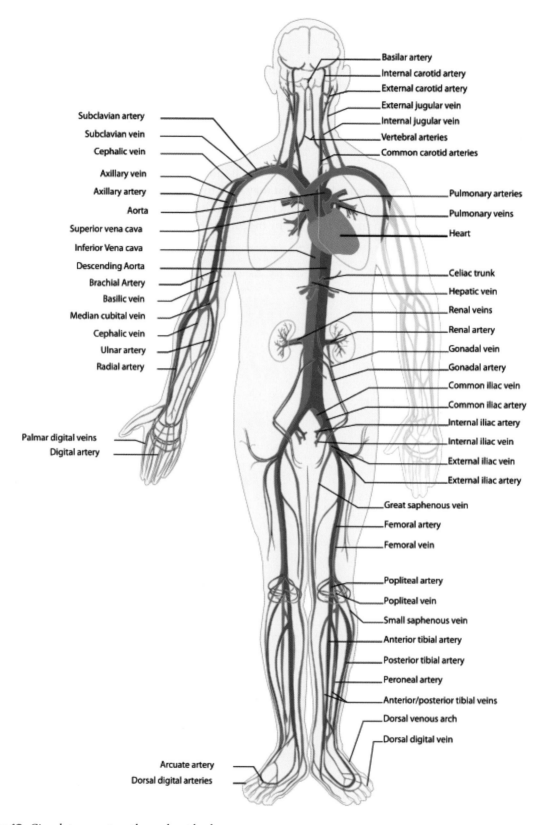

Figure 12. Circulatory system throughout body.

Blood vessels are lined with endothelial cells, which are structurally similar to epithelial cells, with the exception that they contain the protein vimentin, rather than keratin. Endothelial cells play a major role in vascular physiology, including functioning as a selective barrier between blood vessels and the rest of the tissue of the body, as well as mediating inflammation, vasodilation and vasoconstriction, blood clotting, and angiogenesis (the development of new blood vessels). Endothelial dysfunction has been implicated in a range of serious diseases, such as hypertension, atherosclerosis, and some of the negative complications of diabetes mellitus. The details go beyond the scope of the MCAT, but endothelial physiology is an area of active research with direct clinical implications, and so the MCAT expects you to be aware of its importance in general terms.

5. Cardiovascular Physiology

In this section, we'll move beyond the simple anatomy of the circulatory system to consider some of the ways in which it intersects with other systems of the body.

First, let's review how the heart contracts. It can set its own rhythm, which is controlled by the sinoatrial (SA) node, which is found at the roof of the right atrium. The cells in the SA node periodically send out action potentials, much like nerve cells. Gap junctions between the cardiac muscle cells allow the action potential to propagate throughout the tissue, causing contraction. The action potential flows from the SA node into the atria, but not into the ventricles because of a layer of insulating tissue. This causes both atria to contract, pushing the blood forward into the ventricles.

The atrioventricular (AV) node allows the action potential to pass through to the ventricles after the atria have contracted. At this point, the ventricles must contract to push the blood out of the heart. Since the ventricles are larger than the atria, it is a bit more difficult to get them to contract together, so the signal is sped through the bundle of His and Purkinje fibers to all the muscle cells of the ventricles.

The rhythm of the heart is regulated by both the nervous and endocrine systems. The autonomic nervous system, which is subdivided into the sympathetic and parasympathetic nervous systems, regulates heart rate. The parasympathetic nervous system, which is responsible for the "rest and digest" response, slows the heart rate. In contrast, the sympathetic nervous system response ("fight or flight") raises the heart rate. The heart rate is also increased by the hormones epinephrine and norepinephrine, which are released by the adrenal medulla.

One of the reasons why the circulatory system is important for the MCAT is because it provides a way to test the physics of fluids in a biological context. With that in mind, it is very important to review how the fundamental topics of fluid dynamics apply to the circulatory system. Let's start off with a high-level perspective on how flow throughout the circulatory system works on the most basic level: a pressure differential is used to drive flow through a network of tubes that provide resistance. In particular, we can formalize this intuition by saying that $Q = \Delta P/R$, where $Q =$ the flow through the system (equivalent to cardiac output for the systemic circulation), ΔP is the overall change in pressure, and R is peripheral resistance (i.e., the resistance provided by the blood vessels).

Equation 1.
$$Q = \frac{\Delta P}{R} \text{ or } RQ = \Delta P$$

Simply rearranging this equation to $RQ = \Delta P$ provides us with an important conclusion: given constant flow, resistance and ΔP are proportional to each other. This means that if we increase resistance, ΔP goes up as well (if we maintain the same flow). With this fundamental equation in mind, let's take a closer look at resistance. Note that this is analogous to the equation $V = IR$ that is often used for circuits, where V for electric potential is analogous to ΔP (both are forms of potential energy), I for electrical current is analogous to Q (blood flow), and R is used for resistance in both contexts.

Resistance in blood vessels can be modeled using a form of Poiseuille's law that is modified to focus on resistance:

Equation 2.
$$R = \frac{8L\eta}{\pi r^4}$$

You may note that the r^4 term in Equation 2 is in the denominator, not the numerator (on the bottom, not on the top), unlike the form of Poiseuille's law that is most commonly given in discussions of fluids. This is because Equation 2 is an adaptation of Poiseuille's law that focuses on resistance, rather than laminar flow, which is given by $Q = \pi \Delta P R^4 / 8\eta L$. In Equation 2, R again refers to resistance. L refers to the length of the artery, η to the viscosity of the blood, and r to the radius of the blood vessel. Let's work through the physiological implications of these variables.

The first variable we mentioned, L, is the most straightforward. The length of a blood vessel generally cannot be altered, so it is not a parameter used to regulate resistance/blood pressure physiologically. The viscosity of blood (η) turns out to be related to the proportion of erythrocytes in the blood, or hematocrit (as discussed above). All things being equal, the greater the hematocrit, the greater the resistance, which can either correspond to less flow or greater pressure, according to Equation 1. Of note, increased hematocrit is an adaptation to being at higher altitudes due to the lower availability of oxygen at higher pressures. The MCAT could absolutely ask you to combine those insights and ask how adaptation to high-altitude conditions could affect blood flow and/or pressure. However, in normal circumstances, our final variable (r, the radius of the blood vessel) is the most important for explaining how pressure decreases as blood moves along its path through the circulatory system. Resistance is not only inversely related with radius, but the relationship is to the fourth power! This means that as the total radius increases as the blood moves from arteries to arterioles to capillaries, the resistance (and therefore pressure) drops dramatically.

Wait a minute, you might say: what do you mean that the total radius increases as you go from arteries to arterioles to capillaries? Aren't capillaries much narrower than arteries? That point is correct, but it's important to understand that this equation can be applied *both* to a simple system consisting of a single vessel, in which narrowing the vessel would increase the pressure, *and* to the more complex system present in the body, where one artery may branch out into thousands of capillaries. The total cross-sectional area, and therefore the total radius, increases dramatically when evaluating the capillary *system* as a whole in comparison to the artery or arteries supplying it.

The continuity equation can also be applied to the circulatory system, with the same need to be clear about whether it is used to analyze a single vessel or a more complex system in which a single larger vessel branches into multiple smaller vessels. For a given volume of fluid, the continuity equation relates the velocity of blood flow to the cross-sectional area through which flow takes place.

Equation 3.
$$A_1 v_1 = A_2 v_2$$

Care must be taken when applying this equation to think through the anatomical and physiological context correctly. As discussed above, this equation could be applied directly to modeling the effect of, for example, narrowing a blood vessel through a plaque. However, what if we were apply it to predicting the rate of blood flow in the arteries compared to in the capillaries? We might be tempted to start solving this problem by saying that the cross-sectional area of a capillary is much smaller than that of an artery. While that is true, it fails to adequately account for the assumptions of the continuity equation: namely, we have to hold the volume constant. This means that we have to consider *all* of the capillaries fed by a given artery. The total cross-sectional area of these capillaries is much greater than that of the artery. This means that blood flow slows down dramatically in the capillaries compared to the arteries located "upstream," which is actually a useful fact because it provides adequate time for the necessary gas and solute exchange to take place.

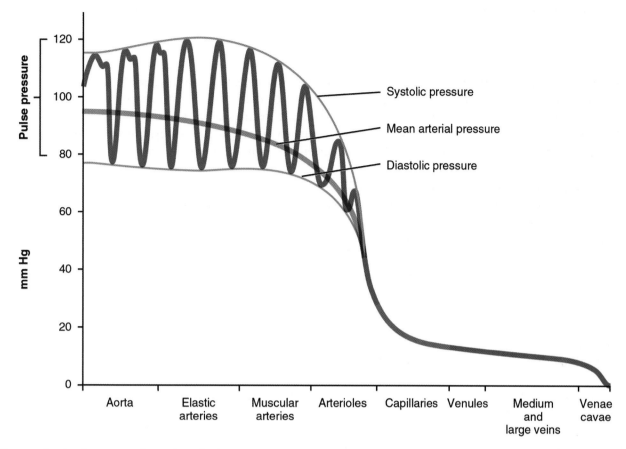

Figure 13. Blood pressure throughout body.

If you have already carefully reviewed your content on fluids, you may wonder whether the Bernoulli equation can be applied here. It is given below as Equation 4, for reference.

Equation 4.
$$P_1 + \frac{1}{2}pv_1^2 + pgh_1 = P_2 + \frac{1}{2}pv_2^2 + pgh_2$$

As a brief review, the Bernoulli equation is essentially conservation of energy applied to fluids. The terms $\frac{1}{2}pv^2$ and pgh are the fluid equivalents of kinetic energy and potential energy, respectively, while the term P refers to the potential energy corresponding to pressure. Essentially, the Bernoulli equation is just the familiar $KE_1 + PE_1 = KE_2 + PE_2$ equation that you have likely studied multiple times in physics, with appropriate adjustments for fluids. One of its most important consequences is that a fluid flowing through a narrower pipe will have higher velocity and exert less pressure on the walls of the pipe. You might notice that this contradicts our reasoning above about resistance using Poiseuille's law. So, which is correct? The issue here is that the Bernoulli equation *doesn't actually apply to blood*, because it is used to describe the behavior of an ideal liquid, and blood is far from ideal. In particular, narrowing a blood vessel means that more of the blood proportionally is in contact with the interior surface of the vessel, and those interactions cause turbulence and slow down the flow of blood, thereby tending to increase the pressure.

> **MCAT STRATEGY > > >**
>
> How can this abstract discussion be translated to simple guidelines for the MCAT? Easy. <u>Don't use Bernoulli's law for blood unless a question tells you to assume that blood is an ideal liquid.</u> In that case, they may give you a question that asks you to recognize that for an ideal liquid, a narrower vessel goes together with increased velocity and lower pressure.

In addition to viewing the system of vessels through the lens of fluid dynamics, the proper balance of fluid must be maintained between the blood vessels and the surrounding interstitial cells. This is accomplished through the interplay between hydrostatic and osmotic forces within the capillary bed. Hydrostatic pressure is the "pushing" pressure due to the force of water on its container (in this case a blood vessel) and oncotic pressure is the "pulling" pressure due to the presence of solutes in a solution (in this case, blood). The key point here is that the hydrostatic pressure drops as you move from the arterial end of the capillary bed to the venous end, but the oncotic pressure remains more or less constant. Therefore, the hydrostatic pressure pushes water into the interstitial tissue and the oncotic pressure pulls it back in on the venous end. Dysregulation of this process, either due to excessive hydrostatic pressure or insufficient oncotic pressure, can lead to fluid buildup, known as edema.

6. Overview of Gas Transport

Finally, now that we've reviewed the anatomy and physiology of the respiratory and circulatory systems, let's step back and re-review the ultimate point of both systems: providing tissue with the oxygen necessary for aerobic metabolism and removing carbon dioxide and other waste products. In particular, we'll focus on gas exchange, because the next chapter will describe how other forms of waste are removed through the excretory system.

It's not random that the respiratory and the circulatory system were grouped together into the same chapter here. Although they are often studied separately, and it is true that they have distinct anatomical structures, the reality is that they work together as a single unit from the point of view of respiration. As you study the physiology of respiration, you should be sure not to limit it to just the respiratory system, but to be able to trace the path of gas transport from the very first steps of air entering the nostrils to the ways that oxygen is supplied to the tissues that need it. In this section, we'll place a particular focus on the latter question, and review the mechanics of hemoglobin in depth.

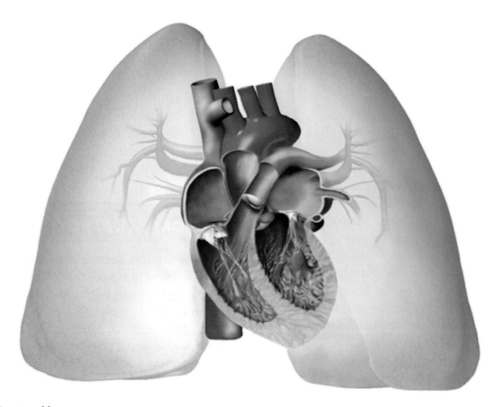

Figure 14. Heart and lungs.

The key to gas exchange is hemoglobin. Understanding how hemoglobin works is absolutely fundamental for the MCAT, and although there are no absolute guarantees, you should study hemoglobin with the expectation that you will encounter a couple questions either on hemoglobin specifically or on the principles that explain how it functions.

Hemoglobin is a metalloprotein composed of four subunits. Each subunit is a globular protein that contains an heme group, which consists of an Fe^{2+} ion held at the center of a heterocyclic porphyrin ring. The Fe^{2+} ion is what binds oxygen for transport. There are two key facts about hemoglobin-oxygen interactions that you must understand for the MCAT. First, the affinity between hemoglobin and oxygen varies depending on the chemical composition of the environment, which is what allows it to function as a delivery system. Second, the binding between hemoglobin and oxygen is cooperative; when the first heme group on a hemoglobin molecule binds with oxygen, it facilitates subsequent binding.

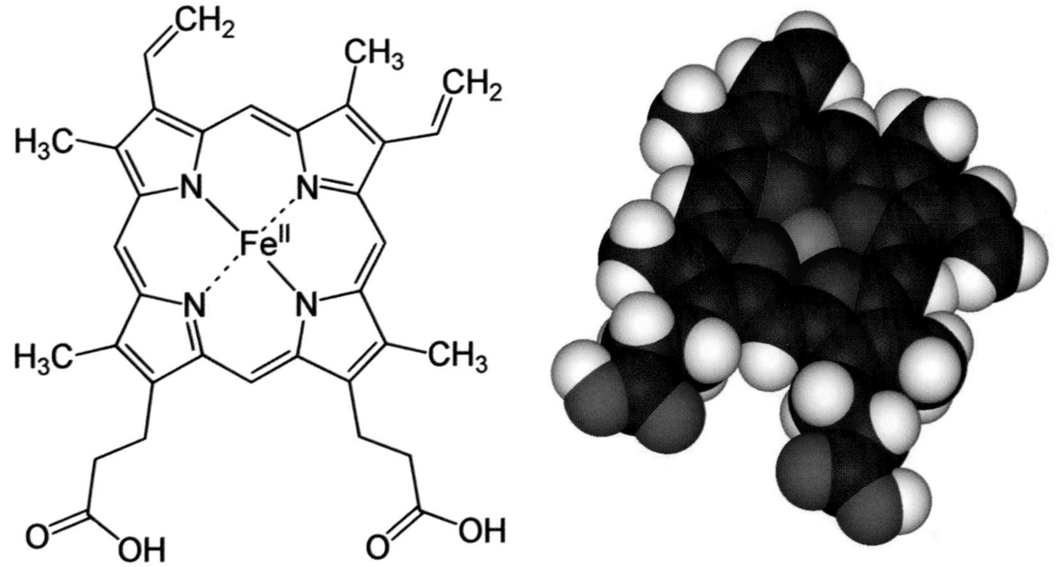

Figure 15. Heme.

Let's first review the cooperativity of hemoglobin, because it underlies some terminology that is then used to discuss other factors that affect hemoglobin-oxygen interactions. Hemoglobin has two forms: taut/tense (T) and relaxed (R). The T form has a low affinity for oxygen, and the R form has a high affinity for oxygen. When oxygen binds to the first heme group, it shifts the hemoglobin molecule from the T form to the R form, facilitating further binding. This, technically speaking, is what makes hemoglobin-oxygen binding cooperative. Additionally, hemoglobin-oxygen binding is relatively favored when large amounts of oxygen are present, as indicated by a high partial pressure of oxygen. This results in a sigmoidal shape for the oxygen-hemoglobin dissociation curve shown below:

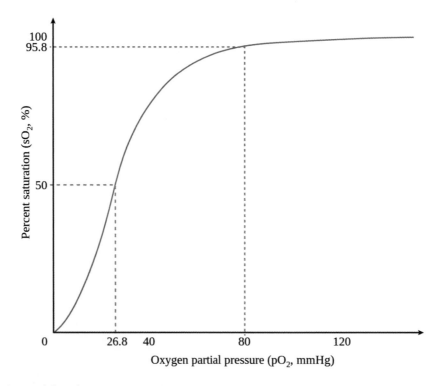

Figure 17. Oxygen-hemoglobin dissociation curve.

Be careful to understand what is shown on the dissociation curve. The x-axis indicates the partial pressure of oxygen—that is, roughly speaking, the amount of oxygen in the blood. The y-axis indicates the percentage of saturation of heme binding sites on hemoglobin. As you can see, the more oxygen is present in the blood, the more likely hemoglobin is to bind oxygen. The next step is to connect this with the physiological distribution of oxygen versus other gases. Oxygen is very plentiful in the alveolar capillaries of the lung, allowing hemoglobin to "load up" with oxygen. Then, hemoglobin is transported to blood vessels in other tissues of the body, where the partial pressure of oxygen is lower; the resultant higher levels of dissociation between hemoglobin and oxygen allow oxygen to be "delivered" to the tissues. Recall that carbon dioxide is a product of anaerobic metabolism, which is commonly used in muscle cells during sustained exertion. Therefore, the partial pressure of oxygen is even lower in areas where exercise is happening, allowing even more oxygen to be delivered precisely where it is needed.

However, the regulation of hemoglobin is even more complicated due to allosteric regulation by carbon dioxide, H^+, and a byproduct of glycolysis known as 2,3-bisphosphoglyceric acid (2,3-BPG). Let's start with the effects of carbon dioxide and pH. Recall the bicarbonate equilibrium reaction, discussed earlier in the chapter but reproduced below:

$$CO_2 + H_2O \rightleftharpoons H_2CO_3 \rightleftharpoons HCO_3^- + H^+$$

The bicarbonate equilibrium reaction means that an increase in carbon dioxide due to anaerobic respiration is manifested as a lower pH due to a higher concentration of H^+ ions. H^+ ions allosterically regulate hemoglobin, and in particular they stabilize the T form, which has a lower affinity for oxygen. This means that H^+ causes hemoglobin to have less affinity for oxygen at a given partial pressure of oxygen, which is manifested as a rightward shift of the oxygen-hemoglobin dissociation curve. This is known as the Bohr effect. 2,3-BPG also causes a rightward shift of the curve. A leftward shift of the dissociation curve would reflect a greater affinity for oxygen; in fact, this takes place in fetal hemoglobin because fetal hemoglobin is less strongly affected by 2,3-BPG. This allows fetal hemoglobin to "take" oxygen from maternal hemoglobin.

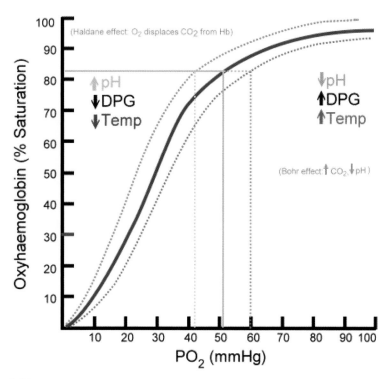

Figure 19. Shifted hemoglobin curves.

Carbon dioxide can be carried by hemoglobin, but is not responsible for the majority of carbon dioxide transport. Again, the bicarbonate equilibrium reaction is crucial for understanding how carbon dioxide is excreted. The enzyme carbonic anhydrase converts carbon dioxide gas to carbonic acid (H_2CO_3), a process that would otherwise take much longer. Carbonic acid then dissociates into bicarbonate ion and H^+; since bicarbonate ion is charged, it moves freely through the aqueous blood. Carbon dioxide as a gas is then exhaled in gas exchange in the lungs, where it diffuses down its concentration gradient and out of the body, as oxygen diffuses down its concentration gradient to bind with hemoglobin in the newly oxygenated blood.

MCAT STRATEGY > > >

As always, the key to MCAT success is going from passive learning in the initial stages of your content review to active mastery. Shifted hemoglobin curves are an excellent place to practice this. Set yourself the goal of explaining to an intelligent but not biochemically sophisticated friend (perhaps a non-premed humanities major?) what a shifted hemoglobin curve means. You will find that to do so, you truly have to master the content. This is what you want on Test Day: actually taking the MCAT is not the time to derive the implications of leftward versus rightward shifts from scratch. You want it to have become a reflex by then.

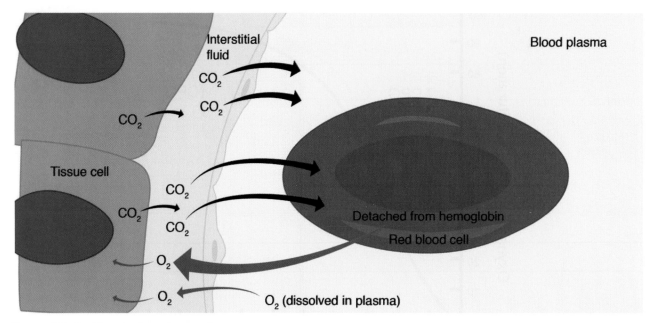

Figure 20. Capillary beds and gas exchange.

7. Must-Knows

> Respiratory anatomy: nasal/oral cavity → pharynx → trachea → bronchi → bronchioles → alveoli; pleurae surround lungs in the thoracic cavity; surfactant covers alveoli to decrease surface tension and prevent them from collapsing.

> Negative-pressure respiration: diaphragm contracts, expanding lungs; greater volume = lower pressure, air comes in from outside.

> Ciliated cells & mucus in trachea and bronchi help trap particulate matter and push it up to be either expelled or swallowed.

> Basic point of respiration: carbon dioxide produced as waste product of anaerobic metabolism needs to be exhaled, and oxygen for aerobic respiration needs to be inhaled.

> Connection between CO_2 and pH due to bicarbonate equilibrium:

$$CO_2 + H_2O \rightleftharpoons H_2CO_3 \rightleftharpoons HCO_3^- + H^+$$

> Blood contains plasma (non-cellular component), platelets, white blood cells (leukocytes) and red blood cells (erythrocytes).

> Erythrocytes lack nuclei and membrane-bound organelles; rely on anaerobic metabolism; have biconcave shape; are packed with hemoglobin (which carries oxygen)

> Basic cardiovascular anatomy: venae cavae → right atrium → tricuspid valve → right ventricle → pulmonary semilunar valve → pulmonary artery → capillaries (gas exchange) → pulmonary veins → left atrium → bicuspid (mitral) valve → left ventricle → aortic semilunar valve → aorta → systemic circulation

> Arteries take blood *away* from heart, veins take blood *to* heart

> Aorta > arteries > arterioles > capillaries > venules > veins > venae cavae

> Pressure decreases as blood moves through the circulatory system, and velocity decreases from arteries to capillary beds. Key point here: large cross-sectional area of capillaries increases peripheral resistance.

> Hemoglobin: protein composed of four units, each with a heme group that contains an iron ion which binds oxygen.

> Hemoglobin-oxygen binding is cooperative. Hemoglobin has T form, which is resistant to binding, and R form, which facilitates easier binding. The first bond stabilizes the R form.

> Rightward shift of oxygen-hemoglobin dissociation curve means a lower affinity; caused by ↑ CO_2, ↑ H+, ↓ pH, (Bohr effect), and ↑ 2,3-BPG. Leftward shift means higher affinity; caused by opposite of above conditions and in fetal hemoglobin.

> Biochemical properties of hemoglobin allow it to pick up oxygen in the lungs and deliver it to where it is needed in tissues undergoing active metabolism.

Practice Passage

Cardiac arrest is the absence of productive mechanical activity in the heart, though significant electrical activity may still be present. Tissue oxygen levels plummet and most muscle activity ceases. Periods of untreated cardiac arrest longer than six minutes result in permanent neurological damage due to brain anoxia. A worldwide study into the causes of cardiac arrest identified the 6 most common factors: hypoxia, hypoglycemia, hypovolemia, acidosis, thrombosis, and elevated serum potassium.

The first-line treatment for cardiac arrest is cardiopulmonary resuscitation (CPR). Chest compressions simulate the mechanical action of the heart, while artificial ventilation provides the lungs with fresh oxygen in the absence of diaphragm contractions. The administration of electric shocks to the heart is used to restore productive cardiac electric activity. A common electrical rhythm during cardiac arrest is ventricular fibrillation (VF), which is a disorganized and unproductive movement of the ventricles, leading to an absence of cardiac output.

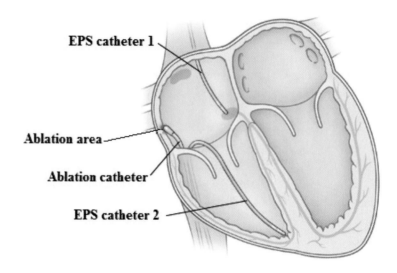

Figure 1. Cardiac ablation procedure

Resuscitation from cardiac arrest due to cold water drowning is generally more successful than warm water drowning. People have been resuscitated by emergency room physicians after experiencing core body temperatures as low as 19°C. Another technique used to treat abnormal rhythms is called ablation (Figure 1). Wire electrode-tipped catheters are threaded to the heart chambers to record and locate the electrical origin of the abnormal heartbeats. Once found, a specialized catheter tip is aimed at the small area of myocardium, and a CO_2 laser (λ = 10.6 μ) destroys the tissue to create a scar called the ablation line. This scar forms a barrier that prevents electrical impulses from crossing between the damaged heart tissues to the surrounding areas, stopping abnormal electrical signals from traveling to the rest of the heart.

Adapted from Seo, J., Joung, B. (2017). High Prevalence and Clinical Implication of Myocardial Bridging in Patients with Early Repolarization. Yonsei Medical Journal, 58(1), 67–74. under CCBY 3.0

1. Which of the following physiological responses probably occurred in a woman who suffered cardiac arrest as a result of submersion into freezing (<0°C) water?
   I. Peripheral vasodilation
   II. Piloerection
   III. Shivering
   A. I and II only
   B. I and III only
   C. II and III only
   D. I, II, and III

2. Given information in the passage, which of the following conditions would most plausibly result from extended cardiac arrest?
   A. Acidosis
   B. Alkalosis
   C. Hyperglycemia
   D. Hypoglycemia

3. When the human body is at rest, which of the following vessels carries blood with the lowest pH?
   A. Gastroduodenal artery
   B. Arterioles
   C. Pulmonary arteries
   D. Pulmonary veins

4. According to Figure 1, which vessel is used to access the right ventricle for electrophysiological study?
   A. Superior vena cava
   B. Inferior vena cava
   C. Carotid artery
   D. Coronary vein

5. While VF is deadly if not treated immediately, many people live years with atrial fibrillation. What is the most probable explanation for this?
   A. The atria are smaller than the ventricles.
   B. The atria are not responsible for pumping blood.
   C. The ventricles pump blood into circulation, while the atria move blood into the ventricles.
   D. The ventricles are less well-perfused by the coronary arteries than the atria.

6. If a cardiologist sees a patient with an abnormal signal conduction in their left ventricle, where should the physician target the ablation catheter?
   A. Near the SA node
   B. Near the AV node
   C. Within the bundle of His
   D. Within the Purkinje fibers

7. Under physiological conditions, vascular endothelial cells prevent thrombosis by means of anticoagulant and antiplatelet factor release. Which molecules will be directly targeted by these endothelial mechanisms?
   I. Thromboxane
   II. Thrombin
   III. Angiotensin II
   A. II only
   B. I and II only
   C. I and III only
   D. I, II, and III

Practice Passage Explanations

Cardiac arrest is the absence of productive mechanical activity in the heart, though significant electrical activity may still be present. Tissue oxygen levels plummet and most muscle activity ceases. Periods of untreated cardiac arrest longer than six minutes result in permanent neurological damage due to brain anoxia. A worldwide study into the causes of cardiac arrest identified the 6 most common factors: hypoxia, hypoglycemia, hypovolemia, acidosis, thrombosis, and elevated serum potassium.

Key terms: cardiac arrest, causes

Cause and effect: 6 causes → cardiac arrest = lack of blood circulation/O_2 delivery by heart → damaged tissues

The first-line treatment for cardiac arrest is cardiopulmonary resuscitation (CPR). Chest compressions simulate the mechanical action of the heart, while artificial ventilation provides the lungs with fresh oxygen in the absence of diaphragm contractions. The administration of electric shocks to the heart is used to restore productive cardiac electric activity. A common electrical rhythm during cardiac arrest is ventricular fibrillation (VF), which is a disorganized and unproductive movement of the ventricles, leading to an absence of cardiac output.

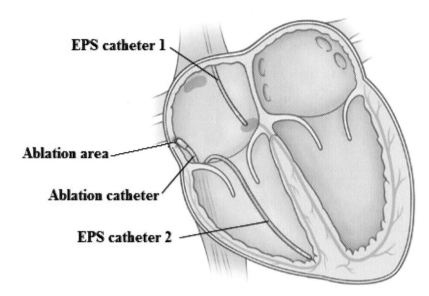

Figure 1. Cardiac ablation procedure

Key terms: CPR, VF, cardiac output

Cause and effect: CPR/defibrillation are used to restart or simulate mechanical actions of heart

Resuscitation from cardiac arrest due to cold water drowning is generally more successful than warm water drowning. People have been resuscitated by emergency room physicians after experiencing core body temperatures as low as 19°C. Another technique used to treat abnormal rhythms is called ablation (Figure 1). Wire electrode-tipped catheters are threaded to the heart chambers to record and locate the electrical origin of the abnormal heartbeats. Once found, a specialized catheter tip is aimed at the small area of myocardium, and a CO_2 laser (λ = 10.6 µ) destroys the tissue to create a scar called the ablation line. This scar forms a barrier that prevents electrical impulses from crossing between the damaged heart tissues to the surrounding areas, stopping abnormal electrical signals from traveling to the rest of the heart.

Key terms: drowning, body T, ablation,

Contrast: cold drowning more survivable than warm drowning

Cause and effect: ablation scar blocks faulty electrical impulses from causing irregular heart contractions

Adapted from Seo, J., Joung, B. (2017). High Prevalence and Clinical Implication of Myocardial Bridging in Patients with Early Repolarization. Yonsei Medical Journal, 58(1), 67–74. under CCBY 3.0

1. C is correct. As the woman is submerged in the water, her body would immediately respond to the cold by attempting to increase thermogenesis (heat production) and heat conservation. This can be accomplished by peripheral vasoconstriction, piloerection, shivering, or non-shivering thermogenesis.
   I: Peripheral vasodilation is a response to hyperthermia, not hypothermia.
   II: Piloerection is the erection of the hair of the skin due to contraction of the tiny muscles that elevate the hair follicles above the rest of the skin to trap heat.
   III: Shivering is a bodily response to hypothermia. When the body temperature drops, shivering is triggered to maintain heat. Skeletal muscles begin to shake in small movements, generating heat by expending energy.

2. A is correct. The passage states that cardiac arrest results in the cessation of muscular activity, including that of the diaphragm. This would result in reduced gas exchange, increased serum $[CO_2]$ (respiratory acidosis) and increased lactic acid production due to anaerobic metabolism. These factors would decrease blood pH, aka acidosis.
   B. The opposite would occur.
   C, D: The passage does not mention anything about hyperglycemia. Though hypoglycemia may be a cause of cardiac arrest, the passage does not suggest that it would be a result.

3. C is correct. Blood is oxygenated in the lungs and returns to the left atrium through the pulmonary veins. Venous blood is typically colder than arterial blood and has a lower oxygen content and thus, a lower pH. The pulmonary arteries carry blood from the right side of the heart to the lungs to be oxygenated so they actually carry deoxygenated blood similar to systemic veins.
   A, B, D: These all carry oxygenated blood.

4. B is correct. We need to look at Figure 1 and see which catheter the question is asking about. The right ventricle is located in the lower left of the image. According to the figure details, this is EPS catheter 2, which appears to snake up from a vessel beneath the heart, enter the right atrium, and then pass through the tricuspid valve into the right ventricle.
   A. This is an alternative route to the right side of the heart, as the SVC drains the blood from the head, neck and, upper limbs into the heart. However, the figure shows that the SVC is used to snake EPS catheter 1 into the right atrium.
   C, D: These vessels would not allow direct access to the right side of the heart.

5. C is correct. The passage states that VF is chaotic and unproductive movement of the ventricles, so one can reasonably infer that AF is unproductive movement of the atria. This question basically asks why someone can survive with poor atrial function but not with poor ventricular function. This is because the ventricles are the workhorses that pump blood into pulmonary and systemic circulation at high pressure, while the atria do the much less taxing job of moving blood into the ventricles in the first place. Answer choice C most closely matches this explanation
   A. While this may be true, it does not answer the question nearly as well as choice C.
   B. This is false; the atria pump blood into the ventricles.
   D. This is false; the ventricles must be well-perfused with oxygen due to their heavy workload.

6. D is correct. The patient's irregular rhythm is originating in the left ventricle, so the nerve area likely to be responsible should be targeted. The Punkinje fibers provide electrical conduction to the ventricles.
   A. The sinoatrial node is located in the right atrium, and coordinates the initiation of atrial contraction.
   B. The atrioventricular node electrically connects the right atrium and right ventricle.
   C. The bundle of His coordinates the passage of the electrical signal of the heart from the AV node to the Purkinje fibers (i.e. from the atria to the ventricles).

7. B is correct. We want to find molecules that are related to blood coagulation and/or blood clotting.
   I. Thromboxane is a hormone released from blood platelets. It induces platelet aggregation and arterial constriction.
   II. Thrombin is an enzyme in blood plasma that causes the clotting of blood by converting fibrinogen to fibrin.
   III. Angiotensin is a peptide hormone that causes vasoconstriction in order to increase blood pressure.

Independent Questions

1. Pneumothorax is a situation in which air accumulates in the pleural space, eventually inhibiting normal expansion of the lung within the thoracic cavity. Treatment may include the insertion of a large-bore IV catheter through the chest wall into the pleural space. If such a procedure were successful, one would notice a rush of air through the catheter:
   A. into the lungs, because pressure in the lungs is less than atmospheric pressure.
   B. into the pleural space, because pressure in the pleural space is greater than atmospheric pressure.
   C. out of the pleural space, because pressure in the pleural space is greater than atmospheric pressure.
   D. out of the lungs, because pressure in the lungs is greater than atmospheric pressure.

2. An emergency room physician suspects that a patient suffers from a respiratory disease. The patient is observed to actively exhale even at rest, visibly struggling to force air out of his lungs. Which of the following is true of this patient?
   A. He is likely healthy, as exhalation is typically active even at rest.
   B. His diaphragm is contracting more forcefully than the diaphragm of an individual performing passive exhalation.
   C. His internal intercostals are contracting more forcefully than the diaphragm of an individual performing passive exhalation.
   D. His residual volume is likely dramatically decreased.

3. All of the following protect the respiratory system from inhaled pathogens and foreign objects EXCEPT:
   A. mucus produced by goblet cells.
   B. cilia lining the epithelium of the trachea.
   C. surfactant that coats the tracheal surface.
   D. the epiglottis.

4. Divers will sometimes hyperventilate prior to free dive, which allows them to remain submerged longer without experiencing the urge to breathe. Divers who employ this technique risk blacking out and drowning because:

   A. increasing the partial pressure of alveolar oxygen inhibits carbon dioxide exchange.
   B. decreased arterial oxygen is the primary stimulus of respiratory drive.
   C. decreased arterial carbon dioxide decreases the affinity of hemoglobin for oxygen.
   D. increased arterial carbon dioxide is a primary stimulus of respiratory drive.

5. Dipalmitoylphosphatidylcholine (DPPC) is produced in abundant quantities by certain alveolar cells and is secreted onto the alveolar surface. The structure of DPPC is shown below.

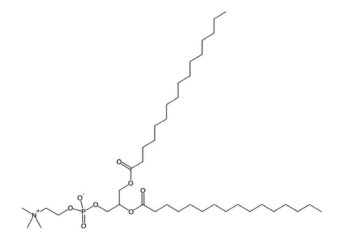

   Based on the given structure, which of the following is a likely function of DPPC?
   A. DPPC is an energy carrier with a high-energy phosphate bond.
   B. DPPC coats the hydrophobic surfaces of microbes so they can be identified by alveolar macrophages.
   C. DPPC acts as an extracellular buffer because of its basic ammonium group.
   D. DPPC disrupts intermolecular interactions between water molecules.

6. Alveolar collapse, known as atelectasis, can greatly reduce the area of respiratory epithelium available for gas exchange. Which of the following might contribute to increased atelectasis?
   A. Decreased production of pulmonary surfactant
   B. Expiration through pursed lips
   C. Providing positive airway pressure, such as with a mechanical ventilator
   D. Increased interstitial fluid in the alveoli

7. Which of the following is the mechanism by which gases are exchanged between the alveoli and the capillaries?
    A. Osmosis
    B. Active transport
    C. Simple diffusion
    D. Carrier proteins

8. Which of the following is true of a person with a blood type of AB⁻?
    A. They are a universal recipient.
    B. They can receive blood from both A⁻ and O⁻ individuals.
    C. They can receive blood from both A⁺ and B⁺ individuals.
    D. They can donate blood to both A⁻ and B⁻ individuals.

Independent Question Explanations

1. C is correct. Choice B can be eliminated immediately, because air would not spontaneously move from a region of low pressure to a region of higher pressure. We are told that the catheter rests in the pleural space, which is not contiguous with the interior of the lungs, leaving only Choice C. The accumulation of air in the pleural space results in an increase in intrapleural pressure that is relieved when the catheter is inserted.

2. C is correct. Exhalation at rest is typically passive in healthy individuals, so this patient may be displaying symptoms of a respiratory disease. In contrast to passive exhalation, active exhalation involves contraction of the internal intercostal muscles. Contraction of the diaphragm is associated with inhalation, not exhalation. Finally, residual volume is the volume of air remaining in the lungs after an individual has exhaled as much as possible. If anything, trouble exhaling would increase, not decrease, this volume.

3. C is correct. Surfactant is found in the alveoli and serves to reduce surface tension; it does not coat the tracheal surface to protect against pathogens. Goblet cells do produce mucus, which traps small particulate matter; additionally, the tracheal epithelium contains cilia to push mucus and particles toward the back of the throat. Finally, the epiglottis closes while eating to protect the lungs from swallowed objects, in particular food.

4. D is correct. Hyperventilation can markedly decrease the amount of carbon dioxide in the blood. Carbon dioxide-sensing chemoreceptors typically stimulate ventilation in response to increased arterial carbon dioxide levels. Divers who practice hyperventilation may extend their dive times by eliminating this respiratory drive, relying instead on oxygen chemoreceptors, which may not elicit a strong urge to breathe before cerebral hypoxia leads to loss of consciousness.

5. D is correct. DPPC is a pulmonary surfactant. Surfactants are amphipathic molecules, meaning they contain both hydrophobic and hydrophilic regions. This allows them to disrupt hydrogen bonding between water molecules, thus reducing alveolar surface tension and preventing alveolar collapse. DPPC does not contain any high-energy phosphate bonds, and quaternary ammonium ions cannot accept protons.

6. A is correct. One function of pulmonary surfactant is the reduction of alveolar surface tension. High surface tension leads to poor alveolar compliance and can ultimately prevent the alveoli from inflating at all. For this reason, decreased production of surfactant can contribute to increased atelectasis, as it is described in the question stem. Atelectasis can be reduced by measures that increase airway pressure and keep the alveoli inflated. Adults with chronic lung disease may exhale through pursed lips, which increases positive airway pressure and prevents alveolar collapse.

7. C is correct. Oxygen and carbon dioxide diffuse directly through the walls of alveolar capillaries and through the alveolar epithelium. No proteins are required to allow small, hydrophobic gas molecules to pass through these membranes.

8. B is correct. Individuals can receive blood if it does not contain antigens that the recipient makes antibodies against. A person will make antibodies against any antigen that is foreign; for this AB⁻ individual, the only foreign antigen is the Rh factor, since the person has the A and B antigens but lacks the Rh factor. As such, this person cannot receive blood with any positive (+) blood type, but he or she can receive blood from those with any negative (-) blood type, including A⁻ and B⁻. It is AB⁺, not AB⁻, that is the universal recipient. Finally, note that any individual with an AB blood type can only donate to others with an AB blood type.

This page left intentionally blank.

Digestive and Excretory Systems

CHAPTER 10

0. Introduction

In this chapter, we'll deal with some of the most basic realities of human existence: obtaining nutrients from food, processing those nutrients, and excreting the resultant waste products. From the point of view of MCAT preparation, you should approach this chapter with two goals in mind. First, you should study the anatomy carefully, because basic anatomy/structure questions are absolutely fair game on Test Day. While any single point of anatomy is relatively unlikely to be tested, the cumulative likelihood of getting one or two questions that require you to draw on an understanding of the anatomy of these systems is relatively high. Second, and more importantly, you must master the underlying physiology, which means understanding how the digestive and excretory systems allow the organism to obtain nutrients and maintain homeostasis. As you have seen, this is a recurring theme for physiology-related topics on the MCAT: you're not generally expected to have a complete command of all of the details, but you are absolutely expected to have a solid understanding of the fundamental principles and how all of the main physiological systems of the body fit together.

1. Digestive System Anatomy

Let's begin this chapter by reviewing the path of a piece of food. In this section, we'll cover the relevant anatomy and the basic functions of the organs of the digestive system, and then in the next section we'll take a closer look at digestion from a physiological standpoint. We should start, though, by clarifying some terminology. First, we need to distinguish digestion from absorption. Digestion refers to the breakdown and processing of food, while absorption refers to how nutrients actually enter the body. Digestion does not necessarily imply absorption; unabsorbed but digested food is a major component of feces.

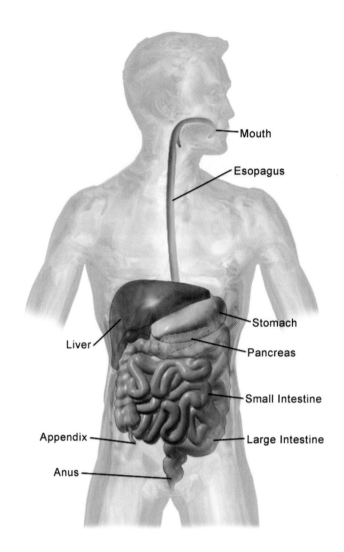

Digestive System

Figure 1. High-level anatomy of digestive system.

Food is first ingested and chewed in the mouth, where saliva, which is produced by the salivary glands, provides lubrication. What enters your mouth as a piece of food exits it as a "bolus"—a term used in digestive anatomy and physiology to describe a ball-shaped mixture of food and saliva (in fact, "bolus" means "ball" in Latin). Think of the bolus as being what you actually swallow. Saliva has other functions in addition to lubrication. Most notably, it contains some enzymes, including alpha-amylase (or salivary amylase), which begins to break down starch. The activity of salivary amylase explains why starchy foods such as rice or potatoes begin to taste sweet if you chew on them for long enough: amylase breaks down starch to form disaccharides, which are perceived as sweet. You may remember this as an experiment in Biology 101. Saliva also contains the antimicrobial enzyme lysozyme, as do tears; although the antimicrobial properties of saliva are nowhere near strong enough to kill off the extensive microbiota of the oral cavity, they are strong enough for saliva to be considered part of the innate immune system.

> **> > CONNECTIONS < <**
>
> **Chapter 11 of Biology**

Once food is swallowed, it passes down the esophagus, a fibromuscular tube that runs behind the trachea and passes through the diaphragm, thereby bypassing the thoracic cavity. The esophagus empties into the stomach through a sphincter that goes by various names: the lower esophageal sphincter, gastroesophageal sphincter, or the cardiac sphincter (this name is somewhat confusing; it refers to the fact that the esophagus enters into the upper part of the stomach, which is known as the cardia). Dysfunction of the esophageal sphincter can lead to gastrointestinal reflux, in which the highly acidic contents of the stomach back up into the esophagus. This leads to a painful condition known as heartburn, and when it persists, it can result in gastroesophageal reflux disease (GERD).

The stomach is a highly acidic digestive organ, in which proteases such as pepsin begin to break down proteins, turning the bolus of food into a semi-digested substance known as chyme. The stomach stores food, churns it, and continues to digest it, although very little absorption happens in the stomach. Exceptions to this guideline include water, some medications, caffeine, and, to some extent, ethanol (although most ethanol is absorbed later). The gross anatomy of the stomach is shown in Figure 2. Some features of note include the general division of the stomach into the greater curvature and the lesser curvature, the presence of folds known as rugae along the lining of the stomach, and the fact that the top of the stomach is known as the fundus and the bottom area as the pylorus. Gastric acid is secreted by parietal cells, and contains highly concentrated HCl that is used to keep the stomach at a pH of 1.5-3.5. This low pH is optimal for the functioning of the digestive enzymes in the stomach, and also helps to kill off bacteria.

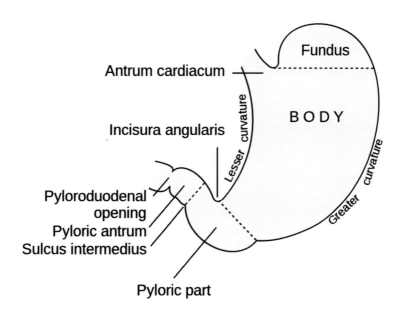

Figure 2. Stomach.

A major challenge the body faces with the stomach is how to protect itself from the low pH and digestive enzymes that it contains. On a conceptual level, a similar point can be made regarding acidic lysosomes in cells, but the stomach is much larger and has an even lower pH, making this an especially important task. Foveolar cells secrete bicarbonate-rich mucus that helps protect the stomach lining from the acidity of its content. Additionally, protections are built into the sequence of events leading to the activation of digestive proteins. In particular, chief cells do not secrete pepsin directly, because doing so would run the risk of proteolytic activity being initiated immediately. Instead, chief cells release the precursor pepsinogen (an example of a zymogen), which is then cleaved under intensely acidic conditions to create the active form, pepsin.

As mentioned, pepsin is a digestive enzyme secreted in the stomach. Pepsin primarily cleaves proteins at the site of aromatic residues; as such, it breaks proteins down into smaller peptides but does not complete their digestion. Additionally, the stomach secretes intrinsic factor, which is necessary for the proper absorption and processing of vitamin B12. The stomach also secretes water to dilute the bolus, as well as signaling molecules to help regulate digestion, as discussed further in Section 2.

The next step in the journey that food takes through the body is to pass through the pyloric sphincter, which connects the stomach with the small intestine. The small intestine is where we really shift gears from digestion to absorption, although this is not a watertight distinction; as we've seen, a little bit of absorption does happen in the stomach, while digestion continues in the small intestine in addition to absorption. The small intestine is subdivided into the duodenum, which is a fairly short structure, and the longer structures of the jejunum (the midsection of the small intestine) and the ileum.

> **MCAT STRATEGY** > > >
>
> The acronym "Dow Jones Industrial" can be used to remember the sequence of the duodenum → jejunum → ileum in the small intestine.

A lot happens in the small intestine, so it's worth stepping back and reviewing the main things that need to be accomplished. Having a clear sense of these tasks will help keep track of which organs are responsible for which components.

> The chyme coming from the stomach is highly acidic and needs to be neutralized.
> When the chyme enters the small intestine, little chemical digestion has happened, with the exception of the contribution of salivary amylase and proteases such as pepsin. Digestion needs to continue.
> Nutrients and vitamins need to be absorbed.

Let's first briefly review how digestion continues in the small intestine. Several organs actually contribute to this process. The small intestine itself releases brush-border enzymes through cells contained in structures known as microvilli (which are discussed more below). Some brush-border enzymes, known as disaccharidases, break down disaccharides (recall that disaccharides are a common form in which carbohydrates are consumed), while others break down proteins (peptidases). The pancreas also contributes significantly to digestion in the duodenum by directly secreting an alkaline fluid containing several types of digestive enzymes, capable of digesting all major classes of biomolecules. The liver also contributes to digestion via the secretion of bile, which is an alkaline, dark green to yellowish fluid that contains bile salts, bilirubin, and some fats. Its main function is to emulsify lipids and help convert them into micelles. The reason this is important is because the enzymes that digest lipids are water-soluble, so it is important to break up lipids and expose the greatest amount of surface area possible to the action of those enzymes. An interesting fact about bile is that it is secreted by the liver but stored and concentrated in the gall bladder, from which it is released into the small intestine.

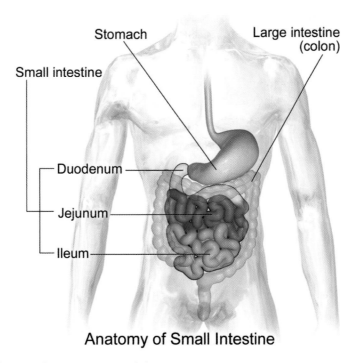

Anatomy of Small Intestine

Figure 3. Small intestine: large scale w/ anatomic subdivisions.

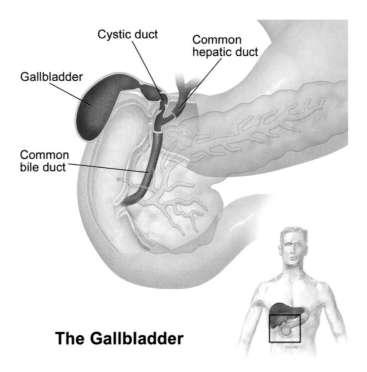

The Gallbladder

Figure 4. Gall bladder.

Next, let's look at how the highly acidic chyme from the stomach is neutralized. An elegant aspect of this process is that it is, to a great extent, combined with the digestive processes reviewed above. As mentioned, the fluid secreted by the pancreas that is rich in digestive enzymes happens to be an alkaline solution rich in bicarbonate. Likewise, bile is also slightly alkaline, with a pH when it is synthesized of roughly between 7.5 and 8. Additionally, the duodenum itself secretes bicarbonate buffer via the Brunner's glands. The additive effect of these secretions results in the duodenum actually becoming a slightly alkaline environment, which is optimal for the various digestive enzymes at work there.

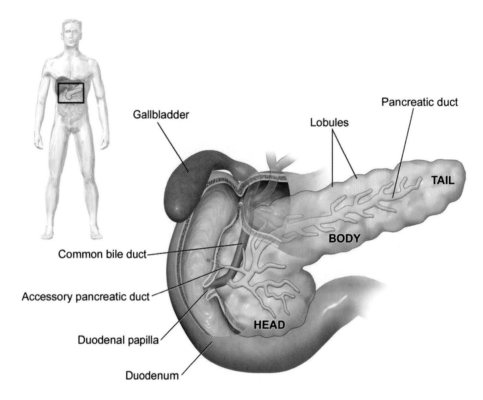

Figure 5. Pancreas.

Once food is sufficiently digested, the resulting nutrients need to be absorbed. This is primarily the job of the rest of the small intestine: the jejunum and the ileum. The small intestine is characterized by structures known as villi, which are finger-like projections that extend into the lumen of the intestine and dramatically increase the available surface area. The surfaces of villi are lined with enterocytes (the cells of the intestinal lining), and the enterocytes themselves are characterized by microvilli, which are villi-like projections from the cell membranes of enterocytes that greatly increase the surface area available for cellular functions.

Food now travels to the large intestine. The large intestine is subdivided into the cecum (and appendix), followed by the ascending colon, transverse colon, descending colon, sigmoid colon, and rectum. The cecum is a pouch that is connected with the ileus of the small intestine through the ileocecal valve. The appendix is attached to the cecum. Traditionally, the appendix has been thought to be a vestigial organ—that is, an organ that has lost whatever function it had in our evolutionary ancestors—but emerging research has called this into question. The last component of the large intestine is the rectum, which serves to store feces before it is expelled through the anus.

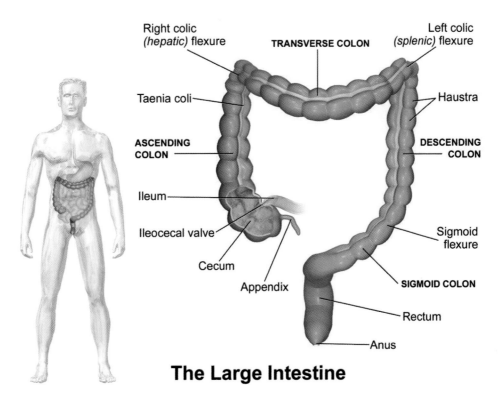

Right colic
(hepatic) flexure

TRANSVERSE COLON

Left colic
(splenic) flexure

Taenia coli

Haustra

**ASCENDING
COLON**

**DESCENDING
COLON**

Ileum

Ileocecal valve

Sigmoid
flexure

Cecum

Appendix

SIGMOID COLON

Rectum

Anus

The Large Intestine

Figure 6. Large intestine.

The large intestine has the following main functions. First, it absorbs water from the food undergoing digestion, which is a large component of how watery chyme becomes solid feces. Second, it hosts the largest community of bacteria in the human body, referred to as the gut microbiota or the gut flora. The relationship of these bacteria to their human host ranges from commensal to symbiotic. Bacteria that provide a benefit to the human body by synthesizing necessary vitamins such as vitamin K and vitamin B_7 (biotin), and commensal bacteria provide no benefits or harms to their host. While you do need to be aware of these terms for the MCAT, on one hand, on the other hand you should also be aware that they are simplifications, not least because widespread but tentative recent research into the gut flora suggests that they may have complex effects on human health that we are only now coming to be aware of. No chemical digestion takes place in the large intestine, but absorption of remaining nutrients (either from food or the metabolic products of bacteria) takes place to some extent; you don't have to be aware of the details for the MCAT, but it could conceivably come up in a passage.

After passing through the large intestine and into the rectum, food has now been fully transformed into feces. Feces primarily contain indigestible material and water. In healthy individuals, a major example of indigestible material would be plant cellulose, because humans lack the enzymes to break down the carbohydrate polymers contained in cellulose. However, pathological conditions can result in different substances becoming indigestible, with ramifications for the content of feces. For example, liver dysfunction can lead to impaired production of bile, which leads to impaired digestion of lipids because bile plays a major role in emulsifying lipids to allow digestive enzymes to do their work. If lipid digestion is impaired, more fat can be excreted in the feces, a condition known as steatorrhea. Steatorrhea itself is not required content for the MCAT, but this is an example of the kind of chain of logical reasoning that the MCAT often incorporates into passage-based questions.

2. Overview of Digestion

In this section, we'll take a closer look at some of the physiological processes that underpin digestion, and also review digestion from the perspective of how specific nutrients are digested.

First, we may ask ourselves: how, exactly, does the bolus/chyme/feces move through the digestive system? The answer is a combination of peristalsis and sphincters. Peristalsis refers to an involuntary process of contractions and relaxation of the smooth muscle surrounding the canal in various parts of the digestive tract. These contractions proceed in a concerted manner to create a peristaltic wave that pushes material along. As we saw in our review of the anatomy of the digestive tracts, various sphincters connect different digestive organs, such as the esophageal sphincter, which connects the esophagus and the stomach, the pyloric sphincter, which connects the stomach and small intestine, the ileocecal valve (also known as the ileocecal sphincter), which connects the small intestine and the large intestine, and finally, the anal sphincter, which regulates the release of feces from the rectum.

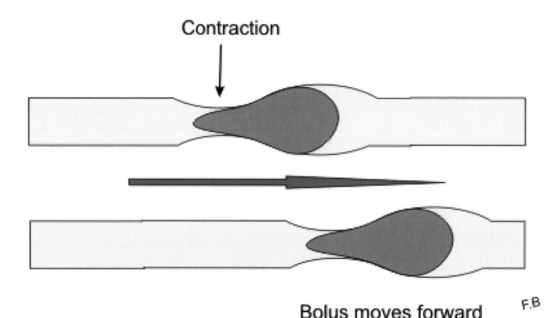

Figure 7. Peristalsis.

Additionally, digestion is subject to complex patterns of endocrine and nervous control, which makes sense, since it must be regulated closely in order to ensure that the organism responds appropriately to various external and internal stimuli. The hormonal control of digestion incorporates everything from our perceptions of hunger to very fine-grained control over the release of enzymes from one digestive organ to another.

Hunger is principally regulated by the hormones ghrelin and leptin. Ghrelin is often known as the hunger hormone (think "grrr," like how your stomach growls when you're hungry). Ghrelin is secreted by specialized cells in the upper part of the stomach and in the pancreas, and is released when the stomach is empty. It has the effect of promoting appetite. In contrast, leptin is secreted by adipocytes (fat cells) and promotes feelings of satiety, or fullness. Interestingly, emerging research has demonstrated that these hormones have effects on a surprisingly broad range of target organs throughout the body, but this goes well beyond what is necessary for the MCAT.

In the stomach, G cells secrete gastrin. Gastrin generally promotes digestion, with the main effect of stimulating parietal cells to secrete gastric acid (HCl). Acidic chyme in the duodenum of the small intestine triggers the release of secretin from S cells; as the name suggests, secretin triggers the secretion and release of bicarbonate-rich mucus from the pancreas to neutralize the acidic chyme and promote the optimal functioning of the digestive enzymes that do their work in the small intestine. Cholecystokinin (CCK) is also secreted by cells lining the small intestine, and stimulates the secretion and release of digestive enzymes from the pancreas and the release of bile from the gall bladder. You can therefore think of secretin and CCK as being on the same team, in a sense, with secretin having the responsibility for pH levels and CCK being responsible for the actual enzymes and compounds that do the work of digestion. CCK also inhibits appetite, which makes sense in that it is only secreted if the body is already working on digesting food and therefore doesn't need any more at the moment.

However, digestion also sometimes needs to be slowed down. This is where somatostatin comes in. Somatostatin is released from several areas of the digestive tract and has the effect of inhibiting the release of many hormones involved in digestion, including some that we have already discussed, such as gastrin, CCK, and secretin, as well as decreasing the rate of emptying from the stomach and inhibiting the secretion of pancreatic hormones such as insulin and glucagon. Somatostatin also inhibits the release of growth hormone, leading to its use as a treatment for gigantism; this gives a sense of its broad-range inhibitory effects, as a result of which it is most effective to think about somatostatin as a signaling molecule that basically puts the brakes on digestion.

> **MCAT STRATEGY > > >**
>
> Somatostatin is an example of how the name of a compound can provide useful hints about its function. "Somat-" means "body," and you can associate "stat" with "static," indicating that it means slowing something down. So, somatostatin is basically what slows your body down. This is a perfect indication of its very general effects on the body.

In addition to endocrine control, the digestion process is also regulated by nervous control. In fact, it has an entire subdivision of the nervous system: the enteric nervous system, which is sometimes called a "second brain" due to its complexity and autonomy. Although the enteric nervous system is connected to the rest of the nervous system, it can actually function autonomously even if important connections with the rest of the nervous system are severed. The autonomic nervous system also has important effects on the gastrointestinal system. Recall that the sympathetic nervous response (also known as "fight or flight") is triggered in response to acute stresses and generally predisposes the body to urgent responses, while the parasympathetic system ("rest and digest") has the opposite effect. What this means for the digestive system is that the sympathetic nervous system contracts the vessels supplying the digestive tract, reducing blood flow and shunting it towards muscles—the idea being that in times of danger, digestion can wait while you run away or fight. In contrast, the parasympathetic nervous system kicks in when the acute stress has passed, at which point digestion becomes a good idea again—therefore, the vessels supplying the digestive system are dilated, increasing blood flow.

Next, let's take a closer look at how nutrients are absorbed. Although it is easy to skim over this point in an anatomically-focused review of digestion along the lines of what was presented in section 1, this is a complicated question that leads us to important physiological topics such as the hepatic portal system and the functions of the liver.

As discussed above, the main action in terms of absorption takes place in the small intestine, although some absorption of certain compounds happens in the stomach and water and vitamins can be absorbed in the large intestine. To understand how absorption takes place, we need to take a closer look at the anatomy of villi and microvilli in the lining of the small intestine. To review, villi are finger-like projections that dramatically increase the surface area available for absorption, and microvilli are similar projections from individual cells located on the villi that increase the available surface projection even more. Villi contain capillaries and a lacteal; capillaries drain into the hepatic portal vein, which takes water-soluble nutrients for the liver for what is often referred to as first-pass metabolism, while lacteals drain lipids into the lymph vessels.

Therefore, what needs to happen in absorption is for nutrients to get into the epithelial cells lining the small intestine and then get out of those cells to enter the capillaries or lacteals. This process is different for amino acids and carbohydrates (which are soluble in aqueous solution) than it is for lipids (which are non-soluble in aqueous solution). This is a common recurring theme when it comes to membranes; note, for instance, how the membrane interactions for steroid hormones (lipids) and peptide hormones are fundamentally different, with functional implications as discussed in Chapter 7.

> > CONNECTIONS < <

Chapter 7 of Biology

Carbohydrates must be broken down into monosaccharides to be absorbed. Secondary active transport coupled to Na$^+$ is used to transport glucose and galactose into the epithelial cells, while facilitated diffusion is used for fructose. All three of these monosaccharides then leave the epithelial cells and enter the circulatory system via facilitated diffusion. Similarly, single amino acids and short chains of two to three amino acids enter the epithelial cells through secondary active transport (via specific transporters), and then leave the epithelial cells and enter the bloodstream through facilitated diffusion. Facilitated diffusion can be used to push these molecules into the bloodstream because the constant flow of blood through the capillaries means that they will always be moving down their concentration gradient.

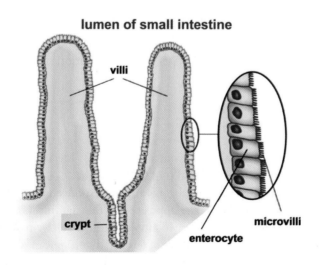

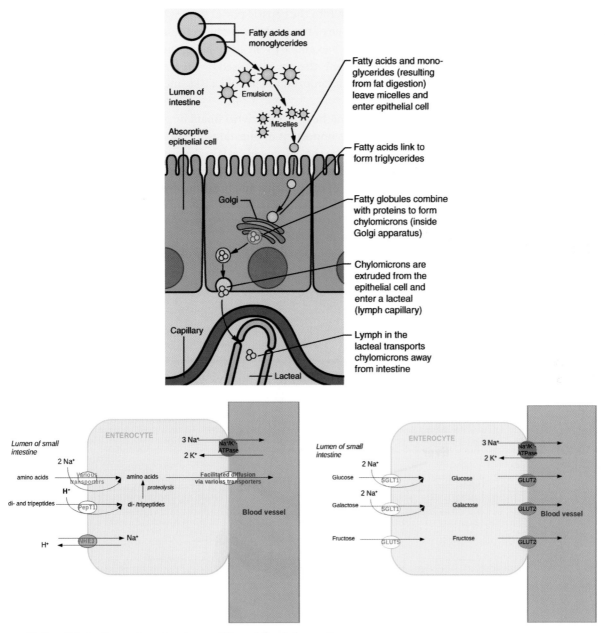

Figure 8. Small intestine: microstructure, villi, and food absorption.

Lipids, however, are more complicated. Lipids are formed into micelles with the aid of bile salts, and individual lipid molecules break away from those micelles to be absorbed into the epithelial cells. No special transport mechanism is necessary for this, because fatty acids and cholesterol can diffuse through the plasma membrane. This actually creates an interesting challenge, though: if simple diffusion can handle this process, how can the body prevent the concentrations from simply equalizing, at which point the absorption would stop? The solution to this is that the epithelial cells in the small intestine combine fatty acids and monoglycerides to form triglycerides. This reduces the concentration of free fatty acids and monoglycerides to the point that they can continue to diffuse into the cells. Next, the cell needs to get rid of the lipids. Triglycerides and other lipids (as well as lipid-soluble vitamins) are combined into fat droplets known as chylomicrons, which are then released into the interstitial space, from which they move on to the lacteals. Lipids pass through the lymphatic system and eventually drain into the venous circulation of the body.

The capillaries of the small intestine eventually drain into the hepatic portal vein, which runs to the liver and the hepatic portal system. The hepatic portal system is one of two portal systems in the body; these are systems of blood vessels with a capillary bed at each end, with the other example in the body being the hypophyseal portal system in the hypothalamus. The blood from the small intestine is thereby processed by the liver before entering the systemic circulation. This gives the liver the chance to perform important metabolic tasks, including the following:

> Detoxifying compounds, either absorbed from the external environment or produced by metabolic processes
> Metabolizing medications and drugs (this has important implications for routes of drug delivery, because this "first-pass" metabolism can dramatically reduce the efficacy of certain drugs when administered orally)
> Storing excess carbohydrates as glycogen or excess fatty acids as triglycerides
> Mobilizing lipids into circulation in the form of lipoproteins and breaking down glycogen to release more glucose if necessary

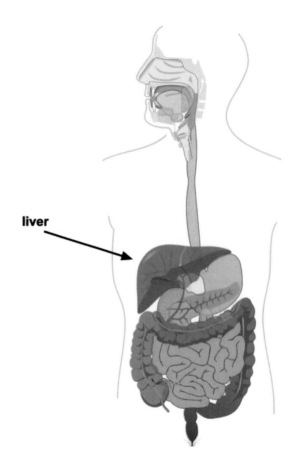

Figure 9. Liver.

Finally, let's review the path taken by each major class of nutrient (proteins, carbohydrates, and lipids) as they go from your mouth to a state where they can be used by the cells of the body.

Proteins start to be broken down in the stomach by pepsin, and they continue to be broken down in the small intestine by peptidases, the most notable of which are trypsin and aminopeptidase. Trypsin cleaves proteins on the carboxyl end of lysine or arginine (except when followed by proline), and aminopeptidases are a class of enzymes that break down proteins from the amino end. Single amino acid residues then enter the epithelial cells of lining the lumen of the small intestine, from which they pass into the circulatory system.

Carbohydrates start to be broken down in the mouth, where starch is broken down into disaccharides by salivary amylase, but they are primarily broken down in the small intestine by various enzymes. The enzymes active in the small intestine include pancreatic amylase, which continues the breakdown of starch, and disaccharidases, such as sucrose, lactase, and maltase. The monosaccharides produced by disaccharidases enter the epithelial cells of the small intestine and from there move into the circulatory system. Cellulose and undigested starch then move into the large intestine, where they may be broken down or digested by the gut flora, resulting in short-chain fatty acids that are used by the body and may mediate some of the health effects associated with the gut microbiota, and gas, which is expelled as flatulence.

Triglycerides begin to be digested in the mouth by lingual lipase. An interesting fact about lingual lipase is that it functions at slightly acidic pH levels, so it continues to some extent as the bolus continues into the stomach. The majority of the digestion of triglycerides, though, occurs through pancreatic lipase. The resulting free fatty acids and monoglycerides are separated by bile salts into micelles that also contain cholesterol and other lipids. Lipids then enter the cells lining the small intestine, are packaged into chylomicrons, and released into lacteals, which drain into the lymphatic system and venous circulation.

3. Vitamins

Vitamins are non-macronutrient compounds that are vital for healthy functioning and cannot be synthesized in adequate quantities by the body, meaning that they must be obtained from external sources. They are an interesting topic for the MCAT, because they have many different effects on a variety of physiological systems, so they often come up piecemeal in various biology chapters—even in biochemistry, because the B vitamins function as coenzymes. However, it can be useful to review the functions of vitamins in one place, which is the goal of this section.

An important distinction is between lipid-soluble and water-soluble vitamins. Vitamins A, D, E, and K are lipid-soluble, while the other vitamins—vitamin C and the B vitamins (B_1, B_2, B_3, B_5, B_6, B_7, B_9, and B_{12})—are water-soluble. Water-soluble vitamins circulate in the blood and are easily excreted, whereas lipid-soluble vitamins accumulate in adipose tissue. This has ramifications for the use of vitamins as dietary supplements: it is almost impossible to take too much of vitamin C or the B vitamins, because the body will simply excrete excess amounts of those substances in the urine. That is to say, to put it bluntly, that so-called "megadosing" with vitamins B and C will just result in very expensive, vitamin-dense urine. (Some cases have occurred in which individuals have experienced negative physical effects due to overdoses of water-soluble vitamins, but this is rare). In contrast, it is quite possible to take too much of lipid-soluble vitamins, resulting in conditions known as hypervitaminosis A, hypervitaminosis D, hypervitaminosis E, and hypervitaminosis K.

Table 1 below presents the basic functions of all the vitamins, followed by a further discussion of some vitamins of special note for the MCAT.

VITAMIN	CHEMICAL NAME	MAJOR FUNCTION
Lipid-soluble		
Vitamin A	Retinol, retinal (+ carotenoids)	Vision (low-light and color)
Vitamin D	Cholecalciferol (D_3), ergocalciferol (D_2)	Calcium and phosphate absorption from gut
Vitamin E	Tocopherols, tocotrienols	Antioxidant
Vitamin K	Phylloquinone, menaquinoines	Coagulation
Water-soluble		
Vitamin C	Ascorbic acid	Cofactor for reactions in collagen synthesis, antioxidant
Vitamin B_1	Thiamine	Coenzyme in important metabolic reactions
Vitamin B_2	Riboflavin	Coenzyme involved in electron transport chain, precursor of FAD (which is involved in many key reactions)
Vitamin B_3	Niacin, niacinamide	Precursor of NAD and NADP, which are involved in many key reactions
Vitamin B_5	Pantothenic acid	Required for synthesis of CoA, as well in metabolism
Vitamin B_6	Pyridoxine, pyridoxamine, pyridoxal	Used as a coenzyme in many metabolic reactions
Vitamin B_7	Biotin	Cofactor for several carboxylase enzymes in metabolic reactions
Vitamin B_9	Folic acid	Ensures proper neurological development in pregnancy, required for fertility
Vitamin B_{12}	Cyanocobalamin + derivatives (ending in -balamin)	Coenzyme in metabolic reactions, especially DNA synthesis and lipid/amino acid metabolism

Table 1. Vitamins.

A few background points are helpful for understanding vitamins. First, you might wonder why several of the vitamins, especially the lipid-soluble ones, correspond to multiple chemical names. You may also wonder about the naming conventions. In a sense, both of these points can be thought of as a historical legacy from the initial period of research into vitamins, which was conducted before modern techniques for characterizing molecular structures emerged.

Vitamins were discovered as a result of research into nutritional deficiencies. The most famous example is probably vitamin C deficiency, which used to be common among sailors who spent extended periods of time away from land without access to fresh food; in fact, scurvy caused the deaths of millions of sailors over the centuries. As is not surprising for a deficiency of a compound needed for collagen synthesis, scurvy involves symptoms of weakness, gum disease, and excess bleeding, and can eventually be fatal. (As a side note, it still occurs today, in the developing world and in the developed world among individuals with mental disorders, alcoholism, or intense patterns of binge drug use). In 1753, a surgeon in the Royal Navy proved that consuming citrus fruit could prevent scurvy. However, the fact that ascorbic acid in particular was responsible for this effect was not shown until 1932. In 1912, the biochemist Casimir Funk discovered niacin (now known as vitamin B_3), and proposed that it be called "vitamine," short for "vital amine." The name stuck, although the final "-e" was dropped when it became clearer that not all vitamins have amine groups. With all of that in mind, there are a few takeaway points you should know about vitamins in general for the MCAT:

> Vitamins are compounds essential for healthy life that cannot be synthesized in adequate quantities by the body and therefore must be obtained externally (generally from the diet, although vitamin D is synthesized in the skin in response to sunlight).
> Some vitamins actually reflect families of related compounds that are interconverted metabolically and/or contribute to the same overall effect.
> Vitamins and vitamin derivatives often serve as coenzymes/cofactors in essential reactions.
> The descriptions of vitamins given in Table 1 only scratches the surface of their range of functions, covering the most important points that are testable on the MCAT. In reality, vitamins play an astonishingly diverse and complex set of roles in the human body, and are still the subject of ongoing research.

For the most part, knowing the difference between fat-soluble and water-soluble vitamins and the short descriptions presented in Table 1 is enough for the purposes of the MCAT. There are a few vitamins, however, that require a bit more attention.

Vitamin A is essential for vision because it binds with opsin to form a protein known as rhodopsin, which is present in the rods of the retina and is used for low-light vision. It turns out that the way that vitamin A contributes to the function of visual processing is interesting chemically in ways that overlap surprisingly closely with some high-yield organic chemistry processes. This means that it is worth having a detailed overview of how vitamin A functions.

First, vitamin A occurs in a variety of forms characterized by different terminal functional groups. Although it's not exactly correct to say that any one form is the base form biochemically, it's useful to consider the alcohol form, retinol, to be the base form from which others are derived. In fact, retinol is the form in which we absorb vitamin A in the small intestine. However, retinol, like

CLINICAL CONNECTIONS > > >

A range of studies have shown correlations between vitamin D deficiencies and poor health outcomes. Does this mean that supplementation of vitamin D is a good preventive measure? Interestingly, research into this question remains controversial. It has been surprisingly difficult to document the benefits of vitamin D supplementation in a way that rules out the possibility of vitamin D deficiency and poor health outcomes both stemming from underlying disease processes, meaning that vitamin D supplementation would just be covering up the underlying problem. The utility of supplementation remains a controversial question that primary care physicians (for example) address frequently in their patients.

alcohols in general, is fairly reactive and is therefore not ideal for long-term storage. To solve this problem, a fatty acid can be used to create a retinyl ester. Retinyl esters are used for long-term storage and are actually the form in which we consume vitamin A in food (the conversion to retinol happens during absorption). You may see references to retinol as a storage form of vitamin A; this is true, but is more the case for shorter-term storage. Retinol itself is not biologically active. It can become biologically active in one of two ways: (1) being converted into retinal, which is used for vision; or (2) being further oxidized to retinoic acid, which is used in various pathways involving growth. The conversion between retinol and retinal is reversible under physiological conditions, whereas the oxidation of retinol to retinoic acid is an irreversible step. Thus, as you can see, vitamin A provides an excellent real-life example of the oxidation and reduction of oxygen-containing organic compounds.

The mechanism through which retinal triggers visual input also overlaps with a high-yield organic chemistry concept: in this case, the stereochemistry of double bonds. The form of retinal that binds to opsin is 11-cis-retinal. Light causes 11-cis-retinal to isomerize to all-trans-retinal, which triggers the transduction of a signal along the optic nerve and the temporary dissociation of retinal from opsin.

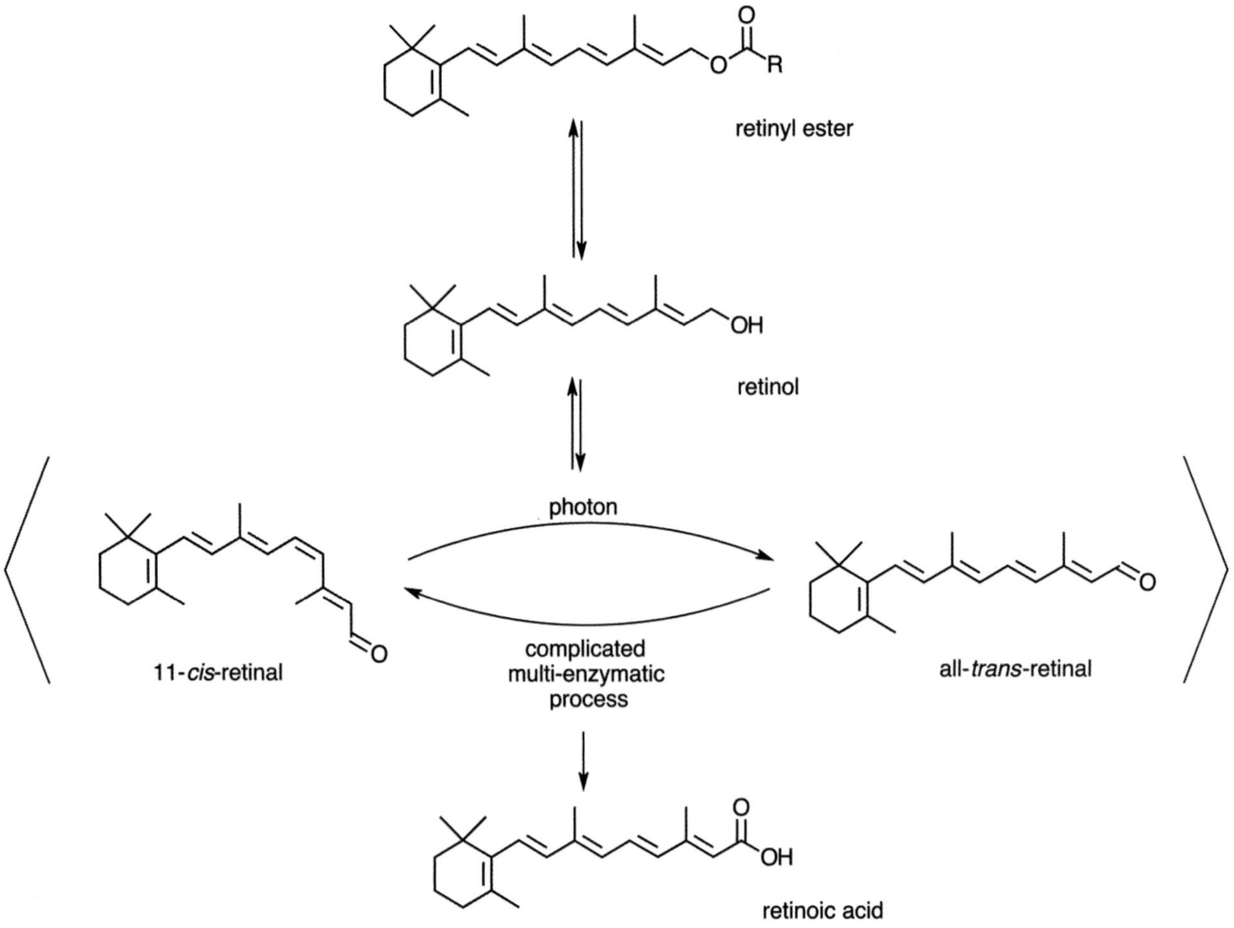

Figure 11. Forms of vitamin A.

Vitamin D is also of note because it has multiple forms and acts as a hormone, regulating calcium and phosphate concentrations in the bloodstream and promoting growth, as well as increasing the absorption of calcium, phosphate, and other minerals from the intestine. The major forms of vitamin D are vitamin D_2 (ergocalciferol) and vitamin D_3 (cholecalciferol), which are metabolized by the liver to form 25-hydroxyvitamin D_2 or $25(OH)D_2$. This compound is then converted to calcitriol, which exerts the hormonal effects of vitamin D.

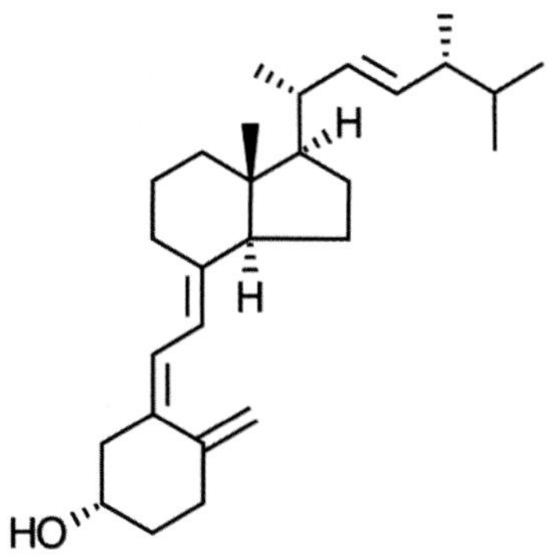

ergocalciferol
(vitamin D$_2$)

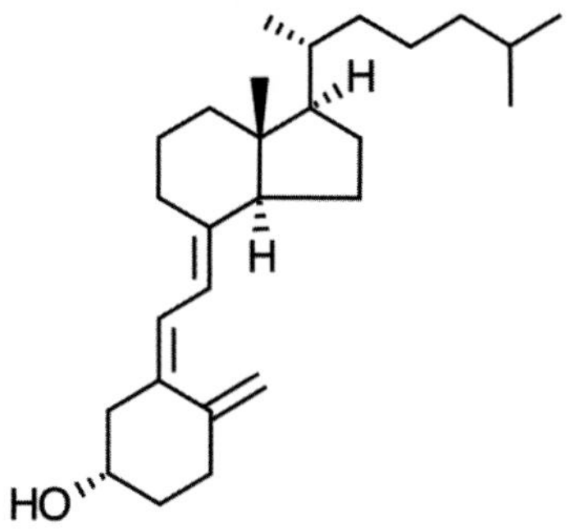

cholecalciferol
(vitamin D$_3$)

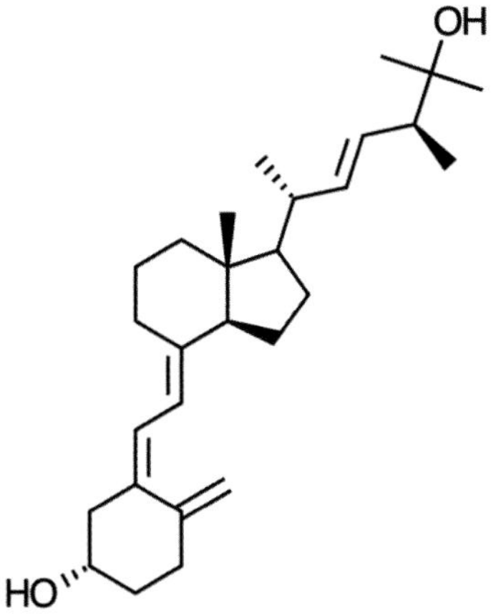

25-hydroxyvitamin D$_2$

Figure 12. Forms of vitamin D.

For the other vitamins, a general knowledge of their function suffices for the MCAT, although there are some isolated points of information that may prove useful. The bacteria in the gut play a major role in the synthesis of vitamin K. In particular, plants contain ample amounts of vitamin K$_1$, but bacteria in the gut transform it to vitamin K$_2$, which then goes on to be the source of various active derivatives in the body. This is another piece of evidence pointing towards the idea that bacteria play an integral role in human health. Vitamin B$_{12}$ is similarly of note because it cannot be produced by plants, fungi, or animals. However, humans can obtain vitamin B$_{12}$ from animal sources in their diet. This may seem paradoxical, but the idea is that some animals (such as cows) can absorb the vitamin B$_{12}$ produced by their gut flora and concentrate it in their tissues, making meat, liver, eggs, and milk sources of B$_{12}$ for humans. A consequence of this is that vegans must be very careful regarding vitamin B$_{12}$, which they can obtain from fortified foods or supplements.

4. Anatomy of the Excretory System

Next, let's turn to the excretory system. Urination may at first seem like a simple topic, but in reality, it is tremendously important physiologically. Defecation played a relatively small role in our discussion of the digestive tract above, whereas multiple sections of this chapter are dedicated to urination. Why the discrepancy? Essentially, with a few exceptions such as pancreatic secretions and bile salts, the contents of feces (primarily water, fiber, bacteria, and bile salts) are derived from substances external to our body. In fact, the entire gastrointestinal tract can be thought of as a series of tubes that pass material through our body while minimizing and tightly regulating the

CLINICAL CONNECTIONS > > >

The need to tightly regulate contact with food is why IV injections of non-sterile substances can be quite dangerous. If you've been in a hospital, you may have observed parenteral nutrition, in which a patient is administered nutrients intravenously. Specialized solutions are needed for this, because running food through a blender and injecting it intravenously would be catastrophic. This point may seem obvious, but you can use it as a reminder of this critically important function of the gastrointestinal tract.

transfer of substances between the body and the lumen of the gastrointestinal tract, because it would be disastrous to simply absorb food directly.

In contrast, though, we also have to get rid of waste products generated in the body. This is the role of the excretory system. As such, the excretory system plays a crucial role in maintaining homeostasis in the body, as discussed in more depth in section 6. First, though, let's review the basic anatomy of the excretory system.

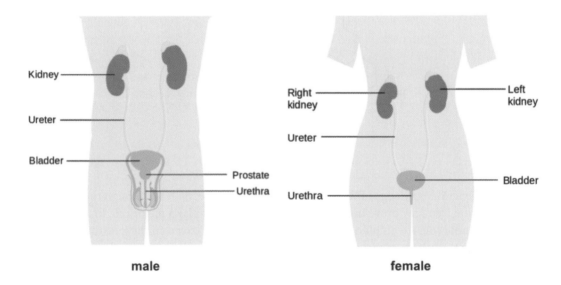

Figure 13. High-level diagram of excretory system.

Blood is filtered to form urine in the kidneys, which are located towards the back of the abdominal cavity. Humans have two kidneys, one on each side. They are supplied with blood by the renal arteries, and then drain into the renal veins. The outside of the kidney is surrounded by the protective tissue of the renal capsule, and then the kidney itself is divided into the outer region of the renal cortex and the inner region of the renal medulla.

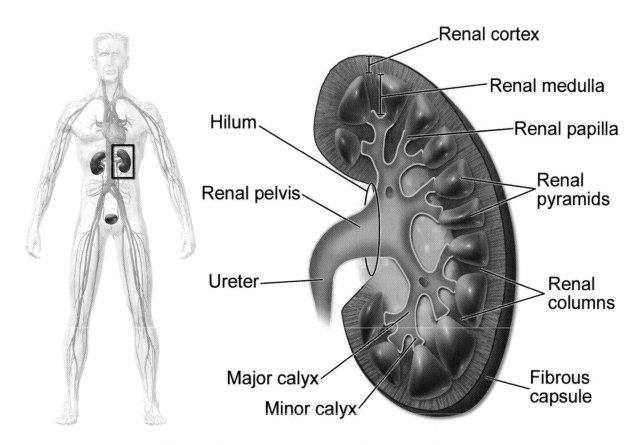

The Structure of a Kidney

Figure 14. Kidney anatomy.

Nephrons are the functional unit of the kidneys that produce urine. They are divided into two major parts. The renal corpuscle is the part of the nephron that carries out the initial filtration, and is located in the renal cortex. The renal tubule then projects downward into the medulla before returning up to the cortex, at which point urine drains into a collecting duct. Collecting ducts empty via structures known as the medullary pyramids into minor calyces (singular = calyx), which drain into major calyces, which drain in turn into a structure at the heart of each kidney known as the renal pelvis. The renal pelvis then becomes the ureter.

The ureters drain downwards from the kidneys into the urinary bladder, which rests on the pelvic floor. The bladder is a muscular and flexible structure that can generally hold approximately 400 mL of urine. Urine is then released from the bladder into the urethra, where it exits the body. The anatomy of the urethra differs between males and females; in females, the urethra exits the body anteriorly to the vagina, while in males the urethra exits the body through the penis, where it is used both for urination and ejaculation.

Release of urine through the urethra is controlled by the urethral sphincter, which has two components: the external urethral sphincter (which differs anatomically between males and females but has the same basic function) and the internal urethral sphincter. The internal urethral sphincter is composed of smooth muscle and is controlled by the autonomic nervous system, meaning that it is not subject to voluntary control. The external urethral sphincter, in contrast, is formed of skeletal muscle and is under voluntary control. Both sphincters must be open for urine to flow.

5. Physiology of the Excretory System

In this section, we'll take a closer look at how urine is produced in the nephron and how urination is regulated.

As mentioned above, the nephron can be divided into the renal corpuscle and the renal tubule. The renal corpuscle contains the glomerulus and Bowman's capsule. The glomerulus is a bunched-up set of capillaries through which water, ions, and small molecules filter out and are gathered into Bowman's capsule, which wraps around the glomerulus. Blood is supplied to the glomerulus through an afferent arteriole and exits through an efferent arteriole. The fluid collected in Bowman's capsule is known as the glomerular filtrate.

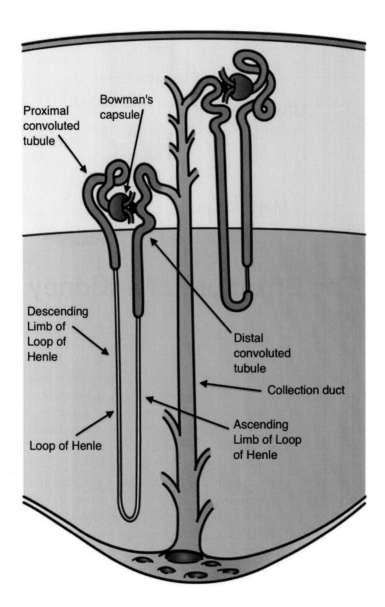

Figure 15. Nephron.

The renal tubule is composed of three main parts: the proximal convoluted tubule, the loop of Henle, and the distal convoluted tubule. The body must solve one basic problem in the renal tubule: adjusting the volume and concentration of urine appropriately. A tremendous amount of blood is filtered by the kidneys on a daily basis—in fact, the entire blood volume is filtered many times per day! It would be tremendously wasteful to eliminate even a small but meaningful fraction of that blood. Therefore, the body has to figure out how to keep enough water to maintain health while getting rid of the wastes that need to be removed. The activity and structure of the renal tubule are relatively complex because this is a critically important task that must be regulated carefully.

In the proximal convoluted tubule (PCT), two-way exchange happens. From the perspective of sheer volume, absorption predominates in the PCT; in particular, large amounts of sodium ions are re-absorbed, as well as other salts, water-soluble vitamins, free amino acids, and glucose. However, secretion of waste products into the urine also happens in the PCT. In particular, hydrogen and potassium ions, nitrogen-containing compounds such as urea and ammonia, and some medications are secreted into the urine via the PCT. This may seem surprising at first, because you might wonder where these waste products are coming from. In fact, a rich vascular plexus supplies the renal cortex, so the wastes in question come from the blood but are mediated via the cells of the PCT.

The loop of Henle is the next step in the nephron. It is a U-shaped tube that dives from the renal cortex to the renal medulla in the descending limb of the loop of Henle, before returning to the cortex in the ascending lib of the loop of Henle. The basic goal of the loop of Henle is to reduce the volume of water in urine in a way that can be closely regulated in response to various conditions. The need for tight regulation is why the structure itself is quite complex. An important point to have in the back of your mind while studying the loop of Henle is that the deeper you go into the medulla, the greater the concentration of solutes is, which facilitates the processes of osmosis and active/passive transport throughout the loop of Henle.

MCAT STRATEGY > > >

The loop of Henle is one of the most common points of confusion in terms of MCAT physiology. The secret to understanding it is first to focus on its overall function (to reduce the volume of filtrate dramatically without producing over-concentrated urine) and then break that down into two subtasks: first, the descending loop pushes out the water, and then the ascending loop pushes out solutes. This topic contains a general lesson about studying physiology topics for the MCAT: always focus on the function *first*, and learn the anatomy in the context of that function.

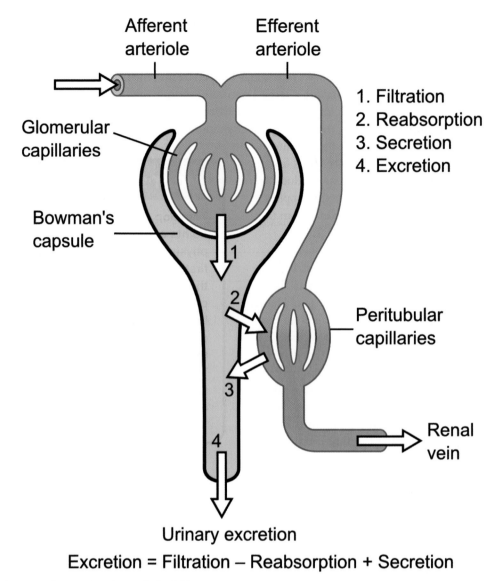

Afferent arteriole

Efferent arteriole

1. Filtration
2. Reabsorption
3. Secretion
4. Excretion

Glomerular capillaries

Bowman's capsule

Peritubular capillaries

Renal vein

Urinary excretion

Excretion = Filtration − Reabsorption + Secretion

Figure 16. Diagram of excretion through the kidney.

The descending limb of the loop of Henle is permeable to water but not to ions. This means that, as the descending limb plunges deeper into the increasingly hypertonic medulla, more and more water flows out of the loop of Henle and into the medulla, where it is eventually absorbed by the vasculature in the region (efferent arterioles known as the vasa recta) and brought back into circulation. Thus, the filtrate at the bottom of the loop of Henle is quite concentrated. The ascending loop of Henle, in contrast, is impermeable to water, but allows sodium and potassium ions to flow through. They diffuse down their concentration gradient at each stage, resulting in a much lower osmolarity by the time the filtrate completes its path through the loop. The top part of the ascending limb is known as the thick ascending limb, and this area also allows the active transport of sodium, potassium, and chloride ions. The end product of this is filtrate that is not actually much more concentrated in terms of osmolarity than the initial filtrate, but with a significantly decreased volume.

The mechanism through which the loop of Henle operates is known as a countercurrent multiplier. This seemingly abstract term essentially just describes how the concentration gradients leading to solute and water flow are established and maintained. If the blood vessels responsible for draining the solutes back into the systemic circulation went in the same direction as the flow through the loop of Henle, the whole process would bog down, because the concentration gradients would just equalize and transport would grind to a halt. To visualize this better, you may want to keep in mind that the blood supply near the loop of Henle is provided by arterioles known as the vasa recta (or "straight vessels"), which run parallel to the loop.

The nephron has two more areas where water balance can be adjusted: the distal convoluted tubule (DCT) and the collecting duct. Aldosterone can act on both sites to promote sodium reabsorption, which in turn promotes water reabsorption mediated by the osmotic effects of this process. The DCT can also increase calcium reabsorption in response to parathyroid hormone, and can contribute to pH regulation by secreting or absorbing protons as needed. The collecting duct, in turn can be affected by antidiuretic hormone (ADH, or vasopressin), which increases water reabsorption directly. Atrial natriuretic peptide (ANP) has the opposite effect of aldosterone; that is, it promotes retention of sodium in the urine, which draws water with it, increasing the amount of water expelled in the urine and decreasing blood pressure. At this point, once the urine drains into the renal pelvis, its composition and concentration are established.

6. Homeostasis and the Excretory System

The details of the excretory system can be overwhelming, but the MCAT often expects you to apply your detailed knowledge to evaluate hypotheticals or in the context of new information. To do so, you must understand the principles of how the excretory system regulates homeostasis. In this section, we'll review the four major domains of homeostasis regulation through the excretory system: blood pressure, osmoregulation, acid-base balance, and the removal of soluble nitrogenous waste.

As we reviewed in the previous chapter, blood pressure can be influenced by many parameters, such as the elasticity of the blood vessels, the velocity of blood flow, and the total cross-sectional area of a given part of the circulatory system. However, this list omits a physiologically fundamental contributor to blood pressure: total fluid volume, which is regulated by the excretory system, which can "choose" to either push out more water in the urine or to make the urine more concentrated in order to preserve water. As briefly reviewed in the previous section, there are three main hormones that affect fluid balance:

> Aldosterone promotes water retention by increasing sodium absorption: ↑ aldosterone = ↑ Na^+ reabsorption = ↑ H_2O reabsorption = ↑ plasma volume of blood = ↑ blood pressure

> Antidiuretic hormone (ADH; vasopressin) promotes water retention directly by increasing water reabsorption in the collecting duct: ↑ ADH = ↑ H_2O retention = ↑ plasma volume of blood = ↑ blood pressure. Because it only promotes water retention, ADH has the effect of reducing the osmolarity of the blood.

> Atrial natriuretic peptide (ANP) is the opposite of aldosterone; it promotes sodium retention in the urine: ↑ ANP = ↓ Na^+ reabsorption = ↓ H_2O reabsorption = ↓ plasma volume of blood = ↓ blood pressure.

Aldosterone release is actually regulated by the kidneys via the renin-angiotensin-aldosterone axis. Juxtaglomerular cells in the afferent arterioles of the kidneys release a substance known as renin in response to reduced blood pressure (detected by baroceptors), reduced sodium levels, or signaling from the sympathetic nervous system (which raises blood pressure as part of the "fight or flight" response). Renin causes angiotensinogen to be cleaved to form angiotensin I, which is then converted to angiotensin II by an enzyme known as angiotensin-converting enzyme (ACE). Angiotensin II increases blood pressure through vasoconstriction and also triggers the release of aldosterone.

> > CONNECTIONS < <

Chapter 7 of Biology

Renin-angiotensin-aldosterone system

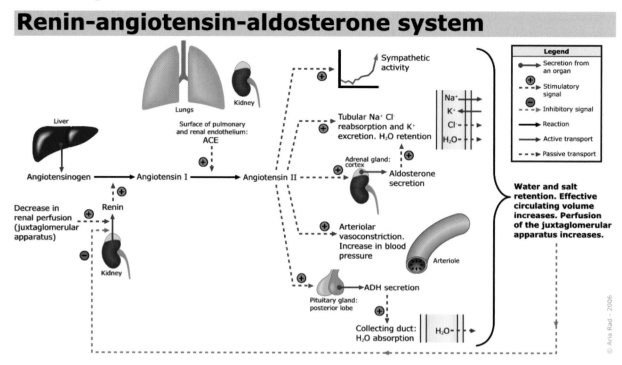

Figure 17. Renin-angiotensin-aldosterone axis (from endocrine chapter).

As suggested by the fact that the mechanisms of aldosterone and ANP involve modulating sodium reabsorption, the excretory system is also involved in regulating solutes. The overall osmolarity of the blood (as distinct from the specific concentrations of individual solutes) is important to maintain fluid balance within the body. As discussed in Chapter 9 on the respiratory and circulatory systems, an interplay between hydrostatic pressure and oncotic pressure (the osmotic pressure due to proteins in blood) drives fluid exchange between capillaries and the interstitial space. Blood osmolarity must be maintained within a very tight range, and this is largely accomplished by fluctuations in the relative quantities of water and solute reabsorption or excretion.

MCAT STRATEGY > > >

As we have seen again and again, the MCAT requires you to develop an integrated understanding of physiological systems. In a sense, this section is the core of this half of the chapter, and the preceding sections on the anatomy and physiology of the excretory system just provide details to bolster your mechanistic understanding of these points. Once you finish this chapter, read this section again, and then go back and reread the previous sections. Work towards allowing your understanding of the fundamentals to assist your study of the details and vice versa.

The excretory system also regulates blood pH, which must be kept within a narrow range (between 7.35 and 7.45). Many factors can impact blood pH, such as active anaerobic metabolism that generates H^+ as a byproduct, or levels of CO_2, which increases the acidity of blood by participating in the bicarbonate buffer equilibrium. However, one easy way to decrease the acidity of blood is to excrete more H^+ in the urine, and one way to increase the acidity of blood is to inhibit the excretion of H^+. As discussed in Chapter 9, the respiratory system also modulates pH; it is useful to think of the respiratory system providing the short-term response to pH changes (because respiratory rate can either increase or decrease very quickly), while the excretory system helps regulate pH on a medium-term to longer-term scale.

Soluble nitrogenous waste is also removed by the excretory system. In particular, this applies to urea. Urea ($CO(NH_2)_2$) can be thought of as a carbonyl-containing carrier of excess amine groups that need to be excreted.

Ammonia (NH_3) is a byproduct of the metabolism of nitrogen-containing compounds such as amino acids, but in excessive levels becomes toxic to the body. Therefore, the liver converts ammonia to urea, which is secreted into the nephron for excretion.

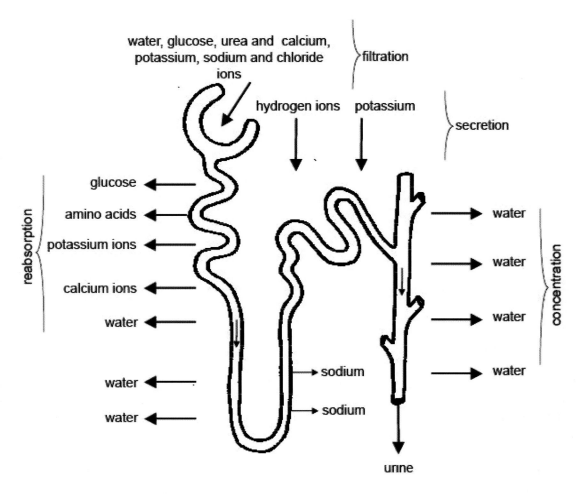

Figure 19. Steps in the formation of urine.

7. Must-Knows

> Basic path of food through the digestive system: oral cavity → esophagus → stomach → small intestine (duodenum, jejunum, ileum) → large intestine (cecum, ascending colon, transverse colon, descending colon, sigmoid colon) → rectum
> Stomach has very low pH due to gastric acid; pH becomes slightly alkaline in small intestine
> Bile: generated in liver, stored in gall bladder, released to small intestine to emulsify fats
> Pancreas: secretes digestive enzymes & bicarbonates and releases them to small intestine
> Small intestine: main site for digestion & absorption of nutrients
   – Villae multiply surface area of small intestinal lining; microvillae on surface of cell increase surface area available for absorption
> Large intestine: re-absorption of H2O, large microbial community, absorption of microbe-generated substances (vitamin K, short-chain fatty acids)

> Carbohydrates: salivary amylase in mouth → digestive enzymes (pancreatic amylase + disaccharidases) in small intestine → monosaccharides absorbed into small intestine cells → hepatic portal vein for liver processing → bloodstream
> Proteins: pepsin in stomach → various peptidases in small intestines; isolated amino acids primarily absorbed in small intestine, as well as some dipeptides → absorbed into small intestine cells → hepatic portal vein for liver processing → bloodstream
> Fats: lingual lipase starts digesting triglycerides → pancreatic lipase continues → bile salts in small intestine emulsify → absorbed into small intestinal cells → lacteals in villi → drain into lymphatic system as chylomicrons → bloodstream
> Vitamins: A, D, E, K = fat-soluble; B vitamins and C = water-soluble
> Vitamins have range of functions; notably A helps in function of vision, D in calcium/phosphate metabolism, K in clotting, C in collagen synthesis, and B vitamins are many important coenzymes/factors.
> Basic urination path:
  – Nephron: glomerulus (blood vessels) → Bowman's capsule → proximal convoluted tubule → loop of Henle (descending & ascending), distal convoluted tubule → collecting duct
  – Collecting duct → minor calyx → major calyx → renal pelvis → ureters → urinary bladder → urethra
> Nephron has two major functions: (1) filtering various substances in blood; (2) appropriately regulating fluid/salt content of urine.
> Loop of Henle has countercurrent multiplier mechanism to greatly reduce liquid volume in urine by first making urine concentrated (descending limb) and then removing solutes (ascending limb)
> Aldosterone: ↑ Na^+ reabsorption = ↑ H_2O reabsorption = ↑ plasma volume of blood = ↑ blood pressure; ADH = ↑ H_2O retention = ↑ plasma volume of blood = ↑ blood pressure; ANP = ↓ Na^+ reabsorption = ↓ H_2O reabsorption = ↓ plasma volume of blood = ↓ blood pressure.
> Excretory system: regulates blood pressure, pH, excretion of nitrogenous wastes

This page left intentionally blank.

Practice Passage

Fuzzy logic is a set of mathematical principles used for representing the ambiguous knowledge and vague "common sense" physicians employ when they reason and think about disease. Fuzzy logic deals with the degree of truth, using a more detailed continuum from 0 (completely false) to 1 (complete true). In recent years, fuzzy logic methods (FLM) have been increasingly used to predict the progress of diseases.

Because of the dynamic nature of chronic kidney disease (CKD), predicting the renal failure progression with accuracy is difficult. Renal failure progression is a function of various parameters including blood pressure, hypertension, proteinuria, and age. Researchers investigating this phenomena found that when the glomerular filtration rate (GFR) reaches less than 15 ml/kg/min/1.73 m^2, dialysis or transplant is necessary for the patient's survival. If it is possible to predict the time to reach the GFR failure threshold, the time for renal replacement therapy (i.e. hemodialysis or transplant) is effectively predicted.

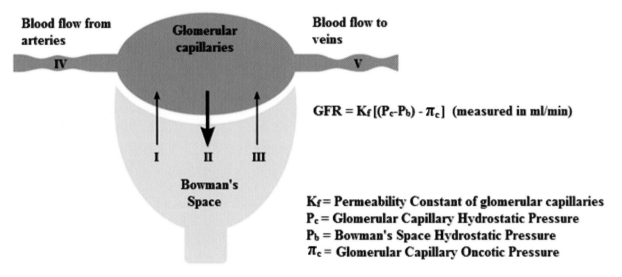

$$GFR = K_f [(P_c - P_b) - \pi_c] \text{ (measured in ml/min)}$$

K_f = Permeability Constant of glomerular capillaries
P_c = Glomerular Capillary Hydrostatic Pressure
P_b = Bowman's Space Hydrostatic Pressure
π_c = Glomerular Capillary Oncotic Pressure

Figure 1. Visualization and quantification of the glomerular filtration rate

A total of 593 CKD patients were evaluated in the study to evaluate the accuracy of the FLM. Prior to study onset, the mean patient GFR value was 60 ml/kg/min/1.73 m^2 with a standard error of 19 ml/kg/min/1.73 m^2. Table 1 lists 10 factors, identified via analysis of patient records, which can be correlated with GFR.

Table 1. Correlation Coefficients Between Inputs and Target Output (GFR$_{t+2}$) for 6-month Period (Note: dbp = diastolic blood pressure; Cr: creatinine; Ca: calcium; P: phosphorus; underlying disease)

Input	Input number	Correlation coefficient between input i and output
Underlying disease$_{(t)}$	1	0.2505
Sex$_{(t)}$	2	0.0706
Age$_{(t)}$	3	−0.1043
dbp$_{(t)}$	4	0.7145
Cr$_{(t)}$	5	0.0322
Ca$_{(t)}$	6	−0.6224
P$_{(t)}$	7	−0.1444
Uric acid$_{(t)}$	8	0.1089
Weight$_{(t)}$	9	0.8120
GFR$_{(t)}$	10	0.5196

After reviewing the relationships between the 10 independent variables, the four independent variables with the strongest correlation with the dependent variable were selected. After training the FLM with patient data, output was generated to predict daily GFR values for each patient for 12 months. Next, GFR in all patients was measured daily for 12 months. Finally, at 12 months, a comparison was made between the GFR values predicted by the FLM and the measured GFR values (Figure 2).

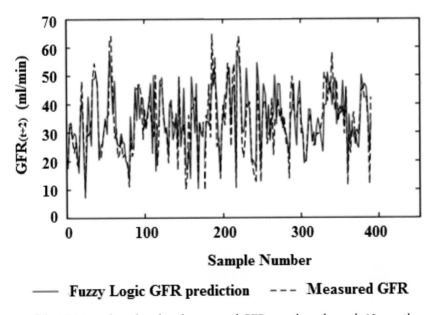

Figure 2. Comparison of the FLM predicted and real measured GFR$_{(t+2)}$ values through 12 months

Adapted from Norouzi, J & Hosseini, A. (2016). Predicting Renal Failure Progression in Chronic Kidney Disease Using Integrated Intelligent Fuzzy Expert System. Computational and Mathematical Methods in Medicine, 2016, 6080814 under CCBY

1. Which independent variable identified by the researchers was NOT included in the FLM training?
   A. $dbp_{(t)}$
   B. $Weight_{(t)}$
   C. $Ca_{(t)}$
   D. Underlying disease$_{(t)}$

2. Which set of pressure values in Figure 1 will result in a net filtration pressure of 5 mm Hg?
   A. I = 10 mm Hg, II = 20 mm Hg, III = 10 mm Hg
   B. I = 15 mm Hg, II = 10 mm Hg, III = 20 mm Hg
   C. I = 10 mm Hg, II = 20 mm Hg, III = 5 mm Hg
   D. I = 20 mm Hg, II = 30 mm Hg, III = 15 mm Hg

3. ABCB10 is a mitochondrial protein suspected to be involved with process of active transport. A student who performs an assay to measure the presence of ABCB10 in the cells of the nephron is most likely to obtain which results?

A.

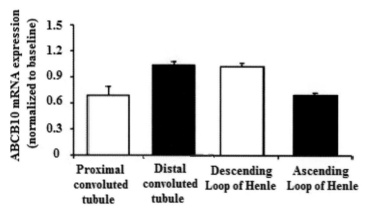

B.

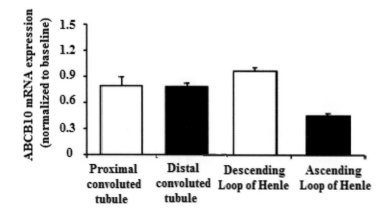

C.

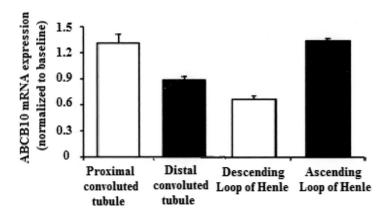

D.

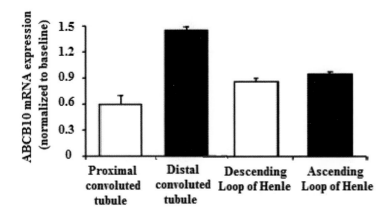

4. Which of the following is closest to the number of the study patients who would be expected to need renal replacement therapy at the onset of the study?
    A. 10
    B. 50
    C. 150
    D. 300

5. Which molecule is the primary contributor to the value represented by π_c?
    A. Fibrinogen
    B. Clotting factor III
    C. Globulin
    D. Albumin

6. Which of the following graphs correctly shows the effect of efferent arteriole resistance (R_E) on glomerular filtration rate?

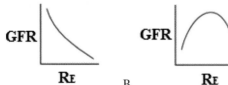

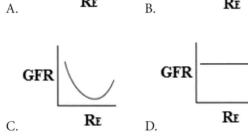

A.   B.

C.   D.

7. The study revealed that 56% of the patients in the study have a nonfunctional renal autoregulation response. Which input factor identified in these patients is most likely to trigger the actions of the juxtaglomerular apparatus in their nephrons?

A. $Na_{(t)}$
B. $P_{(t)}$
C. $dbp_{(t)}$
D. Uric acid$_{(t)}$

Practice Passage Explanations

Fuzzy logic is a set of mathematical principles used for representing the ambiguous knowledge and vague "common sense" physicians employ when they reason and think about disease. Fuzzy logic deals with the degree of truth, using a more detailed continuum from 0 (completely false) to 1 (complete true). In recent years, fuzzy logic methods (FLM) have been increasingly used to predict the progress of diseases.

Key terms: Fuzzy Logic, progress of disease

Cause and effect: FL allows for nonspecific or vague medical information to be modeled so that disease progression can be predicted (0 = false; 1 = true)

Because of the dynamic nature of chronic kidney disease (CKD), predicting the renal failure progression with accuracy is difficult. Renal failure progression is a function of various parameters including blood pressure, hypertension, proteinuria, and age. Researchers investigating this phenomena found that when the glomerular filtration rate (GFR) reaches less than 15 ml/kg/min/1.73 m², dialysis or transplant is necessary for the patient's survival. If it is possible to predict the time to reach the GFR failure threshold, the time for renal replacement therapy (i.e. hemodialysis or transplant) is effectively predicted.

Key terms: CKD, renal failure, GFR failure threshold

Cause and effect: GFR can be used to determine the point of kidney failure, and FLM may predict GFR changes

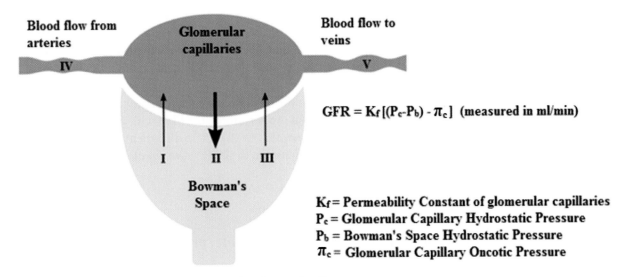

Blood flow from arteries

Glomerular capillaries

Blood flow to veins

$$GFR = K_f[(P_c - P_b) - \pi_c] \text{ (measured in ml/min)}$$

Bowman's Space

K_f = Permeability Constant of glomerular capillaries
P_c = Glomerular Capillary Hydrostatic Pressure
P_b = Bowman's Space Hydrostatic Pressure
π_c = Glomerular Capillary Oncotic Pressure

Figure 1. Visualization and quantification of the glomerular filtration rate

Figure 1 should be familiar; anticipate questions on movement of fluids, pressure balance, and possibly calculating GFR using the equation; note the RN-labeled sections which are likely to be asked about (I = P_b or π_c; II = P_c; III = P_b or π_c; IV = afferent arteriole; V = efferent arteriole)

A total of 593 CKD patients were evaluated in the study to evaluate the accuracy of the FLM. Prior to study onset, the mean patient GFR value was 60 ml/kg/min/1.73 m² with a standard error of 19 ml/kg/min/1.73 m². Table 1 lists 10 factors, identified via analysis of patient records, which can be correlated with GFR.

Key terms: accuracy of the FLM, 10 factors correlated with GFR values, standard error

Table 1. Correlation Coefficients Between Inputs and Target Output (GFR_{t+2}) for 6-month Period (Note: dbp = diastolic blood pressure; Cr: creatinine; Ca: calcium; P: phosphorus; underlying disease)

Input	Input number	Correlation coefficient between input i and output
Underlying disease$_{(t)}$	1	0.2505
Sex$_{(t)}$	2	0.0706
Age$_{(t)}$	3	−0.1043
dbp$_{(t)}$	4	0.7145
Cr$_{(t)}$	5	0.0322
Ca$_{(t)}$	6	−0.6224
P$_{(t)}$	7	−0.1444
Uric acid$_{(t)}$	8	0.1089
Weight$_{(t)}$	9	0.8120
GFR$_{(t)}$	10	0.5196

Table 1 provides too much information to be of use right now, note the diverse magnitudes and directions of the correlations, but save details for the questions, if necessary; weight has the strongest positive correlation (as it increases, GFR increases) while Ca has the strongest negative correlation (as it increases, GFR decreases)

After reviewing the relationships between the 10 independent variables, the four independent variables with the strongest correlation with the dependent variable were selected. After training the FLM with patient data, output was generated to predict daily GFR values for each patient for 12 months. Next, GFR in all patients was measured daily for 12 months. Finally, at 12 months, a comparison was made between the GFR values predicted by the FLM and the measured GFR values (Figure 2).

Key terms: strongest correlation, GFR measured, comparison

Cause and effect: FLM was "trained" using select past patient data; prediction and actual 6 month GFR were compared for accuracy

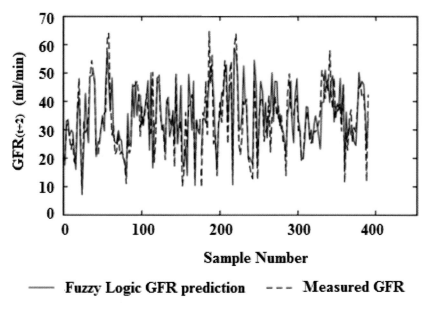

Figure 2. Comparison of the FLM predicted and real measured GFR$_{(t+2)}$ values through 12 months

Figure 2 shows that the FLM predictions of GFR appear to be accurate at 6 months, though no meaningful conclusions can be drawn without statistical findings

Adapted from Norouzi, J & Hosseini, A. (2016). Predicting Renal Failure Progression in Chronic Kidney Disease Using Integrated Intelligent Fuzzy Expert System. Computational and Mathematical Methods in Medicine, 2016, 6080814 under CCBY

1. D is correct. The question asks us to determine which variable from Table 1 the researchers chose to train the FLM. Paragraph 4 tells us that the four independent variables with the strongest correlation to the dependent variable (i.e. GFR) were chosen to train the FLM. If we examine Table 1, we can identify these four values. A good test day rule of thumb for "strength" of correlation is as follows:
   ± (0.7 – 1.0) = strong; ± (0.3 – 0.69) = moderate; ± (0.0 – 0.29) = none to weak
   Thus, we can see that the variables with the strongest correlations with GFR are: weight$_{(t)}$, dbp$_{(t)}$, Ca$_{(t)}$, and GFR$_{(t)}$.
   A, B, C: These all have correlation coefficient values in the top 4 of the 10 variables listed.

2. C is correct. To have a net filtration pressure, the net pressure must favor movement of fluid from the capillary into the Bowman's Space. If we define fluid movement into the Bowman's Space (i.e. filtration) as positive, and fluid movement into the glomerular capillary as negative, we want the net sum of all the pressures to be positive.

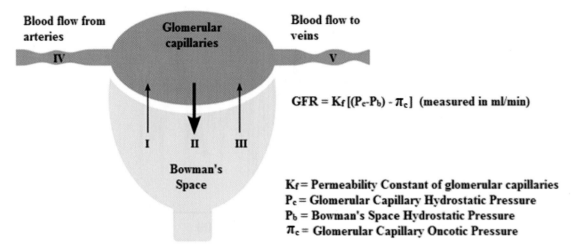

$$GFR = K_f[(P_c - P_b) - \pi_c] \quad (\text{measured in ml/min})$$

K_f = Permeability Constant of glomerular capillaries
P_c = Glomerular Capillary Hydrostatic Pressure
P_b = Bowman's Space Hydrostatic Pressure
π_c = Glomerular Capillary Oncotic Pressure

I is a pressure gradient pointing into the capillary, so we will make it negative.
II is a pressure gradient pointing into the Bowman's space, so we will make it positive.
III is a pressure gradient pointing into the capillary, so we will make it negative.
Thus, we get the formula: Net filtration pressure = II – III – I .
A. II – III – I → 20 – 10 – 10 = 0 mm Hg, no net movement of fluid, no good.
B. II – III – I → 10 – 20 – 15 = -25 mm Hg, net movement into the capillary, no good.
C. II – III – I → 20 – 5 – 10 = +5 mm Hg, net movement into the Bowman's space, correct!
D. II – III – I → 30 – 15 – 20 = -5 mm Hg, net movement into the capillary, no good.

3. C is correct. If ABCB10 is a mitochondrial protein associated with active transport, we would expect to find more of it in nephron location where there is more active transport. The proximal tubule contributes the majority of transport along the nephron. The descending loop of Henle only allows for passive reabsorption of water so we can eliminate choices A and B. The ascending loop of Henle is impermeable to water, and has to actively pump ions out of the nephron. As a result, it has thick walls filled with mitochondria to help satisfy the energy needs of this active transport. Thus, we would expect the expression of ABCB10 to be highest in these two regions. The test makers would not expect us to know more detail than that, so if we check the answers, only 1 choice fits the limited renal biology we have to know for the exam.
A, B, D: These do not show the PT or ascending loop of Henle as the locations with the highest number of mitochondria.

4. A is correct. This is a stats question about interpreting the data from the study. Study demographics were given in paragraph 3. We have approximately 600 patients, and we are given the average GFR (60 ml/min) and the standard error (19 ml/min). Paragraph 1 tells us that a GFR less than 15 ml/min indicates the need for renal replacement therapy. How do we use this information? We should know for test day that in a given data set with a given mean, we expect 68% of our sample values to fall within 1 standard error of the population mean. 95% would fall within 2 standard errors and about 99.7% of the sample values will be within 3 standard errors of the population mean. Thus only 2.5% of the study population would have a GFR more than two standard errors below the mean. With a mean of 60 and a standard error of 19, this means only 2.5% of the group would have a GFR of 22 ml/min or less (60-19*2). Even fewer would have a GFR of 15 or lower. Thus, our answer must be less than 2.5% of 600, or less than 15. Only choice A is anywhere close.

5. D is correct. The question asks about the identity of π_c which Figure 1 tells us is the glomerular capillary oncotic pressure. Oncotic pressure, also known as colloid osmotic pressure, is a form of osmotic pressure exerted by proteins in a blood vessel's plasma. This pressure usually acts to pull water into the circulatory system. The major proteins in the blood are: albumins (55%), globulins (38%), fibrinogen, also known as clotting factor I (7%), and clotting factors (<1%). The test makers do not expect us to know all of these, but we should know the most abundant plasma protein is albumin.

   A, B, C: these proteins are all present in far lower amount than albumin. Thus, they will not contribute as much to the colloid osmotic pressure.

6. B is correct. The primary physiological modulators of GFR are the afferent and efferent arteriolar resistances (R_A and R_E). The relationship between the efferent arteriolar resistance (R_E) and GFR is two-fold. Initially, increasing R_E lowers flow exiting the capillary, which increases the pressure within the glomerulus and thus increases GFR. However, at higher values of R_E the kidneys compensate and total blood flow through the glomerulus decreases causing GFR to drop back down.

   A. This is the relationship between increasing afferent arteriole resistance and GFR. Increasing R_A drops the pressure within the glomerulus and thus reduces GFR.

   C. This shows and decrease in GFR, followed by an increase. This is the opposite effect of increasing R_E.

   D. This shows no effect of efferent arteriole resistance on GFR, which is impossible.

7. C is correct. The juxtaglomerular apparatus is a specialized structure formed by the distal convoluted tubule and the glomerular afferent arteriole. It is located near the vascular pole of the glomerulus and its main function is to regulate blood pressure and the filtration rate of the glomerulus. This dbp is the diastolic blood pressure, a value which is directly related to the mean arterial pressure (systemic bp). In healthy individuals, changes in systemic bp do not affect the pressures in the glomerular capillaries. This is because of renal autoregulation. Renal autoregulation involves feedback mechanisms within the kidney that cause either dilation or constriction in the afferent arterioles to counteract systemic blood pressure changes and keep GFR nearly constant. For instance, if the mean arterial pressure increases, renal autoregulation causes the afferent arteriole to constrict, preventing the pressure increase from being transmitted to the glomerular capillaries, and keeping the GFR from increasing.

   A. While sodium (Na) content in the blood will affect blood pressure and the signals received by the juxtaglomerular apparatus (specifically the macula densa), Na was NOT identified by the study as an input factor. The question specifically asks for a factor included in the study. Always remember to answer the question asked, do not just look for correct science.

   B, D: Phosphorus and uric acid concentrations are unlikely to activate the monitoring mechanism in the juxtaglomerular apparatus.

Independent Questions

1. Which of the following is not found in saliva?
   A. Mucin
   B. Pepsin
   C. Amylase
   D. Lysozyme

2. A gallbladder removal, termed a cholecystectomy, is often recommended to patients who have gallstones. Which of the following would be considered an appropriate dietary recommendation for a patient with a recent cholecystectomy?
   A. Begin cardio exercise immediately following surgery
   B. Avoid carbohydrate intake during the immediate days following surgery
   C. Reduce consumption of protein-rich foods, such as red meat
   D. Avoid fatty foods during the immediate days following surgery

3. Which of the following correctly matches the macronutrient with the location of digestion by digestive enzymes?
   A. Disaccharides—small intestine
   B. Proteins—pancreas
   C. Disaccharides—mouth
   D. All of the above are correct.

4. Humans lack digestive enzymes that break down beta acetal linkages, rendering us unable to digest or absorb cellulose. Which of the following is most likely to result from excess consumption of cellulose?
   A. Less water would be secreted into the lumen of the large intestine.
   B. Less water would be absorbed from the lumen of the large intestine.
   C. More water would be absorbed from the lumen of the large intestine.
   D. Less waste material would be found in the rectum.

5. In 2007, a woman competing in a water-drinking competition, "Wee for Wii," died after drinking seven liters of water in a radio contest. Which of the following would have been an appropriate treatment for water intoxication?
   A. Administration of an aldosterone receptor agonist
   B. Administration of a vasopressin receptor antagonist
   C. Treatment with a renin analog
   D. Treatment with an antidiuretic hormone receptor agonist

6. Which of the following pairings of a part of the nephron with its function is NOT correct?
   A. Proximal convoluted tubule—hormone-controlled reabsorption and secretion
   B. Loop of Henle—creation of osmotic gradient
   C. Ascending limb of the loop of Henle—NaCl reabsorption
   D. Collecting duct—concentration of urine

7. The digestive and excretory systems have multiple sphincters that gate the passage of material from one organ to the next. Which of the following sphincters is under voluntary control?
   A. The cardiac sphincter
   B. The external anal sphincter
   C. The gastroesophageal sphincter
   D. The pyloric sphincter

8. The process of consuming a meal, from anticipating the food to eating it, can be characterized as a feed-forward process. Which statement below best exemplifies this?
   A. Smelling food stimulates salivary secretion, which stimulates hormone secretion in the stomach.
   B. Seeing food stimulates the parasympathetic nervous system, increasing bowel movements.
   C. Consuming food stimulates secretion of GLP-1 from intestinal enteroendocrine cells, thus lowering blood glucose.
   D. The process of mastication reduces vascular resistance, thereby increasing blood flow to facial muscles.

Independent Question Explanations

1. B is correct. Pepsin is a protease found in gastric juice, not the saliva. Pepsin is produced in the form of pepsinogen by the chief cells of the stomach. Mucin lubricates the bolus, amylase digests polysaccharides, and lysozyme is an antimicrobial enzyme. All three are found in the saliva.

2. D is correct. The gallbladder releases stored bile into the small intestine to help emulsify fats. A gallbladder removal has a small associated risk of fat malabsorption, resulting in diarrhea.

3. A is correct. Disaccharides, including sucrose and lactose, are broken down in the small intestine by enzymes known as disaccharidases. The pancreas is the source of the zymogen form of trypsin, a protease, but proteins are not actually digested in the pancreas. Finally, starch is partially digested in the mouth by salivary amylase, but starch is a polysaccharide, not a disaccharide.

4. B is correct. The large intestine is typically the site of the absorption of significant amounts of water into the body. Since cellulose cannot be digested or absorbed, it will remain in the digestive tract, increasing its osmolarity (solute concentration). This will reduce the concentration gradient of water, resulting in less water absorption. Note that cellulose consumption would cause more, not less, waste material to be found in the rectum.

5. B is correct. Vasopressin (ADH) activity results in retention of water via reabsorption in the collecting duct of the nephron. A vasopressin receptor antagonist would interfere with vasopressin receptors, thus decreasing water retention. This would allow the patient with water intoxication to excrete more water, reducing blood volume and helping to re-establish equilibrium.

6. A is correct. The proximal convoluted tubule is the site of major reabsorption and secretion, but this is largely driven by sodium transport, not hormone activity. It is the distal convoluted tubule that is involved with hormone-controlled reabsorption and secretion.

7. B is correct. The external anal sphincter is composed of skeletal muscle and is under voluntary control. The gastroesophageal sphincter and the cardiac sphincter are interchangeable terms for the same structure, which separates the esophagus from the stomach. This structure is not under voluntary control. The pyloric sphincter, which separates the stomach from the small intestine, is similarly involuntary.

8. A is correct. Feed-forward mechanisms are characterized by the anticipatory regulation of certain actions. In choice A, smelling the food initiates physiological responses to prepare the body for food intake. Answer choice C is factually correct, but it illustrates a direct cause-and-effect relationship rather than a feed-forward mechanism.

This page left intentionally blank.

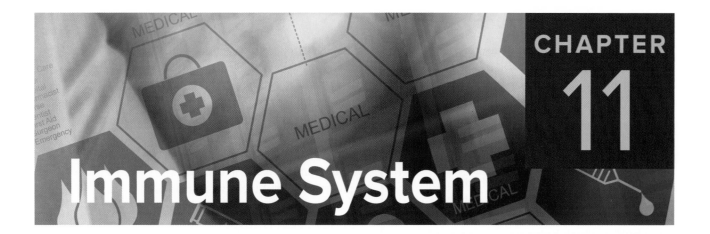

Immune System

CHAPTER 11

0. Introduction

The immune system refers to the complex set of mechanisms that the body uses to protect itself against foreign invaders and malfunctioning cells originating from the body itself. The immune system is remarkably complex. From an evolutionary point of view, you can think of the immune system as being as old as life itself, because the necessity to defend against viruses/bacteria/external threats has existed ever since organisms emerged. Evolutionary developments both on the part of microbes and the organisms affected by microbes have accumulated over a tremendous amount of time, resulting in a bewilderingly complex, intricate, and elegant set of defensive mechanisms. On one hand, the MCAT only expects you to have a relatively basic knowledge of the fundamental components and principles of the immune system, but on the other hand, this itself is a non-trivial task. For the MCAT, you should break your approach to the immune system into two parts: first, becoming familiar with the components of the immune system, how they are classified, and how they relate to each other; and second, developing a thorough understanding of the key principles of immunology, such as antigen-antibody interactions and how the body distinguishes between self and non-self.

Special care must be taken when studying the immune system because of the abundance of classifications that are applied to its components, and especially because those classifications sometimes have been outpaced, or at least complicated, by modern research. For example, the distinction between "humoral" and "cell-mediated" immune responses (discussed in more detail below in section 3) dates from the early stages of modern research into immunology, and the term "humoral" itself derives from the ancient Greek system of medical thought. In reality, these two aspects of the immune response interact with each other, and can only fully be understood in relation to one another. Therefore, you have a twofold task as you study the immune system: first, to know the definitions, and second, to understand how the actual immune response is coordinated on a physiological level.

The highest-level distinction in the immune system is between the innate (or non-specific) immune system, which responds generally to threats but does not learn to recognize specific foreign bodies/molecules, and the adaptive immune system, which does. In this chapter, we will first cover some fundamental concepts in immunology, explore the differences between the innate and adaptive immune systems, and then move on to discuss the anatomy of the immune system, the lymphatic system, and allergies and autoimmune disorders.

1. Concepts in Immunology

In order to make sense of the details of the immune system, which can be somewhat overwhelming even at the relatively basic level that is tested on the MCAT (don't worry, more awaits in medical school!), it's key to have a solid understanding of the basic principles that govern its function. It may be worth reading this chapter twice, because understanding the principles will help you make sense of the tremendous diversity of cells and pathways discussed later in this chapter, but it may also be the case that familiarity with the cell types and components of the immune reaction can help you obtain a deeper understanding of the basic principles.

The most basic principle of the immune system is the interaction between antigens and antibodies. This is also one of the most common and preventable sources of confusion among students preparing for the MCAT, so let's review the details carefully. One way of thinking about antigens and antibodies that is not commonly presented in textbooks but may prove useful is to visualize it as a system through which information is communicated. The idea is that the body has ample resources that it can mobilize to destroy cells/viruses/debris, but it has to do so *if and only if necessary*. Failure in either direction can have major negative consequences: if the body fails to recognize and respond to a real threat, it could potentially die, but if the body responds inappropriately to objects that aren't actual threats (like body cells), serious illness can result. Such illnesses are known as autoimmune disorders and are discussed in section 6.

The job of antibodies is to let the body know when it needs to mobilize the immune response. To do this, they have to be able to do two things: to recognize substances/cells that need to be eliminated, and to be recognized by other components of the immune system. The term "antigen" is used to refer to what antibodies recognize. Note that this definition is circular. There is no specific structural property that defines an antigen, although they often happen to be macromolecules (especially proteins) expressed on the surface of a cell or a viral envelope/capsule. However, external substances like pollen can also serve as antigens, causing pollen allergies.

The structure of an antibody provides a bridge between these two functions. As shown in Figure 1, antibodies have a Y-shaped structure consisting of two heavy chains and two light chains that are linked by disulfide bonds. Five classes of antibodies exist, classified according to the details of their heavy chains: immunoglobulin (Ig) A, IgD, IgE, IgG, and IgM. The details of these classes go beyond the scope of the MCAT, however. The "top" ends of the Y-shaped structure (that is, the part with both the heavy and the light chains) have a hypervariable antigen-recognizing area, and the rest of the antibody structure can be recognized by other cells of the immune system. The specific site on an antigen that is recognized by an antibody is known as the epitope. Extensive random recombination of the antigen-recognizing area of the antibody (also known as the paratope) allows the generation of antibodies that recognize potentially infinitely many types of antigens. Antibodies are used in the adaptive immune system, most notably by B cells; the details of this process are described in section 3 below.

Antigens

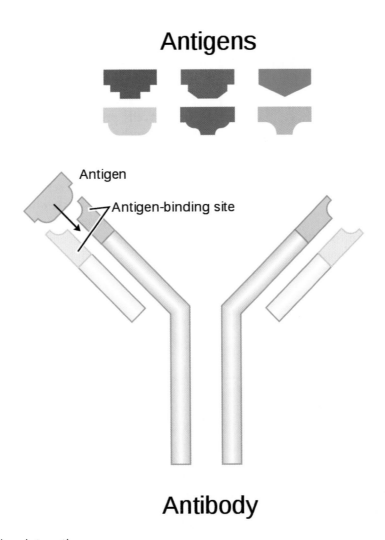

Antigen

Antigen-binding site

Antibody

Figure 1. Antibody-antigen interactions.

Another fundamental issue for the immune system is how to distinguish between self and non-self/damaged-self materials and cells. This is often framed just in terms of self versus non-self, but it is also important for the immune system to be able to recognize cells that were originally self, but have been damaged by viral infections or have malfunctioned in ways likely to turn them into cancer cells. This is primarily the job of T cells, which are discussed in more detail in section 3; for the purposes of this discussion, it is enough to know that various subgroups of T cells either directly attack compromised/foreign cells or mobilize responses to them based on antigen fragments that are presented by major histocompatibility complex (MHC) class I and II.

MHC class I is a protein expressed on the plasma membrane of all nucleated cells that is unique in each individual. Its job is to receive fragments of the proteins being expressed inside of a cell and to present them on the outside of the cell as antigens that T cells can respond to. If all is well, T cells will not respond to MHC I-antigen complexes, because the "antigens" in question are just normal pieces of cellular machinery, and T cells that would inappropriately respond to such stimuli were eliminated during their maturation process. However, cells infected

> ## MCAT STRATEGY > > >
>
> The best way of thinking of MHC class I is as a spot-check, in which the cell presents a sample of its products to T cells, which play the role of quality control checkers.

by viruses can present viral antigens on MHC class I,
and incipient tumor cells are likely to fail to present
appropriate proteins.

MHC class II, on the other hand, is expressed in a smaller
range of cells: primarily, macrophages, macrophage-
like cells such as dendritic cells, and B cells. Whereas
MHC class I serves as an *internal* checkpoint that relays
information about the internal health of the body's
own cells, MHC class II serves as a source of *external*
information. For instance, when macrophages consume a
microbe (or any foreign object), some fragments of it will
be displayed in a complex formed with MHC class II on the cell membrane. This complex is recognized by helper T
cells, and a larger immune response then ensues.

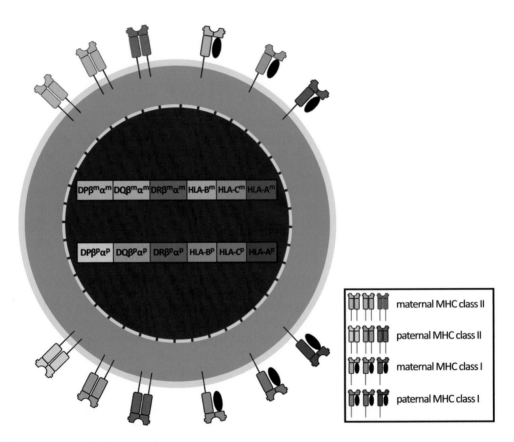

Figure 2. Major histocompatibility complex.

In a rare example of intuitive naming conventions in the immune system, the process by which cells present antigens
on their membranes is known as antigen presentation. Technically speaking, all nucleated cells in the body can
be considered antigen-presenting cells because they express MHC class I, whereas the more specialized cells that
express MHC class II are considered professional antigen-presenting cells. Antigen presentation is also a major
mechanism in the maturation and activation of B and T cells; this is discussed in more detail below, but the basic
idea is that B cells need to recognize antigens in order to generate specific antibodies, while T cells need to learn how
to appropriately respond to foreign stimuli.

Interestingly, immunological principles can be applied not just in the study of physiology, but are also commonly used in laboratory techniques. In western blotting and enzyme-linked immunosorbent assays (ELISA), a technique broadly known as immunohistochemistry or immunostaining is used to visualize specific proteins. In a nutshell, in these techniques, the protein of interest serves as an antigen that is visualized after it reacts with an antibody that has been modified so that it can be visualized using fluorescence or staining with an appropriate dye.

> > **CONNECTIONS** < <

Chapter 5 of Biology

2. Innate Immune System

As mentioned above, the innate (or non-specific) immune system is the component of the immune system that mounts a broad-spectrum defense against threats, but does not involve the recognition of specific foreign bodies and molecules. The innate immune system can be split into non-cellular and cellular components. The non-cellular component of the innate immune system includes anatomical barriers and signaling molecules such as cytokines and complement proteins, while the cellular component includes a range of white blood cell types (leukocytes) that play various roles in responding to threats. The various components of the innate immune system can act independently or be coordinated in the process of inflammation.

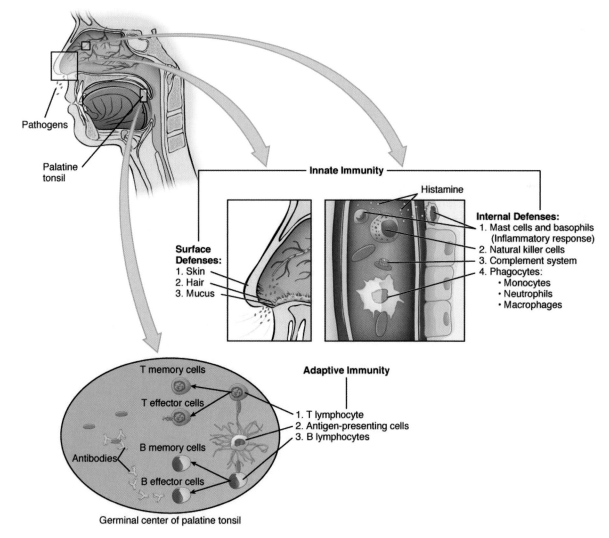

Figure 3. Innate immune system.

The most obvious anatomical barrier to external pathogens is the skin. The tightly packed cells of the epidermis on the top of the skin provide a formidable physical barrier to the entry of pathogens, and mechanisms such as sweat and the shedding/replacement of skin cells also contribute to the ability of the skin to function as a barrier. Additionally, cellular components of the adaptive immune system are "stationed" in and around the skin, allowing a prompt response to any incursions. The gastrointestinal tracts and the respiratory system are the other two main pathways through which external materials enter the body, and therefore it is not surprising that they also provide anatomical barriers against infection.

The protection that the gastrointestinal tract provides against infections starts with the oral cavity, in which the lysozyme contained in saliva helps to break down bacterial cell walls. Interestingly, lysozyme is also present in other fluids, such as mucus, breast milk, and tears. The extremely low pH of the stomach also constitutes a physical barrier against pathogens, as many microorganisms cannot survive in such acidic conditions. The gastrointestinal tract also contains some less obvious physical features that contribute to immunity. First, peristalsis provides a physical way of moving microbes through the digestive tract, meaning that bacteria/viruses that do not immediately find a way to adhere to the gastrointestinal lining or invade body cells will be rapidly flushed out. Second, the abundant bacterial flora of the large intestine actually can be considered an anatomical barrier. This may be counterintuitive, and you may ask how it is possible for a giant community of bacteria to be a defense against bacterial infections. The idea here is that in a healthy person, the gut flora are well-balanced and play a role in maintaining intestinal health, and actually prevent pathogenic bacteria from colonizing the intestine by potentially outcompeting them.

CLINICAL CONNECTIONS > > >

Cholera is a diarrheal disease caused by the bacterium *Vibrio cholerae* that has caused the deaths of millions of people in the 19th and 20th centuries, and has been estimated by the World Health Organization to kill in the range of 42,000-142,000 people a year even now, mostly in the developing world. The subspecies of *V. cholerae* that cause serious disease express a structure known as the toxin-coregulated pilus, which allows them to "hang on" in the human intestine and not simply be washed away in the feces. This points to the ability of the large intestine to function as part of the innate immune system.

The point regarding healthy microflora playing a role as a barrier in the innate immune system can be extended to other areas of the body with sizable microbial populations, such as the skin, oral cavity, and female reproductive tract. For instance, recent research has indicated that maintenance of a healthy vaginal microbiome, with abundant lactobacilli, can help prevent bacterial vaginosis and yeast infections.

The respiratory system also contains mechanisms for protecting the body from invasion. The mucus secreted throughout the upper respiratory tract contains lysozyme, which has antibacterial effects, and mucus also provides a way of physically trapping microbes in a viscous fluid that can either be expelled from the body or swallowed into the highly-acidic stomach. The mucociliary escalator in the bronchi and trachea combines mucus with the ability of cilia to push trapped microbes up the pharynx.

Next, let's turn to the cellular component of the innate immune system, which is composed of white blood cells (WBCs, or leukocytes) that play a diverse range of functions. The sheer variety of WBCs can be overwhelming, as well as the fact that multiple ways have been proposed to classify them. In this section, we will review the various types of WBCs, proceeding from the most common types to the least common types, and then briefly discuss how they can be classified. However, despite their diversity, WBCs have some common features: namely, they all have nuclei (unlike red blood cells) and they are all produced in the bone marrow.

Neutrophils are the most common type of WBC, making up over 60% of WBCs in circulation. Their main role is to phagocytose invading bacteria, and can be thought of as the first responders to infection. As a result of this, an elevated neutrophil level in a complete blood count may be a sign of an acute inflammatory response or an acute infection.

The next most common type of WBC, comprising about 30% of circulating WBCs, are lymphocytes. This is a tricky category because lymphocytes span the innate and adaptive components of the immune system. The major categories of lymphocytes are B cells, T cells, and natural killer (NK) cells. B cells and T cells are involved in the adaptive immune system and are therefore discussed in section 3. NK cells, on the other hand, are considered to be part of the innate immune system. Their role is to respond to cells infected by viruses and tumor cells—that is, body cells in which something has gone wrong. NK cells can recognize such cells by alterations in how affected cells present themselves as "self" (see section 1 for a review). Additionally, NK cells can be thought of as straddling the innate and adaptive immune systems because they respond to destroy cells that have been "tagged" by antibodies.

Next come monocytes, which make up about 5% of circulating WBCs. The main role of monocytes is to travel to various tissues in the body and then differentiate further into macrophages or dendritic cells. Dendritic cells tend to be found in parts of the body in contact with the external environment, and bridge the innate and adaptive immune systems by interacting with external substances to present antigens to T cells. Macrophages (Greek for "big eaters"), in contrast, are large white blood cells that can be thought of as the non-specific garbage processors of the body, as they phagocytose cellular debris, tumor cells, non-cellular foreign substances, microbes, and so on. Eosinophils make up approximately 3% of circulating WBCs, and primarily target parasitic infections. Basophils make up well under 1% of the circulating WBC count and are involved in allergic responses, particularly the release of histamine and heparin (an anticoagulant) as part of inflammatory responses. Mast cells function similarly to basophils, but tend to be located specifically in mucous membranes and connective tissue.

The term "phagocyte" can be used in general to refer to any cell that engages in phagocytosis, or the engulfment and destruction of one cell by another. Phagocytes include neutrophils, monocytes, macrophages, dendritic cells, and mast cells. The MCAT expects you to know the difference between macrophages and phagocytes—don't be fooled by the fact that they both have "phag" in their name! Macrophages are a specific subset of phagocytes.

However, the innate immune system is not limited to cells. A system known as complement is also a major component of the innate immune response. The complement system received its name in 1899 as it was recognized at the time to be a poorly-understood substance that "complemented" the function of cell-based immunity. Complement refers to a signaling cascade of many proteins (over 30, if receptors and regulatory proteins are counted) that function to tag pathogens for destruction (a process also known as opsonization), to recruit phagocytes to destroy the pathogens in question, and/or to initiate an inflammatory process. There are actually three main pathways of complement activation, but the details go beyond the scope of the MCAT. Antibodies play a role in determining which cells are "tagged" by complement proteins, but the complement system is still considered to be part of the innate immune system because its components do not change over time.

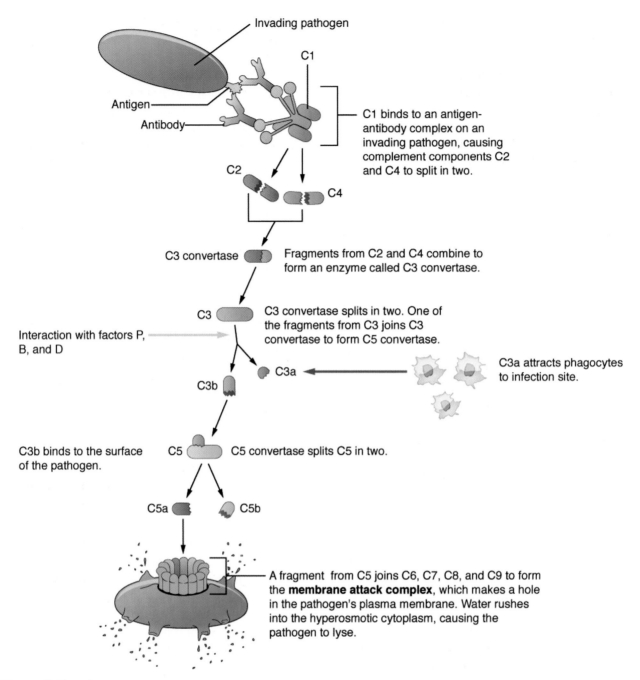

Figure 4. Complement.

The details of the complement system can be challenging to study because its constituent proteins were named C1, C2, …, C9 in order of their discovery, with Roman numerals used to indicate cleaved forms (e.g., C4b or C1s); while this naming system may have been reasonable at the time, an unfortunate consequence is that there is no logical connection between the name of a complement protein and its function, and very little traction for mnemonics to help. The good news, though, is that the MCAT does not expect you to be aware of the specific steps of the complement system (that's what medical school is for!). For the time being, just be aware of its existence and general function.

In addition to the complement system, cytokines are a broad and diverse class of signaling proteins (at least dozens) that are involved in coordinating the immune response and inflammation. Technically, they are classified as immunomodulatory molecules, although their precise functions remain a subject of research. Many cytokines have been found to exert multiple functions: for example, the interleukin 1 (IL-1) family is involved in body temperature control, liver protein synthesis, cell-based immunity, and neuroinflammation, just to name a few examples. The details certainly go beyond the MCAT, but you should be aware that cytokines exist and what their general function is.

Interferons are a subset of cytokines that are best known for having antiviral effects. They are released by infected cells when receptors located in the cytoplasm or the plasma membrane recognize certain microbial biomolecules (such as viral glycoproteins). Once released, they have two major effects: they signal nearby cells to prepare themselves to defend against a viral infection and they upregulate the overall immune response.

In this section, we've already mentioned inflammation a few times, but it's worth focusing on in somewhat greater depth. Inflammation is a response to cellular injury or the presence of pathogens that results in the clinically noticeable signs/symptoms of redness, heat, pain, and swelling. On a mechanistic level, acute inflammation is actually initiated by cells belonging to the innate immune system, including macrophages, dendritic cells, and mast cells. The inflammatory signal cascade ultimately results in vasodilation in the affected area and increased permeability of blood vessels. Vasodilation results in increased blood flow, and increased permeability results in plasma being able to migrate from the blood into the affected tissue. Combined, these two factors result in redness and swelling, but also have the physiologically useful result of allowing a large number of immune cells to move in quickly to address the situation. Similarly to the complement system, the details of the inflammatory signaling cascade are quite complex and go beyond the scope of the MCAT. However, you should also be aware that chronic inflammation—that is, low-level inflammation that persists for a long time—has been increasingly associated with the pathogenesis of a range of major health conditions, including cardiovascular and cerebrovascular disease.

CLINICAL CONNECTIONS > > >

A phenomenon known as the "cytokine storm" may be responsible for abnormal deaths among young healthy adults who were victims of the 1918 influenza pandemic and the SARS epidemic in 2003. In a cytokine storm, a pathological positive feedback emerges between white blood cells and the cytokine system, resulting in a hyperintense immune reaction that can cause organ failure and death. It is also thought that cytokine storms are part of what makes the Ebola virus so deadly.

CLINICAL CONNECTIONS > > >

Until recently, interferon was commonly used, along with an antiviral drug, as part of the treatment of hepatitis C, a chronic liver infection estimated to affect 3.5 million people in the United States. One of the disadvantages of interferon treatment is that it causes side effects like flu-like symptoms, fever, and vomiting, which are ultimately due to the upregulated immune response.

MCAT STRATEGY > > >

You can remember the features of acute inflammation using the acronym "SLIPR" (like "slippers"): swelling, loss of function, increased heat, pain, redness.

---

3. Adaptive Immune System

The adaptive immune system, in contrast to the innate immune system, is the part of the immune system that "learns" to recognize specific invaders/pathogens. There are two main classes of cells at work in the adaptive immune response: B cells and T cells. Both B cells and T cells are lymphocytes that are produced in the bone marrow and mature in the lymphatic system.

When you hear B cells, think antibodies, because the basic job of B cells is to learn to recognize antigens and to secrete large amounts of antibodies in response (they can also present antigens and secrete cytokines, but the MCAT is unlikely to test you on these points). After being produced in the bone marrow, B cells move to lymphatic tissue such as the lymph nodes and the spleen. At this point, before they have "seen" an antigen, they are known as naïve B-cells. Through random recombination, naïve B cells express receptors for many different antigens, and some may never actually encounter a matching antigen at all. However, once a B cell is presented with a matching antigen, generally by antigen-presenting cells such as dendritic cells, it proliferates in a process known as clonal selection. Activated B cells have one of two fates: either they become plasma cells, which are short-lived cells that secrete massive amounts of antibodies in response to an infection, or they become memory cells, which may persist for the entire life of the host. As the name implies, memory cells "remember" the antigen that they were activated by, allowing the body to mount a significantly quicker and stronger response the next time it encounters the antigen in question.

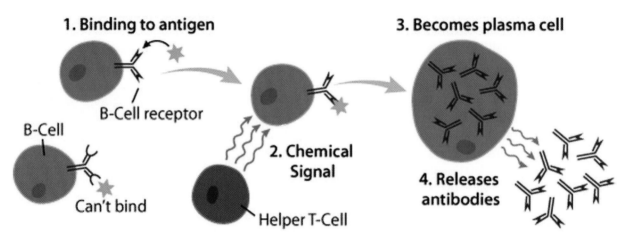

Figure 5. B cells.

B cells are involved in what has traditionally been termed humoral immunity, which refers more specifically to the immune effects of antibodies, whereas T cells, as we'll discuss below, are involved in cell-based immunity. You may object that this distinction doesn't make sense, in that the elements of humoral immunity (antibodies) are secreted by cells and are therefore cell-mediated in a sense. This objection is logical, but as mentioned above, many divisions of the immune system reflect scientific progress as it happened. In particular, the division between the humoral and the cell-based systems of immunity arose from the observation that some properties of the immune response can be retained and transferred in the absence of cells (very similarly to how vaccines work). These properties were dubbed "humoral immunity," based on a reference to the ancient Greek medical system of the humors.

MCAT STRATEGY > > >

You can remember which T cells interact with which MHC class proteins by remembering that the numbers involved must multiply to 8. Therefore, CD8$^+$ T cells interact with MHC class I (8 × 1 = 8) and CD4$^+$ T cells interact with MHC class II (4 × 2 = 8).

T cells correspond to the cell-mediated branch of the adaptive immune system. As briefly sketched out above in section I, the basic job of T cells is to respond to the major histocompatibility complex (MHC) classes I and II. MHC class I is present in all nucleated cells, and presents proteins from inside the cell as antigens. Cytotoxic CD8$^+$ T cells recognize and destroy cells that present abnormal MHC class I proteins, which are indicative of viral infection or of transformation into a tumor. Unlike macrophages, which engulf target cells, CD8$^+$ T cells inject their target cells with substances that induce apoptosis. MHC class II is expressed in a smaller range of cells in the immune system, and is used to present antigen fragments from external sources. CD4+ helper T cells respond to these cells by secreting specialized cytokines that recruit other immune cells to mount a reaction.

In addition to these two main classes of T cells, memory T cells "remember" antigens that they have been exposed to, similar to memory B cells, and suppressor T cells function to reduce the immune response once an infection has been adequately dealt with and to help prevent self-reactivity, which can cause autoimmune diseases (see section 6 below).

CLINICAL CONNECTIONS > > >

Human immunodeficiency virus (HIV) is a retrovirus that attacks CD4$^+$ T cells. When the population of CD4$^+$ T cells declines beyond a certain point, the body becomes very vulnerable to infections that would otherwise be unlikely to harm a healthy individual. This condition is known as acquired immunodeficiency syndrome (AIDS). HIV is fatal without treatment; it emerged in the late 1970s and 1980s. Its effects in the United States peaked around 1995, when nearly 42,000 Americans died from AIDS. Subsequently, highly effective combination treatments were introduced, allowing individuals with HIV to potentially live full lifetimes. However, AIDS remains a major public health issue worldwide.

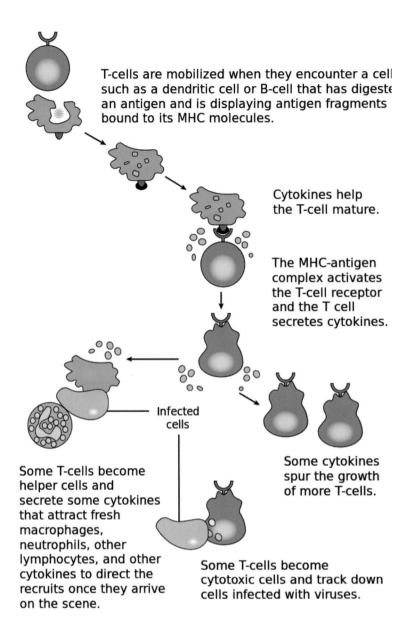

T-cells are mobilized when they encounter a cell such as a dendritic cell or B-cell that has digeste an antigen and is displaying antigen fragments bound to its MHC molecules.

Cytokines help the T-cell mature.

The MHC-antigen complex activates the T-cell receptor and the T cell secretes cytokines.

Infected cells

Some T-cells become helper cells and secrete some cytokines that attract fresh macrophages, neutrophils, other lymphocytes, and other cytokines to direct the recruits once they arrive on the scene.

Some cytokines spur the growth of more T-cells.

Some T-cells become cytotoxic cells and track down cells infected with viruses.

Figure 6. T cells.

Although T cells are produced in the bone marrow, they mature in the thymus, and in fact, the vast majority of immature T cells are discarded. T cells that fail to respond appropriately to MHC class I and II proteins are eliminated in a process known as positive selection, while T cells that are over-reactive—in particular, reactive against self cells—are eliminated in a process known as negative selection. The combination of positive and negative selection means that, ideally, T cells in the body will reliably respond against invaders and not against anything else.

Figure 8 below presents an overview of the immune response that ties together the contributions of the innate and adaptive immune systems.

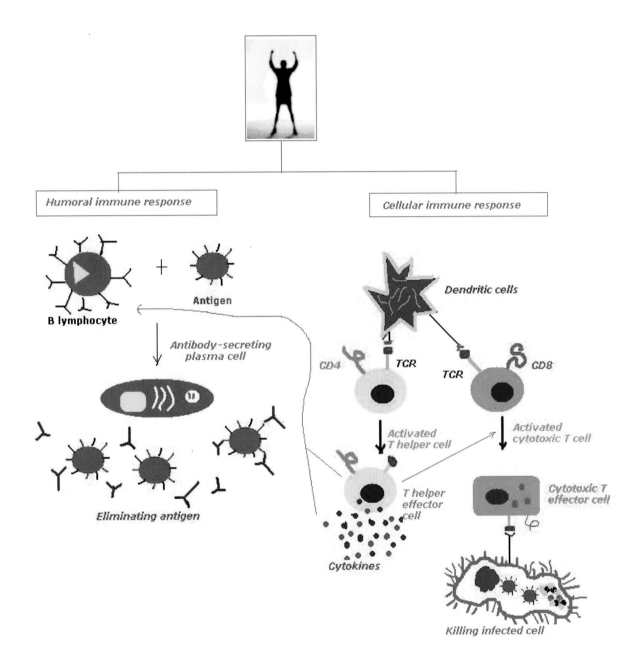

Figure 7. Diagram of immune response.

4. Anatomy of the Immune System

The anatomy of the immune system is quite distributed; as we've seen already, the immune system can be thought of comprising, in a broad sense, everything from the skin to the bone marrow and the blood in between. However, there are some structures that are particularly important for the immune system that you need to be familiar with for the MCAT. They are distributed throughout the body, which also makes sense on an intuitive level because if crucial functional aspects of the immune system were concentrated in a single organ, that could create a potentially disastrous single point of failure.

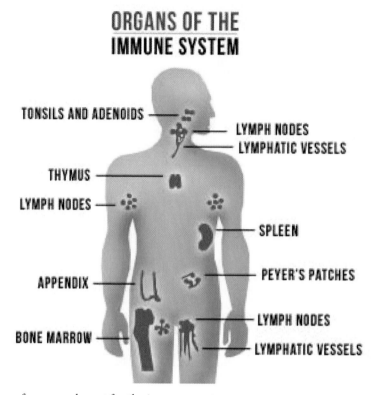

Figure 8. Anatomical view of organs relevant for the immune system.

As briefly discussed in section 2, white blood cells (WBCs) are produced in the bone marrow, as are red blood cells (although they do not play a role in the immune system). In general, you can think of bone marrow as what is on the inside of bones, and its main role is the production of blood cells, known as hematopoiesis. In hematopoiesis, hematopoietic stem cells divide into either lymphoid stem cells or myeloid stem cells. Lymphoid stem cells further differentiate into lymphocytes (B cells, T cells, and NK cells), while myeloid stem cells differentiate into all other types of blood cells, including other types of WBCs as well as red blood cells. The structure of the bone marrow is further discussed in Chapter 12.

> **> > CONNECTIONS < <**
>
> **Chapter 12 of Biology**

The spleen is another organ that plays an important role in the immune system. It is located in the left upper quadrant of the abdomen, and is of historical note in that in the ancient Greek humoral system of medical thought, it was equated with melancholy. The spleen contributes to the circulatory system by breaking down senescent red blood cells and holding a reserve of blood, but the area of the spleen known as the white pulp contributes to the immune system. It is rich in lymphocytes and is a site for the activation of B cells, which produce great quantities of antibodies. Since the spleen does double duty as a blood filtration/processing center and a lymph node-like structure rich in T and B cells, it is an especially important nexus for coordinating the immune response. Lymph nodes (and the lymphatic system in general) are quite important for the immune system, and are discussed separately in section 5 below.

A final immune organ to be aware of is the thymus, which is located in the central part of the anterior chest. The thymus is where T cells mature, as discussed above in section 3.

5. Lymphatic System

The lymphatic system can be thought of as being part of both the circulatory and immune systems. Let's review its circulatory function first, and then explore how it operates as part of the immune system.

In a nutshell, the lymphatic system is a parallel circulatory system that drains interstitial fluid from the space surrounding the cells of the tissue. At any given moment, an adult human has about 10 liters of such fluid, which moves from the capillary beds into the extracellular space in the issues. In order to regulate fluid balance throughout the body, some of this fluid must always be in the process of being recycled through the circulatory system. Lymph capillaries collect this fluid, and empty into lymph vessels, which converge into the right and left lymphatic ducts, which in turn empty into the circulatory system at the intersection of the internal jugular veins and the right and left subclavian veins, respectively. The lymphatic system also has a connection with the digestive system because it is used to transport lipids, in the form of chylomicrons, to the circulatory system.

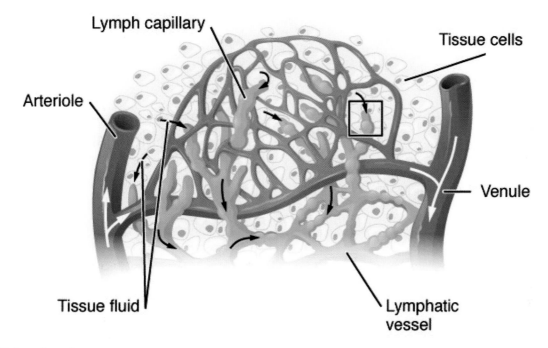

Figure 9. Lymph node.

The lymphatic system is dotted by hundreds of lymph nodes, which are organized clusters of lymphatic system that can be thought of as filtration points for the lymphatic fluid where reservoirs of B and T cells are stored. Distinct clusters of lymph nodes are located in the head, neck, chest, underarms, abdomen, and groin, and are often palpated as a part of routine physical examinations because swollen lymph nodes may be a sign of conditions such as systemic infections or cancers.

CLINICAL CONNECTIONS > > >

Lymphedema is peripheral swelling (edema) caused by blocked lymphatic vessels. It can be an aftereffect of the treatment of cancer that has spread to the lymph nodes, and in developing countries, can be caused by parasitic infections.

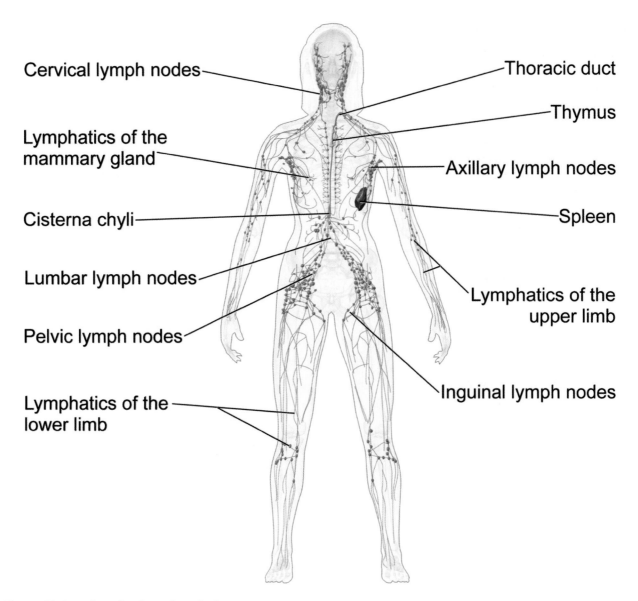

Cervical lymph nodes

Lymphatics of the
mammary gland

Cisterna chyli

Lumbar lymph nodes

Pelvic lymph nodes

Lymphatics of the
lower limb

Thoracic duct

Thymus

Axillary lymph nodes

Spleen

Lymphatics of the
upper limb

Inguinal lymph nodes

Figure 10. Lymph nodes throughout body.

The thymus, where T cells mature, is considered to be part of the lymphatic system, as is the spleen, because it is connected both to the lymphatic and systemic circulation. The red bone marrow, which is where blood cells are produced, is also a key organ in the lymphatic system.

Thus, the lymphatic system can be thought of as having the following major functions:

> Maintenance of fluid balance. It accomplishes this by draining fluid out from the extracellular space in tissues and returning it to circulation.
> Transport of other materials from the extracellular space back into the bloodstream.
> Lipid transport from the digestive system into the bloodstream.
> Production and maturation of lymphocytes.

6. Allergies and Autoimmune Disorders

In light of how intricate the machinery of the immune system is, and how many checks and balances exist to ensure its proper function, it is not surprising that the immune system can become dysregulated. In fact, disorders of the immune system, in the form of allergies and autoimmune disorders, are mainstays in the daily clinical practice of medicine.

Allergies occur when the immune system mounts a response against some exogenous stimulus that is actually harmless. Common examples include pollen and food allergies. Technically speaking, an allergic response is the reason why blood typing is so important, because the immune system will mount a response against antigens that are present in donor blood but not in the body's own blood.

Autoimmune disorders, in contrast, occur when the body mistakenly recognizes self cells as being non-self and mounts an immune response against them. Lupus is an autoimmune condition that is familiar to fans of the TV show *House*, but other common examples include inflammatory bowel disease, multiple sclerosis, and rheumatoid arthritis. The MCAT does not expect you to know the details of all of these conditions, but it does expect you to be aware of the general concept of an autoimmune disorder and of the steps that the body takes to minimize the likelihood of such disorders emerging.

Figure 11 shows how autoimmunity can be thought of as the result of an 'overactive' immune system, in contrast to an underactive immune system that leaves one vulnerable to infection. Although the actual mechanisms underlying autoimmune attacks are more complicated, this way of visualizing autoimmune disorders helps contextualize them within the overall spectrum of immune function.

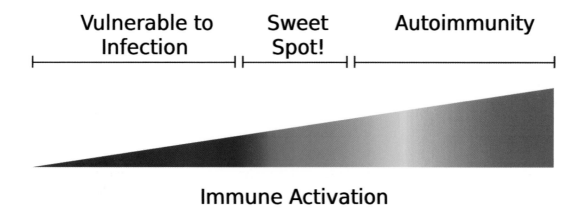

Figure 11. Autoimmune disorders.

7. Must-Knows

> Antigen: any substance that stimulates an immune response
> Antibody: Y-shaped molecule that recognizes antigens and allows an immune response to be mobilized; has 2 heavy and 2 light chains linked by disulfide bonds
> Antigen-antibody interactions: like lock in a key, antibodies are specific for certain antigens
> Self/non-self: mediated by major histocompatibility complex (MHC) class I and II:

- MHC = unique to every person
- MHC class I: expressed in all nucleated cells, shows fragments of proteins from inside cell; can be thought of as internal quality check; abnormal in cases of viral infections or tumorigenesis; $CD8^+$ T cells destroy
- MHC class II: expressed in some immune cells (macrophages, etc.), shows fragments of antigens from external invaders that have been engulfed; $CD4^+$ helper T cells recruit response

> Innate immune system
- Anatomical barriers: skin, digestive enzymes, lysozyme in saliva/tears/breastmilk, mucociliary elevator in respiratory tract
- White blood cells: neutrophils (phagocytose bacteria), NK cells, monocytes (differentiate into macrophages ("big eaters") and dendritic cells), eosinophils, basophils, mast cells.
- Complement: proteins involved in signaling cascade to tag pathogens, recruit phagocytes, and initiate inflammatory process
- Cytokines: signaling proteins that coordinate immune response/inflammation; interferons are cytokines that specialize in response to viruses

> Adaptive immune system
- B cells: *antibody production*; produced in bone marrow and are activated in lymph nodes/spleen. When activated, clonal selection → many copies; short-lived plasma cells produce antibodies in response to current infection, memory cells remain present and react next time a threat appears
- T cells: mature in thymus through positive/negative selection; most are discarded
- $CD4^+$ helper T cells: coordinate response to abnormal MHC class II (bacterial/fungal/other infection)
- $CD8^+$ cytotoxic T cells: kill cells with abnormal MHC class I (virus/tumor)
- Other T cells: regulatory T cells moderate immune reaction when response has been sufficient; memory T cells "remember" previous antigens

> Anatomy of immune system: bone marrow, lymphatic system, spleen, thymus
> Lymphatic system: regulates fluid balance, is home for lymphocytes (B and T cells), drains fats from digestive system into bloodstream, returns substances from extracellular space to circulation

This page left intentionally blank.

Practice Passage

Lambert–Eaton syndrome (LEMS) is an autoimmune disorder that is characterized by muscular weakness in the extremities. In LEMS, antibodies are formed against presynaptic voltage-gated calcium channels in the neuromuscular junction. This leads to a decrease in the release of acetylcholine (ACh) from presynaptic vesicles. The gold standard of LEMS therapy is the potassium channel blocker 3,4-diaminopyridine (3,4 DAP), whose effect on LEMS pathology is shown in Figure 1.

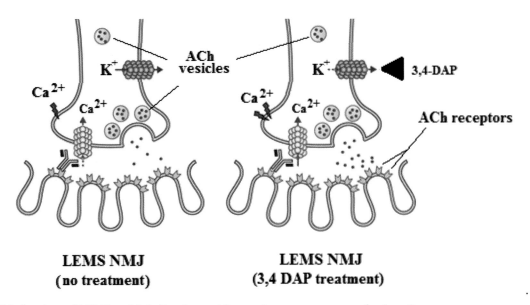

Figure 1. Mechanism of LEMS and 3,4-diaminopyridine action on neuromuscular junction

Myasthenia gravis (MG) also causes muscle weakness, but this weakness is caused by antibodies that impair the binding of ACh to its receptors at the neuromuscular junction. Some isotypes of the antibody impair ACh binding, while other isotypes destroy the ACh receptors. Receptor destruction occurs either by complement fixation or by inducing the muscle cell to eliminate the receptors through endocytosis.

MG antibodies are derived from plasma cells, whose construction from B cells is shown in Figure 2. To carry out plasma cell production, T helper cells must first be activated. Activation is accomplished by binding of the T cell receptor (TCR) to the ACh receptor antigenic peptide fragment (epitope) resting within the major histocompatibility complex of antigen presenting cells.

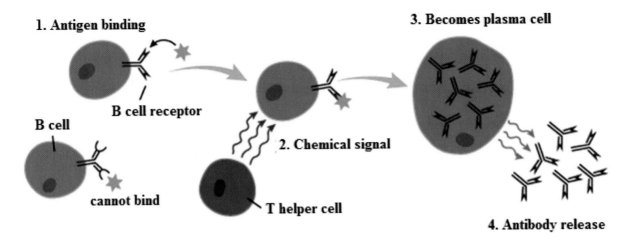

Figure 2. Plasma cell production

Adapted from Schneider, I. and Hanisch, F. (2015). Long-term observation of incremental response and antibodies to voltage-gated calcium channels in patients with Lambert–Eaton myasthenic syndrome: two case reports. Journal of Medical Case Reports, 9, 59. under CCBY 4.0 and from Arizona Science Center via Wikimedia commons under CCBY 3.0

1. Treatment with an anti-acetylcholinesterase antibody is most likely to improve the clinical status of patients with which autoimmune disease?
   A. MG only
   B. LEMS only
   C. Both MG and LEMS
   D. Neither MG nor LEMS

2. What is the cause of the antibody-mediated weakness seen in LEMS?
   A. Receptor binding by acetylcholine is blocked.
   B. Calcium reuptake through voltage-gated channels is inhibited.
   C. Action potential transmission is inhibited.
   D. Pre-synaptic vesicular release of ACh to the plasma membrane is reduced.

3. Surgical removal of which organ in MG patients is most likely to result in a significant reduction in the number of mature, circulating T cells available for B cell activation?
   A. Thyroid
   B. Spleen
   C. Thymus
   D. Pituitary gland

4. Which of the following findings would have been used as evidence to establish the autoimmune nature of LEMS when the disease was first studied?
   I. An LEMS-specific antigen was identified and found only in the neuromuscular junction of LEMS patients
   II. Infants of breastfeeding mothers with LEMS were observed to exhibit transient muscular weakness after feeding sessions
   III. Mice injected with IgG from LEMS patients demonstrated the same physiological changes seen in the patients
   A. I only
   B. III only
   C. II and III only
   D. I, II, and III

5. Which of the following correctly shows the structure of the LEMS treatment discussed in the passage?

A.

B.

C.

D.

6. If LEMS related antibodies mutated to recognize parts of the innate immune system, which cell types are least likely to be targeted?
   A. Mast cells
   B. Macrophages
   C. Neutrophils
   D. Cytokines

7. Myasthenia gravis patients are often put on immunosuppressive therapies which may indiscriminately target the lymph tissues of the patient. Damage to which tissue will most seriously impair the patients' ability to fight off *S. pyogenes* infection?
   A. Red pulp
   B. White pulp
   C. Peyer's patches
   D. Yellow bone marrow

Practice Passage Explanations

Lambert–Eaton syndrome (LEMS) is an autoimmune disorder that is characterized by muscular weakness in the extremities. In LEMS, antibodies are formed against presynaptic voltage-gated calcium channels in the neuromuscular junction. This leads to a decrease in the release of acetylcholine (ACh) from presynaptic vesicles. The gold standard of LEMS therapy is the potassium channel blocker 3,4-diaminopyridine (3,4 DAP), whose effect on LEMS pathology is shown in Figure 1.

Key terms: LEMS, voltage-gated, presynaptic NMJ

Cause and effect: LEMS AI disorder = Ab against ion channels → muscle weakness

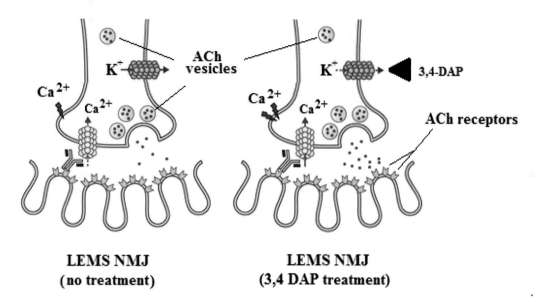

Figure 1. Mechanism of LEMS and 3,4-diaminopyridine action on neuromuscular junction

Figure 1 illustrates mechanism of LEMS: Ab binds Ca channel → blocks Ca influx → reduced ACh release from presynaptic membrane; drug treatment blocks K^+ efflux → elongated depolarization → Ca channels open longer → increased Ca^{2+} influx and intracellular Ca^{2+}

Myasthenia gravis (MG) also causes muscle weakness, but this weakness is caused by antibodies that impair the binding of ACh to its receptors at the neuromuscular junction. Some isotypes of the antibody impair ACh binding, while other isotypes destroy the ACh receptors. Receptor destruction occurs either by complement fixation or by inducing the muscle cell to eliminate the receptors through endocytosis.

Key terms: MG, complement fixation, isotypes

Cause and effect: Ab blocks ACh-R binding OR Ab destroys ACh receptor → MG muscle weakness (2 destruct mechanisms)

MG antibodies are derived from plasma cells, whose construction from B cells is shown in Figure 2. To carry out plasma cell production, T helper cells must first be activated. Activation is accomplished by binding of the T cell receptor (TCR) to the ACh receptor antigenic peptide fragment (epitope) resting within the major histocompatibility complex of antigen presenting cells.

Key terms: plasma cell, epitope, major histocompatibility complex, antigen presenting cells

Cause and effect: TCR-epitope binding → [B cells → plasma cells] → anti ACh-R antibodies produced

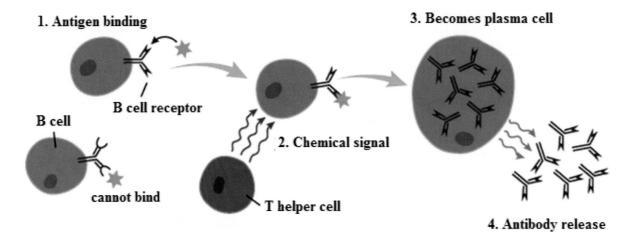

Figure 2. Plasma cell production

Figure 2 shows how T helper cell activation → B cell conversion to plasma cell → Ab release

Adapted from Schneider, I. and Hanisch, F. (2015). Long-term observation of incremental response and antibodies to voltage-gated calcium channels in patients with Lambert–Eaton myasthenic syndrome: two case reports. Journal of Medical Case Reports, 9, 59. under CCBY 4.0 and from Arizona Science Center via Wikimedia commons under CCBY 3.0

1. C is correct. Acetylcholinesterase blocking antibodies would increase the relative concentration of acetylcholine in the synapse (by blocking AChE effects). As discussed in the passage, an increase in synaptic ACh would alleviate the cause of the symptoms in both MG and LEMS patients.

2. D is correct. In normal neuromuscular function, a nerve impulse is carried down the axon until reaching the neuromuscular junction, where the impulse is transferred to the muscle cell, leading to the opening of voltage-gated calcium channels, the influx of calcium ions into the nerve terminal, and the calcium-dependent triggering of synaptic vesicle fusion with plasma membrane. These synaptic vesicles contain acetylcholine, which is released into the synaptic cleft and stimulates the acetylcholine receptors on the muscle. In LEMS, antibodies against these channels decrease the amount of calcium that can enter the nerve ending, hence less acetylcholine can be released from the neuromuscular junction
   A. Receptor binding by acetylcholine is unaffected; instead, less acetylcholine is released.
   B. LEMS only interferes with the flow of extracellular calcium ions into the nerve terminal.
   C. The transmission of the action potential is unaffected.

3. 3) C is correct. T cells mature within the thymus. More specifically, T cells that recognize and attack self-antigens are eliminated in a 2-step process. First, T cells undergo positive selection, whereby the cell comes in contact with self-MHC expressed by thymic epithelial cells; those with no interaction are destroyed. Second, the T cell undergoes negative selection by interacting with thymic dendritic cells whereby T cells with high affinity interaction are eliminated through apoptosis, avoiding autoimmunity. Only those with intermediate affinity survive, promoting the development of self-tolerance. Removal of the thymus would decrease the pool of mature, circulating T cells available for B cell activation.
   A. The thyroid gland controls regulates metabolism and helps maintain calcium homeostasis via its secretion of thyroid hormone and calcitonin. It is not directly involved in T cell maturation.
   B. As part of the mononuclear phagocyte system, it removes senescent red blood cells from circulation and initiates processing of the hemoglobin which they contained. The spleen also synthesizes antibodies in its

white pulp and removes antibody-coated bacteria and antibody-coated blood cells by way of blood and lymph circulation; it is however, not directly involved in T cell maturation.

D. The pituitary gland is an endocrine gland that synthesizes and stores a variety of hormones, but it is not directly involved in T cell maturation.

4. D is correct. We need to find evidence that there is an autoimmune mechanism responsible for LEMS. With RN questions, work smarter by determining which RN appears the most often (if possible) and start with that RN. Here we see RN I appears twice, RN II appears twice, and RN III appears 3 times.
I: This would indicate there is a unique molecule (the antigen) associated with LEMS and identifiable by the host immune system. This antigen is exclusively found in the NMJ. This is solid evidence LEMS is autoimmune related.
II: Breastfeeding is an example of passive immunity, where the mother passes her antibodies to the infant via breast milk. The onset of muscle weakness in infants after drinking LEMS mother's milk would serve as evidence the disease is autoimmune-related.
III: This is another example of passive immunity conferring LEMS-like disease in mice. This would serve as evidence the disease is autoimmune related.

5. A is correct. According to paragraph 1, the "gold standard" LEMS treatment is a molecule called 3,4-diaminopyridine. IUPAC rules, the N atom that forms the imine in the ring serves as our high-priority reference point for numbering the remaining atoms in ring. We want to give our amine substituents the lowest possible numbering. Starting at the N atom and going counterclockwise, we get 3,4-diaminopyridine in choice A.
B. This would be 2,3-DAP.
C. This ring has 2 N atoms in it, which means it is not a pyridine. This is an azole ring.
D. This would be 2,4-DAP.

6. D is correct. The innate immune system is also called the non-specific immune system. These are host defense mechanisms that do not target specific pathogens nor do they adapt or provide long-lasting immunity to the host. Even if you are a bit weak on the immune system, read carefully. The question asks for *cells* involved with the immune system. Cytokines are not cells, they are small proteins that are involved with cell signaling within many systems, including the innate immune system.
A, B, C: These cells are all part of the innate immune system.

7. B is correct. Notice the italicized text. This questions revolves around the part of the immune system that fight off bacteria (in this case, *Streptococcus pyogenes*). The white pulp of the spleen is associated with the lymphatic function of the spleen. The white pulp produces and stores white blood cells, but most of the white pulp is made up of nodules called Malpighian corpuscles. The white pulp works as part of the host immune system, producing antibodies that recognize and neutralize foreign antigens such as bacteria and viruses in the blood.
A. Red pulp is red because it has many small cavities (sinusoids) where the spleen stores blood in case of injury or other situations where the body needs extra blood.
C. Do not panic when you see unfamiliar terms. The MCAT is not testing your ability to memorize biology factoids. This answer is a distractor. Peyer's patches are small masses of lymph tissue found throughout the ileum. These clusters monitor intestinal bacteria populations and prevent the growth of pathogenic bacteria in the small and large intestines.
D. Yellow bone marrow is responsible for producing fat, cartilage, and bone in the body. The tissue is yellow because of the carotenoids in the fat droplets in the many fat cells found in the tissue.

Independent Questions

1. Suppose an individual is exposed to a bacterial pathogen and develops symptoms of infection. This individual successfully recovers from the infection without the need for medical intervention, but six months later he is exposed to the exact same pathogen. Compared to the immune response during the first exposure, the immune response to the second exposure will develop:
   A. more rapidly and will be greater in magnitude.
   B. more rapidly, but will be of similar magnitude.
   C. in a similar amount of time, but will be greater in magnitude.
   D. in a similar amount of time and will be of similar magnitude.

2. Which of the following immune cells will act most immediately against a bacterial pathogen following infection of a naïve host?
   A. CD4+ (helper) T cells
   B. CD8+ (cytotoxic) T cells
   C. Plasma B cells
   D. Neutrophils

3. HDC/ABMT was an experimental cancer treatment strategy that involved administration of extremely high doses of cytotoxic agents, ultimately destroying the hematopoietic progenitor cells in the patient's bone marrow. A patient who recently underwent such high-dose chemotherapy would be expected to be deficient in:
   A. T cells, but not B cells.
   B. B cells, but not T cells.
   C. both T cells and B cells.
   D. neither B cells nor T cells.

4. Which of the following is the site of antigen binding to an immunoglobulin molecule?
   A. The constant region, which is located on the heavy chain only
   B. The variable region, which is located on the light chain only
   C. The variable region, which is located on the light and heavy chains
   D. The variable region, which is located on the heavy chain only

5. Which of the following are not professional antigen-presenting cells?
   A. Macrophages
   B. Dendritic cells
   C. B lymphocytes
   D. CD4+ T lymphocytes

6. Immune cells are capable of generating antibodies with variable regions that are highly specific for an immense number of antigenic epitopes. The number of potential epitopes that can be recognized far exceeds the number of genes coding for immunoglobulin molecules. This variation is made possible by:
   A. alternative RNA splicing.
   B. recombination of DNA sequences.
   C. post-translational modifications.
   D. histone modifications.

7. During adulthood, the spleen functions in which of the following processes?
   A. Production of erythropoietin
   B. Production of red blood cells
   C. Storage of leukocytes
   D. Education of T lymphocytes

8. Which of the following is not a component of the adaptive immune response?
   A. B lymphocytes
   B. CD8+ T lymphocytes
   C. Immunoglobulins
   D. Macrophages

Independent Question Explanations

1. A is correct. The adaptive immune response involves the development of lines of plasma B cells and memory B cells specific for the infectious agent. Plasma B cells proliferate in large numbers and are responsible for clearing the primary infection, while memory B cells survive for years after the primary infection. The existence of memory cells allows the generation of a more rapid and more robust immune response to a secondary infection. Often, the response is so rapid and specific that the infection is cleared before the individual shows any symptoms.

2. D is correct. Neutrophils are a component of the innate immune system. They recognize nonspecific molecular motifs common to a wide range of pathogens. This allows them to respond more rapidly than B cells or T cells, which must be generated via clonal expansion from their activated precursors. This process occurs on the order of hours to days.

3. C is correct. All lymphocytes (including B cells and T cells) originate in the bone marrow from hematopoietic progenitor cells. Destruction of the bone marrow would thus result in a deficiency of both B cells and T cells.

4. C is correct. The variable region is the amino acid sequence that is complementary to the antigenic sequence. Antigens bind to the variable region through noncovalent interactions. The variable region includes amino acids from both the light and heavy chains of the immunoglobulin molecule.

5. D is correct. Professional APCs are those which express MHC class II. These include B cells, dendritic cells, and macrophages, but not CD4+ T lymphocytes. APCs are responsible for processing antigens and presenting antigenic peptide fragments to cells of the adaptive immune system.

6. B is correct. The DNA sequence coding for the antibody variable region is developed randomly via recombination of a relatively small number of genes. This process results in a cell with a genome that differs from that of all other somatic cells. Cells that happen to express genes coding for variable regions specific for self antigens are selected against, while those not specific for self antigens are allowed to develop.

7. C is correct. The spleen holds a large reserve of leukocytes, particularly monocytes, which become macrophages or dendritic cells upon reaching their target tissue. Aged erythrocytes are removed from circulation by the spleen, but erythrocytes are produced in the bone marrow. The kidneys produce erythropoietin. T cells are educated in the thymus.

8. D is correct. Adaptive immunity is the branch of the immune response that recognizes and responds to specific pathogens. (In contrast, innate immunity provides general, non-pathogen-specific protection.) Adaptive immunity includes B lymphocytes, which produce antibodies (alternatively termed immunoglobulins). T lymphocytes are also a component of the adaptive immune response, but macrophages are part of innate immunity.

This page left intentionally blank.

Musculoskeletal System and Skin

0. Introduction

In the final chapter of the Biology book, we'll focus on the musculoskeletal system and skin. These topics are important for the MCAT in their own right and because they interact with other physiological systems that we have already discussed, which means that they provide an opportunity for the MCAT to test you on important themes in physiology. In this chapter, we'll first review the broad category of connective tissue, discuss some aspects of skeletal anatomy, and then review bone from a physiological perspective. Next, in sections 4 and 5, we will discuss muscle tissue and how it contracts, and then finally, in section 6, we will discuss the skin, the largest organ of the body.

1. Connective Tissue

Connective tissue is an extremely broad category that corresponds to one of the four basic types of tissue (the others being epithelial, nervous, and muscle). The MCAT does not expect you to have a detailed knowledge of the anatomical and histological properties of connective tissue, but you should know that it generally carries out the role of holding the body and its organs together (hence its name) and that it includes bone, blood, and adipose tissue as well as cartilage, ligaments, and tendons.

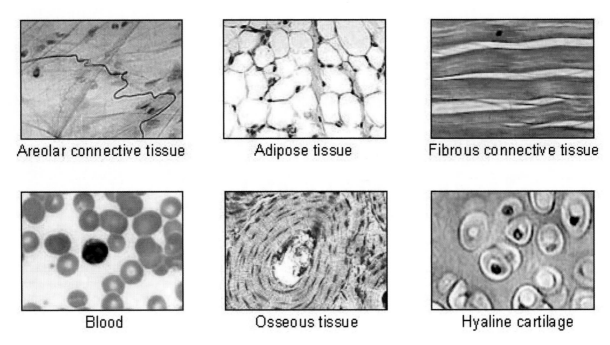

Figure 1. Connective tissue types.

Cartilage is a type of connective tissue that does not contain nerves or blood vessels, and is primarily made up of cells known as chondrocytes. Chondrocytes produce abundant amounts of collagen, which is a structural protein that is the most common protein by mass in the human body, and is found in the extracellular matrix of many types of connective tissue. Cartilage is also a very accessible tissue type in that it comprises the tip of the nose and the ear, so you can easily reach and feel the texture of collagen in and around your face. Additionally, cartilage protects the ends of bones at joints, and is part of many other structures in the body, including but not limited to the rib cage.

Ligaments and tendons are tough bands of collagenous fibers that connect components of the body. The main difference between ligaments and tendons is simply the kind of connections that they make: ligaments connect bones with other bones, whereas tendons connect muscles with bones.

2. Anatomy of the Skeletal System

The skeletal system has multiple important functions. It provides the body with structural support, and some specific skeletal structures provide important protection for organs. For example, the bones of the skull protect the brain, and the rib cage protects the heart and lungs within the thoracic cavity.

It is absolutely not necessary to know all of the 200+ bones of the human body for the MCAT (there will be plenty of time for that in medical school!), but it is worth investing some time to obtain a general sense of the major bones and skeletal structures of the body, because they may be mentioned in passages.

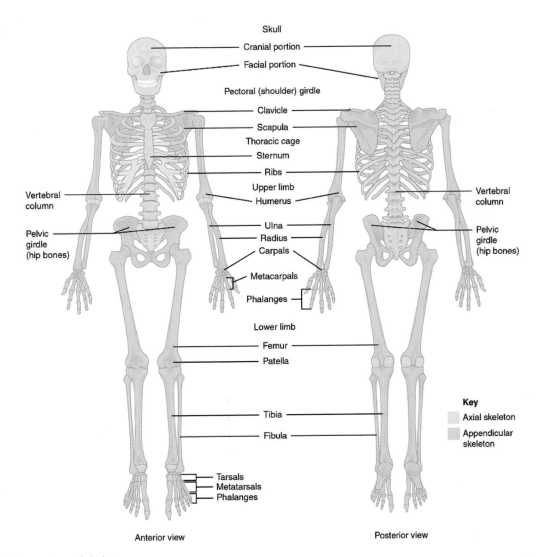

Figure 2. Gross view of skeleton.

The skeleton is subdivided into the axial skeleton and the appendicular skeleton. The axial skeleton starts with the skull and runs downward to the bottom of the vertebral column, while the appendicular skeleton accounts for the upper and lower extremities (medical speak for the arms/hands and the legs/feet, respectively), the shoulder girdle, and the pelvic girdle. On a basic level, the axial skeleton can be thought of forming the core of the organism, including the critical elements of both the central and peripheral nervous system and the skeletal elements necessary to support respiration and circulation, whereas the appendicular skeleton can be thought of as comprising the structures needed for mobility. Some of the most important skeletal structures are listed below:

> Skull. The skull contains 22 bones (8 cranial bones and 14 facial bones). The frontal, parietal, occipital, and temporal bones of the skull correspond to important brain regions that are discussed in Chapter 6. The facial bones form intricate structures that go beyond what you are required to know for the MCAT, although it may come in handy to remember that the mandible is the lower jaw bone, while the maxilla is the upper jaw bone.
> Vertebral column. The vertebral column includes 24 distinct vertebrae, the sacrum, and the coccyx. The sacrum and the coccyx are single bony structures that form from vertebrae that fuse during development. Moving from top to bottom, the vertebral column is divided into the cervical spine (7 vertebrae, C1-C7), the thoracic spine (12 vertebrae, T1-T12), the lumbar spine (5 vertebrae, L1-L5), and the sacrum and the coccyx. Although the sacrum and the coccyx fuse in adults, from a developmental perspective it can be helpful to speak of the sacral and coccygeal vertebrae.

> > <u>Rib cage</u>. A total of 12 pairs of ribs curve out from the spine and meet at the sacrum in the front of the chest. The rib cage protects critical organs such as the heart and the lungs.

> > <u>Upper extremities</u>. The bones of the hand are quite complicated and go beyond the scope of the MCAT, but you should know the basic structure of the arm. The humerus is the upper bone of the arm, stretching from the elbow up to the shoulder. The forearm is composed of two bones: the ulna and the radius. If you place your arms to your side with your palms facing forward (in what is known as anatomical position), the ulna is closest to the body.

> > <u>Lower extremities</u>. The uppermost bone in the leg is the femur, which is the largest bone in the body. The patella is the kneecap, and is an interesting example of a sesamoid bone (or a bone that is encased in tendon or muscle). The lower leg includes two bones: the tibia and the fibula. The tibia is the larger and more anteriorly located of the pair, while the fibula is more slender and ultimately runs down to become part of the ankle joint.

Bones can be classified into five major types:

1. Long bones are probably the most familiar type of bone, and are exemplified by bones in the upper and lower extremities such as the humerus, ulna, radius, femur, tibia, and fibula. Long bones have a long shaft, known as a diaphysis, and a rounded head, known as an epiphysis, at each end.

2. Flat bones are exemplified by the bones of the skull: they are relatively thin and curved.

3. Short bones include those present in the hand and foot. As the name implies, they are about as wide as they are long.

4. Sesamoid bones are embedded in tendons. The most well-known example is the patella, or kneecap.

5. Irregular bones, such as the ethmoid in the face, do not fit into any of the above categories.

Joints are where bones meet, and they can be classified in several different ways. The basic idea, though, is that different degrees of flexibility are required in various joints, and the anatomical structure of joints therefore varies accordingly to meet those functional requirements.

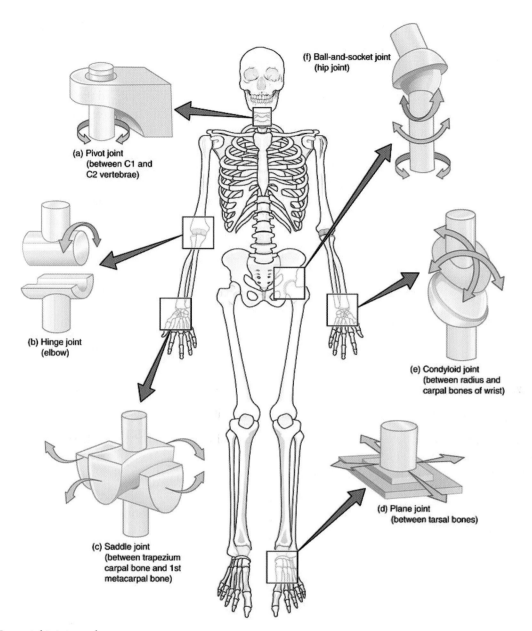

Figure 3. Synovial joints and movements.

When you think of "joints," synovial joints are probably what come to mind. These are freely movable joints in which the bones are not actually directly joined together. Instead, the bones meet in an area known as the synovial cavity, which is a fibrous, lubricated capsule that allows the bones to have a wide range of motion without scraping onto each other. The term "diarthrosis," which refers to free movement, is applied to synovial joints.

On the opposite side of the spectrum, some bones are joined together in a way that allows little to no motion. For example, it is very important that the bones of the cranium stay in place. These joints are known as fibrous joints from a structural point of view, because they are held in place by fibrous connective tissue, and the term "synarthrosis" (referring to little or no movement) is applied from a functional point of view. The fibrous joints connecting the skull bones are specifically known as sutures, and are somewhat flexible in fetuses to allow the head to be compressed while passing through the birth canal.

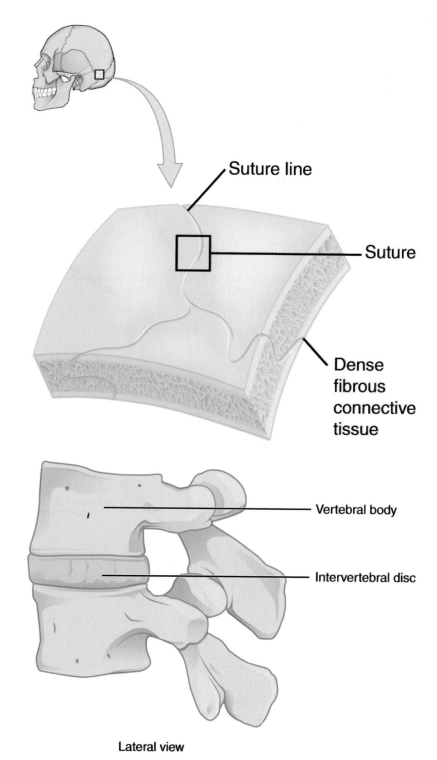

Figure 4. Fibrous (skull) and cartilaginous (spinal column) joints.

In between are cartilaginous joints (to which the term "amphiarthrosis" can be applied). A classic example of these joints are the intervertebral discs. In such joints, the bones are connected by a layer of cartilage that allows some movement, while stopping short of the freedom offered by synovial joints.

An additional distinction you should be aware of is the difference between an exoskeleton and an endoskeleton. Humans, as members of the broad class of vertebrates, contain an endoskeleton: that is, a skeletal system that provides structural support from within the body. Many other organisms have an exoskeleton, which is a tough "shell" that provides structural support on the outside of the body. Exoskeletons in insects, arachnids, and crustaceans are formed of chitin, which is a fibrous polymer of N-acetylglucosamine that is also found in the cell walls of fungi.

> **MCAT STRATEGY >>>**
>
> As you study the mechanical aspects of the musculoskeletal system, keep in the back of your mind the possibility that the MCAT could draw on this system to test physics concepts such as force and torque in a physiological context.

3. Bone Structure and Physiology

The structural role of the skeleton, as well as the fact that we generally see skeletons either in the form of artificially constructed display models or as bone samples from no-longer-living organisms, makes it easy to think of bones as static structures that passively provide support. This viewpoint is actually quite misleading: in living organisms, bone is a physiologically active structure that actively participates in the regulation of calcium and phosphate levels in the body, and new blood cells are produced in the bone marrow.

On the most basic level, you can think of bone structure as involving an interplay between non-cellular structural components of the bone and cellular structures. The non-cellular structural components of bone are referred to as the matrix of the bone, which consists of water, collagen fibers, and crystallized minerals (primarily hydroxyapatite, which has a chemical formula of $Ca_{10}(PO_4)_6(OH)_2$ and can be thought of as a storage depot of sorts for calcium and phosphate). The cellular components of bone tissue are quite diverse, and include epithelial, adipose, and nervous tissue as well as cells and structures unique to the bones.

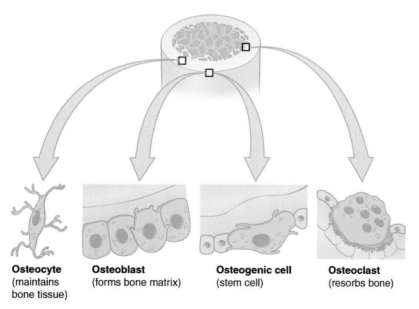

Osteocyte (maintains bone tissue)　　**Osteoblast** (forms bone matrix)　　**Osteogenic cell** (stem cell)　　**Osteoclast** (resorbs bone)

Figure 5. Structural view of bone.

An important division in terms of bone cells is the distinction between osteoblasts and osteoclasts. Osteoblasts are cells that produce hydroxyapatite and deposit it into the bone matrix, while osteoclasts break down the bone matrix, mobilizing calcium and phosphate if serum levels of those minerals are too low. Osteocytes are the most common type of bone cell, and can be thought of as osteoblasts that become somewhat inactivated; osteocytes do have a range of roles in regulating bone mass, but for the purposes of the MCAT you can think of them as being relatively inert components of the bone mass.

MCAT STRATEGY > > >

You can remember the distinction between osteoblasts and osteoclasts by remembering that osteoblasts <u>b</u>uild up bone.

The balance of activity between osteoblasts and osteoclasts is maintained by hormones. Parathyroid hormone (PTH) and calcitriol, a derivative of vitamin D, work to increase blood calcium and levels through various mechanisms, including the promotion of osteoclast activity. In contrast, calcitonin comes into play when serum levels of calcium are too high. Calcitonin is released by the thyroid and reduces osteoclast activity; this allows the balance to tip in favor of the osteoblasts, reducing serum calcium levels and promoting bone growth

In addition to having various cellular components, different types of bone tissue are distinguished based on how their small-scale structures are arranged. Compact bone, also known as cortical bone because it forms the exterior shell (cortex) of most bones, is a hard, dense, and stiff form of bone. As mentioned, it forms the outer layer of bones, providing protection and contributing to the mechanical functions of bone, such as structural support, protection, and leverage for movement. Cancellous, or spongy/trabecular bone, can be thought of as the spongy interior of bone. It is less dense, and correspondingly has a greater ratio of surface area to mass. Different types of bone have specific distributions of compact and cancellous bone.

Bone marrow is primarily contained in the flat bones and the heads of the long bones. It is the location of hematopoiesis, or the creation of blood; this process includes the constant generation of both red blood cells and white blood cells. As discussed in Chapter 11 on the immune system, the bone marrow can also be classified as part of the immune system due to its role in creating white blood cells that mediate important immune processes. There are actually two types of bone marrow: red and yellow. Red bone marrow is where hematopoiesis takes place, whereas yellow bone marrow is predominantly made up of adipocytes (fat cells). The bone marrow is highly vascularized tissue, as newly synthesized red blood cells must enter the circulatory system. It is also connected to the lymphatic system, which is the destination of newly produced lymphocytes.

4. Muscle Tissue

If bones provide the basic structure for our bodies, muscles can be thought of as what put our bodies into motion, including voluntary activities like walking or moving and involuntary but physiologically essential activities like pumping blood through the body, expanding our lungs so that we can breathe, and moving food through the digestive tract. In addition to the intuitively obvious function of providing support and mobility, muscles also help ensure that circulation takes place as needed in the peripheries (the smooth muscle surrounding deep veins contracts to help push the blood back to the heart), and also play a role in thermoregulation via the shivering reflex.

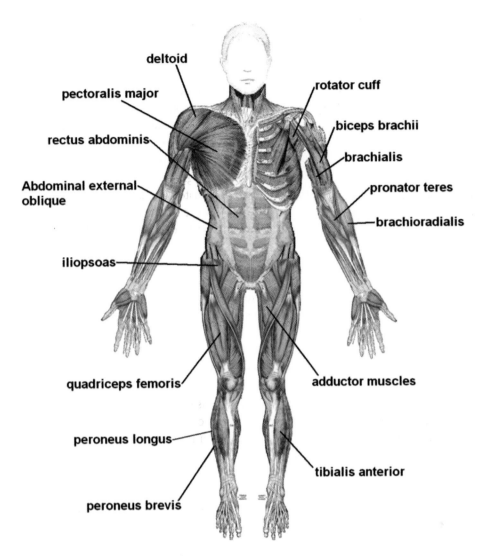

Figure 6. Gross view of muscles throughout body.

There are three basic types of muscle: skeletal, smooth, and cardiac. Skeletal muscle and smooth muscle can be thought of as opposites in many regards, with cardiac muscle occupying an intermediate role. However, in order for the distinctions among these types of muscle to make sense, we have to step back and consider the structure of a muscle cell. Historically, the study of muscle structure was somewhat of a different specialty from the study of basic cell biology, which led to the emergence of different terms for muscle cell structures than are used for the corresponding eukaryotic cell structures in general.

First, let's address one common point of terminological confusion: muscle cells (myocytes) and muscle fibers are different terms that refer to the same thing. This is because muscle cells have structures that are profoundly different from what you may think of as "normal" eukaryotic cells (that is, the standard diagram of a more-or-less circular cell with organelles that is included in most texts on cell biology). Recall, though, that eukaryotic cells can specialize considerably within organisms, to the point of developing very distinct structures. Common examples of this include neurons and spermatozoa, and you should add myocytes to this category of structurally anomalous but physiologically fundamental cell types.

Skeletal muscle is the primary focus of the MCAT in terms of cellular structure, so the discussion below will focus on the structure of myocytes in skeletal muscle, and then the ways in which this discussion does not apply to smooth and skeletal muscle will be explored.

Myocytes are long, tubular cells that principally contain myofibrils. Myofibrils are long, rod-like bundles of actin, myosin, and other proteins. Actin and myosin form thin and thick filaments, respectively, which are organized into repeating units called sarcomeres. The contraction of sarcomeres produces muscle contractions, as discussed in more detail in the next section. Specialized names, generally starting with the prefix "sarco-," exist for the other structures of myocytes. Relatively intuitively, the sarcoplasmic reticulum corresponds to the smooth endoplasmic reticulum, and the sarcoplasm corresponds to the cytoplasm. Somewhat less intuitively, the cell membrane of myocytes is known as the sarcolemma, and mitochondria in myocytes are referred to as sarcosomes.

Myofibrils are the essential structures of myocytes from a functional point of view, but myocytes also contain additional structures that allow myofibrils to do their job. Mitochondria (sarcosomes) are present to various extents in different types of muscle fibers, and the sarcoplasm also contains myoglobin and glycogen. Myoglobin is a red-colored protein that stores oxygen. Its general structure and function are similar to hemoglobin, but it only contains one heme group, and bonds to oxygen with a greater affinity than hemoglobin. This allows it to "pull" oxygen from the bloodstream, similarly to how fetal hemoglobin can obtain oxygen from maternal hemoglobin by having a higher affinity. The glycogen stores in the sarcoplasm allow the quick mobilization of glucose for anaerobic metabolism.

The sarcoplasmic reticulum wraps around the myofibrils, and has the basic function of storing Ca^{2+} ions at a lower concentration than outside the cell, but at a higher concentration than elsewhere in the cell. As such, it plays a role in mediating the transmission of nerve impulses and the resulting contractions. In turn, in non-smooth muscle, the sarcoplasmic reticulum is in contact with structures known as T-tubules. T-tubules can be thought of as projections of the sarcolemma (the cell membrane) that reach toward the center of the cell. They contain abundant ion channels that facilitate the rapid transmission of action potentials that initiate muscle contraction.

> **> > CONNECTIONS < <**
>
> **Chapter 9 of Biology**

> **MCAT STRATEGY > > >**
>
> Take this opportunity to review your knowledge of the physiology and biochemistry of hemoglobin. What would the dissociation curve of myoglobin look like compared to that of hemoglobin? The dissociation curve of myoglobin is left-shifted, because it has a higher affinity for oxygen than does hemoglobin. Its shape is also different. Hemoglobin has a sigmoidal curve due to the cooperative binding among its four subunits, whereas myoglobin has a hyperbolic curve that is more similar to what you see in discussions of enzyme kinetics.

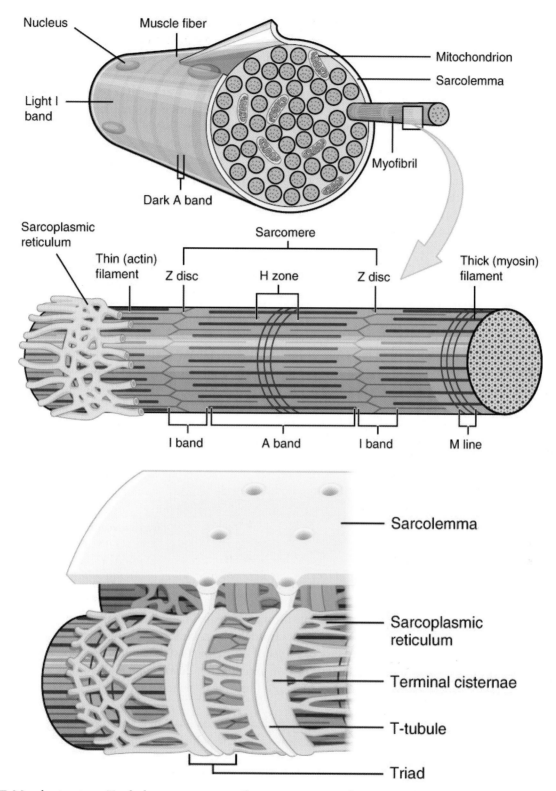

Figure 7. Muscle structure: T-tubule system, contractile apparatus, sarcoplasmic reticulum.

With these preliminary considerations in mind, we can now make more sense of the different types of muscles.

Skeletal muscle is innervated by the somatic nervous system, meaning that it is under conscious control. It is striated, which means that it has extensive linear myofibrils that form striations when viewed with a microscope. Myocytes in skeletal muscles also have multiple nuclei on the periphery of the cell, as they are formed via the fusion of multiple precursor cells. There are two different types of fibers within skeletal muscles: red fibers (slow-twitch fibers) and white fibers (fast-twitch fibers). Red fibers obtain their color from the presence of abundant reserves of myoglobin, and are also rich in mitochondria. This means that they prefer oxidative metabolism, and therefore are present in large quantities in muscles that specialize in performing less intense actions over a longer period of time. White fibers, in contrast, lack those elements, and tend to mobilize glycogen for quick bursts of intense action followed by fatigue. It has been argued that individuals with a relative predominance of white fibers are natural sprinters, whereas individuals with proportionally more red fibers are natural endurance athletes.

Smooth muscle, as mentioned before, is essentially the opposite of skeletal muscle. It is innervated by the autonomic nervous system, meaning that it is not under voluntary control. Smooth muscle is found throughout the body, but a particularly common and intuitive example is the digestive tract, where it is responsible for peristalsis. However, it is also found in blood vessel walls, the bladder, the uterus, and other locations. It is non-striated because it does not contain well-organized, linear myofibrils (although it does contain actin and myosin filaments that engage in contraction). Smooth muscle cells contain only one nucleus, and it is found towards the center of the cell.

Cardiac muscle shares some features of skeletal muscle and some features of smooth muscle, but it also has some unique features of its own. Like smooth muscle, it is not under voluntary control. Similarly to smooth muscle, cardiac muscle cells tend to only have one nucleus, although some cells may have two or more. However, like skeletal muscle, cardiac muscle is striated. A unique feature of cardiac muscle is that its cells are connected by structures known as intercalated discs, which connect the cytoplasm of adjacent cardiac muscle cells, allowing ions to pass from cell to cell. These connections are known as gap junctions, and they allow action potentials to pass rapidly from one cardiac muscle cell to another, facilitating the rapid propagation of action potentials.

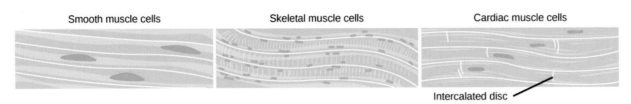

| Smooth muscle cells | Skeletal muscle cells | Cardiac muscle cells |

Intercalated disc

Figure 8. Skeletal, smooth, and cardiac muscle.

Myogenic activity, or the ability to contract even without external neural signaling, is an important characteristic of cardiac muscle (although it is also a property of smooth muscle). Cells in an area known as the sinoatrial (SA) node periodically send out action potentials, which propagate through the gap junctions, causing contraction. The action potential flows from the SA node into the atria, but not into the ventricles because of a layer of insulating tissue. The atrioventricular (AV) node allows the action potential to pass through to the ventricles, via the bundle of His and Purkinje fibers to all the muscle cells of the ventricles.

> > **CONNECTIONS** < <

Chapter 9 of Biology

While the SA node can fire on its own, it is also connected to the autonomic nervous system, which is subdivided into the sympathetic and parasympathetic nervous systems. The parasympathetic nervous system, which is responsible for the "rest and digest" response, slows the heart rate. In contrast, the sympathetic nervous system response ("fight or flight") raises the heart rate. The heart rate is also increased by the hormones epinephrine and norepinephrine, which are released by the adrenal medulla.

5. Muscle Contraction

Next, let's take a closer look at the mechanism of muscle contraction. There are a few levels on which muscle contraction can be analyzed: how the sarcomere changes structurally during contraction, the actual molecular mechanism of contraction, and how contraction happens in response to signals from the nervous system.

To review from the previous section, striated muscle fibers contain long rod-like myofibrils that are composed of alternating units of thick (myosin) and thin (actin) fibers that overlap with each other. The basic mechanism of contraction is for the interwoven myosin and actin fibers to slip past each other, in what is sometimes known as the sliding filament model.

The fundamental unit of contraction is the sarcomere, which is defined as consisting of a band of thick myosin fibers and half of each of the two adjacent bands of thin fibers, as seen in Figure 9. Sarcomeres are divided into the I-band, A-band, H-zone, Z-line, and M-line. This may seem like pointless alphabet soup, but there is some logic to this system. The lines are just definitional: the M-line defines the middle of the sarcomere, running through the middle of the thick filaments, while the Z-lines define the edges, running through the middle of the thin filaments. The two bands are a way to subdivide the sarcomere. The I-band refers to the region where only thin actin filaments are present, and the A-band is everything else, that is, the entire region where thick filaments are present, including areas of overlap with the thin filaments. However, it would still be useful to have some way of describing the inverse of the I-band; that is, the area where only thick filaments are present. It would be good to use a word that is not "band" to describe this to avoid confusion, so the term "zone" was deployed here: the H-zone refers to this area.

To envision what happens to the sarcomere during contraction, imagine holding a myofibril fragment composed of two or three sarcomeres between your hands and pushing your hands together. Recall that in the sliding filament model of the sarcomere, contraction happens because the actin and myosin fibers slide past each other, not because they are themselves compressed. Therefore, the thin fibers would be pushed towards the center, or the M-line. Let's work through the changes step by step, because this is often a point of confusion.

> M-line: If we place a single M-line at the center of our sarcomere fragment as a point of reference, it would not change, but since the whole system is being compressed, the distance *between* M-lines is decreased.

> Z-line: As the system is compressed, the Z-lines move closer together by the same reason.

> A-band: Recall that the A-band is defined as the zone where thick filaments are present, *regardless* of whether they overlap with thin filaments. Since the filaments themselves are not compressed during contraction, the A-band stays the same.

> I-band and H-zone: These two areas are defined by the lack of overlap. Recall that the I-band is where *only* thin filaments are present and the H-zone is where *only* thick filaments are present. Since contraction operates by filaments sliding past each other, the overall effect of contraction is to increase areas of overlap between actin and myosin filaments, thereby shrinking areas defined by the lack of overlap.

The shortest way to summarize this would be to say that during contraction, only the A-band does not shrink, because it is the only interval not defined relative to other structures.

MCAT STRATEGY > > >

If you are rushing to memorize the structures of the sarcomere, slow down and make sure you really *understand* what the different terms refer to. Consider interlocking your fingers and using that as a model for sarcomere contraction, perhaps with lines drawn on your skin to correspond to various structures. Alternately, consider using differently colored slips of paper to correspond to actin and myosin filaments and visualize the structures. Quickly memorizing the features of a structure like this is the path to quickly forgetting them as soon as you turn your energy elsewhere; your goal should be to connect the terminology to an internalized sense of how the system works, and that takes time.

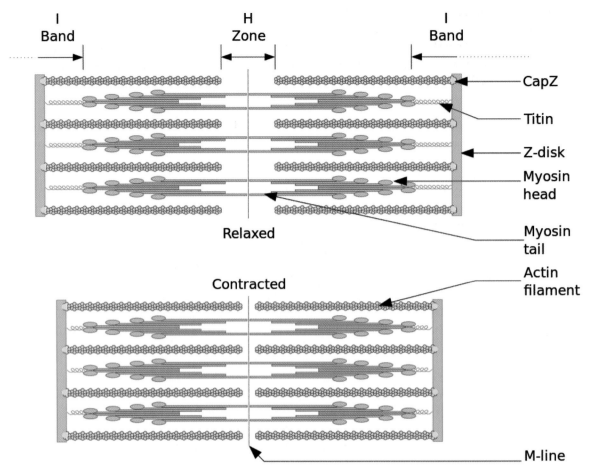

Figure 9. Sarcomeres.

Next, let's look at how the actual mechanism of contraction works. The actin and myosin filaments slide past each other through what is known as a cross-bridge cycle, in which a cross-bridge is formed between myosin and actin, and a power stroke provides the force of contraction. This is a topic where it pays to slow down and even draw out the structures involved—merely learning the names of the structures involved without a real understanding of the principles may allow you answer a low-level multiple-choice question right, but it will not be of much help if you encounter a passage that presents this information in a new light or asks you to apply it to solve a novel problem.

Both the actin and myosin filaments have structures in place that permit them to bind to each other when the conditions are right, and then disassociate as needed, and this interplay between binding and disassociation is what drives the whole process, along with conformational changes that take place in response to other factors. Myosin filaments have so-called heads that project from the filament. Each head has one site that can bind to ATP and another to actin. Actin filaments have a myosin-binding site that is blocked by the regulatory protein tropomyosin in the absence of Ca^{2+}.

As with any cycle, there is no starting point in the absolute sense, but a relatively straightforward place to start is immediately after a power stroke has happened and a cycle of contraction has ended. At this point, myosin and actin are bound together, and the cycle needs to begin again. The first step is for ATP to bind to the myosin head, causing a conformational change that releases it from actin. At this point, tropomyosin is free to move back into place to block strong interactions between actin and myosin. The ATP molecule is then hydrolyzed to form ADP + P_i (recall that P_i is inorganic phosphate). This is a strongly exergonic reaction and is used to move the myosin head into the "cocked position." In this position, it can interact weakly with actin, but tropomyosin prevents stronger interactions. Tropomyosin is ultimately removed by Ca^{2+} through a somewhat complex mechanism: Ca^{2+} binds to a protein known as troponin that is also located on actin, and the complex formed by Ca^{2+} and troponin causes tropomyosin to dissociate from the actin-myosin binding site. At this point, the myosin head can bind tightly to actin. The final step is for the power stroke to happen. This occurs via a conformational change that happens when P_i is released, resulting in a force of about 2 pN. After the power stroke happens, ADP is released and actin and myosin are essentially stuck together until another ATP binds to myosin so that the process can start again.

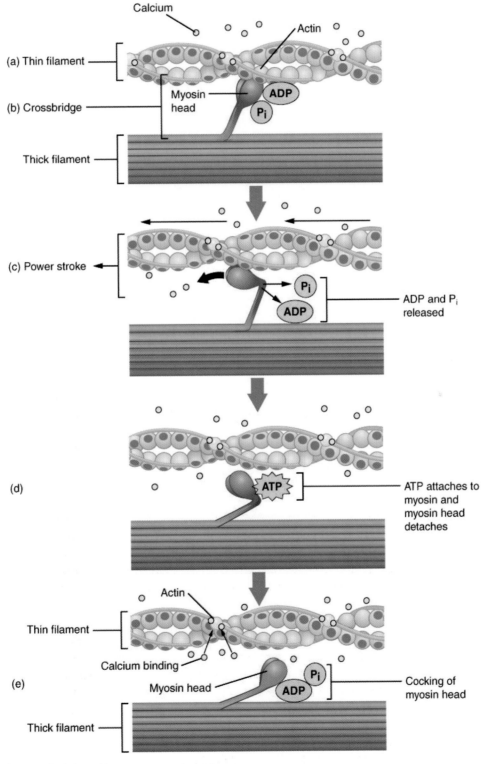

Figure 10. Actin-myosin interactions.

CLINICAL CONNECTIONS > > >

Rigor mortis refers to muscle stiffness that sets in several hours after death. It occurs because ATP is required to release myosin and actin, such that when the body has completely exhausted its stores of ATP post-death (interestingly, anaerobic respiration can continue in cells for a short time postmortem), the muscles become trapped in a state of contraction.

Next, let's turn to how muscles receive the signal to contract. An action potential propagates down a motor (efferent) neuron, until it reaches the nerve terminal at the neuromuscular junction. The neurotransmitter acetylcholine is then released into the neuromuscular junction. As a point of background terminology, the muscle cells innervated by a single neuron are known as a motor unit.

Acetylcholine binds to receptors on the cell membrane, which is known as the sarcolemma in muscle cells, and the sarcolemma then depolarizes in response. This results in an action potential, and when the action potential reaches the sarcoplasmic reticulum, Ca^{2+} is released into the sarcoplasm (recall that this is just muscle-speak for the cytoplasm). Once in the sarcoplasm, Ca^{2+} can bind to troponin, which allows contraction to take place.

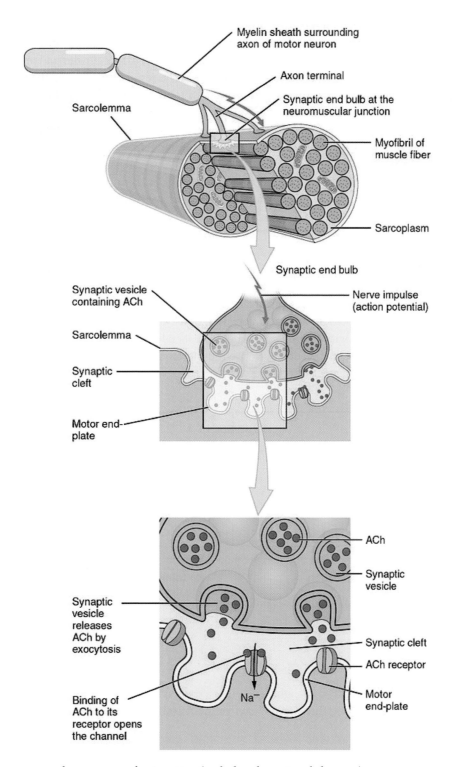

Figure 11. Motor neurons and neuromuscular junction (including how signals happen).

To summarize, contraction has two basic ingredients: ATP and Ca^{2+}, and the job of acetylcholine is to regulate the availability of Ca^{2+} in response to neural signaling.

An isolated contraction is known as a twitch, and more coordinated contractions occur in a process known as summation. In summation, frequent action potentials mean that muscle fibers do not relax completely between stimuli, and the overall contraction becomes stronger. Of note, even at maximum conscious exertion, fewer than half of the fibers in a muscle are actively contracting. Hyperstimulation can continue, resulting in a condition known as tetanus that should be differentiated from the disease known by the same name. Tetanus occurs when muscles have been maximally stimulated for some period of time, and to some degree it can occur during normal life, such as if you carry a heavy load for a sustained period of time. It can also be the result of pathological processes (as in the infectious disease tetanus, in which *Clostridium tetani* produces a toxin that causes spasmodic contractions).

> > **CONNECTIONS** < <

Chapter 9 of Biology

All the time that we've spent focusing on contraction should not cause us to overlook the fact that we also must account for relaxation. An enzyme known as acetylcholinesterase breaks down the acetylcholine that is released into the neuromuscular junction. In the absence of further stimulation, this allows the sarcolemma to repolarize and for Ca^{2+} to be taken back up into the sarcoplasmic reticulum.

As we've seen, ATP is essential for muscle contractions to happen. The abundant mitochondria and myoglobin in muscle cells help to ensure the constant production of ATP via oxidative respiration, but it is of course entirely possible for the muscle to run out of oxygen, even though the body does have a range of adaptations to help mobilize oxygen to active muscle tissue. If insufficient oxygen is present, muscles switch to glycolysis. Extensive glycolysis results in a buildup of lactic acid, and lactic acid buildup is associated with fatigue. Ultimately, the lactic acid is mostly converted to pyruvate. This discrepancy between the oxygen actually needed by active muscles and the amount of oxygen present is known as the oxygen debt.

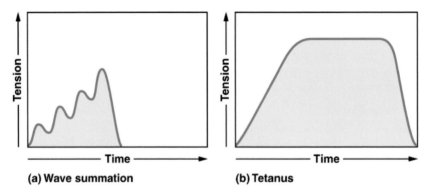

(a) Wave summation　　**(b) Tetanus**

Figure 12. Summation and tetanus.

6. Skin

The skin is the largest organ of the body by weight, and plays a crucial role in physiology both by serving as a physical barrier dividing the body from the external environment and by making significant contributions to homeostatic regulation.

The skin is divided into three major layers. The epidermis is the most external layer, and the basement membrane divides it from the dermis, which lies underneath. Below the dermis is the hypodermis. We'll review the anatomical features of these structures in some detail, and then review the physiological contributions made by the skin to the overall function of the organism.

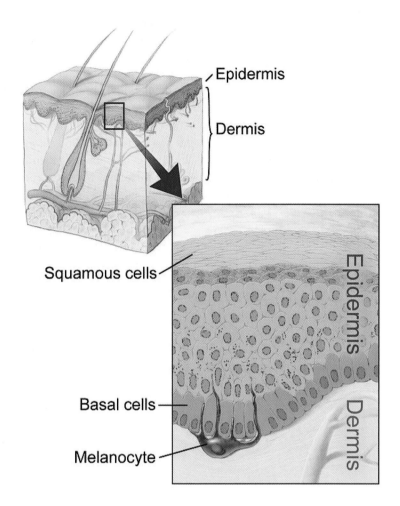

Figure 13. Layers of skin.

The epidermis is itself divided into five layers: the stratum corneum (most external), the stratum lucidum (only present in skin on the palm and the soles of the feet), the stratum granulosum, the stratum spinosum, and the stratum basale (most internal).

The stratum corneum is the layer that most directly provides a physical barrier against the outside world. It is made up of approximately 15 layers of dead keratinous cells known as corneocytes, which are gradually shed as part of the process through which the stratum corneum is regenerated. A lipid matrix surrounds the corneocytes, contributing to the fact that the skin forms a barrier that is largely impermeable to water. The stratum lucidum is a clear layer of dead cells only present in the palms of the hands and the soles of the feet. The stratum granulosum is where skin cells die and lose their nuclei after forming keratohyalin granules that link keratin filaments together into larger structures capable of serving as a hydrophobic barrier. The stratum spinosum and the stratum basale are responsible for the formation and development of keratinocytes (skin cells that produce keratin). Keratinocytes are produced from stem cells in the stratum basale, and then move upwards into the stratum spinosum where they begin to undergo keratinization and form connections to each other. The stratum spinosum also contains Langerhans cells, which are antigen-presenting dendritic cells that help alert the immune system to pathogens invading the body via the skin (or abrasions).

The stratum basale contains some additional cell types. Melanocytes produce the pigment melanin, which protects against damage induced by ultraviolet light. The expression of melanin is upregulated in response to ultraviolet damage, which is the mechanism behind tanning. Interestingly, differences in the skin color of individuals are not due to the *number* of melanocytes but due to their activity level, which is responsive to a range of stimuli. Merkel cells present in the stratum basale are mechanoreceptors that allow us to perceive the stimulus of touch. They are densely present in highly sensitive parts of the skin, such as the fingertips.

The dermis is a much more physiologically active place. It is largely composed of dense connective tissue consisting of collagen and elastic fibers, but has a diverse range of cell types. One particularly notable difference between the dermis and the epidermis is that the dermis is vascular tissue; that is, it contains capillaries and small lymphatic vessels that supply and drain blood and other fluids. It also contains hair follicles and sweat glands, as well as a broader range of sensory cells. The sensory cells present in the dermis include Ruffini endings, which sense stretching, Pacinian corpuscles, which sense deep vibration and pressure, and Meissner corpuscles, which sense gentle touch.

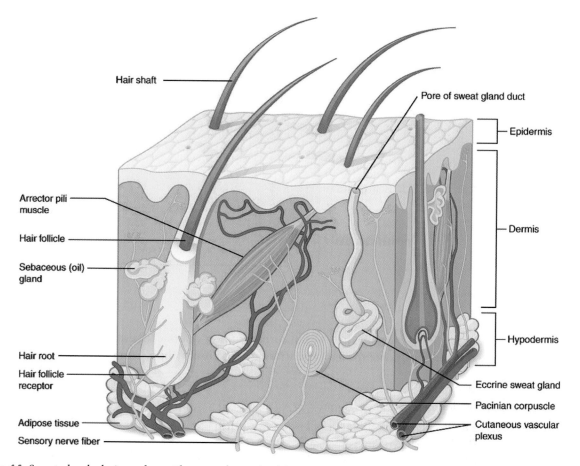

Figure 14. Sweat glands, hair, and erectile musculature in skin.

The hypodermis lies beneath the dermis, and its main job is to provide structural and immune support. It provides structural support by containing abundant adipocytes (fat cells) that provide padding and insulation, and it also contains macrophages that can respond to invaders.

With all of the above in mind, we can review the major physiological functions of the skin.

The epidermis provides a physical barrier, and this functionality is enhanced in certain parts of the body by the presence of fingernails/toenails and hair (which are both made of keratin) and calluses, which are thicker and tougher areas of skin that emerge in response to friction. In addition to being a physical barrier, the skin protects against invasive microorganisms by hosting abundant populations of immune cells in the dermis.

The skin additionally plays a major role in thermoregulation, starting with the fat layer of the hypodermis that provides insulation. Additionally, sweat glands, which are located in the dermis, are a major way in which the organism can avoid overheating. Sweat consists of water combined very small amounts of minerals. The evaporation of sweat on the skin absorbs heat energy from the body, thereby cooling the blood close to the skin. The arterioles that supply the skin can also be dilated to deal with excess heat (bringing more blood close to the skin to be cooled) or constricted to deal with excessively cold temperatures (minimizing blood flow to the skin to conserve heat). These processes are referred to as vasodilation and vasoconstriction, respectively. Body hair also plays a role in conserving heat in cold conditions. The arrector pili muscles that surround hair follicles contract, causing the body hairs to become vertical, trapping warm air close to the skin. This manifests as goose bumps, and is technically known as piloerection. Since body temperature must be maintained within a very close range, it is tightly controlled by the hypothalamus in response to various stimuli.

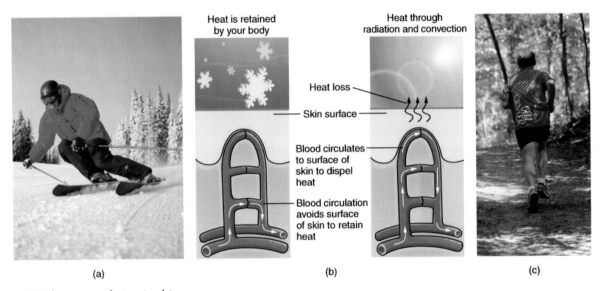

Figure 15. Thermoregulation in skin.

7. Must-Knows

> Connective tissue: includes bone, blood, adipose tissue as well as cartilage, ligaments, tendons
  - Cartilage: avascular, flexible connective tissue
  - Ligaments: tough tissue connecting bones to bones
  - Tendons: tough tissue connecting muscles and bones
> Bone types: long (example: humerus, femur), flat (example: skull), short (example: hand/foot bones), sesamoid (example: patella [kneecap]), irregular (example: ethmoid in face)
> Joints:
  - Synovial/diarthrosis: free movement; bones connected by lubricated synovial cavity; example: elbow.
  - Cartilaginous/amphiarthrosis: limited movement; bones connected by cartilage; example: vertebral discs.
  - Fibrous/synarthrosis: no movement; bones connected by tough fibers; example: skull bones
> Bone structure:
  - Matrix: minerals (hydroxyapatite), collagen, water; acts as calcium/phosphate storage
  - Osteoblasts: build up bone; osteoclasts: break down bone
  - PTH: ↑ Ca^{2+} from bone; vitamin D: ↑ Ca^{2+} from intestine; calcitonin: ↓ Ca^{2+} in blood by promoting osteoblast activity
  - Bone marrow: blood production
> Muscle types:

- Skeletal: voluntary (autonomic nervous system), striated, multinucleated; red (slow-twitch) fibers contain much myoglobin, specialize in long-lasting actions requiring oxidative metabolism; white (fast-twitch) fibers contain less myoglobin and specialize in short bursts of action using glycolysis
- Smooth: involuntary (somatic nervous system), non-striated, uninucleated; can undergo myogenic activity (contraction in absence of nervous stimulation)
- Cardiac: involuntary (somatic nervous system), striated; usually uninucleated; sinoatrial node sets pace of contractions that can be modified by other signaling; intercalated discs/gap junctions allow signals to spread

➤ Muscle contraction: sliding actin/myosin filaments; ATP required to dissociate actin & myosin; ATP → ADP to "cock" myosin head; Ca^{2+} dissociates tropomyosin to allow actin & myosin to bind; P_i is lost to generate power stroke.

➤ Sarcomere: I-band (thin filaments only), H-zone (thick filaments only), distances between M-lines (center of H-zone) and Z-lines (center of I-band) contract; A-band (entire area where thick filaments are present) stays the same during contraction.

➤ Skin:
- Epidermis > dermis > hypodermis
- Epidermis contains layers of dead keratocytes that provide physical protection; as well as melanocytes (pigment) and Merkel cells (touch)
- Dermis: capillaries, lymph vessels, hair follicles, sweat glands, sensory cells
- Skin → thermoregulation via sweating, vasodilation/vasocontraction, piloerection

This page left intentionally blank.

Practice Passage

Human bone cells are subjected to vibration forces through activities or exercise. However, the biomechanical responses of osteoblasts and their mechanisms are unclear when it comes to vibration stimuli of different accelerations and/or frequency. An orthopedic group aimed to investigate the biomechanical responses of osteoblasts, functional bone strength, and bone density to whole-body mechanical vibration training (WBVT).

A total of 40 adolescents (20 per group, age-matched, bone density-matched) with cerebral palsy participated in the study. Participants stood barefoot on the plate with feet apart and knees slightly bent for the duration of training. WBVT sessions each consisted of three 3-minute bouts of training, with a 3-minute rest between them. Sessions were performed four times a week, over a 20-week period. All participants started with sessions of three 1-minute bouts at 12 Hz. Physical function was assessed by a 5-minute walk test. Participants were asked to walk as fast as possible for exactly 5 minutes, with the total distance covered and the time taken to reach individual milestones recorded (Figures 1 and 2).

Group 1

Beginning at week 5, participants were trained at 3 sets of 3 minutes at 15 Hz, four times a week until the end of week 20.

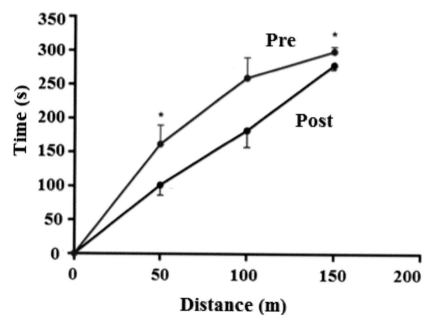

Figure 1. Performance of Group 1 participants in the 5-minute walk test prior to (Pre) and after (Post) 20 weeks of whole-body vibration training

Group 2

Beginning at week 5, participants were trained for 2 minutes at 15 Hz until the end of week 10, for 3 minutes at 16 Hz until week 15, and for 3 minutes at 20 Hz until the end of week 20.

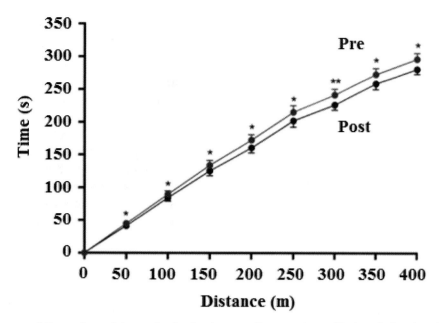

Figure 2. Performance of Group 2 participants in the 5-minute walk test prior to (Pre) and after (Post) 20 weeks of whole-body vibration training

Another cause of bone weakness is menopause, a period where older women experience significant estrogen deficiency and bone loss. It is believed that estrogen acts through high affinity receptors on osteoblasts and osteoclasts, to maintain bone density and prevent osteoporosis. Figure 3 shows the estimates of bone density for a typical man and woman.

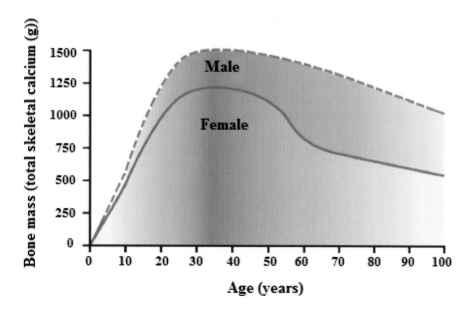

Figure 3. Bone mass changes with age

(Note: Data are means ± standard errors of the mean. *p < 0.05, **p < 0.01 for baseline vs. post-training)

Adapted from Gusso, S., & Hofman, P. L. (2016). Effects of whole-body vibration training on physical function, bone and muscle mass in adolescents and young adults with cerebral palsy. Scientific Reports, 6, 22518. under CCBY 4.0

1. Scientists looking to summarize the results of the WBVT study are most likely to conclude that:
   A. graduated WBVT improves measure bone properties significantly more than steady-dose WBVT.
   B. graduated WBVT improves measure bone properties significantly less than steady-dose WBVT.
   C. WBVT significantly improves the strength of the human appendicular skeleton
   D. WBVT significantly improves the strength of the human axial skeleton.

2. A comparison of the composition of ligaments and tendons is shown below:

COMPONENT	LIGAMENT	TENDON
Fibroblasts	20%	25%
Collagen (Type 1)	90%	95%
Collagen (Type 2)	10%	5%
Elastin	2X collagen	1.5X collagen
Degrees of Freedom	6	

   What is the order of tendon structure, from least to most complex?
   A. Tendon → Sub-fibril → Fascicle → Fiber
   B. Collagen → Sub-fibril → Fascicle → Tendon
   C. Microfibril → Fibril → Tendon → Collagen
   D. Fibril → Microfibril → Collagen → Fascicle

3. Which of the following osteoblast and osteoclast activity levels would result in the porosity of bone seen in patients suffering from osteoporosis?
   A. High levels of osteoblast activity and low levels of osteoclast activity
   B. High levels of osteoblast activity and high levels of osteoclast activity
   C. Low levels of osteoblast activity and low levels of osteoclast activity
   D. Low levels of osteoblast activity and high levels of osteoclast activity

4. According to the passage, the rate of bone mass loss is highest, on average, during which years of a woman's life?
   A. From age 20 to 30
   B. From age 30 to 40
   C. From age 50 to 60
   D. From age 80 to 90

5. Sutures, a specialized type of fibrous joint designed to allow no movement of the bones, are found in the:
   A. Skull
   B. Ribs
   C. Ankle
   D. Pubic bone

6. If calcitonin release is found to be an effective defense against the bone loss experienced by some menopausal women, which gland will be directly responsible for mounting this defense?
   A. Parathyroid
   B. Thyroid
   C. Hypothalamus
   D. Adrenal medulla

7. Which of the following is the best explanation for the differences in bone mass observed between genders after age 40 years?
   A. Men over 40 have increased testosterone compared with women over 40
   B. Women over 40 have increased levels of Vitamin D_3 compared with men over 40
   C. Women over 40 have increased sensitivity to calcitonin compared with men over 40
   D. Men over 40 have increased levels of serum Ca^{2+} compared with women over 40

377

Practice Passage Explanations

Human bone cells are subjected to vibration forces through activities or exercise. However, the biomechanical responses of osteoblasts and their mechanisms are unclear when it comes to vibration stimuli of different accelerations and/or frequency. An orthopedic group aimed to investigate the biomechanical responses of osteoblasts, functional bone strength, and bone density to whole-body mechanical vibration training (WBVT).

Key terms: vibration force, osteoblasts, WBVT

Cause and effect: vibration → increased bone strength/density/osteoblast activity?

A total of 40 adolescents (20 per group, age-matched, bone density-matched) with cerebral palsy participated in the study. Participants stood barefoot on the plate with feet apart and knees slightly bent for the duration of training. WBVT sessions each consisted of three 3-minute bouts of training, with a 3-minute rest between them. Sessions were performed four times a week, over a 20-week period. All participants started with sessions of three 1-minute bouts at 12 Hz. Physical function was assessed by a 5-minute walk test. Participants were asked to walk as fast as possible for exactly 5 minutes, with the total distance covered and the time taken to reach individual milestones recorded (Figures 1 and 2).

Key terms: age-matched, bone density-matched, WBVT, 5-minute walk

Cause and effect: Schedule of WBVT training → changes in bones as measured by walking test

Group 1

Beginning at week 5, participants were trained at 3 sets of 3 minutes at 15 Hz, four times a week until the end of week 20.

Cause and effect: at week 5, training intensity was increased, and then kept constant until the end

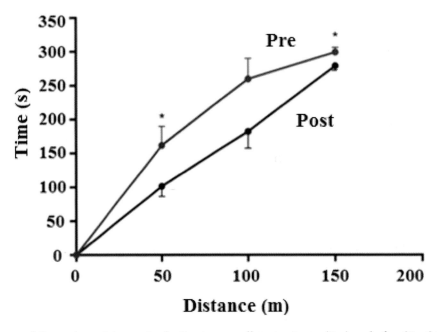

Figure 1. Performance of Group 1 participants in the 5-minute walk test prior to (Pre) and after (Post) 20 weeks of whole-body vibration training

Figure 1 shows a significant improvement in walking speed was a result of training, but no increase in total distance walked was observed

Group 2

Beginning at week 5, participants were trained for 2 minutes at 15 Hz until the end of week 10, for 3 minutes at 16 Hz until week 15, and for 3 minutes at 20 Hz until the end of week 20.

Contrast: group 2 participants had a graduated schedule of increasing WBVT session intensity throughout the 20 week study, while Group 1 participants had a near constant dose of WBVT

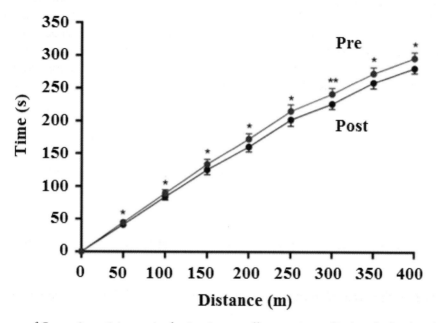

Figure 2. Performance of Group 2 participants in the 5-minute walk test prior to (Pre) and after (Post) 20 weeks of whole-body vibration training

Figure 2 x-axis reveals that Group 2 subjects reached much greater distances before and after training, suggesting that the 2 groups were not equal in their initial musculoskeletal ability (a flaw in the study)

Another cause of bone weakness is menopause, a period where older women experience significant estrogen deficiency and bone loss. It is believed that estrogen acts through high affinity receptors on osteoblasts and osteoclasts, to maintain bone density and prevent osteoporosis. Figure 3 shows the estimates of bone density for a typical man and woman.

Key terms: menopause, osteoblast, osteoclast, osteoporosis

Cause and effect: menopause → decreased estrogen → ↑osteoclasts ↓osteoblasts → bone loss

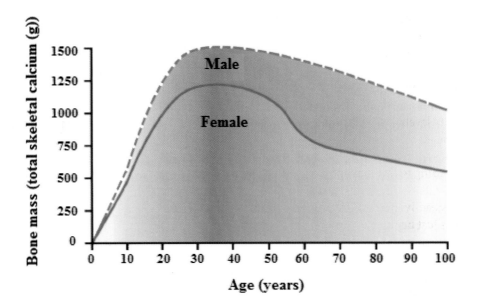

Figure 3. Bone mass changes with age

Figure 3 shows similar trends for male and female, but males have greater bone mass from age 10 onward and women drop off quickly between ages 45 and 60 years

(Note: Data are means ± standard errors of the mean. *$p < 0.05$, **$p < 0.01$ for baseline vs. post-training)

Adapted from Gusso, S., & Hofman, P. L. (2016). Effects of whole-body vibration training on physical function, bone and muscle mass in adolescents and young adults with cerebral palsy. Scientific Reports, 6, 22518. under CCBY 4.0

1. C is correct. The only results we are given regarding the WBVT is significant improvement in walking distances and speeds for both groups. The appendicular skeleton supports the attachment and functions of the upper and lower limbs of the human body. The human appendicular skeleton is composed of the bones of the upper limbs (which function to grasp and manipulate objects) and the lower limbs (which permit locomotion).
   A, B: We have no statistics comparing the two group results to each other, so the researchers cannot make any definitive conclusions about which approach is more effective.
   D. The axial skeleton forms the central axis of the human body and consists of the skull, vertebral column, and thoracic cage. The only test we have involves walking, which involves the appendicular skeleton.

2. B is correct. Do not get distracted by the table. Not all data presented is relevant or needed for the question. The table tells us (and we should know for Test Day) that both structures contain collagen, which is the fundamental protein that makes up both of these structures and muscle tissue (eliminate choices C, D). The correct answer should also end with tendon (eliminate choice A).

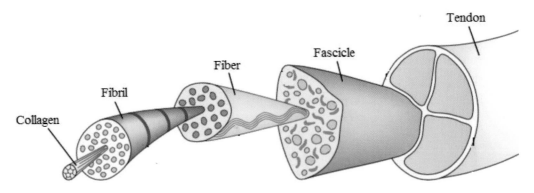

3. D is correct. Osteoporosis is the loss of bone density/mass. According to the passage, osteoblasts build bone while osteoclasts break it down. Thus, high levels of osteoclast activity, without high levels of osteoblast activity to build bone back up, would result in increasing porosity of bone.
   A. This would result in increasing bone mass over time, not decreasing bone mass.
   B. The high activity levels of both of these cells would have opposing effects, resulting in an insignificant net change in bone mass.
   C. The low activity levels of both of these cells would have opposing effects, resulting in an insignificant net change in bone mass.

4. C is correct. According to the chart provided in the figure, the slope is most negative for women between ages 50 and 60 years.
   A. Bone mass is steadily increasing during this period, not decreasing.
   B. Bone mass has just begun to decrease during this period, but the rate of decrease is not yet at its maximum.
   D. The rate of bone mass loss is not as high here as it is between the ages of 50 and 60 years.

5. A is correct. Fibrous joints are held together by fibrous connective tissue. There is no space present between the bones, so most fibrous joints do not move at all. There are three types of fibrous joints: sutures, syndesmoses, and gomphoses. Sutures are found only in the skull and possess short lengths of connective tissue that hold the skull bones tightly in place.
   B. Most rib joints are hyaline cartilage joints which allow little movement, while others are synovial joints (connected to the vertebrae) which allow some movement.
   C. The ankle joint is an example of a syndesmosis fibrous joint and allows significant movement. The degree of movement in these types of joints is determined by the length of the connective tissue fibers.
   D. The pubic bone joints are cartilaginous joints and allow slight movement.

6. B is correct. Calcitonin is a peptide hormone secreted by cells which, in humans, are found mainly in the thyroid gland. The musculoskeletal function of calcitonin is the long-term maintenance of the skeleton achieved by control of bone resorption.

7. B is correct. Examining Figure 3, we can see that men have more bone mass after age 25, but the gap widens as women's bone mass drops of much faster after age 40 years. This could be due to upregulation of the bone-resorbing hormones (parathyroid hormone and 1,25 dihydroxyvitamin D) or by decreased activity of bone-depositing (aka bone reabsorption) factors such as calcitonin and estrogen. According to the passage, it seems likely that the increased bone resorption which leads to post-menopausal bone loss is due mainly to the decrease in circulating levels of estrogen and calcitonin. Thus, increased activity of Vitamin D_3, a bone-resorbing factor, could do it.
   A. This is true for almost the entire life of a man/women, so this does not explain the increased separation of the values after age 50
   C. Increased sensitivity to calcitonin would cause women to have more calcium deposited back into their bones.
   D. While this might be true (though we have no way of knowing), high serum calcium would not cause decreased bone mass, it would be a result of increased bone resorption.

Independent Questions

1. Which of the following is most likely true of the structure that connects the patella (kneecap) to the tibia?
   A. It is a tendon.
   B. It is a ligament.
   C. It is composed largely of epithelial tissue.
   D. It does not contain collagen.

2. The main mineral component of bone, termed hydroxyapatite, contains all of the following EXCEPT:
   A. phosphate.
   B. calcium.
   C. vitamin D.
   D. hydroxide ions.

3. Of the following types of muscle, which are striated?
   I. Muscle composed of red (slow-twitch) fibers
   II. Muscle composed of white (fast-twitch) fibers
   III. Muscle lining the digestive tract
   IV. Cardiac muscle of the heart
   A. IV only
   B. I and IV only
   C. I, II, and IV only
   D. I, II, III, and IV

4. Muscle contraction can be initiated when acetylcholine is released at the neuromuscular junction. In a typical muscle contraction, what second messenger is necessary for the contraction of a muscle?
   A. cAMP
   B. cGMP
   C. Calcium
   D. Sodium

5. Which region of the sarcomere is neither composed of nor overlaps with actin filaments?
   A. The H-zone
   B. The A-band
   C. The I-band
   D. None of the above

6. The length of a single sarcomere can be described as:
   A. the distance between its M line and an adjacent Z line.
   B. twice the distance between its Z lines.
   C. the sum of half of the lengths of the two flanking I-bands and the A-band.
   D. the sum of the A-band and the H-zone.

7. Which of the following is true of skeletal muscle when intracellular calcium is absent?
   A. Actin heads are bound to ATP.
   B. The myosin-binding site on actin is blocked by tropomyosin.
   C. The actin-binding site on myosin is blocked by tropomyosin.
   D. Actin is able to freely and tightly bind myosin.

8. Which of the following does NOT accurately describe a thermoregulatory role of the skin and its associated structures?
   A. Embedded muscles around hair follicles contract during piloerection.
   B. Sweat glands in the dermis release sweat to cool the body.
   C. The fatty layer of the hypodermis provides insulation against the cold.
   D. Capillaries vasoconstrict to keep blood close to the body in cold weather.

Independent Question Explanations

1. B is correct. Ligaments and tendons are similar in that both are bands of connective tissue, specifically composed of collagen. However, ligaments connect bones (such as the patella) with other bones (such as the tibia). In contrast, tendons connect bone to muscle.

2. C is correct. Vitamin D does aid in the intestinal absorption of calcium, but it is not a direct component of hydroxyapatite. Hydroxyapatite contains calcium, phosphate, and hydroxide ions.

3. C is correct. Skeletal and cardiac muscle are striated. Skeletal muscle consists of white (fast-twitch) muscle fibers and red (slow-twitch) muscle fibers. In contrast, muscle lining the digestive tract is smooth muscle and is therefore not striated.

4. C is correct. Calcium released from the sarcoplasmic reticulum binds to troponin C, which initiates the crossbridge cycle that allows for muscle contraction to occur.

5. A is correct. The H-zone is the region where only myosin filaments are present. It does not overlap with actin filaments, so it is our answer here. The A-band is also composed of myosin, but it can overlap with actin fibers. Finally, the I-band is itself made of actin.

6. C is correct. A sarcomere is flanked by one I-band, or region of actin alone, on each side. Since each I band extends into the adjacent sarcomere as well, only half of each is actually found in the sarcomere in question. In contrast, the A-band represents the length of "all" the myosin in the sarcomere, including that which overlaps with actin. The sum of all of the myosin (the A-band) and all of the actin that does *not* overlap with myosin equals the length of the entire sarcomere.

7. B is correct. When calcium is not present within the muscle cell, the site on actin that would otherwise bind myosin is blocked by a protein known as tropomyosin. This prevents tight actin-myosin binding. Note that it is myosin, not actin, fibers that contain "heads" that can bind ATP.

8. D is correct. Vasoconstriction of peripheral arterioles, not capillaries, helps protect the body from cold external conditions. Capillaries cannot constrict or dilate because their walls do not contain smooth muscle. Piloerection, or the contraction of hair follicle muscles colloquially termed "goosebumps," helps trap air near the skin and insulate the body. Sweat glands in the dermis do release sweat, which evaporates and cools the skin, and the fat present in the hypodermis does play an insulating role.

This page left intentionally blank.

IMAGE ATTRIBUTIONS

Chapter 1

Fig 6: https://commons.wikimedia.org/wiki/File:Protein_structure_(full).png under CC BY 4.0

Fig 15: https://commons.wikimedia.org/wiki/File:DNA_chemical_structure.svg under CC BY 2.5

Fig 16: https://commons.wikimedia.org/wiki/File:Diagram_showing_a_double_helix_of_a_chromosome_CRUK_065.svg under CC BY-SA 4.0

Chapter 2

Fig 3: https://commons.wikimedia.org/wiki/File:Blausen_0212_CellNucleus.png under CC BY 3.0

Fig 5: https://commons.wikimedia.org/wiki/File:Blausen_0350_EndoplasmicReticulum.png under CC BY 3.0

Fig 6: https://commons.wikimedia.org/wiki/File:0314_Golgi_Apparatus.jpg under CC BY 4.0

Fig 8: https://commons.wikimedia.org/wiki/File:Actin_filament_atomic_model.png under CC BY-SA 4.0

Fig 8: https://commons.wikimedia.org/wiki/File:Microtubule_structure.png under CC BY-SA 4.0

Fig 9: https://en.wikipedia.org/wiki/File:Difference_Between_Prokaryote_and_Eukaryote_Flagella.svg under CC BY-SA 4.0

Fig 10: https://commons.wikimedia.org/wiki/File:Cell_membrane_detailed_diagram_4.svg under CC BY-SA 4.0

Fig 11: https://en.wikipedia.org/wiki/File:Mitosis_Stages.svg under CC BY-SA 4.0

Fig 13: https://commons.wikimedia.org/wiki/File:Chromosomal_Crossover.svg under CC BY-SA 3.0

Fig 15: https://commons.wikimedia.org/wiki/File:Ana.png under CC BY-3.0

Fig 16: https://commons.wikimedia.org/wiki/File:Prokaryote_cell.svg under CC BY-SA 4.0

Fig 17: https://commons.wikimedia.org/wiki/File:Binary_Fission_2.svg under CC BY-SA 3.0

Fig 18: https://commons.wikimedia.org/wiki/File:Bacterial_growth_en.svg under CC BY-SA 3.0

Fig 19: https://commons.wikimedia.org/wiki/File:Bacterial_horizontal_gene_transfer.jpg under CC BY-SA 3.0

Fig 20: https://en.wikipedia.org/wiki/File:TMV_structure_simple.png under CC BY-SA 3.0

Chapter 3

Fig 2: https://commons.wikimedia.org/wiki/File:Gene_structure_eukaryote_2_annotated.svg under CC BY 4.0

Fig 4: https://commons.wikimedia.org/wiki/File:Nucleosome_structure.png under CC BY-SA 3.0

Fig 10: https://commons.wikimedia.org/wiki/File:Eukariotische_Genexpression.png under CC BY-SA 2.0 Germany

Fig 11: https://commons.wikimedia.org/wiki/File:TRNA-Phe_yeast_1ehz.png under CC BY-SA 3.0

Fig 13: https://commons.wikimedia.org/wiki/File:Peptide_syn.png under CC BY-SA 3.0

Fig 14: https://commons.wikimedia.org/wiki/File:Point_mutations-en.png under CC BY-SA 4.0

Chapter 4

Fig 6A: https://en.wikipedia.org/wiki/File:Co-dominance_in_Roan_Cattle.svg under CC BY-SA 4.0

Fig 6B: https://commons.wikimedia.org/wiki/File:Mendelian_inheritance_intermed.svg under CC BY-SA 3.0

Fig 8: https://commons.wikimedia.org/wiki/File:TwoPointCrossover.svg under CC BY-SA 3.0

Fig 8: https://commons.wikimedia.org/wiki/File:OnePointCrossover.svg under CC BY-SA 3.0

Fig 11: https://commons.wikimedia.org/wiki/File:Selection_Types_Chart.png under CC BY-SA 3.0

Fig 12: https://commons.wikimedia.org/wiki/File:Bottleneck_effect_Figure_19_02_03.jpg under CC BY 4.0

Chapter 5

Fig 2: https://en.wikipedia.org/wiki/Trp_operon#/media/File:Trpoperon.svg under CC BY-SA 3.0

Fig 4: https://commons.wikimedia.org/wiki/File:Enhancer_Nucleotide_Sequence.svg under CC BY-SA 4.0

Fig 5: https://en.wikipedia.org/wiki/File:Sha-Boyer-Fig1-CCBy3.0.jpg under CC BY 3.0

Fig 6: https://en.wikipedia.org/wiki/File:Lysine_acetylation.png under CC BY-SA 3.0

Fig 7: https://commons.wikimedia.org/wiki/File:Cytosine_DNA_methylation.png under CC BY-SA 4.0

Fig 8: https://en.wikipedia.org/wiki/File:Ch1-oncogene.svg under CC BY-SA 3.0

Fig 11: https://en.wikipedia.org/wiki/File:Recombinant_formation_of_plasmids.svg under CC BY-SA 3.0

Fig 12: https://commons.wikimedia.org/wiki/File:PGEX-3X_cloning_vector.png under CC BY-SA 1.0

Fig 13: https://commons.wikimedia.org/wiki/File:Gel_Electrophoresis.svg under CC BY-SA 4.0

Fig 15: https://commons.wikimedia.org/wiki/File:Northern_blot_diagram.png under CC BY-SA 4.0

Fig 17: https://commons.wikimedia.org/wiki/File:Sanger-sequencing.svg under CC BY-SA 3.0

Fig 18: https://commons.wikimedia.org/wiki/File:Polymerase_chain_reaction.svg under CC BY-SA 3.0

Chapter 6

Fig 1: https://commons.wikimedia.org/wiki/File:Patellar-knee-reflex.png under CC BY SA 3.0

Fig 3: https://commons.wikimedia.org/wiki/File:Ion_channel_activity_before_during_and_after_polarization.jpg under CC BY 4.0

Fig 4: https://commons.wikimedia.org/wiki/File:Action_potential.svg under CC BY SA 3.0

Fig 5: https://commons.wikimedia.org/wiki/File:Propagation_of_action_potential_along_myelinated_nerve_fiber_en.svg under CC BY SA 4.0

Fig 6: https://commons.wikimedia.org/wiki/File:1225_Chemical_Synapse.jpg under CC BY 4.0

Fig 8: https://commons.wikimedia.org/wiki/File:Components_of_the_Nervous_System.png under CC BY SA 3.0

Fig 9: https://commons.wikimedia.org/wiki/File:Brain_parts.jpg under CC BY 2.0

Chapter 7

Fig 1: https://commons.wikimedia.org/wiki/File:Endocrine_vs._Exocrine.svg under CC BY-SA 4.0

Fig 7: https://commons.wikimedia.org/wiki/File:HPA_Axis_Diagram_(Brian_M_Sweis_2012).png under CC BY-SA 3.0

Fig 9: https://commons.wikimedia.org/wiki/File:Blood_glucose_control.png under CC BY-SA 3.0

Fig 10: https://commons.wikimedia.org/wiki/File:Verlauf_Insulin-Glucagon-GLP1_nach_Habener.svg under CC BY-SA 4.0

Fig 13: https://commons.wikimedia.org/wiki/File:Renin-angiotensin-aldosterone_system.png under CC BY-SA 3.0

Fig 16: https://commons.wikimedia.org/wiki/File:Blausen_0536_HypothalamusLocation.png under CC BY-3.0

Fig 17: https://commons.wikimedia.org/wiki/File:Figure_28_03_01.jpg under CC BY-3.0

Chapter 8

Fig 1: https://commons.wikimedia.org/wiki/File:Male_anatomy_en.svg under CC BY-SA 3.0

Fig 2: https://commons.wikimedia.org/wiki/File:Female_anatomy_with_g-spot-en.svg under CC BY-SA 3.0

Fig 2: https://commons.wikimedia.org/wiki/File:Vagina_1.jpg under CC BY-SA 3.0

Fig 4: https://commons.wikimedia.org/wiki/File:Figure_28_01_04.jpg under CC BY 3.0

Fig 5: https://commons.wikimedia.org/wiki/File:Blausen_0404_Fertilization.png under CC BY 3.0

Fig 6: https://commons.wikimedia.org/wiki/File:Human_Fertilization.png under CC BY-SA 3.0

Fig 7: https://commons.wikimedia.org/wiki/File:2912_Neurulation-02.jpg under CC BY 3.0

Fig 8: https://commons.wikimedia.org/wiki/File:Germ_layers.jpg under CC BY-SA 3.0

Fig 10: https://commons.wikimedia.org/wiki/File:MenstrualCycle.png under CC BY-SA 3.0

Chapter 9

Fig 3: https://commons.wikimedia.org/wiki/File:Quiet_breathing.jpg under CC BY-SA 4.0

Fig 3: https://commons.wikimedia.org/wiki/File:Forceful_breathing.jpg under CC BY-SA 4.0

Fig 4: https://commons.wikimedia.org/wiki/File:Gas_exchange.jpg under CC BY-SA 4.0

Fig 5: https://en.wikipedia.org/wiki/File:Lungvolumes_Updated.png under CC BY-SA 3.0

Fig 6: https://en.wikipedia.org/wiki/File:2325_Carbon_Dioxide_Transport.jpg under CC BY 3.0

Fig 7: https://commons.wikimedia.org/wiki/File:CO2_%26_pH.png under CC BY-SA 4.0

Fig 8: https://commons.wikimedia.org/wiki/File:Blausen_0425_Formed_Elements.png under CC BY 3.0

Fig 8: https://commons.wikimedia.org/wiki/File:1901_Composition_of_Blood.jpg under CC BY 3.0

Fig 9: https://commons.wikimedia.org/wiki/File:Red_blood_cells.svg under CC BY-SA 4.0

Fig 10: https://commons.wikimedia.org/wiki/File:Diagram_of_the_human_heart_(cropped).svg under CC BY-SA 3.0

Fig 11: https://commons.wikimedia.org/wiki/File:2101_Blood_Flow_Through_the_Heart.jpg under CC BY 3.0

Fig 12: https://commons.wikimedia.org/wiki/File:2109_Systemic_Blood_Pressure.jpg under CC BY 3.0

Fig 14: https://commons.wikimedia.org/wiki/File:Heart_%26_Lungs.png under CC BY-SA 4.0

Fig 20: https://commons.wikimedia.org/wiki/File:2320_Fig_23.20_NEW_KGX.jpg under CC BY 3.0

Chapter 10

Fig 1: https://commons.wikimedia.org/wiki/File:Adult_Digestive_System.png under CC BY-SA 4.0

Fig 3: https://commons.wikimedia.org/wiki/File:Blausen_0817_SmallIntestine_Anatomy.png under CC BY 3.0

Fig 4: https://en.wikipedia.org/wiki/Gallbladder#/media/File:Gallbladder_(organ).png under CC BY-SA 4.0

Fig 5: https://commons.wikimedia.org/wiki/File:Blausen_0699_PancreasAnatomy2.png under CC BY 3.0

Fig 6: https://commons.wikimedia.org/wiki/File:Blausen_0604_LargeIntestine2.png under CC BY 3.0

Fig 7: https://commons.wikimedia.org/wiki/File:Peristalsis.png under CC BY-SA 3.0

Fig 8: https://commons.wikimedia.org/wiki/File:Villi_%26_microvilli_of_small_intestine.svg under CC BY-SA 4.0

Fig 8: https://commons.wikimedia.org/wiki/File:Absorption_of_monosaccharides_in_small_intestine.png under CC BY-SA 4.0

Fig 8: https://commons.wikimedia.org/wiki/File:Absorption_of_proteins_in_small_intestine.png under CC BY-SA 4.0

Fig 8: https://commons.wikimedia.org/wiki/File:2431_Lipid_Absorption.jpg under CC BY 3.0

Fig 13: https://commons.wikimedia.org/wiki/File:Diagram_of_the_male_urinary_system_CRUK_042.svg under CC BY-SA 4.0

Fig 13: https://commons.wikimedia.org/wiki/File:Diagram_showing_the_female_urinary_system_CRUK_301.svg under CC BY-SA 4.0

Fig 14: https://commons.wikimedia.org/wiki/File:Blausen_0593_KidneyAnatomy_02.png under CC BY 3.0

Fig 15: https://commons.wikimedia.org/wiki/File:Kidney_Nephron.png under CC BY 3.0

Fig 16: https://commons.wikimedia.org/wiki/File:Physiology_of_Nephron.png under CC BY 3.0

Fig 19: https://commons.wikimedia.org/wiki/File:Anatomy_and_physiology_of_animals_Summary_of_the_processes_involved_in_the_formation_of_urine.jpg under CC BY 3.0

Chapter 11

Fig 2: https://commons.wikimedia.org/wiki/File:MHC_expression.svg under CC BY-SA 3.0

Fig 3: https://commons.wikimedia.org/wiki/File:2211_Cooperation_Between_Innate_and_Immune_Responses.jpg under CC BY 3.0

Fig 4: https://commons.wikimedia.org/wiki/File:2212_Complement_Cascade_and_Function.jpg under CC BY 3.0

Fig 5: https://commons.wikimedia.org/wiki/File:B_cell_function.png under CC BY-SA 3.0

Fig 9: https://commons.wikimedia.org/wiki/File:2202_Lymphatic_Capillaries_big.png under CC BY-SA 4.0

Fig 10: https://commons.wikimedia.org/wiki/File:Blausen_0623_LymphaticSystem_Female.png under CC BY-3.0

Fig 11: https://commons.wikimedia.org/wiki/File:Inflammation_scale.svg under CC BY-SA 3.0

Chapter 12

Fig 2: https://commons.wikimedia.org/wiki/File:701_Axial_Skeleton-01.jpg under CC BY-SA 3.0

Fig 3: https://commons.wikimedia.org/wiki/File:909_Types_of_Synovial_Joints.jpg under CC BY-SA 3.0

Fig 4: https://commons.wikimedia.org/wiki/File:904_Fibrous_Joints.jpg under CC BY-SA 3.0

Fig 4: https://commons.wikimedia.org/wiki/File:902_Intervertebral_Disk-02.jpg under CC BY-SA 3.0

Fig 5: https://commons.wikimedia.org/wiki/File:604_Bone_cells.jpg under CC BY-SA 3.0

Fig 7: https://commons.wikimedia.org/wiki/File:1022_Muscle_Fibers_(small).jpg under CC BY-SA 4.0

Fig 7: https://commons.wikimedia.org/wiki/File:1023_T-tubule.jpg under CC BY-SA 4.0

Fig 9: https://commons.wikimedia.org/wiki/File:Sarcomere.svg under CC BY-SA 3.0

Fig 10: https://commons.wikimedia.org/wiki/File:1008_Skeletal_Muscle_Contraction.jpg under CC BY-SA 3.0

Fig 11: https://commons.wikimedia.org/wiki/File:1009_Motor_End_Plate_and_Innervation.jpg under CC BY-SA 3.0

Fig 12: https://commons.wikimedia.org/wiki/File:1013_Summation_Tetanus.jpg under CC BY-SA 4.0

Fig 14: https://commons.wikimedia.org/wiki/File:501_Structure_of_the_skin.jpg under CC BY 3.0

Fig 15: https://commons.wikimedia.org/wiki/File:515_Thermoregulation.jpg under CC BY 3.0

A site, 83
acetyl-CoA, 130
ACTH, 199
action potential, 162, 360
activator, 124
active transport, 231, 292
adaptation, 113
adenine, 18
ADH, 204
adipocyte, 358
adrenal, 184, 189, 196, 205
aerobic, 39, 52, 255, 270
albumin, 187
aldosterone, 205, 8, 305-6
allele, 86, 100-7
alveolus, 250
amino acid, 256, 292, 303
amphipathic, 3
amylopectin, 17
amylose, 17
anaerobic, 52, 255
anaphase, 47
androgen, 205, 222
aneuploidy, 48, 87
anneal, 75
antagonist, 197
antibody, 324-5
anticodon, 81
antigen, 103
antiparallel, 20, 72
antisense strand, 80
anus, 288
aorta, 260
apoptosis, 124, 332
archaea, 50
arteriole, 263
artery, 266
ascending colon, 288
astrocyte, 159
ATP synthase, 39
autoimmune, 339
autonomic, 166, 362
AV node, 265
axon, 158, 160, 162
B cell, 324, 332
bacilli, 51
bacteria, 50
bacteriophage, 56
basal metabolic rate, 204
base pair, 20
basophil, 329
beta-oxidation, 38
bicarbonate, 255
bile, 286
bipolar, 160
bladder, 301
blastocyst, 124, 228
blood clot, 258
blood filtration, 301
blood glucose regulation, 191
bolus, 284
bone, 331, 352
bottleneck, 112
Bowman's capsule, 302
brainstem, 167

Bronchioles, 250
bronchus, 250
brush border, 286
bundle of His, 362
calcium, 193, 357
cancer, 133
capillary, 263
capsid, 57
carbohydrate, 15
carbonic anhydrase, 271
carcinogen, 88
cardiac, 265, 285
carrier, 105
cartilage, 352
catalyst, 11
cell body, 158
cell cycle, 46
cellulose, 17
central nervous system, 167
centriole, 43
centromere, 47
centrosome 43
cerebellum, 167
cerebral cortices, 168
chemotaxis, 54
chiasmata, 49
chief cell, 285
cholecystokinin, 291
chromatid, 47
chromatin, 46
chromosomal mutation, 87
chromosome, 20
chylomicron, 293
chyme, 285
cilia, 43
cleavage 42, 84
clonal selection, 332
clone, 139
clotting cascade 258
cocci, 51
codominant, 103
codon, 71
coenzyme, 297
cofactor, 297
collagen, 352
collecting duct, 301
complement, 329
complementary, 72
complete dominance 103
conformation, 186
conjugation, 56
connective tissue, 351
contractile, 361
cooperativity, 269
corpus luteum, 233
cortex, 167, 205
cortisol, 192
cranial nerve, 166
cross-bridge, 364
crossing over, 49
cysteine, 8
cystine, 8
cytokinesis, 48
cytoplasm, 38
cytosine, 18

cytoskeleton, 42
cytosol, 38
degenerate, 236
dehydration, 204
deletion, 85
denature, 20
dendrite, 158
depolarization, 162
dermis, 368
descending colon, 288
determination, 107, 145
diaphragm, 252
diaphysis, 354
diastolic, 261
differentiation, 123
diffusion, 44
digest, 283
dihybrid, 105
diploid, 50
distal convoluted tubule, 305
DNA, 18
DNA-binding protein, 76
DNA helicase, 76
DNA ligase, 76
DNA methylation, 131
DNA polymerase, 76
DNA sequencing, 145
domain, 11
dominant, 99
double helix, 20
duodenum, 286
duplication, 86
dynein, 179
E site, 83
eccrine gland, 185
ectoderm, 123
effector, 157
eicosanoid, 14
elasticity, 305
electrochemical gradient, 160
electron carrier, 38
electron transport chain, 38
elongation, 83
endocrine, 183
endocytosis, 42
endoderm, 123
endoplasmic reticulum, 40
endoskeleton, 357
endothelial cell, 265
endothelium, 244
enhancer, 128
enterocyte, 288
entropy, 10
envelope, 48
enzyme, 11
eosinophil, 329
ependymal cell, 167
epidermis, 229
epididymis, 222
epigenetic, 132
epiglottis, 249
epinephrine, 188
epiphyseal plate, 217
epiphysis, 354
erythrocyte, 36